# WHAT REALLY WORKS

## WITH EXCEPTIONAL LEARNERS

*This book is dedicated to the memory of Dr. Lynne Cook and Fred Weintraub. Lynne and Fred were icons in the field of special education. They were teachers, mentors, friends, and absolute inspirations to those of us lucky enough to know them, work with them, and love them.*

# WHAT REALLY WORKS

## WITH EXCEPTIONAL LEARNERS

EDITORS

## WENDY W. MURAWSKI
## KATHY LYNN SCOTT

Foreword by Ann Turnbull

A JOINT PUBLICATION

**FOR INFORMATION:**

Corwin

A SAGE Company

2455 Teller Road

Thousand Oaks, California 91320

(800) 233-9936

www.corwin.com

SAGE Publications Ltd.

1 Oliver's Yard

55 City Road

London, EC1Y 1SP

United Kingdom

SAGE Publications India Pvt. Ltd.

B 1/I 1 Mohan Cooperative Industrial Area

Mathura Road, New Delhi 110 044

India

SAGE Publications Asia-Pacific Pte. Ltd.

3 Church Street

#10-04 Samsung Hub

Singapore 049483

Council for Exceptional Children

2900 Crystal Drive, Suite 100

Arlington, Virginia 22202

(888) 232-7733

www.cec.sped.org

Program Director: Jessica Allan

Senior Associate Editor: Kimberly Greenberg

Editorial Assistant: Katie Crilley

Production Editor: Melanie Birdsall

Copy Editor: Deanna Noga

Typesetter: Hurix Systems Pvt. Ltd.

Proofreader: Laura Webb

Indexer: Amy Murphy

Cover Designer: Gail Buschman

Marketing Manager: Charline Maher

Printed in the United States of America.

*Library of Congress Cataloging-in-Publication Data*

Names: Murawski, Wendy W., editor. | Scott, Kathy Lynn, editor.

Title: What really works with exceptional learners / Wendy W. Murawski, Kathy Lynn Scott.

Description: Thousand Oaks, California : Corwin, [2017] | "A SAGE Company." | Includes bibliographical references and index.

Identifiers: LCCN 2016036881 | ISBN 9781506363479 (pbk. : acid-free paper)

Subjects: LCSH: Special education—United States | Students with disabilities—United States.

Classification: LCC LC3981 .M87 2017 | DDC 371.9—dc23

LC record available at https://lccn.loc.gov/2016036881

This book is printed on acid-free paper.

18 19 20 21 10 9 8 7 6 5 4 3

# *Contents*

Foreword     vii
*Ann Turnbull*

About the Editors     ix

About the Contributors     x

Introduction     1

**SECTION I. WHAT REALLY WORKS WITH CONTENT**

**Chapter 1. Getting Past "I Hate Math!"**     6
*Sarah A. Nagro, Margaret P. Weiss, and Jaime True Daley*

**Chapter 2. Creating a Cadre of Capable Readers**     23
*Leila Ansari Ricci*

**Chapter 3. When Writing Isn't Easy or Fun:
Techniques for Struggling Writers**     42
*Katie M. Miller and Sally A. Spencer*

**Chapter 4. Instructional Strategies and UDL:
Making Content Accessible**     60
*Ruby L. Owiny, Anne Brawand, and Janet Josephson*

**Chapter 5. Leveling the Playing Field With Technology**     79
*Barbara Serianni, Ela Kaye Eley, and LaToya Cannon*

**SECTION II. WHAT REALLY WORKS WITH INSTRUCTION**

**Chapter 6. Culturally Responsive Teaching
to Support All Learners**     100
*Jacqueline Rodriguez and Stacey E. Hardin*

**Chapter 7. Thanks for the Memories:
Brain-Based Learning at Its Best**     117
*Horacio Sanchez*

**Chapter 8. Positive Behavior Intervention
and Supports in the Inclusive Classroom**     133
*Jennifer D. Walker and Brittany L. Hott*

Chapter 9. Beyond Just "Playing Nicely":
Collaboration and Co-Teaching                                     152
*Amy Kramer and Wendy W. Murawski*

Chapter 10. Progress Monitoring: Your Classroom Itinerary        169
*Kyena E. Cornelius and Kimberly M. Johnson-Harris*

SECTION III. WHAT REALLY WORKS
WITH SPECIAL POPULATIONS

Chapter 11. Addressing the "Invisible Disability":
Supporting Students With Learning Disabilities                    188
*Janet Josephson, Anne Brawand, and Ruby L. Owiny*

Chapter 12. Search for the Miracle Cure: Working With
Students With Emotional and Behavioral Disorders                  207
*Brittany L. Hott, Jennifer D. Walker, Audrey Robinson,
and Lesli Raymond*

Chapter 13. Addressing the Autism Spectrum Disorder
"Epidemic" in Education                                           225
*Claire E. Hughes and Lynnette M. Henderson*

Chapter 14. Teaching Students With Moderate-to-
Severe Disabilities: You've Got This!                             244
*Dawn W. Fraser*

Chapter 15. English Language Learners With Disabilities:
Best Practices                                                    262
*Brenda L. Barrio, Pamela K. Peak, and Wendy W. Murawski*

Chapter 16. Inclusion as the Context for
Early Childhood Special Education                                 282
*Zhen Chai and Rebecca Lieberman-Betz*

Chapter 17. Focusing on Strengths: Twice-Exceptional Students     302
*Claire E. Hughes*

SECTION IV. WHAT REALLY WORKS
BEYOND THE CLASSROOM

Chapter 18. It's the Law! Legal Issues in Special Education       320
*Christine A. Hayashi*

Chapter 19. The Importance of Partnerships: School-to-Home
Collaboration                                                    338
*Bethany M. McConnell and Wendy W. Murawski*

Index                                                            356

# *Foreword*

*58,000,000!*

What does 58,000,000 have to do with your preparation to be an amazing, highly qualified educator in today's diverse classroom?

No, it is not how many students there are. No, it is not how many jobs are available. No, it is not the number of pages you will need to read. Rather, it is the number of hits I got this morning when I Googled "teaching in the field of special education." Yes—58,000,000 hits! How can you possibly be on top of such a colossal amount of knowledge?

It has been suggested that trying to get a question answered these days is likened to trying to get a sip of water from a torrential fire hydrant. Picture yourself trying to do just that! What is your imagined result? Are you able to quench your thirst or are you knocked to the ground?

Wendy Murawski and Kathy Scott have come to the rescue in saving you from drowning in the 58,000,000 online resources! As editors of *What Really Works With Exceptional Learners*, they have selected highly knowledgeable experts to write chapters organized into the following four domains:

- What really works with content
- What really works with instruction
- What really works with special populations
- What really works beyond the classroom

The 19 chapters that comprise these four domains all have a common research-based format including:

- Overview of key concepts
- Priority dos and don'ts related to professional practice
- Most significant websites and apps
- Supplemental resources and references

The organization and content provide for you a map of the field's key knowledge. This map enables you to gain a *breadth* of teacher competency that is rare in terms of current textbooks. Once you grasp the special education field's *breadth*, you can be launched when it comes to exploring your area of specialization in more *depth*.

Let's return to the special education fire hydrant of 58,000,000 resources. Rather than being drowned in knowledge onslaught and overload, *What Really Works With Exceptional Learners*

- *identifies* the most important knowledge for you to master,
- *boils* it down into manageable portions, and
- *presents* it to you in an engaging and time-efficient manner.

What a gift of time, energy, and cost savings to you in your quest to be a highly qualified teacher of students with exceptionalities!

*1 book with **4** domains and **19** chapters*

So much better than a fire hydrant of **58,000,000** resources!

Ann Turnbull
*2016 Council for Exceptional Children Lifetime Achievement Awardee*

# *About the Editors*

 **Wendy W. Murawski, PhD,** is the Michael D. Eisner Endowed Chair and Executive Director for the Center for Teaching and Learning at California State University, Northridge (CSUN). She is a tenured Full Professor in the Department of Special Education, a past president of the Teacher Education Division (TED) for the Council for Exceptional Children, a former Teacher Educator of the Year for the state of California, and the recent recipient of the Outstanding Faculty Award for CSUN. She has authored numerous books, chapters, articles, and handbooks in the areas of co-teaching, collaboration, inclusion, differentiation, and teaching. Wendy owns her own educational consulting company (2 TEACH LLC), loves to travel and speak nationally and internationally, and is a frequently requested keynote speaker. Due to her 12-year-old son Kiernan's expertise in dinosaurs and fish, she is also now able to confidently reference Abelisaurus and Goliath Groupers during presentations, when the need arises—you'd be surprised at how often that happens!

 **Kathy Lynn Scott, PhD,** is the Center Administrative Analyst for the Center for Teaching and Learning (CTL) at California State University, Northridge. Kathy was trained as an old school darkroom photographer, but she fell in love with all things to do with education. After conducting research on art education and adult education in England and coordinating research on learning disabilities in New Jersey, Kathy jumped from coast to coast, finding a new home with the CTL where she gets to do a little bit of everything related to education. When not acting as the "glue" for the CTL (as Wendy calls her) and when she finds the time, she collects passport stamps at National Parks. She's been to 48 of the 50 states, but more often than not, she's just relaxing at home, eating something with entirely too much garlic, watching *Jeopardy!*, and shouting out the (not always correct) answers.

# *About the Contributors*

**Brenda L. Barrio, PhD,** is an Assistant Professor of Special Education at Washington State University. Her work focuses on addressing disproportionality in special education through culturally responsive teaching and social justice in education. While globetrotting, she pretends she is on the *Bizarre Foods with Andrew Zimmern* show and samples as much of the local cuisine as possible.

**Anne Brawand, PhD,** is an Assistant Professor at Kutztown University of Pennsylvania. Most of her teaching experience is in the middle level co-taught setting. She is the 2015 recipient of the Outstanding Researcher Award for the Council of Learning Disabilities. Her research area is mathematics interventions. She looks forward to beach trips with her husband and two little boys (mostly because it keeps the house clean!), and she enjoys running to guarantee some quiet time.

**LaToya Cannon, MAT,** is a graduate student at Armstrong University and native New Yorker, currently residing in Georgia. LaToya's love for teaching prompted her to change careers from mental health counseling to special education. Combining the best of both worlds, LaToya's passion lies in working with children with behavior issues that are affecting learning. In her spare time, LaToya enjoys spending time with her teenage daughter and is an avid writer who has written and published six novels.

**Zhen Chai, PhD,** is an Assistant Professor of Early Childhood Special Education at California State University, Northridge. Her research interests include positive behavior supports and using technology to promote early learning. Full of curiosity, she loves challenges. When she is not busy working, she likes to spend time with her family on road trips.

**Kyena E. Cornelius, EdD,** is an Assistant Professor in Special Education at Minnesota State University, Mankato. Her research interests include teacher preparation practices and the induction and mentoring of early career special educators. She enjoys traveling and seeing new places; she especially enjoys these new places if a winery is on the itinerary.

**Jaime True Daley, EdD,** has spent the past 20 years providing special education to children from PreK through twelfth grade in multiple states then teaching teachers at Johns Hopkins University. She's researching a new *order of operations* that stops *multiplying* her kids' activities and *dividing* her time between multiple projects—while *adding* more time to play and *subtracting* gray hairs! "Anyone? . . . Anyone?"

**Ela Kaye Eley, PhD,** is currently Assistant Professor of Educational Technology in the College of Education at Armstrong State University. Her research interests include online and blended learning, technology integration, augmented reality, and makerspaces. Ela Kaye is always searching for new innovations in teaching and learning and is currently exploring ways to get her cats, Butterscotch and Dumbledore, to allow her to share the space on *their* sofa.

**Dawn W. Fraser, EdD,** is the Education Director for Kennedy Krieger Institute's Partnership Program with Anne Arundel County, a role that allows her to combine her passions for working with students diagnosed with autism spectrum disorder, applied behavior analysis, and coaching special educators. In her spare time, she enjoys making beaded and chainmaille jewelry, knitting, and boxing.

**Stacey E. Hardin, PhD,** is an assistant professor at Illinois State University who enjoys traveling the world to learn about diversity and various cultures. Dr. Hardin is the chair of the Culturally Responsive Campus Community committee and fights very hard to ensure the campus is equitable and just. When not on campus, Dr. Hardin tries to stay relevant with the new-age lingo and dances by spending quality time with her daughter.

**Christine A. Hayashi, JD,** is an Associate Professor in the Educational Leadership and Policy Studies Department and Associate Dean of the College of Education at California State University, Northridge. Her areas of academic interest include education policy and law, disability rights, special education law, and educational leadership. When she can get away, she prefers a sleepy balcony with an ocean view.

**Lynnette M. Henderson, PhD,** serves the Vanderbilt Kennedy Center as the StudyFinder Coordinator and as an Associate Director of Community Services. She led the development of the Employment Area of Emphasis, including TennesseeWorks.org. She has researched and spoken on autism spectrum disorder for more than 15 years and has twice been Volunteer of the Year for Autism Tennessee. Meanwhile, she is content with ruling Goodreads, going to the movies, and keeping a positive energy balance.

**Brittany L. Hott, PhD,** is an Assistant Professor at Texas A&M University–Commerce. Her research interests include school-based interventions for students with, or at risk for, emotional and behavioral disabilities. Brittany spends most of her days trying to determine the function of her naughty bird dogs' behavioral choices. To date, one couch, one coffee table, several sweet treats, and the Diaper Genie have exploded. Any advice is much appreciated.

**Claire E. Hughes, PhD,** lives her life in twos: She received her doctorate in both gifted education and special education from the College of William and Mary. She specializes in twice-exceptional children; and she currently has a position as Principal Lecturer and Faculty Head of the Special Needs and Inclusion program at Canterbury Christ Church University in England, while her two children, two dogs, two cats, two fish, and one husband—the other half of the two-parent team—are in the United States until their house sells.

**Kimberly M. Johnson-Harris, PhD,** is an Assistant Professor in the Department of Special Education at Minnesota State University, Mankato. Her research interests revolve around instructional design that facilitates the meaningful inclusion of students with high-incidence disabilities. In an effort to find more balance in her life, she has recently taken up running, cycling, and yoga . . . again.

**Janet Josephson, PhD,** is an Assistant Professor in the Department of Early, Middle, and Exceptional Education at Millersville University in beautiful Lancaster County, Pennsylvania. When she is not preparing the future superheroes of America, she can be found plotting escape routes for dogs in local shelters and smuggling two (or five!) of them into her foster home.

**Amy Kramer, MEd,** is a doctoral candidate at Bowling Green State University. As a practitioner in the field, she has been a teacher, a principal, and a university instructor. Her research and expertise focuses on inclusion and co-teaching. Considering her house is filled with all males (a husband, three boys, and even a male puppy), she relishes in those few-and-far-in-between moments of a clean house and a good Lifetime movie.

**Rebecca Lieberman-Betz, PhD,** is an Assistant Professor of Special Education at the University of Georgia. Her research interests include communication, play, and parent-implemented intervention in young children with autism spectrum disorder. Although living in places such as Maine, Alaska, and Oregon may seem adventurous, Rebecca is now quite convinced that nothing compares to careening around tight corners on hardwood floors in socks to race airplanes with her 3-year-old son. She has yet to win a race.

**Bethany M. McConnell, PhD,** is an Assistant Professor at the University of Pittsburgh at Johnstown. She spends her days creating and teaching a newly developed dual certification special education program. Bethany is writing/performing a reality series on sticky notes with her husband and their children. You can find her "YouTubing" *how to tie a karate belt* or *second position in ballet* to maintain her "family collaboration" credentials as a mom in higher education.

**Katie M. Miller, PhD,** is an Assistant Professor in the Department of Exceptional Student Education at Florida Atlantic University. She has worked as both a general and special educator. Her teaching and research interests center around literacy, technology, and teacher preparation. Originally from Western New York, she enjoys cheering for the Buffalo Sabres and Bills in a different scene these days—the beach!

**Sarah A. Nagro, EdD,** is an Assistant Professor in Special Education at George Mason University. Her research and teaching focus on preparing reflective, profession-ready special educators who effectively implement evidence-based practices to improve the learning experiences of all students. When not writing, Sarah enjoys gardening, playing softball (because she is overly competitive), and spoiling her two golden retrievers.

**Ruby L. Owiny, PhD,** is an Assistant Professor of Education at Trinity International University in the northern Chicago suburbs. Her teaching focuses on approaches to connect general and special education principles to benefit and include all students. Growing up on a farm provided her the training necessary to corral the neighborhood kids and college students who flock to her house on a regular basis!

**Pamela K. Peak, PhD,** is a Senior Lecturer of Special Education at the University of North Texas. Her work focuses on the knowledge and skills required for the effective educational assessment of individuals from culturally and linguistically diverse backgrounds. Living out in the country, she regularly chases armadillos out of the flowerbeds, wrangles dogs away from snakes, and reroutes chickens back into their free range spaces.

**Lesli Raymond, MS,** is a doctoral student in Supervision, Curriculum, and Instruction at Texas A&M University–Commerce. She has 21 years of teaching experience in both special and general education classrooms and was named the 2016 Council for Learning Disabilities Texas Teacher of the Year. Lesli's part-time job is subsidizing her daughter's highly successful (yet largely unprofitable) cookie making business.

**Leila Ansari Ricci, PhD,** is an Associate Professor at California State University, Los Angeles. She coordinates the special education pathway of the *Los Angeles Urban Teacher Residency*, and has coauthored a book on teaching reading to children with visual impairments. When she's not busy with her three daughters, three cats, dog, and (sometimes) foster kittens, you can find her at CrossFit deadlifting nearly 200 pounds, cursing burpees, or running like a turtle stampeding in peanut butter.

**Audrey Robinson, PhD,** is a school counselor at a large, urban elementary school in Mesquite, Texas, and an Adjunct Professor at Texas A&M University–Commerce. She is a Licensed Professional Counselor and a Registered Play Therapist. A classic overachiever, Audrey enjoys filling her plate with her many jobs, including running a part-time photography business, but her favorite job title of all is Mom. She welcomed her first child in May!

**Jacqueline Rodriguez, PhD**, is an Assistant Professor at The College of William & Mary where she codirects the Holmes Scholar Program. Jackie is keenly interested in inclusive education policy and practice, especially related to vulnerable populations including culturally and linguistically diverse learners, refugees, and displaced persons. Most often you can find her trail running with her Belgian Shepherd through sun, rain, sleet, snow, and yes, hail.

**Horacio Sanchez, MEd,** received his master's degree from Duke University and is currently the President/CEO of Resiliency Inc. He has authored several books, and The Maladaptive Council (Academy of Science) recognizes him as a leading authority in emotional disorders and resiliency. When not lecturing and conducting training on helping schools close the achievement gap, he can be found concocting new culinary dishes and accompanying beverages for friends (at least those brave enough to test his next creation).

**Barbara Serianni, PhD,** is an Assistant Professor of Special Education at Armstrong State University in Savannah, Georgia. Her research interests include co-teaching, inclusion, including students with autism spectrum disorder, and the tech tools that support those endeavors. As "Grammie" to seven little digital natives, she is constantly challenged to stay one step ahead and is long past thinking she can beat any of them at their favorite digital game.

**Sally A. Spencer, EdD,** is a Professor of Special Education at California State University, Northridge. She has published three books, two for Corwin, and is a passionate advocate for good teaching and good teachers. In her spare time she works to rescue dogs and cats and currently has 12 of them (12!!) in her home. A good housekeeper is mandatory!

**Jennifer D. Walker, PhD,** is an Assistant Professor at the University of Mary Washington in Virginia. Her research interests include students with emotional and behavior disabilities, functional analysis, and positive behavior supports. In an effort to teach, research, provide professional development, and parent three children, two dogs, a cat, and six chickens, Jennifer's preferred superpower would be the ability to successfully function without sleep.

**Margaret P. Weiss, PhD,** is an Assistant Professor in Special Education at George Mason University. Her research and writing are focused on co-teaching in secondary schools and in higher education. She has been a middle school and high school special educator as well as a learning specialist in student athlete academic support at the college level. Outside of work, she enjoys learning new things by taking on home improvement projects that are way beyond her current capabilities.

# Introduction

This book is called *What Really Works With Exceptional Learners*, but when you think about it, what students *aren't* exceptional, or special, learners at some point in their lives? Which one of us has not struggled with content or pedagogy or even just sitting, focusing, being organized, or listening . . . especially before our coffee in the morning? It would be lovely if we could have a book that addressed *all* our special needs and gave us the perfect answer to all questions. Unfortunately, there are simply too many needs to address them all and this book is not an encyclopedia. (For those of you who do not know what an encyclopedia is, it was a paper version of the Internet before the Internet was created.) So we have limited our focus in this book to special learners with identified disabilities, those who are English language learners, and those who are gifted or twice exceptional. That is plenty to tackle in one book, don't you agree?

It is amazing to us when we hear teachers say, "I wasn't taught how to deal with that type of student." We wish we knew who "*that* type" of kid was! Every student we have worked with has been unique, different, special. However, we do know that there are techniques that teachers can try to help improve the learning or behavior or social skills of students. We also know that labels have been created to help us categorize and make sense of the special needs that some students have. We definitely capitalize on those labels through the chapters of this book. But we implore you to read this text, not as a guide to specific categories of students, but as a reference manual for numerous strategies to try for *any* child.

As with our first two texts of this series, we selected authors we knew are not only content experts but who also are practitioners. We wanted people who knew the research base, but also who really knew kids and what works with students! We asked them to write *to* the reader (that's you!), not *at* the reader. We asked for practical strategies and bulleted lists, not ivory tower, theoretical, or esoteric information. The research provided for each chapter will help you recognize how important it is that the things you do in school are evidence-based, and will be given to you in a way that respects that you are a busy educator with a lot to process. We know that you will find this book accessible and helpful. We hope you will share the strategies you learn with your colleagues, as you hear them venting in the teachers' lounge or crying in the parking lot after school.

How will you use this book? That's up to you. You can read it from beginning to end or you can pick and choose. We organized it so that content areas are first, followed by instructional strategies and pedagogy. In the third section, we include information on working with students in specific disability areas. Finally, when working with exceptional learners, there is no way we could (or should) avoid addressing legal issues and school-home partnerships! While some chapters may be more or less relevant to you and your teaching, we hope you consider reading them all. You may be surprised what you pick up in a chapter on working with students who are twice-exceptional, for example, even if you don't think you have any of those students in your classes yet!

We'd also like to point out that we have interspersed quite a few "Making Connections" boxes throughout the chapters. This is so you can see how all our chapters interrelate and support one another. If you want, you can make this a "Choose-Your-Own-Adventure" book and follow the Making Connections boxes throughout the text! Want to keep learning? We certainly hope you do. If so, please look at the plethora of references and websites our authors have included and cited. We also provide an "Additional Recommended Reading" section, but be aware, if an item was cited in the References section, it is not in the Recommended Reading section as well. We hope you will know that the author recommends it by the fact that it was important enough to reference.

We must thank each and every one of our authors for their hard work on this book. When we approached them and said, "We want you to write this chapter on your topic of expertise and passion, but please keep it practical and short," we were so excited by the responses. Not only did they meet that challenge, but they also met our very quick deadlines and were positive every time we gave editing feedback. They, like us, felt this book was important and needed to be out there. They understood that educators are busy and looking for a reference that is based in research but is a quick read, chock-full of ideas and doable strategies. We thank each and every one of our authors for working with us and for adding their expertise to the field through their chapters.

We must also thank the Eisner Foundation for creating and supporting the Center for Teaching and Learning (CTL) at California State University, Northridge (CSUN). Their vision of ongoing professional development for urban education has enabled us to create this What Really Works series in the first place. Our Dean at the CSUN Michael D. Eisner College of Education, Dr. Michael Spagna, also continues to constantly encourage us to pursue cutting edge practices in education and to remain the professional development and research hub of the college. Our Provost, Dr. Yi Li, has also demonstrated his support—in words and funds—for our commitment to sharing What Really Works with the community. We would like to thank Steve Holle, the CTL Coordinator of Professional Development for keeping our PD going as we were in the weeds of this book. We would also like to thank the CTL student assistants who have helped us with this book. Dani Lavoie, Jessica Bandarizadeh, and Soraya Fallah provided us with much support throughout this manuscript, while also helping us run a myriad other events. Special thanks to student assistant Josh Mandell for assisting with the permissions of this book—Josh, we wish you the best of luck in your impending career as an English teacher! We are so grateful for all our CTL student assistants; they are wonderful additions to our CTL family.

Finally, we would like to encourage each of you to subscribe to our mailing list at ctl@csun.edu. We promise no spamming or selling; our goal is merely to keep you abreast of our publications, presentations, events, and research opportunities. We look forward to you becoming part of our larger CTL family as well.

All our best,

*Wendy J. Murawski* and *Kathy Lynn Scott*

# SECTION I

## *What Really Works With Content*

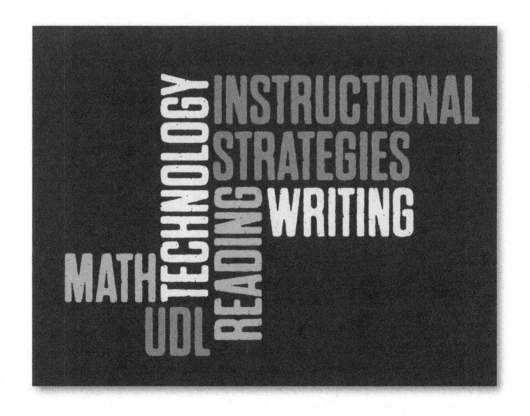

# 1

# *Getting Past "I Hate Math!"*

Sarah A. Nagro
*George Mason University*

Margaret P. Weiss
*George Mason University*

Jaime True Daley
*Johns Hopkins University*

## THE RUB: MATHEMATICS AND STUDENTS WITH DISABILITIES

Wait, what? A student with a disability who doesn't like math? Say it isn't so! But yes, we all know this far too well. We also know that responding to "Why do I ever have to know how to write a geometry proof" with "Because it'll be on the test" simply isn't a good strategy. What can we do, and why has there been such a push for problem-based mathematics?

Improving student outcomes through effective academic instruction has always been key. The passage of the No Child Left Behind Act (NCLB) of 2001 provided an even bigger push to do so (NCLB, 2002). The consensus was that to better prepare students for postsecondary success, greater focus needs to be on improving academic outcomes for students across content areas and particularly in mathematics (NCLB, 2002). The Common Core State Standards Initiative (CCSSI, 2010) was enacted to do just that by introducing more rigorous national mathematics standards that promote critical thinking and problem solving. Even though not all states embrace the Common Core State Standards (CCSS), all national mathematics standards indicate that students must be able to reason abstractly and quantitatively to be career and college ready, yet these skills are challenging for even the best students. As a result, mathematics curriculum persists as one of the most difficult aspects of school for students with disabilities (Miller & Hudson, 2007).

Despite higher standards for student learning and improved instructional approaches, students with disabilities continue to struggle in math. Nationwide, students with disabilities are performing far below the national averages. That might not surprise you—naturally, students with special needs would struggle more than students without disabilities. But will this surprise you? Only 18% of fourth graders and 8% of eighth graders performed at a proficient or advanced level on the 2013 Nation's Report Card (National Center for Education Statistics, 2013). Ouch! Compared to the 42% of all fourth graders and 35% of all eighth graders without disabilities nationwide who are performing at or above proficient in mathematics, the differences are striking. Put simply, students with disabilities are failing math at much higher rates than their nondisabled peers. (Though, obviously, we need to do better in teaching math across the board.)

The reasons students with disabilities struggle in math are well documented. Many students with disabilities lack number sense or the ability to interact with numbers in a fluid and flexible manner (Gersten & Chard, 1999). Number sense is the ability to seamlessly translate abstract mathematical expressions into real-world concepts. Students with disabilities who lack number sense and experience additional cognitive difficulties often experience deficits in organizational skills, higher order thinking, working memory, learning and retaining operational skills, connecting conceptual knowledge with tangible representations, and academic risk taking (Montague, Krawec, Enders, & Dietz, 2014). Additionally, students with more pervasive disabilities tend to struggle with fine motor skills due to the "inability to plan, organize, and coordinate movement" (Gibbs, Appleton, & Appleton, 2007, p. 534). These students tend to struggle with spatial representation of numerical values, misinterpret visually represented material, and face deficits in writing and reading comprehension when accessing the general curriculum (Geary, 2004). Just imagine struggling with math concepts only to be introduced to word problems and learn that now you get to struggle with math, reading, and writing . . . all at once!

Many of the challenges students with disabilities face when trying to learn mathematics align to shifts in the CCSS focus. For example, key mathematical practices that span across all grades under the CCSS require students to persevere in problem solving, reason abstractly, construct viable arguments, communicate with precision, and identify structural patterns and relationships. Do any of those sound like they might be challenging for a student with a disability? We think so, too. In fact, difficulties in information processing, including working memory and executive functioning problems, as well as making meaning from text and generalizing strategies across contexts will have an impact on a student's success in mathematical practices. Steps can, and should, be taken to mitigate the many challenges faced by students with disabilities in mathematics education. That's where this chapter comes in.

## WHAT RESEARCH SAYS REALLY WORKS IN MATHEMATICS FOR STUDENTS WITH DISABILITIES

Researchers have identified several research- and evidence-based practices that promote positive student learning dispositions, flexible concept understanding, reflective decision making, greater confidence in mathematics abilities, and improved academic performance for students with disabilities (Gurganus, 2007). With all this information, it should be a piece of cake to teach math effectively to students with disabilities, right? Not quite, but at least there are confirmed strategies that help. The research- and evidence-based practices covered in this chapter can be summarized into three categories: graduated instructional sequence, commonly referred to as the *concrete-representational-abstract* (CRA) sequence; combined cognitive and metacognitive strategies instruction; and schema-based instruction (SBI). This chapter briefly reviews the essential components and gives specific examples of all three.

**Key Concepts**

Your three heavy-hitters in math?

- CRA sequence
- Cognitive and metacognitive structures
- Schema-based instruction

### Graduated Instructional Sequence

Graduated instructional sequence, or CRA, is a three-stage process used to develop conceptual knowledge in mathematics (Mancl, Miller, & Kennedy, 2012). Students learn the conceptual underpinnings of topics, such as factoring equations in algebra, by progressing through stages that include *concrete* demonstrations or introducing physical manipulatives to depictions represent conceptual properties (e.g., holding three apples), followed by *representational* or pictorial depictions (e.g., three tally marks or three pictures of apples), and concluding with *abstract* depictions or problems presented in symbolic notation or written form (e.g., *3* or *three*; Mancl et al., 2012). The CRA stages are taught using the principles of explicit instruction including modeling and identification of critical components, as well as guided and independent practice with examples and nonexamples (Archer & Hughes, 2011).

Mathematics CCSS (CCSSI, 2010) place an emphasis on successive concepts, such as algebra, across grade levels. Though many educators seem to think that manipulatives (the C in the CRA teaching sequence) are for primary or elementary grades only, their use has been advocated for and proven effective in higher level mathematics as well (e.g., Miller & Hudson, 2007). For example, using algebra tiles in the *concrete* phase of the CRA teaching sequence, students with disabilities can "see" all basic algebraic operations (Maccini, Mulcahy, & Wilson, 2007). This often helps students without disabilities as well. Think about how students are typically shown an abstract example on the board, such as $2x + 3 = 9$. Students are then instructed to subtract 3 from both sides of the equal sign, even if they might not grasp why. Setting up and solving the equation with algebra tiles helps students understand the underlying concept behind adding opposites (different colors of the same blocks) to equal zero. Moving students sequentially through the CRA teaching sequence during algebra instruction, and also during the introduction of any new math concept, can help link concrete concepts to abstract mathematical expressions for students who struggle to do so without such structure. So bring on the manipulatives!

## Combined Cognitive and Metacognitive Strategies Instruction

Cognitive strategy instruction includes teaching students reasoning methods to enhance problem-solving skills, since problem solving is both an area of focus in mathematics (CCSSI, 2010) and an area of weakness for students with disabilities (Montague et al., 2014). Montague and Dietz (2009) reviewed the evidence base of cognitive strategy instruction including a 7-step process for attacking and solving word problems. The authors found cognitive strategy instruction showed promise for improving the problem-solving abilities of students with disabilities, particularly students

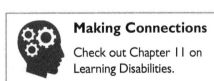

**Making Connections**

Check out Chapter 11 on Learning Disabilities.

with learning disabilities. The 7-step process includes: reading the problem to clear up uncertainty, putting the word problem in their own words, drawing or visually representing the problem, creating a plan to solve the problem, predicting the answer, computing the answer, and then checking the answer. Pretty logical, right?

Despite the success of the cognitive strategy instruction, many students with disabilities require additional help understanding how to approach problem solving (Montague, Warger, & Morgan, 2000). Combining metacognitive strategies instruction with cognitive strategies promotes a holistic approach to effective and efficient problem solving (Jitendra, DiPipi, & Perron-Jones, 2002). One metacognitive strategy is a 3-step process called *Solve it!* where students coach themselves through each of the seven problem-solving steps. Students follow a sequence of *say, ask, check* to say the purpose of the step, ask what is required in that step, and check to assure the step is completed (Montague et al., 2000). Combining cognitive and metacognitive strategies in this way can improve independence for students with disabilities who are learning math.

## Schema-Based Instruction

Even after implementing combined cognitive and metacognitive strategy instruction, students with disabilities may still struggle to *persist in problem solving* (CCSSI, 2010). We know—you're shocked. It's true though; disabilities that impact math just do not go away that easily. Reasons for this enduring struggle include the inability to learn and retain operational skills, gaps in higher order thinking, and failure to apply a systematic strategy (Lerner, 2003). Traditionally, students are taught to recall specific operations based on key words within problems. Focusing on scanning for key words and then recalling rules or procedures rather than emphasizing big picture comprehension of mathematical concepts may actually be perpetuating the challenges students face in mathematics (Dingfelder, 2007). This is just so far away from what we've traditionally done with students with disabilities and math so it can be a difficult shift for many educators.

Schema-based instruction can help address such challenges by teaching students to categorize word problems graphically in a way that guides meaning and structure recognition (Jitendra, Griffin, Deatline-Buchman, & Sczesniak, 2007). For example, students can group word problems into *change* problems (e.g., requiring addition or subtraction), *group* problems (e.g., requiring the combination of groups or sets), or *compare* problems (e.g., describing relationships between numbers) (Dingfelder, 2007; Jitendra, Hoff, & Beck, 1999). Approaching word problem instruction in this manner can build students' schema about ways most problems can be solved (Montague & Jitendra, 2006). Essentially, you are providing students with a visual graphic organizer to help them understand their math.

As we've stated, students with disabilities frequently struggle with math, and yet math is a major area of emphasis in all schools. Using the CRA (concrete-representational-abstract) progression, adding in metacognitive and cognitive strategies to make students aware of their processes, and providing schema to help them see how they are solving their problems, are all evidence-based approaches for helping students learn math.

Here are a few of our major dos and don'ts when it comes to teaching students with disabilities mathematics.

# SABOTAGING MATH INSTRUCTION AND STUDENT LEARNING

**Teachers and Administrators:**

✗ **STOP using drill and fill worksheets that were premade for general consumption.** This style of instruction reinforces passive learning for students with disabilities who do not make connections between procedural probes and mathematical concepts. Plus, they're boring!

✗ **STOP teaching math tricks that do not link the process for solving problems to the mathematical concepts these problems are used to teach.** We all love magic, but if the students don't understand why the trick works, what's the point?

✗ **STOP handing out calculators as a standalone support.** Students with disabilities already struggle with number sense, and using calculators in this way requires additional procedural awareness, a common area of relative weakness. They may be fine as an accommodation, but not as your answer for how to *teach* math.

✗ **STOP jumping from instruction to independent practice without sufficient guided practice.** Many students who lack number sense cannot generalize concepts across probes without supports. Be ready to differentiate. Some of your students may be ready for independent practice before others; prepare for that.

✗ **STOP targeting one type of learning mode (visual, auditory, kinesthetic) during mathematics lessons.** Though the research on learning styles hasn't been validated, we can all agree that students don't learn in one way. Instead, use multiple means of representing the material to account for students' relative strengths (e.g., listening comprehension) and weaknesses (e.g., processing delays). This also goes along nicely with the emphasis on Universal Design for Learning (see www.cast.org).

**Making Connections**

Check out Chapter 4 on Instructional Strategies and Universal Design for Learning.

✗ **STOP giving homework that includes new concepts.** Homework is meant to review and reinforce. It is not meant to help a teacher move ahead in the curriculum more quickly. For students with special needs, homework may already be taking more time than nondisabled peers in completing; to add in information that has not been presented almost guarantees that the student will not do it or will do it wrong. You may even want to watch the film Race to Nowhere (www.racetonowhere.com) to see if it impacts your overall view of homework for all students, not just those who are special learners.

## SUCCESSFULLY TEACHING MATH TO ALL STUDENTS, INCLUDING EXCEPTIONAL LEARNERS

**Teachers and Administrators, DO this:**

**Plugged In**

For a short presentation on Planning Pyramids, see http://www.mindspring .com/~lindaross/Differentiating_ Instruction/Pyramid_Planning.swf.

✔ **USE the Pyramid Planning approach when planning for whole group math instruction.** Most of the time, math teachers are instructing the entire class, including students with special needs, and it can be difficult to differentiate for so many students. The Planning Pyramid for mathematics instruction helps decide what all, some, and just a few students will learn as well as the resources needed to achieve such learning objectives.

✔ **HAVE high expectations for your students' learning**—don't water it down, break it down. This can be done by identifying the big picture, the ultimate learning objective, the "My students will be better off if they just learn this one thing today" concept, and then break that concept down by targeting individual components.

✔ **USE the CRA instructional sequence when introducing new topics.** This gradual release framework will help students make their own connections during learning experiences by blending concrete demonstrations and abstract depictions in a structured way. First model with concrete objects and have students repeat. Then model several examples using pictorial representations and have students repeat the practice with a partner while you prompt them with supportive questioning. Provide an abstract representation of a concept only after students master them with scaffolds.

**Plugged In**

For downloadable visual organizers about scaffolding math instruction using the CRA sequence, visit www.learningequalizer.com.

✔ **VARY the "calculation devices" used as accommodations.** Go beyond the calculator to support students by providing number charts, fraction charts, and place value boards. Again, these suggestions are to support students in *understanding* math, not merely memorizing procedures. Provide visual guides such as t-charts for function tables, time lines for elapsed time, and area models for partial product multiplication and partial quotient division. Use printed examples in page protector sleeves with dry erase markers to provide resources for students to reuse with homework and assignments. Consider creating a *resource binder* with customized tools. We've provided several examples for you at the end of this chapter.

✔ **ASK students to explain their reasoning.** Plugging numbers into a formula for 30 problems straight is not actually showing comprehension of math concepts. Students who can explain their thinking and process for solving a math problem will have an easier time generalizing these concepts across contexts, especially since math in everyday life is not predictable like math textbooks. Build on student strengths by asking, or letting them choose, to explain in writing, orally, on video, or in pictures to build confidence with expressing themselves.

✔ **PROMOTE perseverance in problem solving by providing student-centered supports.** These student-centered supports might include anchor charts, manipulatives, hint cards, self-correcting materials, graphic organizers, and self-monitoring checklists. For ideas of how to make activities student centered, check out

**Plugged In**

Learn about student-centered teaching through teacher blogs!

- http://fishbowlteaching
  .blogspot.ca/p/math-
  resources.html
- https://misstorkelson-
  swiki.wikispaces.com/
  Self+Correcting+Material

what these distinguished math teachers are doing through their blogs listed in the call out box or visit *Math Landing* at http://www.mathlanding.org/content/hint-cards for teacher resources, tools, and videos on effective strategies such as using hint cards in your own math classroom.

✔ **USE schema-based instruction to help students solve word problems.** Teach students that every math problem asks them to find an unknown, but most of the information is given. Provide students with diagrams to show the whole to part relationship, such as a whole rectangle with two smaller rectangles drawn under it (see figures at the end of the chapter). The purpose of schema-based instruction is to help students look at math problems and identify patterns rather than only focusing on solving each problem in isolation. One suggestion is to teach students specific patterns of problems such as change or grouping without any missing information first to help them master the learning technique before having to actually use it.

✔ **USE precision in math language.** Focus on increasing students' comfort in using math language rather than emphasizing the memorization of math rules to help students make connections and generalize abstract math concepts across contexts and across the curriculum. For example, begin by reviewing a stack of 5 to 10 related vocabulary terms with pictorial representations of the terms. Generate a sentence that defines and links the terms to each other. Then expect students to use the terms throughout the lesson. Refer back to vocabulary cards as needed. Challenge yourself and students to use these same terms during future math lessons or even during cross-curricular discussions in science or reading.

✔ **ALLOW for sufficient guided practice that includes verification of accuracy and strategy use.** Start with the "Rule of 9" for how frequently to model concepts (3 times), guide small groups or partners (3 times), and require independent practice (3 times). Students with disabilities may require additional guided practice with models, manipulatives, or self-correcting materials before independent practice such as the customizable self-correcting checklists available at http://www.interventioncentral.org/academic-interventions/math/self-monitoring-customized-math-self-correction-checklists. To help students verify accuracy and strategy use, consider introducing self-monitoring student checklists such as the ones available through *Positive Behavior Interventions and Supports (PBIS) World* at http://www.pbisworld.com/tier-2/self-monitoring.

**Making Connections**

Check out Chapter 8 on Positive Behavior Supports.

✔ **USE cognitive strategies.** Try the 7-step problem solving strategy and metacognitive strategies, such as the 3-step process called *Solve it!*, to coach students through thinking about and attacking problem solving. Cognitive and metacognitive strategies are likely new concepts for students who are not always expected to think about their thinking. This can be overwhelming to introduce all at once, especially with all the other new strategies introduced in this chapter. Introduce one strategy at a time, and practice the selected strategy until it is mastered before introducing another. First, use the strategy as a whole class. Model the steps of the strategy using think-alouds and anchor charts. Then gradually shift the responsibility to the students by asking them to complete one, then two, then three (and so on) steps of the strategy independently before checking back in with a teacher. Once you know they are on the right track, you can provide positive reinforcement and prompt students to continue their learning process (known as the *catch and release technique*). It may take a few lessons to successfully introduce a new cognitive or metacognitive strategy, but once students have the hang of it, you will increase instructional time by reducing confusion and necessary redirection that interrupts learning.

✔ **PROVIDE students with choices when approaching problem solving.** Hard to reach students such as the nonstarters, students who avoid tasks, or those easily frustrated will benefit from having choices when approaching learning. Choice making can increase student motivation and independence. Embed choices into math lessons whenever possible. Simple choice making templates include a tic-tac-toe board where students choose three math problems to complete to successfully win the tic-tac-toe game. Another more complex choice making strategy that can help with differentiating instruction is a learning menu. Students can choose an appetizer (a planning strategy or graphic organizer), an entrée (the problem to solve), and a dessert (an extension activity that links the problem to larger concepts or daily life) from the learning menu to achieve a learning objective.

 **Plugged In**

To see a video of a teacher using a learning menu to introduce choice, visit the teaching channel at https://www.teachingchannel .org/videos/differentiating- instruction-strategy.

✔ **ASK open-ended mathematical questions.** Asking open-ended questions does two things for students. First, it helps them understand that there isn't a definite "this way is the right way" to answer math questions. Second, it allows you the opportunity to say, "Tell me more" so that you can check the metacognitive strategies that students are using to solve problems.

✔ **ASK students what they "notice" and what they "wonder" before teaching a new concept to assess their current levels of understanding.** This allows you to assess their use of vocabulary (precision in language) as well as to see if they can apply previous concepts to new learning. One of the most important components of math is using what you already know to solve problems that don't look exactly the same. If students are encouraged to hypothesize, they take ownership of what they know and are then asking the question of what comes next on their own.

✔ **DRAW CONNECTIONS between students' lives and mathematical concepts to promote desired student learning dispositions such as authentic engagement.** For example, when creating practice or example problems, use students' names and situations they may find around school or at home. Instead of solving endless equations like $2x + 3 = 12$, put students into the problems. "Joe is at the basketball game. His friends ask him to buy some popcorn for them. He has $5 and each bag of popcorn costs $0.75. But he really wants some Skittles. They are $0.50. If he buys the Skittles for himself, how many friends can he buy popcorn for? What should Joe figure out first? Why?" This promotes student engagement and helps students see how they use math every day.

✔ **POSE real-world problems to students that require application of mathematical concepts.** Again, it is so important to show students that math is something we need and use in the real world, not just numbers repeated over and over on a page. Rather than focusing strictly on memorizing math rules, try posing real-life problems that happen to require target math concepts to solve the problem. For example, you can use Google Earth in your math class to "visit" actual crop circles in Wiltshire, England, a fractal coastline in Ireland, or the surface of the Earth and pose questions about complex area, circumference, estimating, distance, exchange rates, line graphs, and so much more.

**Plugged In**

For complete lessons with embedded Google Earth recordings or images, visit http://www.realworldmath.org and create a free teacher account.

✔ **PROVIDE multiple opportunities to practice math concepts and procedures with feedback.** While we continue to stress digging deeper into math concepts, which means more time spent on each math problem, it is still critical to expose students, particularly students with disabilities, to repetition. A major league baseball pitcher throws hundreds of practice pitches to develop muscle memory, and similarly, we want our students to develop math muscle memory. How can you both dig deep into critical math thinking and help students develop math muscle memory through repetition? Find a balance between breadth and depth. Focus on breadth when introducing new concepts and depth when reinforcing previously introduced concepts while always giving students opportunities to respond so that you can "catch" misconceptions and "release" students back to student-centered learning (yes, the catch and release technique again).

✔ **PROVIDE immediate and specific feedback to students during guided practice.** Immediate feedback helps ensure high rates of success and reduces the likelihood of practicing errors. As a colleague likes to say, "Practice makes permanent." You don't want that practice to be incorrect, and then you have to reteach a concept or strategy. As a student is learning new concepts or strategies, make sure you are watching, checking in, and providing immediate and specific feedback in terms the students understands. Then ask them to do it again until they become independent.

✔ **FACILITATE peer-to-peer interactions as well as model appropriate peer feedback routines.** In other words, teach students to work together in math. Put them in pairs or small groups, and give them scripts for giving feedback, correcting their peers, and talking about math. First, have them practice these interactions with material they already know. Provide feedback about their collaboration and dialogue. Then have them practice again!

**Plugged In**

To learn more about *Classwide Peer Tutoring* and *Peer Assisted Learning* in math, visit http://www.council-for-learning-disabilities.org/peer-tutoring-flexible-peer-mediated-strategy-that-involves-students-serving-as-academic-tutors and http://www.readingrockets.org/article/using-peer-tutoring-facilitate-access.

✔ **MONITOR student comprehension throughout the lesson with frequent check-ins.** We've all seen it—as a teacher gives instruction, she asks three questions. The same student answers all three questions. Everyone else seems to be writing things down and following along. "Great! They all get it," she thinks. Wrong. She only knows that the student who answers gets it. Have students answer your questions on whiteboards and raise them up so you can see. Have students use laminated cards with numbers to raise up answers in response to your questions. Teachers must check in with students with disabilities, in particular, throughout instruction to see how they are progressing.

✔ **TRY new techniques that are supported by quality research.** Visit reliable peer-reviewed journals and organization websites to learn about new instructional strategies and techniques. Currently, Whole Brain Math teaching strategies, which combine direct instruction, peer-to-peer interactions, high opportunities to respond, and immediate feedback, are being researched in classrooms across the United States, Canada, Europe, and elsewhere. To read about the research behind this systematic approach to math instruction and to watch videos of actual teachers employing Whole Brain Math, visit http://wholebrainteaching.com.

**Plugged In**

Visit http://trackstudentlearning.weebly.com to download, customize, and print formative assessment templates that align with whole group responding techniques to track student participation and comprehension during math.

## CALCULATION DEVICE OPTIONS ACROSS MATH CONCEPTS

| Key Mathematical Concept | "Calculation Devices" Picture Representations of Concrete Objects | |
|---|---|---|
| Numbers | • Tens frames<br>• Hundreds chart<br>• Place value chart<br>• Multiplication chart<br>• Fractions chart | |
| Geometry | • Labeled diagrams<br>• Large grid<br>• Mnemonics | |
| Measurement | • Charts and diagrams<br>  ○ Analog clock with hours and minutes<br>  ○ Rulers showing inches and fractions of an inch<br>  ○ Capacity units showing volume<br>  ○ Labeled protractor | |
| Statistics | • Bar graph<br>• Line graph<br>• Line plot<br>• Pictograph<br>• Stem and leaf plot | |

## SCHEMA-BASED INSTRUCTION GRAPHIC ORGANIZER

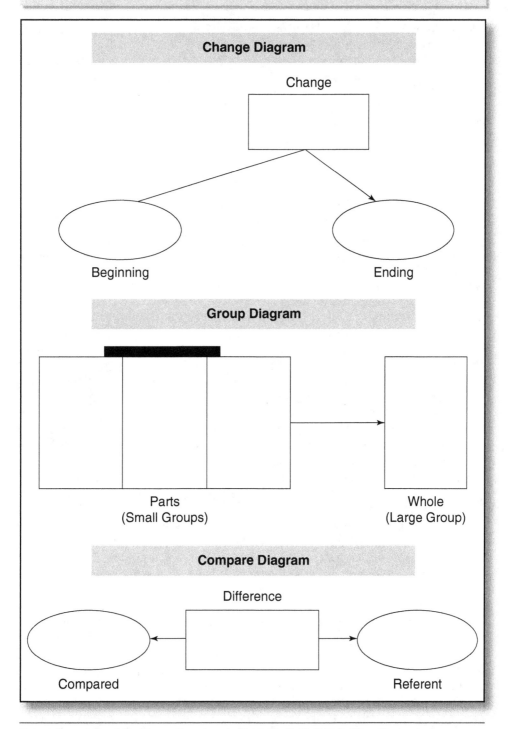

**Change Diagram**

Change

Beginning

Ending

**Group Diagram**

Parts
(Small Groups)

Whole
(Large Group)

**Compare Diagram**

Difference

Compared

Referent

*Source:* http://teachingld.org; Jitendra, A. K., & Hoff, K. (1996). The effects of schema-based instruction on the mathematical word-problem-solving performance of students with learning disabilities. *Journal of Learning Disabilities, 29*(4), 422–431.

# REFERENCES

Archer, A., & Hughes, C. (2011). *Explicit instruction: Effective and efficient teaching*. New York, NY: Guilford Press.

Common Core State Standards Initiative. (2010). *Common core state standards for mathematics*. Washington, DC: National Governors Association Center for Best Practices and the Council of Chief State School Officers. Retrieved from http://www.corestandards.org/the-standards

Dingfelder, S. (2007). Schema-based instruction improves math skills. *American Psychological Association, 38*(4), 10. Retrieved from http://www.apa.org/monitor/apr07/schema.aspx

Geary, D. C. (2004). Mathematics and learning disabilities. *Journal of Learning Disabilities, 37*, 4–15.

Gersten, R., & Chard, D. (1999). Number sense: Rethinking arithmetic instruction for students with mathematical disabilities. *The Journal of Special Education, 33*, 18–28.

Gibbs, J., Appleton, J., & Appleton, R. (2007). Dyspraxia or developmental coordination disorder? Unravelling the enigma. *Archives of Disease in Childhood, 92*(6), 534–539.

Gurganus, S. P. (2007). *Math instruction for students with learning problems* (1st ed.). Boston, MA: Pearson Education.

Jitendra, A., DiPipi, C. M., & Perron-Jones, N. (2002). An exploratory study of schema-based word-problem-solving instruction for middle school students with learning disabilities: An emphasis on conceptual and procedural understanding. *The Journal of Special Education, 36*, 23–38.

Jitendra, A. K., Griffin, C. C., Deatline-Buchman, A., & Sczesniak, E. (2007). Mathematical word problem solving in third-grade classrooms. *Journal of Educational Research, 100*, 283–302.

Jitendra, A. K., & Hoff, K. (1996). The effects of schema-based instruction on the mathematical word-problem-solving performance of students with learning disabilities. *Journal of Learning Disabilities, 29*(4), 422–431.

Jitendra, A. K., Hoff, K., & Beck, M. M. (1999). Teaching middle school students with learning disabilities to solve word problems using a schema based approach. *Remedial and Special Education, 20*, 50–64.

Lerner, J. (2003). *Learning disabilities: Theories, diagnosis, and teaching strategies* (9th ed.). Boston, MA: Houghton Mifflin.

Maccini, P., Mulcahy, C. A., & Wilson, M. G. (2007). A follow-up of mathematics interventions for secondary students with learning disabilities. *Learning Disabilities Research & Practice, 22*, 58–74.

Mancl, D. B., Miller, S. P., & Kennedy, M. (2012). Using the concrete-representational-abstract sequence with integrated strategy instruction to teach subtraction with regrouping to students with learning disabilities. *Learning Disabilities Research & Practice, 27*(4), 152–166.

Miller, S. P., & Hudson, P. J. (2007). Using evidence-based practices to build mathematics competence related to conceptual, procedural, and declarative knowledge. *Learning Disabilities Research & Practice, 22*(1), 47–57.

Montague, M., & Dietz, S. (2009). Evaluating the evidence base for cognitive strategy instruction and mathematical problem solving. *Exceptional Children, 75*, 285–302.

Montague, M., & Jitendra, A. (2006). *Teaching mathematics to middle school students with learning difficulties*. New York, NY: Guilford Press.

Montague, M., Krawec, J., Enders, C., & Dietz, S. (2014). The effects of cognitive strategy instruction on math problem solving of middle-school students of varying ability. *Journal of Educational Psychology, 106*(2), 469–481.

Montague, M., Warger, C., & Morgan, T. H. (2000). Solve it! Strategy instruction to improve mathematical problem solving. *Learning Disabilities Research & Practice, 15*(2), 110–116.

National Center for Education Statistics. (2013). *The Nation's Report Card: A first look: 2013 mathematics and reading* (NCES 2014–451). Washington, DC: National Center for Education Statistics, Institute of Education Sciences, U.S. Department of Education.

No Child Left Behind Act of 2001, Pub. L. No. 107-110, 115 § 1425. (2002).

## ADDITIONAL RECOMMENDED READING

Bouck, E. C., Satsangi, R., Doughty, T. T., & Courtney, W. T. (2014). Virtual and concrete manipulatives: A comparison of approaches for solving mathematics problems for students with autism spectrum disorder. *Journal of Autism and Developmental Disorders, 44*(1), 180–193.

Gersten, R., Beckmann, S., Clarke, B., Foegen, A., Marsh, L., Star, J. R., & Witzel, B. (2009). Assisting students struggling with mathematics: Response to intervention (RtI) for elementary and middle schools. NCEE 2009–4060. Retrieved from http://ies.ed.gov/ncee/wwc/pdf/practice_guides/rti_math_pg_042109.pdf

Rivera, C. J., & Baker, J. N. (2013). Teaching students with intellectual disability to solve for x. *TEACHING Exceptional Children, 46*(2), 14–21.

Satsangi, R., & Bouck, E. C. (2014). Using virtual manipulative instruction to teach the concepts of area and perimeter to secondary students with learning disabilities. *Learning Disability Quarterly, 38*(3), 174–186.

## TOP WEBSITES TO SUPPORT MAKING MATH ACCESSIBLE

→ http://dwwlibrary.wested.org

→ http://www.nctm.org

→ https://www.frontrowed.com

→ http://nlvm.usu.edu/en/nav/vlibrary.html

→ https://www.tenmarks.com

→ http://www.intensiveintervention.org/intervention-type/mathematics

→ http://www.ldonline.org/article/c665

## APPS WE LOVE

- ➡ Math Maze!
- ➡ Monster Math Multiplayer
- ➡ Zap Zap Fractions
- ➡ Math Shake
- ➡ Mental Arithmetic Math Workout

# 2

# *Creating a Cadre of Capable Readers*

Leila Ansari Ricci

*California State University, Los Angeles*

## READING: FAIRY TALES OR FAILURE?

As a young girl, my earliest memories of reading are only that I loved it. When I was 6 years old, I remember begging my mother to take me to the local bookstore, where I would gather up as many books as I could convince her to buy, pouring over the fairy tales and adventures as soon as we got home, and within hours announcing to my then irritated mother that I needed more books right now! Sadly, this is not the experience of many children in the United States, particularly those with disabilities. Unlike my younger self, too many children do not smoothly enter the exciting world of adventures made accessible by their proficient reading. Rather, many struggle to read unfamiliar words, fail to understand the meaning of long passages, or recoil with anxiety when asked to read aloud from a textbook.

As a nation, we have prioritized improving educational outcomes for all children. Just look at the efforts from the Every Student Succeeds Act (2015) and its predecessor, No Child Left Behind (2001), to the Common Core State Standards. We know that reading serves as the foundation for the rest of formal education and is necessary for full access to the educational curriculum (American Federation of Teachers, 2008). However, much work remains in making our national priority a reality, especially for children with special needs. According to the National Assessment of Educational Progress, a staggering 67% of fourth graders with disabilities scored below basic in reading, as compared to 26% of students without disabilities (National Center for Education Statistics, 2015). Seriously. Read that again. Sixty-seven percent of students with disabilities are below basic in reading! That's more than two-thirds. How scary! When asked to read, many of these children think of failure rather than fairy tales. It is prevention, or at least mitigation, of this reading failure that inspired many of us to choose education as our life's work. Our goal is to make reading rewarding for these children rather than a source of frustration. If that sounds good to you, read on.

## EXPLORING ESSENTIAL READING SKILLS

As educators, whether at the elementary or secondary levels and whether teaching in your own solo-taught classroom or co-teaching with a colleague, we need a good understanding of how to teach reading. We need to know how to intervene (or collaborate with others to intervene) most effectively to address the specific needs of children in our classes who struggle with reading. Considering students' unique characteristics and the implications of a particular disability on their reading achievement is also important. In teaching children to become capable readers, we must teach complex reading skills in interconnected ways by building on strengths, diagnosing gaps and challenges, and teaching students skills and strategies to mitigate those challenges.

Fortunately, decades of research studies have helped us identify what really works in reading. We know the essential skills necessary for reading, along with effective approaches for teaching reading to both typical and struggling readers, including children with disabilities. Consider the essential or big ideas of reading instruction and the corresponding effective teaching practices identified by the National Reading Panel (NRP, 2000). Each of these essential components—*phonemic awareness, phonics, reading fluency, vocabulary*, and *comprehension*—are briefly described in this chapter. It is worth noting that these skills are not the *only* ones needed for effective reading and that approaching them as separate skills fails to consider the complexity of the reading process as a whole (Cassidy, Valadez, & Garrett, 2010). We need to weave these skills together—not in a linear sequence—but within a well-balanced,

**Key Concepts**

Your five heavy hitters in reading?
- Phonemic awareness
- Phonics
- Reading fluency
- Vocabulary
- Comprehension

comprehensive program of reading instruction that emphasizes meaning, and, dare I say, enjoyment! It is our responsibility and our greatest achievement if we not only teach our students to read, but also that we inspire their passion and love for reading.

## Explicit Instruction in Phonemic Awareness

*Teach students to be skilled at identifying individual sounds in words.* The ability to distinguish and manipulate the smallest individual units of sound (known as *phonemes*) of spoken words is *phonemic awareness*, which is an important precursor for reading text (NRP, 2000). Within phonemic awareness, the ability to segment or break apart words into their individual phonemes (as *pan* is broken apart into /p/-/a/-/n/) and the ability to blend together individual phonemes to say a word (as /s/-/i/-/t/ together make the word *sit*) are critical for effective reading (O'Connor, 2011). For many students with special needs, teaching phonemic awareness often requires very explicit, structured instruction with frequent repetition and practice. Examples include teaching stretched blending and segmenting (that's where you have students practice isolating and saying each sound in a one-syllable word very slowly), or asking students to jump and clap each time they hear an individual sound in words we say aloud. Obviously, if you are teaching secondary students who are at this very basic level, they might roll their eyes if you ask them to jump and clap, but you get the point. Figure out what's appropriate for them (drumming on the table perhaps) and go with it!

## Systematic Instruction in Phonics and Decoding, Including Multisyllabic Decoding

*Teach students to crack the "code" of reading, both for short words and more challenging multisyllabic words.* All teachers have encountered students who experience difficulty decoding, or sounding out, unfamiliar words. For these children, finally cracking the code of reading and beginning to read even a few words can be highly motivating. Many children with exceptionalities benefit from structured, explicit, systematic instruction in *phonics*, a method of teaching reading that focuses on the acquisition of letter-sound correspondences and their use in reading (O'Connor, 2011). Saying sounds of letters accurately is critical when teaching students to read. For example, sometimes teachers introduce the sounds of the letters *p*, *t*, or *b* by saying /puh/ or /tuh/ or /buh/. This can make it difficult for some students with disabilities when they try to blend the sounds together to read words (e.g., it is much easier to blend /p/, /a/, /t/ to read the word *pat* than blending together the sounds /puh/, /a/, /t/). So what can you do? Begin decoding instruction with teaching the sounds of just a few consonants and vowels that can be combined together to form simple words (such as *m*, *n*, *s*, *t*, *a*, and *i*), along with a few high frequency, irregular words (such as *the, was,* and *said*) that can be combined into short sentences (Carnine, Silbert, Kame'enui, & Tarver, 2010). Did you know that teaching students in an explicit manner how to read multisyllabic words—through teaching syllabication rules or structural analysis—is often very important for students with disabilities who may be more likely to avoid or guess at longer words? Teach students the six syllable types and syllable division strategies, as well as how to break apart longer words into meaningful parts (e.g., prefixes, root words, and suffixes) to allow them to conquer multisyllabic words that are often the source of frustration (Archer, Gleason, & Vachon, 2003). Empower them! Show them they can do it.

## Instruction in Reading Fluency, Particularly Guided Oral Reading

*Teach students to read accurately with appropriate speed and natural expression that mimics spoken language.* This fluency in reading enables students to focus on comprehending the meaning of texts. Many students with disabilities struggle with reading accurately, or with appropriate speed and natural expression (also known as *prosody*), making it quite challenging to remember what they have read (Chard, Ketterlin-Geller, Baker, Doabler, & Apichatabutra, 2009). These are the kids who put their heads on their desk, ask to go to the bathroom, or exhibit behavior problems when you start to have the class read aloud. These students benefit from explicit instruction in reading fluency, particularly guided oral reading, to help them become more fluent, expressive readers. Selecting reading materials that are both motivating and at the appropriate reading level for each student is a critical first step in teaching reading fluency (Allington, 2000). We can effectively teach our students reading fluency through activities such as *repeated readings, choral reading,* and *echo reading,* in which we model fluent reading and guide students as they practice improving their rate, accuracy, and prosody in reading. Miscue (or error) analysis will help us detect patterns of errors in students' oral reading and plan our instruction accordingly. Worried about how to do this in a content class or a secondary class wherein most of your students already read fluently? Consider co-teaching! Having two teachers can help create the space for small groups, alternative teaching, and specially designed instruction (Murawski, 2009).

**Making Connections**

Check out Chapter 9 on Co-Teaching.

## Rich and Explicit Vocabulary Instruction

*Teach students the meanings and uses of vocabulary words to expand their comprehension.* Compared to proficient readers, students with special needs who struggle with reading often have a smaller, less sophisticated repertoire of vocabulary words. These students benefit from rich, explicit vocabulary instruction emphasizing deeper engagement, repetition, and multiple exposures to words to learn and apply new vocabulary in a variety of contexts (Vadasy & Nelson, 2012). We should provide our students with direct instruction of new vocabulary, as well as teach them strategies for figuring out the meaning of unknown words (e.g., knowledge and application of prefixes and suffixes). We can teach vocabulary more effectively by providing student-friendly definitions, offering numerous examples and nonexamples, and connecting new words to students' prior experiences. Rich and explicit vocabulary activities, semantic mapping and semantic feature analysis, and mnemonic strategies such as the keyword method, can all help students better access definitions. Make them feel like detectives unlocking the meanings of words!

**Plugged In**

Find helpful vocabulary activities at sites like Word Generation procedures, www.wordgeneration.org.

## Strategic Instruction in Reading Comprehension

*Teach students skills and strategies for understanding what they read.* Comprehension is the ultimate goal of reading and is defined as "intentional thinking during which meaning is constructed through interactions between text and reader" (Harris & Hodges, 1995, p. 207). Often, students with disabilities and other special needs have challenges in the area of reading comprehension. This may be partly due to gaps in other reading skills and partly because reading comprehension is quite complex. Comprehending written text well requires a variety of skills employed *before* reading (such as predicting what the text will be about or considering the author's purpose), *during* reading (such as visualizing the events of a story or making connections between ideas in the text), and *after* reading (such as summarizing what has been read or answering questions about the topic) (Pak, 2015), all deemed necessary by the NRP (2000). We can develop students' comprehension skills in a variety of ways (Klingner, Vaughn, & Boardman, 2015), such as by teaching them about different types of writing (e.g., narrative and informational text) and using close reading strategies to help students focus on the deeper meanings of passages. We can model effective comprehension

**Making Connections**

Check out Chapter 3 on Writing Strategies.

through our teacher think-alouds during reading. Using graphic organizers such as story maps or Venn diagrams and explicitly teaching reading comprehension strategies (such as predicting, creating mental images, and summarizing) will also increase students' reading comprehension. Focus always on expanding students' understanding of what they read!

### Other Reading Related Skills

*Teach students other skills necessary for successful reading.* Other important factors—such as oral language, prior knowledge, memory, processing skills, attention and focus, and motivation and interest—also contribute to how well children can read. To help students become more capable readers, we can improve their skills in these other areas as well. For example, if you are reading a story involving camping, and your students have never been camping to draw on their prior knowledge for comprehending the story, you can create a "campsite" in your classroom (e.g., set up a tent, show cooking items used when camping, and play a recording of noises heard at night during camping). For application of the five big ideas of reading, along with these additional skills (including a basic assessment of prior knowledge), see *Reading Connections: Strategies for Teaching Students with Visual Impairments* by Kamei-Hannan and Ricci (2015).

## WHAT YOU NEED TO AVOID WHEN TEACHING CHILDREN TO READ

**Teachers:**

✘ **STOP letting the model of service delivery at your particular school dictate how you teach reading.** Focus instead on what your students need. Specially designed intensive instruction does not only have to occur in pull-out or segregated placements. If students are receiving services in a general education class through push-in support or co-teaching, be sure you deliver their intensive, individualized reading intervention in that setting!

✘ **STOP reading instruction that is not based on accurate data.** Take the time to diagnose each student's profile of strengths and areas for growth in reading. Have a clear understanding of students' current skills based on solid diagnostic assessment that informs your instruction. Be aware of reading instruction provided in general and special education classes and work together to provide a well-balanced, comprehensive reading program. Instead of relying on individualized education program (IEP) software goal banks, work as a team to truly individualize the reading goals in your students' IEPs.

✘ **STOP teaching reading as isolated skills and focus on meaning.** Students will be more successful readers if they understand that reading skills are interconnected and the ultimate goal of reading is comprehension. Make sure to connect reading with writing and other content areas, such as history or science.

✘ **STOP underestimating what your students can achieve in reading, even if they are older.** Some children may need different techniques or more repetition but will master skills with our patience and persistence. It is not too late for older students, even those in high school, who still have significant reading difficulty. Consider programs that emphasize basic and advanced decoding or use reading comprehension strategies such as graphic organizers, acronyms and mnemonics, and teaching about text structures. Find the appropriate strategies and materials to teach these students to read, even if others have given up trying or the school curriculum and schedule dictate otherwise!

**Plugged In**

Need a reading program that emphasizes basic or advanced decoding? Consider the Wilson Reading System (www.wilsonlanguage.com) or REWARDS Multisyllabic Word Reading Strategies (www .voyagersopris.com/rewards).

✘ **STOP using worksheets to teach reading.** Worksheets may be easy to use and readily available, but worksheets are neither engaging nor fun. Try as much as possible to plan hands-on, engaging lessons that encourage students' active involvement. At the very least, chop up the portions of worksheets to create matching or puzzle activities that encourage students to interact with each other.

✘ **STOP "helping" students by telling them the word when they come across a word they cannot read.** Resist supplying unknown words, which can make students dependent on you and likely to keep waiting until you come to their rescue. Instead, teach students strategies for tackling those words so they become more independent readers.

✘ **STOP teaching isolated lists of whole words because you think your students may not learn to sound out unfamiliar words.** Research shows that most students, even those with intellectual disabilities, can benefit from instruction in phonics and decoding unfamiliar words (Connor, Alberto, Compton & O'Connor, 2014). This process may take longer and require more repetition for some students, but is worth the effort!

✘ **STOP under-utilizing your paraprofessionals.** Enlist your paraprofessionals strategically to develop the reading skills of your students, including assisting with delivery of research-based reading lessons, collecting data on students' reading progress, and monitoring students' behavior during reading lessons. We see too many classes in which paraprofessionals are just standing around, waiting to be told what to do.

✘ **STOP forgetting that reading is supposed to be fun.** Don't let yourself or your students get so mired down in gaps and deficits that you forget to enjoy reading and celebrate your students' victories. Don't let reading instruction become drill and kill. Remind students that despite any challenges, reading is meant to be enjoyable and expansive!

## TIPS FOR CREATING A CADRE OF CAPABLE READERS

**Teachers, DO this:**

✔ **KNOW the nuts and bolts of a balanced, comprehensive, and effective reading program and evaluate your students' current reading instruction to determine if that is indeed what they are currently receiving.** Students with disabilities often receive an array of services from a variety of professionals. Depending on service delivery models, some students are pulled out of classrooms for services, creating the risk for fragmented learning and missed opportunities for reading instruction. Do your best to collaborate with other professionals to maximize reading instruction for your students. The first step toward this can be an evaluation of current reading instruction (such as the one found at the end of this chapter). Having a clear understanding of your students' current reading instruction will help you fill any gaps and ensure the best for each child.

✔ **BECOME A PRO at data-based individualization of reading!** Use appropriate diagnostic assessments to fully understand your students' strengths and needs in reading. Set reading goals aligned with students' needs and select appropriate reading programs to help them achieve their goals. Be sure to monitor students' progress toward their reading goals, adjust your instruction as needed, and cycle back to diagnostic assessments to reevaluate students' skills. Be strategic, allow the time needed for this process, and let your students surprise you!

✔ **USE effective, explicit instruction when teaching reading to students with disabilities.** Explicit instruction for efficient and effective teaching (Archer & Hughes, 2011) includes focusing on critical content and clearly communicating lesson goals and your expectations of students. Be sure to sequence skills carefully in meaningful instructional chunks. Activate students' prior knowledge, and provide step-by-step instructions and modeling. Use concise and clear language. Offer a variety of examples and nonexamples related to the topic, and provide lots of opportunities for student participation. Monitor your students' performance, and give immediate feedback to create more capable readers.

✔ **PROVIDE appropriate and engaging reading materials for your students, including both narrative and informational texts.** Know your students' instructional, independent, and frustration levels in reading. Keep in mind the Goldilocks rule for helping them select reading materials: Not too easy, not too hard, but just right! Use readability formulas to measure complexity of texts and whether they are appropriate for your students (some readability formulas include the *Flesch Reading Ease Formula*, the *Degrees of Power [DRP] scale of text complexity*, the *Dale-Chall Formula*, and *Lexile scores*. Actively teach students about text structure so that they are better able to tackle different reading materials.

>  **Plugged In**
>
> Looking for an online site to help determine the readability and complexity of texts? Check out www.readabilityformulas.com.

✔ **KNOW and USE evidence-based practices in reading instruction.** When teaching reading, use evidence-based methods, strategies, and programs (such as those found on the *What Works Clearinghouse*, *IRIS Center*, or *Center on Instruction* websites) that meet high standards of rigor in scientific research examining their effectiveness. Examples include repeated readings, structural analysis (or advanced word study), and comprehension monitoring. Be mindful of why and how you are using particular methods and techniques for reading instruction and if you might need to adjust your teaching based on students' individualized needs. For each student, find and use what really works!

✔ **UNDERSTAND that reading is a complex but fun process with meaning as the ultimate goal, and TELL your students that, too!** Give your students interest surveys, and select books that are of high interest to your students to motivate them to read. Create a library of high-interest, low-readability books for your students who need it. Use role playing, videos, and drama activities to bring texts to life for students. Create your own stories using students' names to build their reading fluency and comprehension. Show them what it means to be a good reader, and guide your students in setting their own reading goals. Teach them how to monitor their own growth in reading. Enlist them as partners in their reading development!

✔ **USE less anxiety producing strategies when having students read aloud.** Rather than "round robin" or "popcorn" reading using the same text for a whole class of students (which can increase anxiety in children with disabilities), instead place your students into smaller groups of three to five students at similar reading levels. Consider using the routine of *Successful, Anxiety-Free, Engaged*

*Reading* (SAFER; Bursuck & Damer, 2015), in which you select a passage at the *independent* reading level of a small group of students. Together with students, determine a goal for maximum number of errors (e.g., no more than five errors) when the group reads aloud. Randomly call on individual students to read aloud passages varying from one to a few sentences, while everyone points to every word during the reading. Record and correct student errors during reading by allowing students to read a few words past the error word to see if they self-correct, ask the student who made the reading error to stop and try sounding out the word, model correct pronunciation of the word, and ask the student to read again from the beginning of the sentence. At the end of the reading, review all the errors with students. Reinforce correct pronunciation and the meanings of the words. Find whatever motivates them to engage deeply with the reading!

✔ **TEACH students strategies that will enable them to become more independent readers.** For example, when teaching students how to tackle multisyllabic words, introduce and have them practice the DISSECT (Lenz & Hughes, 1990) word identification strategy for reading unfamiliar, long words (see the DISSECT Strategy at the end of this chapter for a useful resource). For improved reading comprehension, teach students to use the Question-Answer Relationships strategy (QAR; Raphael, 1986) for determining how to find answers to text-related questions. Promote your students' independence in reading!

✔ **CONSIDER the needs of your English learners when teaching reading.** Support English learners as they acquire both English language and reading skills. Ensure that assessments used are valid and reliable in providing information on the skills of English learners. Support these students in learning English sounds if their first language does not contain sounds similar to English phonemes. Teach multiple meanings of vocabulary words and common idioms to English learners. Model fluent reading and give your English learners frequent practice in reading aloud themselves. Be sure to focus on content rather than accents or errors in grammar, and expand on your students' background knowledge to support their comprehension. Be a champion for your English learners.

**Making Connections**

Check out Chapter 15 on English Language Learners.

✔ **PROVIDE uninterrupted reading time for students.** As educators, we want to intervene and help students who struggle or have identified disabilities that impact reading. However, we sometimes forget to allow our students to really delve into and engage with books. Once students have identified a book they enjoy at their independent reading level, give them uninterrupted time to just read. Let them enjoy the worlds opened to them through reading.

✔ **IMPLEMENT positive behavioral incentives.** Particularly if you need to "hook" some of your students into reading, figure out what incentives will reinforce their desire to read. Try to align reading materials and incentives to students' interests as much as possible. Pique their motivation to read!

✔ **ENLIST a "village" to teach reading to your students.** Your support crew for teaching reading can include parents, volunteers from local high schools or agencies, administrators, general and special education teachers, coaches and specialists, and students in upper grades who can be reading buddies. Seek out sources of funding (such as National Education Association [NEA] teacher grants, foundations, or www.donorschoose.org) to build an enviable library of reading materials. Tap into programs at local universities and partner with special education professors in research projects, particularly when it might bring a new app or resource into your classroom.

✔ **BECOME an expert on all things reading!** Research and learn about specialized reading interventions. Continue your own professional development in reading by attending conferences, earning certifications in specialized reading interventions, observing veteran reading teachers, reading research journals on reading, and scouring websites of reading-related organizations.

## A COLLABORATIVE TOOL FOR EVALUATING READING INSTRUCTION FOR STUDENTS WITH SPECIAL NEEDS

Name of Student: _____    Date: _____

Using the scoring instructions below, please work collaboratively to evaluate the student's reading instruction.

**Scoring Instructions:**

**NA** = Instruction not needed; based on diagnostic assessment results, student has already mastered this skill

**1** = Instruction of skill is needed somewhat or occasionally, as student is nearing mastery level

**2** = Instruction of skill is needed most of the time, in mostly explicit, structured, systematic, consistent manner

**3** = Instruction of skill is highly needed, on daily basis, in highly explicit, structured, systematic, consistent manner

**Who:** Who provides this instruction? **GET** = general education teacher; **SET** = special education teacher; **P** = paraprofessional; **COT** = co-teachers together

**Where:** Where does this instruction occur? **GE** = general education classroom; **SE** = special education classroom; **BOTH** = general and special education classrooms

| Essential Components of Reading | NA | 1 | 2 | 3 | Who | Where |
|---|---|---|---|---|---|---|
| Instruction in Phonemic Awareness | | | | | | |
| Instruction in Phonics and Basic Decoding | | | | | | |
| Instruction in Multisyllabic Decoding | | | | | | |
| Instruction in Reading Fluency | | | | | | |
| Instruction in Vocabulary | | | | | | |
| Instruction in Reading Comprehension | | | | | | |
| **Other Factors Related to Reading** | **NA** | **1** | **2** | **3** | **Who** | **Where** |
| Emphasizing meaning as the overall goal of reading | | | | | | |
| Activating student's background knowledge and memory | | | | | | |
| Building student's motivation and interest in reading | | | | | | |

| Other Factors Related to Reading | NA | 1 | 2 | 3 | Who | Where |
|---|---|---|---|---|---|---|
| Maintaining student's attention and focus in reading | | | | | | |
| Addressing processing issues related to reading | | | | | | |
| Connecting reading instruction to writing and teaching reading across content areas | | | | | | |

What are the curriculum, materials, and strategies being used to teach reading to this student?

_____

_____

What are the strengths in this student's reading instruction? What are the gaps or areas of need?

_____

_____

_____

What are our next steps for improving this student's reading instruction?

_____

_____

_____

How will we measure our success?

_____

_____

_Source:_ Adapted from Kamei-Hannan, C., & Ricci, L. A. (2015). _Reading connections: Strategies for teaching students with visual impairments._ New York, NY: American Foundation for the Blind Press.

## ACTIVITY FOR READING LONGER WORDS

Once you have taught students the different types of syllables and/or prefixes and suffixes that they will encounter in long words, a simple activity for reinforcing their knowledge of syllable types is to create a chart with the syllable types written as headings across the top. Give your students time in pairs or small groups to think of as many words (or look in their various reading materials to find) as they can that fit each syllable type. Students write these words on sticky notes and place these under each category of syllable types. For a similar activity on affixes, create a chart with some common prefixes and suffixes across the top, and challenge students to generate their own or find words in texts that contain these prefixes and suffixes. After each of these activities, debrief with students to see what words they found and ensure that they learn the (student friendly!) definitions of these words as well, extending this activity into a writing or journal activity using these new vocabulary words.

| Syllable Types | Closed | Open | Vowel-Consonant-e | Vowel Team | Consonant+le | R Controlled |
|---|---|---|---|---|---|---|
| Examples | Bat | Donut | Namesake | Seat | Example | Starter |
| Post your own words! ⇨ | | | | | | |

## DISSECT STRATEGY

The **DISSECT** strategy is a systematic process for students to use when encountering multisyllabic words, particularly in content areas such as history or science.

| Steps of DISSECT | What Student Does |
| --- | --- |
| **D**iscover the context | Student is taught to discover the context by skipping the unknown word and reading to the end of the sentence and then use the meaning of the sentence to guess the best word that fits in the place of the word in question. |
| **I**solate the prefix | Student is taught to look at the beginning of the word to see if the first several letters create a phoneme that the student can pronounce. If a prefix is recognized, the student isolates it by boxing it off. |
| **S**eparate the suffix | Using similar procedures and a list of suffixes, the student then separates the suffix by boxing it off. |
| **S**ay the stem | Student is taught to say the stem and then say the stem along with any prefixes or suffixes. |
| **E**xamine the stem | If the stem cannot be named easily, the student learns to try using one of three rules: <br><br>1. If the stem or a part of the stem begins with a vowel, separate the first two letters. If the stem or a part of the stem begins with a consonant, separate the first three letters from the rest of the stem and pronounce them. Once the first two or three letters are separated from the stem, the application of the same rules is repeated until the end of the stem is reached. The stem is then pronounced by saying the dissected parts. If the stem can be read, the prefix and suffix are added and the whole word reread. <br>2. If the student cannot read the word using the first rule, the student isolates the first letter of the stem and then tries to apply the first rule again. <br>3. The third rule is applied when two different vowels are together in a word. The student is instructed to pronounce both the vowel sounds in the word. If that does not sound right, the student makes one vowel sound at a time until it sounds right. |
| **C**heck with someone | The student checks with someone else if the word is still unknown. |
| **T**ry the dictionary | If no help is available, the student tries the dictionary. The student looks up the word, uses the pronunciation guide to pronounce the word, and reads the definition if the meaning of the word is unknown. |

*Source:* Adapted from Lenz, B. K., & Hughes, C. A. (1990). A word identification strategy for adolescents with learning disabilities. *Journal of Learning Disabilities, 23,* 149–158.

## FLUENCY ACTIVITIES

Here are some activities for building students' reading fluency. Be sure to attend to the rate, accuracy, and natural expression with which students read selected passages.

| Activity | Description |
|---|---|
| **Echo Reading** | Provides most teacher support and modeling. Teacher reads one or two sentences of text (modeling appropriate rate, accuracy, and prosody), and students read the same sentence(s) right after. Teacher expands length of text read as students learn the procedure. Roles can be reversed, with teacher echoing student. |
| **Choral Reading** | Teacher reads text aloud to students, and then teacher and students read same text aloud together in unison. |
| **Partner Reading** | Students are paired together to read aloud text at their instructional or independent level, taking turns reading a few sentences, paragraph, or a page, and offering each other feedback. Provides opportunity for student collaboration. |
| **Repeated Reading** | The teacher selects a passage that is about 50 to 200 words long for a student. The student reads the same passage aloud several times with the teacher.<br><br>If the student misreads a word or hesitates for longer than 5 seconds, the teacher says the word aloud and asks the student to repeat the word correctly. |

# REFERENCES

Allington, R. L. (2000). *What really matters for struggling readers: Designing research-based programs.* Upper Saddle River, NJ: Pearson.

American Federation of Teachers. (2008). *Improved early reading instruction and intervention.* Washington, DC: Author.

Archer, A. L., & Hughes, C. A. (2011). *Explicit instruction: Effective and efficient teaching.* New York, NY: Guilford Press.

Archer, A. L., Gleason, M. M., & Vachon, V. L. (2003). Decoding and fluency: Foundation skills for struggling older readers. *Learning Disability Quarterly, 26,* 89–101.

Bursuck, W. D., & Damer, M. (2015). *Teaching reading to students who are at risk or have disabilities: A Multi-tier, RTI approach* (3rd ed.). Boston, MA: Pearson.

Carnine, D. W., Silbert, J., Kame'enui, E. J., & Tarver, S. (2010). *Direct instruction reading* (5th ed.). Boston, MA: Merrill Prentice Hall.

Cassidy, J., Valadez, C. M., & Garrett, S. D. (2010). Literacy trends and issues: A look at the five pillars and the cement that supports them. *Reading Teacher, 63*(8), 644–655.

Chard, D. J., Ketterlin-Geller, L. R., Baker, S. K., Doabler, C., & Apichatabutra, C. (2009). Repeated reading interventions for students with learning disabilities: Status of the evidence. *Exceptional Children, 75,* 263–281.

Connor, C. M., Alberto, P. A., Compton, D. L., & O'Connor, R. E. (2014). Improving reading outcomes for students with or at risk for reading disabilities: A synthesis of the contributions from the Institute of Education Sciences Research Centers (NCSER 2014–3000). Washington, DC: National Center for Special Education Research, Institute of Education Sciences, U.S. Department of Education.

Every Student Succeeds Act. PL No 114-95. (2015). Retrieved from https://www.congress.gov/bill/114th-congress/senate-bill/1177/text

Harris, T. L., & Hodges, R. E. (1995). *The literacy dictionary: The vocabulary of reading and writing.* Newark, DE: International Reading Association.

Kamei-Hannan, C., & Ricci, L. A. (2015). *Reading connections: Strategies for teaching students with visual impairments.* New York, NY: American Foundation for the Blind Press.

Klingner, J. K., Vaughn, S., & Boardman, A. (2015). *Teaching reading comprehension to students with learning difficulties* (2nd ed.). New York, NY: Guilford Press.

Lenz, B. K., & Hughes, C. A. (1990). A word identification strategy for adolescents with learning disabilities. *Journal of Learning Disabilities, 23,* 149–158.

Murawski, W. W. (2009). *Collaborative teaching in secondary schools: Making the co-teaching marriage work!* Thousand Oaks, CA: Corwin.

National Center for Education Statistics. (2015). *The Nation's Report Card: Reading 2015.* Washington, DC: National Center for Education Statistics, Institute of Education Sciences, U.S. Department of Education.

National Reading Panel (NRP). (2000). *Teaching children to read: An evidence-based assessment of the scientific research literature on reading and its implications for reading instruction.* Washington, DC: National Institute of Child Health and Human Development.

No Child Left Behind Act of 2001, Pub. L. 107-110, 20 U.S.C. § 6301 *et seq.* (2002).

O'Connor, R. E. (2011). Phoneme awareness and the alphabetic principle. In R. O'Connor & P. Vadasy (Eds.), *Handbook of reading interventions* (pp. 9–26). New York, NY: Guilford Press.

Pak, M. (2015). The before-during-after reading process. *TCARE: Teachers Connecting to Advance Retention and Empowerment, 1,* 2. Retrieved from http://www.csun.edu/sites/default/files/T-Care-Volume-1-Fall-2015.pdf

Raphael, T. E. (1986). Teaching question answer relationships, revisited. *Reading Teacher, 39*(6), 516–520.

Vadasy, P. F., & Nelson, J. R. (2012). *Vocabulary instruction for struggling students.* New York, NY: Guilford Press.

## MORE READINGS ON READING!

Beck, I. L., McKeown, M. G., & Kucan, L. (2002). *Bringing words to life: Robust vocabulary instruction.* London, UK: Guilford Press.

Haager, D., Dimino, J. A., & Windmueller, M. P. (2014). *Interventions for reading success* (2nd ed.). Baltimore, MD: Paul H. Brookes.

Lemons, C. J., Kearns, D. M., & Davidson, K. A. (2014). Data-based individualization in reading: Intensifying interventions for students with significant reading disabilities. *TEACHING Exceptional Children, 46*(4), 20–29.

Weaver, C. (2009). *Reading process: Brief edition of reading process and practice* (3rd ed.). Portsmouth, NH: Heinemann.

## HELPFUL WEBSITES FOR READING

➡ National Center on Intensive Intervention: www.intensiventervention.org

➡ What Works Clearinghouse: http://ies.ed.gov/ncee/wwc

➡ Center on Instruction: www.centeroninstruction.org

➡ Evidence Based Intervention Network: http://ebi.missouri.edu

➡ Florida Center for Reading Research: http://www.fcrr.org

➡ IRIS Center: http://iris.peabody.vanderbilt.edu

➡ Intervention Central: http://www.interventioncentral.org

➡ Colorín Colorado: http://www.colorincolorado.org

➡ International Literacy Association: www.reading.org

## APPS WE LOVE

➡ Sound Literacy

➡ Reading Fluency Builder

➡ Epic! Unlimited books and educational videos for kids

➡ Pictello talking visual story creator

➡ Gro Guided Reading Organizer

➡ Tools 4 Students

➡ Kidspiration Maps

# 3

# *When Writing Isn't Easy or Fun*

## *Techniques for Struggling Writers*

### Katie M. Miller
*Florida Atlantic University*

### Sally A. Spencer
*University of California, Northridge*

Naomi, a fifth-grade student with a learning disability, struggles to begin her writing project. Her teacher, Ms. Smith, just read the writing prompt and told the students to use their strategies. "Strategies?" Naomi wonders. "Hmm . . . is she talking about that graphic organizer thing? I don't remember. Let me just write a couple of sentences so I can finish. Oh wait, what was I supposed to write about?" Naomi puts down her pencil and lays her head on her desk in frustration.

Naomi has strong fine motor skills, and she can tell you verbally about a topic. However, she has difficulty planning and remembering the ideas in time to get them all on paper. She also struggles with spelling words with complex phonics patterns and will frequently swap them out for simpler words. As a result, she writes simple sentences and her work does not reflect her potential. Writing is a struggle for Naomi, and Ms. Smith just isn't sure how to help Naomi get her ideas on paper.

Does the above vignette sound familiar? There are so many students like Naomi and, like her teacher Ms. Smith, so many teachers need to figure out how to most effectively teach writing to our struggling learners—no matter what subject or grade we teach! With the implementation of the Common Core State Standards (CCSS), there has been a shift in focus toward teaching all students to write across the content areas. The bar has been raised, and with those increased expectations comes the responsibility to teach writing with our 21st century learners in mind. Writing itself, though, is complex, and has lots of moving parts. Think about all that needs to happen when students are writing! They need to plan what they will write, process their ideas, and get their thoughts down on paper—all the while thinking about what letter or word comes next, when to capitalize or add punctuation, and what grammatical form the words should take. Each of these in itself is a highly demanding process; together they can be overwhelming. Many times students like Naomi can verbally tell you about a topic but have difficulty getting their thoughts on paper. Additionally, their teachers, like Ms. Smith, are unsure of how to get their "Naomis" to live up to their writing potential! Innovations in technology have also changed how we write and how we teach writing. The features of autocorrect on our phones and text to speech on our devices have opened up doors for all students who struggle—no longer do they necessarily have to focus on spelling a word, and their ideas can be freely written with their voices. So how do we get those working parts to come together—and reduce the demands of writing for our students? This chapter provides concrete instructional strategies that can help you to turn your "Naomis" into a classroom of successful writers.

## KEY RESEARCH ABOUT WRITING AND STRUGGLING LEARNERS

Traditionally, writing is taught using a process approach (think Writer's Workshop) or some variation of it, which includes planning, drafting, revising, editing, and publishing (Calkins 1983; Graves, 1983). The writing process has shown to be powerful enough for many learners (Graham & Perin, 2007). However, for struggling learners, especially those with learning disabilities (LD), just teaching the process is usually not enough to build proficient writers, because writing isn't something that just comes naturally to many young people (Mason, Harris, & Graham, 2011). It's important to think of writing like exercise: The more you do it, the more your muscles build and become stronger. Writing is the same way.

Students need to practice writing to build their writing muscles and become successful. However, just the practice of writing itself is not going to necessarily increase student performance; without explicit modeling and instructional strategies to support writing, many students may be unable to effectively complete the task.

**Making Connections**

Check out Chapter 11 on Learning Disabilities.

So what makes writing so difficult? Let's break it down and think about the cognitive processes that are involved when we ask students to write. Just like a building, students need to have a solid foundation (e.g., mechanics, spelling, organization, fine motor skills, and so forth) to be successful. Many struggling learners, however, lack this solid foundation, and the complex cognitive processes involved in writing can overwhelm them.

### The Cognitive Processes of Writing

For special learners, such as students with disabilities, writing can be a very strenuous task. They often have difficulty with many of the components of the writing process such as composing, organizing and generating ideas, transforming ideas into sentences, and then finally putting those ideas onto paper. But it doesn't stop there—many students also have difficulty with the editing, revising, and publishing processes as well (Graham & Harris, 2003; Troia, 2006). For many of these students who have learning disabilities, the very cognitive weaknesses that give them a special education eligibility, such

**Key Concepts**

What cognitive processes come into play with writing?

- Memory
  - Short-term
  - Long-term
  - Working
- Graphomotor functions
- Language
- Ordering
- Complex thinking

as weaknesses in memory, graphomotor functions, language, ordering, or complex thinking, also fundamentally interfere with the writing process.

Each of these cognitive processes is key to success in writing. Students must have the graphomotor functions to operate a pencil or keyboard, the language to create effective sentences, ordering skills for putting events in a sequence, letters in a word, and words in a sentence, as well as the higher-order thinking skills to help them understand and synthesize concepts for writing.

(For more research and information about any of these areas, we've provided a section on recommended reading at the end of this chapter. Many of them go in more depth on these topics.) Memory is another critical area in which students with LD struggle, and which plays a significant role in many parts of the writing process. Let's look at that in more detail in this next section.

**The role of memory in writing.** Memory is a significant component that affects a student's ability to write (Harris & Graham, 2013). Memory is typically organized into three categories—short-term memory, working memory, and long-term memory. Short-term memory is the type of memory you call on when you are completing an immediate task (e.g., copying from the board, using a dictionary). This can be really difficult for many students, since by the time they look up to copy a word from the board, they may have already forgotten it when they go to write it on paper. Working memory is also an essential and central part of the writing process (Kellogg, 1996; Macaro, 2003) and really contributes to whether or not a child can be successful with navigating all the parts of the writing process. Working memory carries a heavy "cognitive load" when we write (Spencer, 2015; Swanson & Berninger, 1996). When students have to sound out words to write down the order of the letters, remember and choose appropriate grammar rules, or stop to consider how to use punctuation, the cognitive demand is significant. Until these tasks become automatic, students struggle to layer them one on top of the other, thereby increasing the cognitive load and making it more difficult for them to complete any of the tasks successfully. Last, long-term memory is used to recall elements that have been memorized and stored for later retrieval. The process of

**Making Connections**

Check out Chapter 7 on Brain-Based Learning and Memory.

long-term memory is complex and is demonstrated during writing when students remember vocabulary or must activate prior knowledge to write about a given topic (Spencer, 2015). To help students lighten the cognitive load, we need to give them strategies to navigate all these complicated memory processes.

## Make Writing Explicit!

How do we best work with students to break down the demands of writing for struggling learners and those with disabilities? Researchers have conducted meta-analyses for both elementary and secondary students. Overall, the recommendations are clear: *explicit and systematic strategy instruction* has been found effective to increase writing performance for students with and without disabilities across the grade levels (Baker, Chard, Ketterlin-Geller, Apichatabutra, & Doabler, 2009; Graham, McKeown, Kiuhara, & Harris, 2012; Graham & Perin, 2007). So we know what we need to do; how specifically do we do that?

**Teaching writing strategies.** A *strategy* can be defined as a series of steps a person purposively takes to complete a goal (Alexander, Graham, & Harris, 1998). Strategies include ways people think and act when planning, performing, and evaluating their completion of a task (Alley & Deshler, 1979; Deshler & Schumaker, 2006). In writing, strategies may include processes such as a checklist of the elements of an essay, a graphic organizer for a paragraph, or a mnemonic device. Strategy instruction can be especially helpful for students with LD and other struggling learners, because it breaks down and organizes the writing components, giving students a plan to follow and steps to take to complete their plan, but we imagine all students will appreciate these strategies, don't you? Furthermore, strategies make the thinking process within writing more visible and concrete (Harris, Graham, Mason, & Friedlander, 2008). Explicit, interactive, and scaffolded instruction of writing strategies, as well as strategies for self-regulating the writing process, result in improved student writing performance for our "Naomis" (Mason et al., 2011) and peace of mind

**Making Connections**

Check out Chapter 4 on Instructional Strategies and Universal Design for Learning.

for teachers who are trying to reach their struggling writers. See the end of this chapter (Steps for Teaching a Learning Strategy) for details on how to explicitly teach any strategy and for further reading and resources. *Remember: Research tells us that strategies can be counted on to work **only** when we explicitly teach students how to use them, give them plenty of practice and feedback, and help them generalize the strategies to new writing!* No more assuming that students will just figure it out on their own.

**Writing has changed.** As advances in instructional technology continue to occur, the way we write and the tools we use to write impact the instructional content we teach. Literacy itself has changed with the integration of technology and other media, including the Internet. With the implementation of the CCSS, students are required to write about what they have read in the content areas, and for many teachers this is a difficult shift, but here is where technology can be your friend! When given the right types of supports and tools, struggling learners and students with disabilities can become proficient with the writing standards (Mastropieri & Scruggs, 2014; Spencer, 2015). Technology can be that tool that gives struggling writers the ability to express themselves to the best of their ability. Don't be afraid of technology; use it to help both you and your students. At the end of this chapter, you will find some essential tools for making technology work for your students—things to avoid and tips to improve student writing within your classroom.

**Making Connections**

Check out Chapter 5 on Using Technology and Assistive Technology.

## WHAT TO AVOID WHEN TEACHING WRITING

Teachers:

- ✗ **STOP making writing a mystery.** Students who struggle in writing need explicit instruction. Laying the roadmap for how to complete a writing task will take the ambiguity out of writing. Too many teachers simply assume students will be able to put all the different processes together because they have been shown an example or "taught" to write a topic sentence.

✘ **STOP focusing on narrative.** Students need to be exposed to different genres of writing. With the implementation of the CCSS, expository writing is key—and comes easier for some learners. Why? It doesn't rely on students to invent stories. Not all kids have great imaginations. Give them a topic, and you can provide tools to activate their prior knowledge, which will assist them in finding ideas about what to write. A favorite writing task for many students are research projects focusing on topics of interest such as science, animals, types of employment, or interesting places to visit.

✘ **STOP teaching just one strategy.** Mnemonics and other procedural supports, such as graphic organizers, are useless unless you teach students to use them appropriately and give them a variety of tools to choose from. Would you always want to be told what works for you or would you want to have options? Teach students to use a range of strategies and make sure to MODEL them explicitly and repeatedly until they are mastered. Remember, special learners often can't come up with their own strategies.

✘ **STOP having students write out complete sentences on graphic organizers.** Students need to learn how to use graphic organizers as tools. Graphic organizers are meant to be a tool to facilitate the planning process, so they should include only one or two key words in each section, NOT full sentences. Model the process in which you take the words and turn them into sentences on paper. This is the key component!

✘ **STOP focusing so much on spelling.** Sure, spelling is important, but it increases the cognitive load for the reluctant writer because they focus on spelling instead of ideas. Use technology tools for spelling, because in the real world, your phone, your computer, and your iPad all have dictation and autocorrect tools. Start teaching the technology appropriately. That will be a life skill that your special learner will need down the road.

✘ **STOP assuming writing is a natural process for kids.** Writing doesn't come "naturally!" Students who are struggling need explicit examples and strategies for a variety of writing genres. Consider the fact that many of these students are grappling with language, due perhaps to a disability or the fact that they are English language learners or both. Now add on all the processes required for writing and there's nothing "natural" about it; it's work!

✘ **STOP focusing only on fine motor, capitalization, and spelling skills.** We get that you may love cursive and think it's a lost art, but please prioritize what you are trying to teach. If a student finds writing difficult, your time should be spent teaching him or her processes and strategies that work to make writing successful, not drill and kill on the perfect loop on a *p*. As much as we respect proper grammar and punctuation, we first want students to be willing to express themselves. Only then can we work on how it looks and sounds.

✗ **STOP going old school.** Technology continues to change EVERYTHING! By giving our students with disabilities and struggling learners the tools to support these tasks, we open up a whole new world of writing. Do students need to be able to logically put sentences and paragraphs together? Yes, of course! But do they NEED to have perfectly neat handwriting or even write on paper? No! Use of dictation apps and other technology tools may assist our learners in completing their writing tasks, without the problems inherent in the traditional pencil and paper model. Plus, the use of technology often adds an inherent motivator for many students to try something that would otherwise be a nonpreferred task.

## Administrators:

✗ **STOP taking writing for granted.** Ensure you have a high-quality writing program that is based on research.

✗ **STOP forgetting about assessment data.** Just like it is important to track reading and math progress, it is just as important to understand how our students are progressing in writing.

✗ **STOP making it too prescriptive.** You can't assign exactly what a teacher should be teaching in writing on a given day. Good teachers know when to move on from a writing skill; respect the fact that not all classes are the same and some students may need more time.

✗ **STOP being surprised if teachers are not confident in providing writing instruction.** Many teacher preparation programs do not have specific courses in the teaching of writing, and especially for those learners who are struggling. Provide professional development opportunities. Find the experts in your district or state and bring them in!

# INSTRUCTIONAL STRATEGIES FOR SUCCESS IN TEACHING WRITING TO STRUGGLING LEARNERS

**Teachers, please DO:**

✔ **HAVE your students WRITE every day!** Make it authentic, and students will be more likely to gain interest and motivation in completing the writing tasks. For students to improve writing, they need to practice. But for students who struggle with writing, you may want to consider giving them other options for practicing that keep their motivation up. For example, if you are focusing on the literacy skill of summarizing a story, have them create a story map using a technology tool (such as Comic Life) that utilizes illustrations before having students write out the paragraph.

✔ **TEACH students how to set goals and self-monitor.** Make sure you model how to do this and have students graph their progress (e.g., number of words written, time spent writing). It can be very powerful and motivating for students to see their progress in completing their writing tasks. Once you have modeled for your students and they are getting it, let them self-monitor and graph their own progress.

**Plugged In**

Use tech tools that help keep kids motivated to write. These can include:

- Comic Life: www.plasq.com
- Storyboard That: www.StoryboardThat.com
- Story Bird: https://storybird.com
- Buncee: https://www.edu.buncee.com
- PicLits: www.piclits.com
- Pixton: http://www.pixton.com
- Little Bird Tales: https://littlebirdtales.com

✔ **TEACH students a variety of writing strategies and graphic organizers for each.** Graphic organizers can act as a procedural facilitator (Gersten & Baker, 2001). A procedural facilitator is any tool that can assist students in completing a writing task. It could be a graphic organizer, a mnemonic, or a combination of both (Spencer, 2015). Teach one strategy until they can use it independently, and help them generalize it to another structure. *The specific type of graphic organizer you use is not as important as how you use it.* Remember, universal design for learning emphasizes having multiple means of representation, expression, and engagement; give students options! It is important for struggling learners to be comfortable with using the tool on their own. See the end of this chapter for a sample graphic organizer for the expository writing genre.

✔ **USE technology throughout the writing process.** Think about ways you can lighten the cognitive load (e.g., using dictation during the drafting process or letting students dictate words into their graphic organizer during the planning process). Think of the objective you want the technology to assist you in, then find the technology that would serve that purpose, not the other way around. (Find the tool for the job, not the job for the tool!) Tips for using technology and an example of some high-powered technology tools are included at the end of the chapter.

**Plugged In**

Is spelling an issue? Don't let it be! Many successful authors can't spell, but they do know strategies to ensure their work is spelled correctly. Try:

- Dragon Dictation App: http://www.nuancemobilelife.com/apps/dragon-dictation
- CoWriter: http://donjohnston.com/cowriterapp

✔ **GIVE students options for spelling.** Explicitly teach students how to use the appropriate tool for the job. Whether that is dictation software via the Dragon Dictation App, autocorrect options on their smartphone, or word prediction software, you must model for students how to use and implement it. Think of this like any other strategy, and follow the steps laid out in the table at the end of the chapter.

✔ **TEACH students expository writing.** Expository writing (which is to explain, inform, or describe a topic) often makes more sense to struggling learners, because they can understand a clear sequence. Focusing only on narrative writing (otherwise known as story writing) will put some of your students at a disadvantage and in the end will be less applicable to their college and career outcomes. There are seldom times when adults are required to write stories, unless they are an author or taking a creative writing class in college. By not giving students the tools and strategies they need to complete an expository writing task, such as completing an e-mail or writing a report, students are at a disadvantage in the workplace.

✔ **OFFER options.** You may not be a writing teacher, but you still need students to practice writing daily. How do you fit that in when you are supposed to be teaching math? Or Spanish? Or music? You provide a variety of ways for students to write! This could be a quick write that they do to start class on an interesting question or quote of the day related to your topic; it could be written on an index card where they have to be for or against a statement you give them; it could be a 5-minute journal they write to the person of their choosing, living or dead. Mix it up! Ask students for other ideas on how they can incorporate writing into your class in interesting ways, and yet ones that are still connected to your area of focus.

✔ **SHOW the good and the umm . . . not so good.** Students who struggle with writing, especially those with LD, understand less about the nature of the writing process, as well as the features of good writing, different genres, and the purpose and audience for writing, than their general education peers (De la Paz, 2007). It's important to model what good writing looks like, as well as show students writing that needs improvement. Model by using a "think-aloud." Then show some specific areas that need to be refined. Make sure you have prepared before this lesson to perfectly pinpoint what the piece needs and how you will model that for your students. We recommend that you save papers from year to year so that you have authentic examples of the good and the not so good that aren't from your current students. (And of course, always remove the names!)

✔ **TEACH students how to use dictation tools.** Talking and writing are distinctly different from one another. Show students what the differences are and model how to use dictation tools. It is still essential that students plan what they will dictate. It is also important to think about the goal of your writing lesson (e.g., dictation would not be appropriate if you want students to practice their handwriting, whereas dictation would be appropriate if your goal is for them to write a well-organized paragraph). See the end of the chapter for tips for teaching students how to use dictation tools.

### Administrators:

✔ **FIND time for writing in your school's schedule.** With all the demands schools are facing to teach specific content, don't let writing be the first skill to go! Find creative ways to fit it in. Use a writing program schoolwide—one that is based on research. And don't forget to identify and adopt supplemental programs that support the writing process and give students who struggle the interventions they need. Use response to intervention (RTI) to support writing development.

✔ **SUPPORT teachers' use of technology in writing**—and provide professional development for it. So many times technology is given but is not supported. Professional development is crucial for teachers to understand how to use a tool.

✔ **MAKE writing authentic!** Support school and/or community nights where students get to show off their writing to their parents and other community members. Have students write to people in the community (e.g., nursing homes), community leaders (e.g., contact the mayor), or another class (e.g., pen pals). There are many great ideas out there—with the blink of a Google search. Just be sure they align to a standard.

## STEPS FOR TEACHING A LEARNING STRATEGY

| 1. Develop Background Knowledge | During this step, assess and teach the vocabulary and concepts the students will need to learn in the mnemonic or organizer. For example, if you are teaching a strategy for opinion writing, make sure the students understand what an opinion is first. It's important to identify and recognize the prerequisite skills and concepts a student needs for the strategy and to pre-teach the skills in this step. |
|---|---|
| 2. Discuss the Strategy | Motivate your learners to use the strategy provided and help them begin to understand when and why to use it. The research is clear: Struggling learners will not apply strategies unless someone explicitly explains to them how they will help. |
| 3. Model It | In this step, you explicitly teach a strategy by demonstrating how it is used. The most effective way to do this is often through a think-aloud: Step into the role of the learner, and talk yourself through the steps of the strategy, verbalizing your thought processes and questions along the way. This step is critically important to the success of any strategy instruction and may have to be repeated before all your students will master it. Small group instruction may be very effective for those who need a little more practice. |
| 4. Memorize It | By this step, most of your students should have some understanding of how to use the strategy. It's important that they begin to use it on their own. Before they can do that, they will need to know the steps by heart. This doesn't mean they must know the strategy word for word, but they should be able to generate the steps from memory and explain what they mean. Give students opportunities to memorize through activities using flash cards, rehearsal, and picture cues so they can commit the steps to memory. |
| 5. Support It | At this point, students are ready to practice the strategy. Students will need various levels of practice for them to prepare for independent practice. Provide them with opportunities to practice in groups or with partners, and with frequent peer and teacher feedback. This will lead them down the road to mastery and will assist in having them use the strategy independently. |
| 6. Establish Independent Practice | Hooray! Students have begun to internalize the steps of the strategy, and they are ready to use it on their own. Don't stop supporting them yet: Make sure to monitor their use of the strategy and ensure they are using the steps appropriately. Small changes may be okay, but make sure they haven't altered the strategy so much that it becomes ineffective. As students get better at using the strategy, they will begin to work on generalizing it to other settings and other content areas. And congratulations on explicitly teaching your students a strategy to mastery! |

*Source:* Adapted from Spencer, S. A. (2015). *Making the common core writing standards accessible through universal design for learning.* Thousand Oaks, CA: Corwin; adapted from Harris, K. R., & Graham, S. (1996). *Making the writing process work: Strategies for composition and self-regulation.* Cambridge, MA: Brookline Books.

# SAMPLE GRAPHIC ORGANIZER: EXPOSITORY WRITING

Fourth Grade W.4.1.A: Introduce a topic or text clearly, state an opinion, and create an organizational structure in which related ideas are grouped to support the writer's purpose. W.4.1.B: Provide reasons that are supported by facts and details.

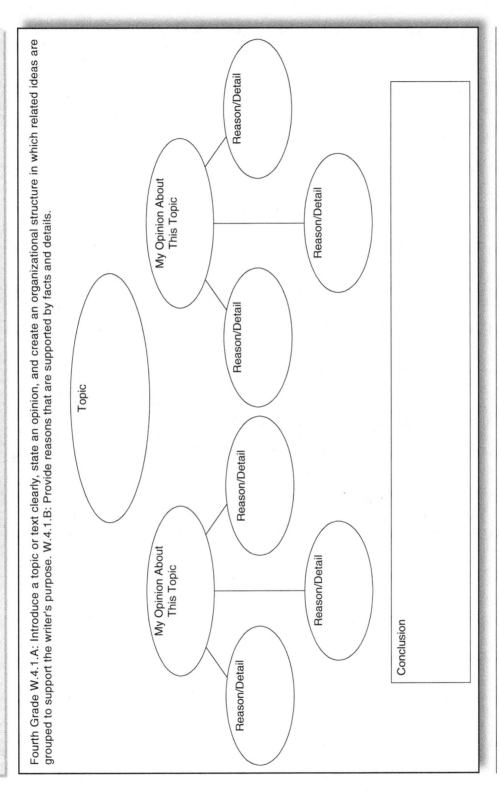

*Source:* Spencer, S. A. (2015). *Making the common core writing standards accessible through universal design for learning.* Thousand Oaks, CA: Corwin.

## USING TECHNOLOGY TOOLS ACROSS WRITING: A CHECKLIST

☐ **Think about the objective.** What do you want the tool to solve? Is it to help with getting students to generate ideas for writing, or is it to help with spelling? Do you want the tool to support students in their organization or in their grammar and punctuation?

☐ **Find the tool!** There are many different types that are frequently changing as technology evolves. Use your peers. There are many suggestions available on teacher websites (http://www.freetech4teachers .com).

☐ **Check out the accessibility features and compatibility with your students.** Can you change components of the tool to meet your students' needs? Can you access it in your classroom? Are there speech-to-text components? Can you change font size or color?

☐ **Try the tool.** Learn how to use it and break down how to use it into small steps. Make sure it does what you thought it would do and that it is student friendly. Remember that what you may find difficult may be simple for your students because many are very tech savvy from a young age; consider having a few of your students try it out and give you their "expert" opinion! On the other hand . . .

☐ **Don't assume kids know!** Many students in lower socioeconomic areas do not have access to technology or may only have whatever access their phone gives them. We have worked with high school students who don't know how to start up a computer, much less access websites and writing tools. So research carefully before you make assumptions!

☐ **Model and teach the student to access and use the tool.** Make sure you fully understand how you would like your students to implement and use the tool prior to showing them. Then, just like all strategy instruction, don't just assume they'll figure it out. Model how the tool is used to support writing and scaffold how the students use it until it becomes second nature.

☐ **Repeat with other tools.**

## TEACHER TOOLKIT FOR THE WRITING PROCESS

| Writing Skill | Barriers | Solutions | |
|---|---|---|---|
| | | No Tech Strategy | Tech-Related Strategy |
| Prewriting: Brainstorm ideas, decide on topic, gather research | Lack of background knowledge | Read a text on topic | www.watchknowlearn.org Use this website to search for free videos across topics. |
| | | | www.pinterest.com Pinterest is a great tool where students can find and organize information before they write. |
| | Difficulty with organizing information | Paper graphic organizer paired with strategy | www.popplet.com Use this app/website to organize information and enhance with graphics. |
| Drafting: Students write down their ideas and organize them around a structure such as a paragraph | Difficulty managing all the cognitive factors involved in writing | Dictate the first draft to a peer | Dragon Dictate This app allows students to dictate their first draft into a phone, tablet, or computer. |
| | | | Siri The speech-to-text features built into Mac products are highly effective and can be used across a variety of devices. |
| Revising: Students review content and work to make it better: focus on content rather than mechanics | Difficulty with identifying content that needs revision | Checklist with steps for revision | Livescribe Pen—record and reread writing piece. Write your text using a Livescribe pen. It has recording abilities so you will be able to either have the computer read what you have written using the Livescribe software or record in your own voice what you have written using the Livescribe pen. |
| | | | Text-to-Speech Software—Naturalreaders.com Listen to piece that was written to identify content or style that may need revising. |

*(Continued)*

(Continued)

| Writing Skill | Barriers | Solutions | |
|---|---|---|---|
| | | No Tech Strategy | Tech-Related Strategy |
| Editing: Focus is on grammar, punctuation, and spelling | Frequent errors in spelling and punctuation | Checklist with steps for editing | Speech-to-Text Software Use software to check spelling and punctuation, then correct in final version. |
| | | | Word Processing Programs (Microsoft Word ) Use spell checker within software program. |
| Publishing: Allow students to finalize and share their work | Unmotivated to finish | Authentic audience, such as their parents, peers, or a younger class of students | Kidblog Edublog Create a different space to share student-published work. |
| | | | VoiceThread An alternative to typical writing. Allow students to speak their piece around graphics or create shared writing pieces. |

## STEPS FOR TEACHING SPEECH-TO-TEXT TOOLS

| | | |
|---|---|---|
| **Step 1: Model and practice spoken punctuation.** Before students can begin to write using speech to text, they need to practice saying punctuation aloud. | **Example:** If a student wants to write, "The dog ran up the hill." The student must say "The dog ran up the hill period." | **Move on** to Step 2 once students master dictating one or two sentences with ending punctuation. |
| **Step 2: Teach basic editing.** Students need to practice editing by giving them the opportunity to move words, add commas, and replace vocabulary. | **Example:** If a student wants to delete a word, they must highlight the text and delete the word. Then they must speak the replacement word. This is different based on the software. | **Move on** to authentic writing after the student can write multiple sentences and can do each of the suggested editing activities independently. |
| **Step 3: Model using speech-to-text software for authentic writing.** Model the writing process using a strategy that was previously learned. Make sure you show them how to plan using the dictation strategy. | **Example:** Read the topic and model your thinking for planning your writing. Make sure to be explicit and talk about how you are using the software. | **Monitor** your students to make sure they continue proficiency. Review when needed. |

*Source:* Adapted from Spencer, S. A. (2015). *Making the common core writing standards accessible through universal design for learning.* Thousand Oaks, CA: Corwin.

# REFERENCES

Alexander, P., Graham, S., & Harris, K. R. (1998). A perspective on strategy research: Prospect and progress. *Educational Psychology Review, 10*, 129–154.

Alley, G. R., & Deshler, D. D. (1979). *Teaching the learning disabled adolescent: Strategies and methods*. Denver, CO: Love.

Baker, S., Chard, D., Ketterlin-Geller, L., Apichatabutra, C., & Doabler, C. (2009). Teaching writing to at-risk students: The quality of evidence for self-regulated strategy development. *Exceptional Children, 75*(3), 303–318.

Calkins, L. M. (1983). *Lesson from a child: On the teaching and learning of writing*. Exeter, NH: Heinemann.

De la Paz, S. (2007). Best practices in teaching writing to students with special needs. In S. Graham, C. A. MacArthur, & J. Fitzgerald (Eds.), *Best practices in writing instruction* (pp. 308–329). New York, NY: Guilford Press.

Deshler, D. D., & Schumaker, J. B. (2006). *Teaching adolescents with disabilities: Accessing the general education curriculum*. New York, NY: Corwin.

Gersten, R., & Baker, S. (2001). Teaching expressive writing to students with learning disabilities: A meta-analysis. *Elementary School Journal, 101*(3), 251–272.

Graham, S., & Harris, K. R. (2003). Students with learning disabilities and the process of writing: A meta-analysis of SRSD studies. In L. Swanson, K. R. Harris, & S. Graham (Eds.), *Handbook of research on learning disabilities* (pp. 383–402). New York, NY: Guilford Press.

Graham, S., McKeown, D., Kiuhara, S., & Harris, K. R. (2012). A meta-analysis of writing instruction for students in the elementary grades. *Journal of Educational Psychology, 104*(4), 879–896.

Graham, S., & Perin, D. (2007). *Writing next: Effective strategies to improve writing of adolescents in middle and high school—A report to Carnegie Corporation of New York*. Washington, DC: Alliance for Excellence in Education.

Graves, D. (1983). *Writing: Teachers and children at work*. Exeter, NH: Heinemann.

Harris, K. R., & Graham, S. (1996). *Making the writing process work: Strategies for composition and self-regulation*. Cambridge, MA: Brookline Books.

Harris, K. R., & Graham, S. (2013). "An adjective is a word hanging down from a noun": Learning to write and students with learning disabilities. *Annals of Dyslexia, 6*(3), 65–79.

Harris, K. R., Graham, S., Mason, L. H., & Friedlander, B. (2008). *Powerful writing strategies for all students*. Baltimore, MD: Brookes.

Kellogg, R. T. (1996). A model of working memory in writing. In C. M. Levy & S. E. Ransdell (Eds.), *The science of writing* (pp. 57–71). Mahwah, NJ: Lawrence Erlbaum.

Macaro, E. (2003). Strategies for language learning and for language use: Revising the theoretical framework. *Modern Language Journal, 90*(3), 320–337.

Mason, L. H., Harris, K. R., & Graham, S. (2011). Self-regulated strategy development for students with writing difficulties. *Theory Into Practice, 50*(1), 20–27.

Mastropieri, T., & Scruggs, M. (2014). *Thirty years of research collaboration: What have we learned and what remains to be learned?* Paper presented at the meeting of the Office of Special Education Programs Project Director's Conference, Washington, DC.

Spencer, S. A. (2015). *Making the common core writing standards accessible through universal design for learning*. Thousand Oaks, CA: Corwin.

Swanson, H. L., & Berninger, V. W. (1996). Individual differences in children's writing: A function of working memory or reading or both processes? *Reading and Writing: An Interdisciplinary Journal, 8*, 357–383.

Troia, G. A. (2006). Writing instruction for students with learning disabilities. In C. A. MacArthur, S. Graham, & J. Fitzgerald (Eds.), *Handbook of writing research* (pp. 324–336). New York, NY: Guilford Press.

## ADDITIONAL RECOMMENDED READING ON WRITING

Ganske, K. (Ed.). (2014). *Write now! Empowering writers in today's K–6 classroom.* Newark, DE: International Reading Association.

Graham, S., MacArthur, C., & Fitzgerald, J. (2013). *Best practices in writing instruction* (2nd ed.). New York, NY: Guilford Press.

Mason, L., Reid, R., & Hagaman, J. (2012). *Building comprehension in adolescents: Powerful strategies for improving reading and writing in content areas.* Baltimore, MD: Brookes.

Straub, C., & Alias, A. (2013). Next generation writing at the secondary level for students with learning disabilities. *TEACHING Exceptional Children, 46*(1), 16–24.

Troia, G. A. (2008). *Instruction and assessment for struggling writers.* New York, NY: Guilford Press.

## TOP FIVE WEBSITES TO SUPPORT WRITING

➡ CAST Tools: Check out Science Writer: http://www.cast.org/our-work/learning-tools.html

➡ IRIS Center: Module on Improving Writing Performance: Persuasive Essays: http://iris.peabody.vanderbilt.edu/module/pow

➡ Project WRITE: Features lesson plans for strategic strategy instruction: http://kc.vanderbilt.edu/projectwrite

➡ ReadWriteThink: www.Readwritethink.org (Look for interactive classroom resources.)

➡ Bubbl.us: An online brainstorming tool for creating graphic organizers: https://bubbl.us

## APPS WE LOVE

➡ StoryWheel

➡ CoWriter for iPad

➡ WordMover

➡ Kidspiration

➡ BitStrips

# 4

---

# *Instructional Strategies and UDL*

## *Making Content Accessible*

### Ruby L. Owiny
*Trinity International University*

### Anne Brawand
*Kutztown University*

### Janet Josephson
*Millersville University*

## THE NEED FOR RESEARCH-BASED SUPPORTS

You're a second-grade teacher, and you look around at the faces in front of you—so many diverse backgrounds, needs, and abilities. Wait! No. You are a high school algebra teacher, so your class is completely different. Or not. You still have students with identified disabilities, students on 504 plans, students who are English language learners (ELLs), students who are gifted, and students who are all the above. Now you are a special education teacher; your students all have the same needs, right?

Of course not. We think we've made our point. No matter what role you play, the need for a variety of instructional strategies to meet students' needs is critical. In this chapter, we identify some of those strategies, clarify some confusing terminology, and emphasize a new trend toward Universal Design for Learning (UDL). We start by focusing on students with identified disabilities, but you'll quickly see how many of the strategies used for this population will extend to other exceptional learners as well.

The Individuals with Disabilities Education Act (IDEA; 2004) requires that multidisciplinary teams develop an individualized education program (IEP) for each student with a disability who qualifies for special education services. In this IEP, the team must plan for an education that will meet the student's needs and allow the student to make appropriate progress in the general education curriculum. To support adequate progress in the general education curriculum, students with disabilities often need accommodations and modifications to level the playing field. What we mean by this is to allow the student to *appropriately* access instruction in general education. Emphasis on appropriately! IDEA requires that a statement explaining these modifications or *supports* be based on peer-reviewed research and meet individual needs to provide for the student's advancement toward academic and behavioral goals (Wright & Wright, 2014). That's where this chapter comes in. We intend to help you identify some of those research-based supports and strategies.

The reauthorization of IDEA extended the requirements for "access to the general education curriculum" (Soukup, Wehmeyer, Bashinski, & Bovaird, 2007), which requires an explanation of peer-reviewed research-based adaptations be provided to students with IEPs in a reasonable manner (Wright & Wright, 2014). The intent of these adaptations is to provide the student with an opportunity to successfully meet annual goals, be included in the general education program and make progress in the curriculum, appropriately participate in nonacademic activities, including extracurricular activities, and be educated with nondisabled peers to the maximum extent possible (Wright & Wright, 2014). Okay, this seems like a lot. Let's boil it down. It means that there are going to be increasing numbers of students with identified disabilities who are in general education classes and we need to be able to meet their needs. We need to provide whatever adaptations, accommodations, modifications, and curriculum augmentations are required to help all students be successful.

## Clarifying Terms

What is the difference between an adaptation, accommodation, modification, and a curriculum augmentation? Often these terms are used interchangeably—especially adaptation, accommodation, and modification—but they are not the same.

- **Adaptation:** The umbrella term that includes accommodations and modifications that support students with disabilities (Johns, 2011) and help level the playing field for students to appropriately access the general curriculum.

- **Accommodation:** Instructional accommodations are those services or supports provided to students with the intent of assisting them to successfully access the general education curriculum (Friend & Bursuck, 2009). The big difference is that accommodations do *not* change the learning objective or assignment expected. Assessment accommodations are supports provided to students with the intent to accurately assess learning while simultaneously removing barriers to students' ability to demonstrate their learning (i.e., provision of a reader). Teachers should remember that accommodations used during instruction should not vary significantly from those used in assessment (Johns, 2011). Edgemon, Jablonski, and Lloyd (2006) provide a guide to considerations for testing accommodations that could be helpful in making accommodation decisions.

- **Modification:** When providing modifications, changes occur in the content expectation or in the performance outcome in some manner (Friend & Bursuck, 2009). These changes can occur in the curriculum, content, or strategies used for instruction (Johns, 2011). Modifications occur as a result of student needs. Most often, modifications are provided when a student's needs are so intense that accommodations alone will not adequately meet the need (Friend & Bursuck, 2009). Teachers are less likely to want to use a modification because it means that students are *not* meeting the same standards as their peers; as they get older, this is increasingly impactful.

- **Curricular augmentation:** Curricular augmentation is the practice of including instruction on strategies and skills that can help students succeed across classes. The various strategies and skills can be categorized into four groups: learning, studying, organization, and self-regulation (Suk-Hyang, Wehmeyer, Palmer, Soukup, & Little, 2008). Learning strategies, like mnemonics and keyword strategies, can be taught so that students can find ways to recall and retrieve information in multiple classes. Strategies for studying and test-taking can also be taught to enhance students' learning. Did you just pick up a set of flashcards one day and instinctively know what to do with them? No. You were *taught* how to make use of flashcards as a support for studying. By teaching strategies for organization, such as managing one's time effectively, students also develop greater independence. The final form of curricular augmentation is strategies for self-regulation, which can include things like problem solving, goal setting, and evaluating one's progress toward a goal. For example, a student may recognize that they ran out of time for their homework and make the determination that they need to begin homework sooner the next day to allow enough time for completion. There are many ways to teach these curricular augmentations, and research shows how influential they are on students.

**Key Concepts**

Adaptations include both *accommodations* (which do NOT change the standard or learning objective) and *modifications* (which DO change the standard or learning objective).

## How Do I Know Which Strategies to Use?

When writing an IEP, co-teaching with colleagues, or planning your own instruction, teachers must consider the adaptations, including accommodations and modifications, that individual students need to be successful in social and academic settings. To appropriately identify which accommodations and modifications are needed, you need to consider the present levels of academic and social performance of each student. Several questions must be addressed when considering accommodations and modifications: What does the student need to be successful during classroom instruction and when learning is assessed? Which supports will lead a student to independence? Which accommodations from the previous IEP should be faded? Answering these questions will allow you to justify your instructional decisions and be intentional with how you are meeting student needs.

## Adaptations: Just a List or Is There More?

Accommodations and modifications—the components of the overarching umbrella of adaptations—are often rendered to a back page of the IEP giving the impression that these are add-ons or something extra the teacher must do. In reality, adaptations go beyond a list on a page. While modifications often do require some forethought and preparation of materials to ensure proper changes to curriculum, and often are made strictly for one student's use, accommodations are most often more easily embedded into instruction to be used by any student, whether diagnosed with a specific dis-

**Making Connections**

Check out Chapter 11 on Learning Disabilities.

ability or not. Students diagnosed with learning disabilities (LD) often require accommodations rather than modifications but may require some modifications as well. The way a teacher designs instruction can go a long way in providing the necessary accommodations for students.

Providing quality instruction with built-in supports without necessarily having to add on anything extra is not difficult with some practice. You can plan to use an accommodation because you know that one student requires it, but find that same accommodation can actually benefit many of your students. Let's take a peek into a classroom as an illustration. Mrs. Wallen has a student with a learning disability that manifests in her reading. Sarah's IEP lists visual cues as an accommodation to aid in memory, retention of skills, and to develop independence. Mrs. Wallen decides to create a poster for math class that lists the steps in solving a story problem. She includes a picture cue for each step to help Sarah remember the steps without becoming bogged down with reading the list each time she solves a story problem. Why a poster and not an index card at Sarah's desk? The poster can help *all* Mrs. Wallen's students! This is not to say Sarah couldn't have an index card of the steps at her desk or that all students couldn't have an index card. The point is that *all* students can use the visual cues. In other words, the *strategy* is naturally embedded for all students' benefit. Not only will Sarah look at the poster to help solve story problems, but other students will likely look at it also for cues in what to do next as they work through a problem. In this instance, more students than just the student with an IEP benefit from the accommodation. Let's be honest—how many of us really *read* the word Stop on the red octagon at an intersection? Most of us see the *symbol* or the *visual cue* and know to apply our brake. We all benefit from visual cues!

## INSTRUCTIONAL STRATEGIES

Accommodations can be provided for students using various methods. Friend and Bursuck (2009) suggest adapting instructional methods as one component to meeting student needs. It is important to remember that "high-quality, intensive instruction" is most beneficial for enhancing achievement for students with disabilities (McLeskey & Waldron, 2011, p. 50) in all settings. Teachers can provide accommodations for their students by using instructional methods that can benefit all students. This can seem very overwhelming though, can't it? Wouldn't it make your life easier if you didn't have to do something different for every single student? Let's talk about some ways that your life can be easier and you can still meet differentiated needs. We'll first review some sure-fire strategies for teaching students with special needs and then go a bit deeper into a framework that can pull all this together for you: UDL!

**Evidence-based practices (EBPs).** In this day and age, it is imperative to provide instruction using practices that are proven to be effective in ensuring that instruction will yield learning. It's fine to teach, but how are you certain your students are *learning*? The use of EBPs provides teachers with assurance that the implemented practice has been determined, by quality research, to be effective (Torres, Farley, & Cook, 2014). Torres and colleagues outline a process for identifying and implementing EBPs. In short, you would carefully identify a practice or program that meets the needs of your particular students, can be implemented in the necessary setting (most likely your classroom), and has a strong level of evidence. The point is, a promising or research-based practice or program is probably the best choice to meet the immediate needs of your students.

**Explicit instruction.** Explicit instruction is an EBP that is "a structured, systematic, and effective methodology for teaching academic skills" that provides a scaffolded approach to errorless learning by structuring learning to occur incrementally (Archer & Hughes, 2011, p. 1). Teachers who use explicit instruction can be confident in meeting students' needs. The teacher is highly involved in the teaching and learning process at the initial concept development stage, but as students develop skills and understandings, teachers fade out supports to more fully develop student independence in using skills, developing understandings, and generalizing learning to other settings and new concepts. Just to clarify, explicit instruction does not mean straight out lecturing!

**Peer tutoring.** Peer tutoring builds fluency and comprehension development, while also developing overall self-esteem for the tutor and higher levels of social acceptance for the tutee (Mastropieri & Scruggs, 2007). In cross-age tutoring, older students tutor younger lower-functioning students, while in same-age tutoring students can challenge each other with flashcards. Classwide peer tutoring increases engaged time on task and opportunities to respond. Stenhoff and Lignugaris/Kraft's (2007) review of the literature provided evidence for peer tutoring to support its use as an evidence-based instructional practice. This is good for students with and without disabilities.

In seeking out appropriate adaptations for students, teachers should consider not only the accommodations and modifications outlined in the IEP, but also how their instructional design meets the academic needs of their students. Often, the accommodations prescribed in a student's IEP can easily be provided through the usual methods a teacher uses with some possible tweaks. In fact, many accommodations are beneficial to all students and are easy to implement. Consider which EBPs are beneficial to all students and can naturally be embedded into the daily routines of the classroom.

## UNIVERSAL DESIGN FOR LEARNING

Have you heard of UDL? Yes? No? Either way, this is a biggie. This is the framework most professional educators are studying, implementing, testing, and trying to make an everyday part of instruction in today's classrooms. UDL is a framework for designing instruction from the planning stages with all learners in mind. The concept comes from the architectural field that developed *universal design*. This promoted the philosophy that designing an accessible building from the ground up promotes a sense of belonging for all users of the building and just flat out makes more sense. Why create a building with only steps just to have to add a ramp or elevator later? Instead, build it with the ramps, larger bathrooms, handrails, and electronic doors right from the get-go. Remember our example of visual cues? Everyone uses them, right? The same is true for universal design. Have you ever pushed the button to open a door electronically because you were pushing a stroller, on crutches, or had your hands full? The same idea holds true in education. All students can benefit from teachers using the principles of UDL in their planning, instruction, and assessment.

Universal Design for Learning is where this concept is applied to the creation of lessons, instruction, and assessment. It's about being *super* proactive in planning lessons and assessments rather than merely reacting to individual needs of students as the lesson is in progress. The main premise of UDL is that the teacher reduces the rigidity of the curriculum by providing student choice and creating flexibility within instructional design. Developing and implementing instruction using the UDL framework will help teachers plan for all students to learn at high levels while providing for accommodations and modifications outlined in IEPs in a seamless manner.

The principles of UDL are based on three networks (UDL Center, 2014). First, "recognition networks," or the *what* of learning, are the ways in which learners gather facts and organize the new material in their brains for later retrieval. This principle of representation works toward multiple ways of presenting concepts to students. What are the various ways concepts could be represented to help students learn the material? Are we always lecturing or are we changing up our presentation? Are we modeling, showing videos, inviting guest speakers, or using text features (i.e., bold, italics, color) to help students learn information?

**Plugged In**

For more ideas on how to use the UDL framework and examples of ways to use each principle, check out http://www.udlcenter.org/implementation/examples.

Second, "strategic networks," or the *how* of learning, are the ways in which learners organize what they are learning and express that learning. This principle, action, and expression gets at how teachers plan for students to express their learning, formatively and summatively, informally and formally. Are students typically writing or speaking? How else could they express their learning? Could they use speech-to-text software to create a report? Could they draw a response or create a model? Could they write a play or a poem instead of an essay? These varied activities allow students to express learning in a way that best makes sense to them to show off their learning.

Third, "affective networks," or the *why* of learning, are the ways in which learners are engaged in learning and maintain attention to what they are learning. This principle of engagement begs the question: How are we keeping students engaged? Do they have multiple ways they can stay engaged in learning? Are we helping them take ownership of their learning by helping them learn how to organize their learning in a way that makes sense to them?

## APPROPRIATE ADAPTATIONS CAN BE SEAMLESSLY EMBEDDED IN INSTRUCTION IF . . .

Teachers:

✗ **STOP keeping the same accommodations year after year.** You must continually evaluate accommodations and assess their effectiveness. Common accommodations on IEPs are "small group setting for testing" and "read tests aloud." So many students balk at these accommodations and say they don't need them. Check to see—do they? Sometimes they've just been rewritten year after year. If these accommodations are not proving helpful to a student, identify what will be effective instead.

✗ **STOP working independently.** You are a team; work together. Unless you've figured out some magical formula, you've experienced times when you just can't figure out what to do with a student. Didn't you want a partner to help you? Two heads are better than one!

✗ **STOP mismatching the student and the accommodation.** Too often, accommodations are used "because we've always used that with this student." For example, perhaps the student once had their test questions read aloud, but now after some additional practice, they don't need this accommodation anymore. Be sure to think about the student's unique characteristics, strengths, and needs when considering the most appropriate changes to make.

✗ **STOP making decisions without the student's input.** Encourage students to take ownership of their education. Invite students to team meetings (like IEP meetings) to discuss their progress, especially if they are in middle or high school. Ask students what is working for them and where they feel they need additional help. Let their voice be heard!

✗ **STOP backing down.** ADVOCATE for your students professionally. When you know programming for students with special needs (e.g., gifted, ELLs, disabilities) could be improved, speak up and make a case for what students need. Be willing to go out on a limb to advocate for students to receive what they need to be successful.

✘ **STOP assuming others know what you are talking about or that they don't care to know.** Avoid jargon and invite questions from your colleagues and from parents. Be willing to explain terms so your colleagues can understand. Not everyone knows what an accommodation or modification is.

✘ **STOP thinking you don't have a voice in IEP development, especially in developing goals, objectives, and identifying appropriate adaptations.** You know the demands of the curriculum at your grade level if you are the general educator. You understand disabilities and know strategies that can enhance students' learning if you are the special educator. You know the school's resources and community connections if you are an administrator. You know your child if you are a parent. Speak up for what would be appropriate to consider in helping a student with an IEP be successful in a general education classroom and access the curriculum appropriately.

✘ **STOP using a one-size-fits-all approach.** All your students are different in their approach to learning and their interests, just like you are different from your colleagues. Use the principles of UDL to help you meet the needs of all your students while providing multiple ways for them to learn concepts, express their learning, and stay engaged in learning.

Administrators:

✘ **STOP enabling the gap between special education and general education.** Special educators and general educators have unique skills and knowledge. When you see one teacher being treated as inferior to another teacher, speak up. Recognize that orchestrating a professional marriage between your special and general education teachers will only serve to enhance instruction in your building (Murawski & Dieker, 2012).

✘ **STOP forgetting that your teachers need time to plan together.** Research has shown that the number one obstacle to collaboration is time (Vannest & Hagan-Burke, 2010). Provide your special education and general education teachers with time to plan, consult, and come up with instructional adaptations. You have oversight of the master schedule; work with others to create an inclusive and collaborative schedule.

## STRATEGIES FOR UDL SUCCESS

GO

If only teachers would . . .

✔ **USE flexible grouping arrangements.** When you use flexible groups in your classes, you provide students with opportunities to work with others and learn in new ways, which is another use of the action and expression principle of UDL. Sometimes, you may need to use homogenous teacher-led groups, while other lessons may be best suited to heterogeneous independent groups.

✔ **INCORPORATE appropriate instructional technology into daily instruction.** Instructional technology, sometimes also called *educational technology*, is one of the many tools that teachers can access to facilitate student learning, increase student engagement, and provide accommodations as needed, while incorporating the principles of UDL. The continuum of instructional technology can range from no-tech options (such as response cards) to high-tech options such as polling applications for iPad. By incorporating the appropriate

**Making Connections**

Check out Chapter 5 on Using Technology and Assistive Technology.

instructional technology into your lessons to enhance instruction, you can make learning a more enjoyable, engaging, and productive experience for students.

✔ **DIFFERENTIATE assignments.** For students with disabilities, assignments, including homework, can be daunting. You can differentiate for your students by modifying the length, task, and procedure for grading. Be clear with directions, model what you are looking for, and review necessary materials needed for completion. We have provided a template to aid in planning for differentiated, or tiered, assignments.

✔ **TEACH strategies.** Students with special needs need strategies from which to approach learning. When tackling a large amount of text, *chunk* the reading into smaller portions. Consider within the chunking *hiding some of the text or a portion of an assignment* to help students feel more confident and less overwhelmed. You may want to also consider providing short breaks as each section of a larger assignment is completed (Mastropieri & Scruggs, 2014). Use *color-coding* to help students categorize or remember. For example, when reading about the Civil War, students can mark a page with a yellow sticky note for the causes for the war, use a green sticky note for the conditions soldiers endured, and use an orange sticky note for the differences between the North and the South. When learning to tell time, the hour hand can be in red and the minute hand in blue to help students distinguish the difference. *Highlighting* keywords in a text, such as vocabulary words, can help students remember those words more easily and find them in the text more easily when referencing the text. Use *mnemonics* (Mastropieri & Scruggs, 2014) to aid in memory. For example, "King Philip cuts open five green snakes" for remembering the order of taxonomy in biology (kingdom, phylum, class, order, family, genus, species).

✔ **TEACH strategies for independence.** A component of engagement in UDL is students taking ownership of their learning. Teaching them how to use graphic organizers, cue cards, guided notes, or other strategies are helpful but go a step further. Don't only teach the strategy or the use of the materials and leave it at that. Deliberately teach students to create their own, decide when to use which one, and prompt them when a particular strategy might be helpful.

✔ **START early.** It's never too early to incorporate UDL strategies. Teachers in early childhood programs can use multiple means of representation, engagement, and expression to identify students' strengths and include more students with disabilities in all programs at an early age.

**Making Connections**

Check out Chapter 16 on Inclusion for Early Childhood Special Education.

## EXAMPLES OF COMMON CLASSROOM ADAPTATIONS[*]

| Area of Adaptation | Examples |
|---|---|
| **Equipment or materials** | Use of a calculator<br>Use of manipulatives<br>Use of a lower-level reading passage<br>Use of an amplification or FM system<br>Use of an audio recorder<br>Use of a magnification device<br>Activate closed-captioning for videos<br>Use of a spell-checking device |
| **Presentation/ instruction** | Directions repeated<br>Read aloud any visual material that is provided<br>Large print format<br>Braille format<br>Present content in multiple ways (e.g., lecture, writing, video, pictures)<br>Reduce the difficulty of assignments |
| **Scheduling** | Extended time for tasks<br>Break up long tasks into multiple smaller tasks<br>Frequent breaks<br>Testing during preferred time of day |
| **Setting** | Use of a study carrel<br>Private testing room<br>Preferential seating in the classroom<br>Special lighting or minimized lighting<br>Use of noise-canceling headphones |
| **Student response** | Mark answers in book<br>Use of a scribe/oral response to test questions<br>Alternative response (eye gaze, point, oral response)<br>Use of computer for extended response<br>Use of a note taker<br>Use of a communication device or native language |
| **Other** | Use of a highlighter<br>Longer tasks broken into smaller increments<br>Use of assistive technology<br>Provide brief, clear instructions<br>Provide models of completed products |

[*]Note that not all these adaptations are permissible in testing situations, and you should consult your testing program guidelines for more information.

## EXAMPLES OF UDL PRINCIPLES IN USE

| | |
|---|---|
| **Representation** | Videos (with closed caption), lecture with PowerPoint, Prezi, or other visual guide, models, use of text features to emphasize important information in handouts or presentations, pictures/images or symbols to accompany text, diagrams, charts, pre-teach academic vocabulary in a manner that promotes understanding and retention, pre-teach symbols (e.g., mathematics, chemistry, geography), connect new concepts to previously learned ones, provide material in dominant language and supplement in first language (e.g., ASL, Spanish, Polish, Swahili), activate prior knowledge, use of graphic organizers, use of mnemonic strategies, checklists, color-coding, allow use of different modalities (e.g., hearing, seeing, touching, doing/action) |
| **Action and Expression** | Provide digital options to allow for easier navigation, text-to-speech capabilities, provide opportunities for choice, alternate keyboards or various app uses, use of manipulatives, creation of models, drawing, writing (using various materials; e.g., markers, colored pencils, pencil grippers, crayons), song, movement, interactive technologies, providing multiple strategies for completing the same task, prompts, scaffolds, clearly state goals and objectives, provide step-by-step directions, provide "wait time," break down long-term projects into smaller steps with due dates for each step |
| **Engagement** | Provide practice in how to organize learning, reinforce appropriate academic and social behaviors, model use of graphic organizers, provide instruction and activities that are culturally relevant, consider age and developmentally appropriate practice, provide opportunities for choice, create authentic learning tasks and assessments, vary activities to keep students actively involved in learning, provide breaks, alter the sensory stimulation in the room (e.g., music, talking/not talking), help students design learning goals for themselves, alter the degree of difficulty of tasks, provide opportunities for group work with clear expectations and roles |

# ELEMENTS OF EXPLICIT INSTRUCTION

| | | |
|---|---|---|
| Focus on critical content. | Sequence skills logically. | Design organized and focused lessons. |
| Begin lessons with a clear statement of the lesson's goals and your expectations. | Review prior skills and knowledge before beginning instruction. | Break down complex skills and strategies into smaller instructional units. |
| Provide an adequate range of examples and nonexamples. | Provide guided and supported practice. | Provide step-by-step demonstrations. |
| | | Use clear and concise language. |
| | Deliver the lesson at a brisk pace. | Require frequent responses. |
| Provide immediate affirmative and corrective feedback. | | Monitor student performance closely. |
| | Help students organize knowledge. | Provide distributed and cumulative practice. |

*Source:* Adapted from Archer, A. L., & Hughes, C. A. (2011). *Explicit instruction: Effective and efficient teaching.* New York, NY: Guilford Press.

## TIERED INSTRUCTION AND ASSESSMENTS: MEETING THE NEEDS OF ALL STUDENTS

**Name:** Mrs. Bauman    **Subject Area:** Science

**Topic:** Waves and Technology Applications    **Grade Level:** 4th

**Pre-Assessment:** Science districtwide assessment—use of the data from the section on waves. Student responses will provide information on prior knowledge to place students within levels for tiering.

| | Level 1: Beginning | Level 2: Developing | Level 3: Advanced |
|---|---|---|---|
| **Outcome/ Performance Indicators:**<br><br>*All students will develop a model of waves to describe patterns.* | Students will develop a model of waves using string pasted on paper to form a wave and label the parts. | Students will develop a model of waves using string pasted on paper to form a wave and label the parts. Students will illustrate three examples of an object's movement caused by vibrations and compose an explanation of the waves created by the vibrations. | Students will develop a model of waves using string pasted on paper to form a wave and construct a paragraph explaining the parts of a wave and their functions. Students will draw and compare a sound wave to a light wave and explain the effects of a sound wave on an object compared to the effects of a light wave on an object. |
| **Assessment:**<br><br>*All students will correctly label the parts of a wave and explain the patterns.* | Students will correctly label the parts of a wave. Students will create three illustrations (using materials of their choice) to explain, in a manner of their choice (e.g., create a Nearpod presentation, an audio file, or create a written explanation), a wave (e.g., a drum emitting sound waves; speakers "bouncing" music notes/emitting vibrations). | Students will correctly label the parts of a wave; create three illustrations (using materials of their choice) to explain, in a manner of their choice (e.g., create a Nearpod presentation, an audio file, or create a written explanation), the different parts of a wave and their functions. They will include examples of how waves can cause objects to move. | Students will create an illustration (using materials of their choice) of a sound wave and a light wave to explain and compare, in a manner of their choice (e.g., create a Nearpod presentation, an audio file, or create a written explanation), the different parts of a wave and their functions. They will include examples of how waves can cause objects to move. |

| | Level 1: Beginning | Level 2: Developing | Level 3: Advanced |
|---|---|---|---|
| **Instructional Learning Activity:** *All students will observe the teacher model making a wave using a Slinky.* | Small groups will experiment using the slinky and attempt to create waves. The teacher will ask for a volunteer to demonstrate making a wave. The students will practice and continue working in small groups to make a wave using a Slinky. They will practice moving their arms in different directions to experiment with what will happen to the wave and its properties. Students will draw pictures of their observation in their science notebooks. | Small groups will practice making different types of waves. The teacher will challenge the groups to make different types of waves, transverse v. longitudinal. The students will draw and label the two types of wave. | After the teacher explains the types of waves to this group of students, they will work in a small group to create different types of waves; transverse v. longitudinal. In their small groups, students will draw and label the types of waves and their properties that they make. Students will record their observations and compare and contrast the waves and their properties and record their observations in their notebooks. |
| **UDL Principles** | *Representation*: video, modeling of activity by teacher, review of vocabulary; review of group expectations; picture examples of light and sound waves<br><br>*Expression*: using Slinkys for a hands-on activity, explaining observations and notes in notebook, creating a wave using string and glue; technology use, as needed, for explanations<br><br>*Engagement*: Slinky wave practice in small groups, giant wave making on the floor, observation records and reflections of what they have seen; choice in assessment | | |
| **Resources** | Slinky<br>String<br>Glue<br>Technology (computers, tablets, etc.)<br>Art supplies<br>Paper<br>Science notebooks | Slinky<br>String<br>Glue<br>Technology (computers, tablets, etc.)<br>Art supplies<br>Paper<br>Science notebooks | Slinky<br>String<br>Glue<br>Technology (computers, tablets, etc.)<br>Art supplies<br>Paper<br>Science notebooks |

*Source:* Template originated from http://www.dcmoboces.com/dcmoiss/staffdev/oinit/ dile/tact2.doc (2003) and has been adapted by Dr. Sandra Fortner, Regent University; Drs. Laurie Matthias and Ruby Owiny, Trinity International University.

## COMPONENTS OF HIGH-QUALITY INSTRUCTION

| | |
|---|---|
| **Grouping** | • Instruction should be provided in small groups (e.g., from 1–3 students for optimal results)<br>• Students should have similar instructional needs |
| **Instructional Design** | • Instruction should focus on a small group of clearly defined skills or concepts<br>• Instruction should be provided using an instructional sequence and materials that meet individual needs<br>• Instruction should be well structured and provide explicit instruction with concrete examples, models, and demonstrations |
| **Delivery of Instruction** | • Allow an appropriate pace and sufficient time for student mastery of targeted skills, with redundant instruction as necessary<br>• Provide cognitive support through the use of carefully sequenced lessons, control of task difficulty, and providing models and scaffolding that ensures a high level of student success<br>• Provide emotional support through encouragement, feedback, and high levels of student success<br>• Provide students with opportunities to practice and response (e.g., guided practice) |
| **Independent Practice** | • Provide practice directly related to the skills being taught<br>• Students should achieve high success rate during independent practice<br>• Independent practice should continue until responses are automatic |
| **Progress Monitoring** | • Monitor student progress weekly or biweekly to evaluate the effectiveness of the intervention, and ensure that students are making sufficient progress<br>• Provide students with feedback regarding their individual progress |

*Source:* McLeskey, J., & Waldron, N. L. (2011). Educational programs for elementary students with learning disabilities: Can they be both effective and inclusive? *Learning Disabilities Research & Practice, 26,* 48–57.

# REFERENCES

Archer, A. L., & Hughes, C. A. (2011). *Explicit instruction: Effective and efficient teaching*. New York, NY: Guilford Press.

Edgemon, E. A., Jablonski, B. R., & Lloyd, J. W. (2006). Large-scale assessments: A teacher's guide to making decisions about accommodations. *TEACHING Exceptional Children, 38*(3), 6–11.

Friend, M., & Bursuck, W. D. (2009). *Including students with special needs: A practical guide for classroom teachers* (5th ed.). Columbus, OH: Merrill.

Individuals with Disabilities Education Improvement Act of 2004, 20 U.S.C. § 1400 *et seq* (2004).

Johns, B. H. (2011). *401 practical adaptations for every classroom*. Thousand Oaks, CA: Corwin.

Mastropieri, M., & Scruggs, T. (2007). *The inclusive classroom: Strategies for effective instruction*. Upper Saddle River, NJ: Prentice Hall.

Mastropieri, M., & Scruggs, T. (2014). *The inclusive classroom: Strategies for effective differentiated instruction*. Upper Saddle River, NJ: Pearson Education.

McLeskey, J., & Waldron, N. L. (2011). Educational programs for elementary students with learning disabilities: Can they be both effective and inclusive? *Learning Disabilities Research & Practice, 26,* 48–57.

Murawski, W. W., & Dieker, L. (2012). *Leading the co-teaching dance: Leadership strategies to enhance team outcomes*. Arlington, VA: Council for Exceptional Children.

Soukup, J., Wehmeyer, M., Bashinski, S., & Bovaird, J. (2007). Classroom variables and access to the general curriculum for students with disabilities. *Exceptional Children, 74,* 101–120.

Stenhoff, D. M., & Lignugaris/Kraft, B. (2007). A review of the effects of peer tutoring on students with mild disabilities in secondary settings. *Exceptional Children, 74,* 8–30.

Suk-Hyang, L., Wehmeyer, M. L., Palmer, S. B., Soukup, J. H., & Little, T. D. (2008). Self-determination and access to the general education curriculum. *The Journal of Special Education, 42*(2), 91–107.

Torres, C., Farley, C. A., & Cook, B. G. (2014). A special educator's guide to successfully implementing evidence-based practices. *TEACHING Exceptional Children, 47,* 85–93.

UDL Center. (2014). What is UDL. Retrieved from http://www.udlcenter.org/aboutudl/whatisudl

Vannest, K. J., & Hagan-Burke, S. (2010). Teacher time use in special education. *Remedial and Special Education, 31,* 126–142.

Wright, P. W. D., & Wright, P. D. (2014). *Special education law* (2nd ed.). Hartfield, VA: Harbor House Law Press.

## ADDITIONAL RECOMMENDED READING

Hall, T. E., Meyer, A., & Rose, D. H. (2012). *Universal design for learning in the classroom: Practical applications.* New York, NY: Guilford Press.

Marchand-Martella, N. E., Slocum, T. A., & Martella, R. C. (Eds.). (2004). *Introduction to direct instruction.* Boston: MA: Pearson Education.

Ralabate, P. K. (2016). *Your UDL lesson planner: The step-by-step guide for teaching all learners.* Baltimore, MD: Paul H. Brookes.

Tomlinson, C. A., & McTighe, J. (2006). *Integrating differentiation + understanding by design.* Alexandria, VA: Association for Supervision and Curriculum Development.

## TOP FIVE WEBSITES TO SUPPORT INSTRUCTIONAL STRATEGIES AND UDL

➡ National Center for Learning Disabilities: www.ncld.org

➡ Council for Learning Disabilities: www.CLDinternational.org

➡ Evidence-based summaries:
http://iris.peabody.vanderbilt.edu/ebp_summaries

➡ http://www.cast.org

➡ http://www.udlcenter.org

## APPS WE LOVE

➡ Notability

➡ iMovie

➡ Inspiration Maps

➡ Memory King

➡ Clicker Sentences

# 5

## Leveling the Playing Field With Technology

Barbara Serianni,
Ela Kaye Eley, and LaToya Cannon
*Armstrong State University*

## MOTIVATING AND ENGAGING STUDENTS WITH SPECIAL NEEDS

Chandra is a low performing seventh-grade student with a learning disability and ADHD (attention deficit hyperactivity disorder) attending school in an urban, Title 1 middle school. During the first 9 weeks, she was disengaged and turned in only one of 17 assignments in her science class. Even hands-on science labs did not motivate her to participate and complete assignments. One Monday morning, Chandra arrived to find a class set of iPads in her classroom and a science assignment that gave her the freedom to choose a partner and explore any of a dozen educational websites on the day's topic. Without hesitation, Chandra and Kala paired up and used their iPads to explore more than half the sites offered. Chandra collected pictures from websites and took pages of notes as they explored. After finishing their research, the two girls chose how they would complete the written assignment, used an app on the iPad to write and organize their information, and met all the assignment objectives. The pair's work demonstrated a strong understanding of the topic and the ability to organize and synthesize information from several sources. For the first time her teacher could remember, Chandra was an active participant in learning. Despite their impoverished backgrounds, both Chandra and Kala had experience using the Internet to get information and communicate outside of school. In school, it proved to be an engaging and effective way for the girls to learn, engage with the content, and demonstrate their new knowledge.

Technology has radically transformed the way we communicate, shop, bank, socialize, and belong. It has changed entertainment, advertising, and even political campaigns. *Disruptive innovation* describes how something like technology takes root in an organization or culture and eventually expands to the point where it changes the way people live, work, or learn (Christensen, Horn, & Johnson, 2008). In the case of education, technology continues to battle the status quo for dominance in the classroom.

In the scenario above, Chandra's experience shows the potential of technology as a tool to engage students in authentic learning in a way that mirrors how they live, learn, and communicate outside the classroom. While there continues to be a digital divide maintained by socioeconomic status, that divide is shrinking. Today's students, regardless of socioeconomic status, are not unfamiliar with technology or how to use it to get information or communicate. Despite racial and economic differences, students have access to the Internet through smart phones in increasing numbers. This chapter explores technology integration and three critical components of effective instruction: (1) learning what works to eliminate barriers to grade level content, activities, and assessment; (2) learning what works to engage and motivate students in today's inclusive classrooms; and (3) creating student-centric classrooms and responsible digital citizens.

**Key Concepts**

**Disruptive innovation:** Something that changes the way people live, work, or learn.

## THE RESEARCH AND THE PROMISE

Technology as a tool for learning has been a hot topic in education for more than 30 years, dating back to discussions about using television in classrooms and Papert's (1980) audacious ideas to have students program computers and participate in project-based learning. Since that time, a number of barriers to technology integration have been identified and mitigated (e.g., access to technology, system capacity, professional development, and policy considerations), yet widespread effective technology integration has not occurred (Davies & West, 2014; Ertmer, 2005). Ertmer suggests it is teachers' pedagogical beliefs that continue to present a barrier to effective technology integration and the anticipated benefits to student learning that may result from the use of digital technologies in teaching and learning.

Project Tomorrow (Speak Up, 2011) conducted a survey of 1,987 pre-service teachers, 38,642 in-service teachers, and 3,890 administrators in a 2009 survey, along with 299,677 students and 26,312 parents in a complementary online survey. These surveys revealed a telling profile of the participants. Students are generally ready and eager for opportunities to engage in technology-based learning. School administrators see the benefit and promote and support the use of technology in the classroom. Teachers, on the other hand, have mixed opinions and varying perceptions of the usefulness, benefits, and practicality of technology integration in the classroom, thus resulting in widespread continued use of traditional, whole-class instruction delivered by a teacher standing in the front of the room (Speak Up, 2011).

Fear not—there is hope! There are teachers, both in special and general education, who are excited about the potential of the Internet, digital devices, and applications to provide accessibility, motivate and engage learners, and support students' unique learning needs (Cheung & Slavin, 2013). In schools and classrooms where there is widespread student use of technology for learning, there is often a blurring of the historical line between assistive and instructional technology (Gray, Silver-Pacuilla, Brann, Overton, & Reynolds, 2011). Devices like word processors, text-to-speech, or speech-to-text tools that were once acquired strictly for use by students with disabilities who required that support are now common classroom tools available to all students. Increasingly, students have access to computers, tablets, and smartphones, whether school-owned or brought into school as part of bring your own device (BYOD) initiatives, making technology-based learning a reality in many of today's classrooms (Johnson, Adams Becker, Estrada, & Freeman, 2014).

The most significant change in the use of technology in the classroom over the last decade is that learners are no longer passive users of technology. Web-based social media tools encourage user socialization and collaboration (Hicks & Graber, 2010).

 **Key Concepts**

**Assistive technology (AT)** is technology that is necessary "to increase, maintain, or improve the functional capabilities of students with disabilities" (IDEA, 1997).

**Educational technology (ET)** is the variety of electronic tools and applications that help deliver learning materials and support learning processes in K–12 classrooms to improve academic learning goals (Cheung & Slavin, 2013).

Learners now embrace their new role as content creators rather than mere consumers of information (Halverson & Smith, 2009). This creation and exchange of user-created content helps students take ownership of their own learning (Kaplan & Haenlein, 2010). In addition, when this ownership happens, they become more empowered. The use of social media provides that sense of empowerment to those who are collaborating, authoring, and sharing content across the web (Lietsala & Sirkkunen, 2008).

The use of desktop computers and the development of applications for educational use has slowed and is being replaced by web-based applications that can be used on a variety of mobile platforms. Schools are no longer investing in devices that must be shared by rotating students into a room but instead are investing their resources in mobile devices that can be moved around the school and shared between classrooms. Increasingly, schools are promoting BYOD initiatives and investing in training teachers to integrate student devices into their lessons and learning activities (Johnson et al., 2014). Special and general education teachers alike are using cloud-based computing, mobile devices, apps, and flipped classroom strategies to support individual student needs (Schaffhauser, 2013). The future is now; digital devices are a staple in today's classrooms.

Much of the current focus in education is being placed on the need for students to learn to use new technologies to engage in learning. The National Education Technology Plan (NETP), *Transforming American Education: Learning Powered by Technology*, was designed by the U.S. Department of Education in 2010. The NETP draws attention to the around-the-clock access that students have to resources and information, their proficiency in creating and sharing content, and the ability to connect with others through the use of online social networks. The report's executive summary acknowledges that this ubiquitous access to resources has become part of the new normal and the challenge for educators is to use the technologies to "create engaging, relevant, and personalized learning experiences for all learners that mirror students' daily lives and the reality of their future" (U.S. Department of Education, 2010, p. x).

So how does all this fit with students with special needs specifically? Students with moderate or severe disabilities are also using more digital assistive technology (AT). Point to communication boards and expensive communication devices have new competition from low cost and no cost tablet apps that serve the same purpose (Schaffhauser, 2013). iDevices and other mobile platforms have made the use of technology in the field of special education and speech pathology affordable, convenient, and user-friendly. Tablets like the iPad are increasingly more accessible, increasing their popularity in classrooms. Apple's iOS operating system and built-in software makes the iPad more accessible for all and reduces the need for AT specific devices for many students.

As an alternative to iPads, many districts are purchasing Chromebooks for student use (Asher-Schapiro & Hermeling, 2013). The keyboard built into the Chromebook makes it more accessible for some students—especially those who need tactile stimulation (Peterson-Karlan, 2015). One of the factors driving the acquisition of

Chromebooks is cost, but the Chromebook has earned a reputation for being rugged; it is able to withstand multiple drops from the height of a desk without damage.

These common and easy to use devices are becoming a mainstay in the American classroom. Their portability and ability to level the educational playing field for students with exceptionalities and below grade level learners are key factors in their rise in popularity in schools. No matter which device schools or districts choose for their students, there is a positive impact by providing all students the opportunity to learn with technology.

A number of recent research studies on the use of iPads have demonstrated benefits for students with autism spectrum disorder, hearing and visual impairments, intellectual disabilities, learning disabilities, and speech and language disabilities (Desai, Chow, Mumford, Hotze, & Chau, 2014; Fernandez-Lopez, Rodriguez-Fortiz, Rodriguez-Almendros, & Martinez-Segura, 2013). The flexibility and adaptability of these devices to transform and impact the lives of students with disabilities elevates classroom performance and increases learning potential (O'Malley, Lewis, Donehower, & Stone, 2014).

iPad versatility allows students to access a wide range of educational features and third party apps that have the potential to engage and support, ultimately with the potential to improve student academic outcomes. Historically, alternative and augmentative communication (AAC) devices, like the Dynavox, were solely dedicated to a singular function (Stoner, Angell, & Bailey, 2010). Now increasingly, there are commercial apps that turn the iPad into an AAC device. A recent study introduced the use of an iPad with the app *Go Talk Now* as an ACC device for a student with comorbid cerebral palsy and autism spectrum disorder. Using the iPad, the student demonstrated a marked improvement in communication skills and nonacademic functioning and a need for fewer prompts (Desai et al., 2014). How cool is that?

Additional studies involving students with disabilities who used various iPad educational apps showed improved performance and autonomy in mathematics (O'Malley et al., 2014) and literacy/language (Fernandez-Lopez et al., 2013). Apps on the iPad and other tablets are proving to be effective tools to support learning for students with disabilities.

There are over 80,000 apps in the App Store that have been categorized as educational, and Google opened its own Play for Education store to market their educational apps, videos, and other supporting materials. With more educational apps being developed every day, it is important to rely on reviews and ratings to select just a few to use with your students. It is easy to overwhelm yourself or your students with the sheer number of choices. There is no end in sight, and the wave of educational app development continues.

## ACCESSIBILITY: ELIMINATING BARRIERS

iOS, Apple's operating system for mobile devices, has a number of built-in accessibility features that allow students with a variety of needs to successfully use the iPad, iPhone, or iPad touch. Most can be accessed through the device settings and are customizable to suit individual needs.

**Making Connections**

Check out Chapter 14 on Moderate-to-Severe Disabilities.

**Students who are blind, have low vision, or reading disabilities** can use VoiceOver, an advanced screen reader; Siri or Alexa, voice command; and Dictation, Apple's voice-to-text app support for students who cannot see or read content on the iPad screen. A number of plug-in third-party Bluetooth braille displays allow students who are blind to navigate, read, and execute iPad commands independently.

**Students with disabilities that affect physical or motor skills** also benefit from those features as well as AssistiveTouch and Touch Accommodations that allow iOS touch screen functionality to be customized to a student's unique needs; Switch Control, which allows easy access to Bluetooth-enabled switch hardware; and Predictive Text, an intuitive word prediction software that reduces keystrokes.

**Students who are deaf or hard of hearing** communicate through features like video platforms (e.g., FaceTime, Skype) and text messaging. Additionally, closed captioning and mono audio both support accessibility to audio content on the iPad for these students.

**Students with autism spectrum disorder or other sensory or attention challenges** who need support to focus or stay on task can benefit from Guided Access, which allows a teacher to limit features and functions of the iPad to help reduce visual stimuli and reduce distractions.

**Students with speech/language or reading disabilities** may benefit from any or all the features described above. Additionally, integrated features such as Dictionary, which allows students to look up unknown words; or read-aloud support such as Screen Speak, which can also highlight text as it is read, or Safari Reader, which reduces sensory overload by minimizing visual clutter as it works with VoiceOver to read webpage content out loud.

## MOTIVATING AND ENGAGING STUDENTS

Regardless of disability, learning requires engagement. Students must connect and interact with content to create new knowledge and develop understanding. It has been suggested that allowing students to use technology can be a motivating factor in the classroom, but any teacher who has added technology to their classroom can attest to the fact that the novelty of new technology wears off and student engagement returns to the classroom norm (Ferriter, 2012).

Researchers have shown that four goals underlie student engagement: success, curiosity, originality, and relationship (Strong, Silver, & Robinson, 1995). Learners who are engaged all exhibit similar characteristics: They have interest in their work, they persist despite obstacles, and they exhibit a sense of accomplishment (Strong et al., 1995). While it is clear that technology in itself is not a motivator (Ferriter, 2012), technology can be used to connect students to topics of interest, investigate and solve problems, and provide creative opportunities for demonstrating new knowledge.

**Making Connections**

Check out Chapter 4 on Instructional Strategies and Universal Design for Learning.

Teachers must design lessons that are authentic tasks that align with student interests to maintain high engagement (Meyer, Rose, & Gordon, 2014). Student interests vary widely, and student perceptions of what is authentic vary as well, requiring extensive differentiation to boost engagement. What might be an impossible task in a traditional learning environment is possible by including technology-enhanced options in learning activities and assessments and designing instruction using Universal Design for Learning (UDL) principles (Meyer et al., 2014).

## CREATING STUDENT-CENTRIC CLASSROOMS WITH RESPONSIBLE DIGITAL CITIZENS

What tech skills are necessary for school and postsecondary success? Conversations among administrators, parents, employers, and community leaders revolve around 21st century skills for 21st century learners. Collaboration, creativity, communication, problem solving, and critical thinking have become this century's buzzwords. They are in every research study, article, professional development, and blog about teaching in today's schools. But these skills are not new; teachers have always expected these things from their students. These skills have simply been repackaged, redefined, and popularized as critical skills for success in the 21st century.

The International Society for Technology in Education (ISTE) created a set of research-based technology standards that K–12 students should demonstrate. The six categories of student standards are (1) creativity and innovation, (2) communication and collaboration, (3) research and information fluency, (4) critical thinking, problem solving, and decision making, (5) digital citizenship, and (6) technology expectations and concepts.

Each of these standards can be met in any and all content areas. To help you address these standards, a list of cloud-based resources has been included at the end of this chapter that will expand your digital technology toolbox.

Keeping your toolbox organized and the resources easily accessible requires a specialized digital tool. Social bookmarking allows you to tag, organize, access, and share your favorite tools from any device or location that has an Internet connection and share them with others. Diigo (https://www.diigo.com) is an easy to use social bookmarking tool that teachers can use to collect useful websites and share them with students.

 **Plugged In**

Check out the technology standards at https://www.iste.org, or this Social bookmarking tool: https://www.diigo.com.

Let's take another look at Chandra, the seventh-grade student we met at the beginning of the chapter. One of the best strategies used by her teacher was allowing Chandra to have choices in her learning. In this particular lesson, Chandra could choose a partner, which content she would access, and how (what product) they would demonstrate what they had learned. By participating in this learning activity, Chandra and her partner were able to express their creativity, collaborate with each other, and communicate with classmates. The two demonstrated the standards of good digital citizenship while building content knowledge and fluency in research and information gathering.

Throughout the entire project, Chandra and Kala were engaged in critical thinking, problem solving, and decision making because they were in control of their learning. If technology is going to be transformative for all learners, teachers must relinquish control, equip students with the skills necessary to complete tasks, and empower them to make choices in learning that will allow them to demonstrate mastery. It is no different for our students with exceptionalities. They too will benefit from preparation and opportunities for creativity and independence. This is a change in mindset for general and special education teachers alike, frightening for some, but critical to the task of creating engaged and self-directed learners who can take those important skills into their postsecondary college and careers.

 ## CHANGES TO CONSIDER

**Teachers:**

✗ **STOP being afraid of your own technology competency (or lack of).** You do not have to be able to use every tool. You simply need to provide opportunities for students to use technology to explore knowledge or develop skills. Besides, there is little more motivating to a student than to be able to teach his or her teacher something!

✗ **STOP worrying about what you don't have in technology or what it will cost.** Invite students to bring their own device and make free apps the "go to" in your classroom. They will be comfortable on devices they use at home and bring a great deal of background knowledge into assignments.

✗ **STOP taking cell phones away from your students.** Instead, challenge your students to fact check you or explore a topic they want to learn more about. Instead of answering students' questions, ask them to "Google it."

✗ **STOP simply using technology as rewards or time fillers.** You want students to use technology to learn rather than merely as entertainment or a break from learning.

✗ **STOP hoarding your classroom technology.** Technology integration requires putting technology in the hands of your students. Empower them to use technology through regular inquiry-based creative learning opportunities. Don't make every other Thursday "technology day."

Administrators:

✗ **STOP creating policy that limits teachers' ability to integrate technology.** Avoid schoolwide directives that limit students' use of personal digital devices or the school Wi-Fi. Allow teachers to hold students accountable for appropriate use of their devices.

✗ **STOP thinking of mobile devices as disruptive and support BYOD practices.** Host a team building session to spark excitement about a BYOD initiative. Model using smartphones to meet session objectives in your staff meetings or flip your own department meetings.

## GETTING YOUR TECHNOLOGY ON

Teachers:

✔ **START taking risks.** Explore new websites, find new tools, and expose your students to learning through technology. Charge groups of students to explore new tools and make a plan to teach their peers how to use those tools or encourage students to find and use a new tool for creating their next project.

✔ **BEGIN by learning one app.** Become an expert and use it often until you are a fluent user. Once you are comfortable and integrating it effectively, continue to build your repertoire by adding another app. Repeat that cycle and watch your toolbox grow!

**Plugged In**

Need money for technology?

- www.edutopia.org
- www.eschoolnews.com
- www.donorschoose.org
- www.gofundme.com

✔ **START writing grants.** There are still many opportunities to apply for grant funding if you need more classroom technology. Often districts have internal grants for teachers to support innovative use of technology in their classrooms, so check out what your district offers. In addition, sites like edutopia.org and eschoolnews.com often have lists and links to funding opportunities. Many teachers find great success in posting classroom needs on crowdfunding sites like donorschoose.org or gofundme.com.

✔ **INTENTIONALLY MODEL how to learn and create new knowledge with technology.** Your students will learn more by what you do than what you say. It's even okay to model how to do something wrong and show them how you learned by screwing something up a few times. Funny stories make a big impression on kids.

✔ **RAISE your expectations for student learning.** Students are no longer bound to their textbook. Through technology, your students have all the knowledge in the world at their fingertips, which has the potential to engage a wide variety of learners. Use it!

✔ **UTILIZE technology to bump up the cognitive level of your learning activities.** Students can move from *locating* a city on Google Maps and *reporting* on its culture to *synthesizing* information about its culture from several sites, or *creating* a model of the city that represents the impact of various cultures on its architecture. They *can* do this . . . but are they?

✔ **MAKE content and learning activities accessible to all students.** Bring your technology specialist into your classroom to teach your students to use the technology features of their devices. Co-teach with that specialist so that you are providing content and he or she is providing the technological application.

✔ **INTEGRATE ISTE-S technology standards into your lesson plans, activities, and rubrics.** Familiarize yourself with the ISTE Standards for students. Add learning objectives to your lessons that are directly aligned with one or more of those standards. For example, an assignment that involves exploring aspects of another culture might include corresponding with a digital pen pal who is a student from another country or culture, which would meet Standard 2.c.

✔ **FLIP your classroom.** The prevalence of personal digital devices and Internet give students the opportunity to access content and continue learning at home or in specially designed afterschool programs that can support your flipped classroom. If your school doesn't provide a program that can support your effort to flip your classroom, it is something you can plan to do after school in your own classroom a couple of times a week (let's face it, it's not like you don't stay late anyway). Keep your expectations for outside-of-class learning realistic. For struggling learners, flipping can activate or create background knowledge or be used to review or pre-teach prerequisite academic language or foundational concepts/skills. This strategy can bring everyone together during class time to engage productively in student-centered learning activities.

Administrators:

✔ **SUPPORT teachers' technology needs with school policies** that support BYOD and wireless Internet access for students such as: *Students may use their personal digital devices to access the Internet by signing on to the school's wireless network.* Other policies can help maintain teacher autonomy in the classroom: *Student use of personal digital devices in the classroom is subject to the policies and discretion of classroom teachers.*

✔ **PROVIDE professional development and ongoing support** for teachers to promote technology integration in classrooms and application of ISTE-S standards in planning instruction. This could be an outside consultant, but don't disregard the expertise on your own faculty. Consider using your own faculty to do lunch sessions on favorite apps, tools, and devices.

✔ **PRIORITIZE technology initiatives by allocating additional funds to technology equipment and training.** Title I-A funds can be used as a part of a district or school plan to acquire digital devices and curriculum. Title II-A funds can be used to hire technology coaches or provide professional development to help teachers integrate technology or identify and use Open Educational Resources in their classrooms. Title III-A funds can support the acquisition and use of digital learning resources or native language resources for English learners. IDEA Part B can be used to support access to the general education curriculum for students with disabilities through the use of assistive technology devices and services.

✔ **EVALUATE teachers' effectiveness in incorporating ISTE-S standards into assignments.** First familiarize yourself with the student standards. During a formal or informal observation, ask to see rubrics or other student product evaluation tools to look for the use of ITSE-S standards in criteria. For example, Standard 3 (Research and Information Fluency on an assignment where students are collecting data) may involve a project rubric that includes a requirement to use software to report data results in charts or graphs.

## IOS COMPATIBLE ALTERNATIVE AND AUGMENTIVE COMMUNICATION APPS

| | My Talk Tools Lite | Go Talk Now | Proloquo2Go |
|---|---|---|---|
| **Price** | Free | $79.99 | $249.99 |
| **Preview** | https://itunes.apple.com/us/app/mytalktools-mobile-lite/id376401959?mt=8 | https://itunes.apple.com/us/app/gotalk-now/id454176457?mt=8 | https://itunes.apple.com/us/app/proloquo2go/id308368164?mt=8 |
| **Platforms** | Requires iOS 6.0 or later. Compatible with iPhone, iPad, and iPod touch. | Requires iOS 6.0 or later. Compatible with iPad. | Requires iOS 8.2 or later. Compatible with iPhone, iPad, and iPod touch. |
| **Voice** | One adult female | • Included text to speech voice<br>• Record own voice<br>• Text-to-speech voices available ($0.99) in 20 languages | Variety of male/female and child (girl/boy) voices available for free download |
| **Selection** | Touch (Direct select) | • Touch (Direct select)<br>• Switch (Scan)<br>• Attainment Switch app<br>• RJ Coopers Bluetooth Interface switch | Touch (Direct select) |
| **Features** | • Syncs across multiple devices<br>• Customizable vocabulary<br>• 20 cell capacity with one or more boards | • Import and edit pictures<br>• Customizable backgrounds borders and text<br>• Record your own speech<br>• Auditory cues<br>• Customize navigation tools<br>• Add custom message to core | • Large collection of premade vocabulary, customizable<br>• Resizable app features and scaling through settings<br>• Auto-conjugation |

## LOW-COST AND NO-COST EDUCATIONAL APPS

| Name | Category | Price | Description | iTunes Preview | Similar Tool for Android |
|------|----------|-------|-------------|----------------|--------------------------|
| **Virtual Manipulatives** | Math | Free | Fraction bars and circles to build conceptual understanding of equivalence in fractions and decimals. iPad only. | https://itunes.apple.com/us/app/virtual-manipulatives!/id471341079?mt=8 | Matholia Tools https://play.google.com/store/apps/details?id=air.sg.com.matholia.Tools |
| **Draw Free** | General | Free | Bring ideas to life. Variety of tools and colors that can be used to draw, paint, and create. iPad only. | https://itunes.apple.com/us/app/draw-free-for-ipad/id366755447?mt=8 | Draw for Kids https://play.google.com/store/apps/details?id=com.iskander.drawforkids&hl=en |
| **Talking Calculator** | Math | $1.99 | Colorful, full function calculator with voice over. Includes recording studio. iPad and iPhone compatible. | https://itunes.apple.com/us/app/talking-calculator/id424464284?mt=8 | Talking Calculator https://play.google.com/store/apps/details?id=pg.talkingcalculator |
| **Notability** | General | $5.99 | Use to take notes, sketch, brainstorm, mark up photos or PDFs, and record lectures. iPad and iPhone compatible. | https://itunes.apple.com/us/app/notability/id360593530?mt=8 | Note Everything (free) https://play.google.com/store/apps/details?id=de.softxperience.android.noteeverything&hl=en |
| **Dragon Dictation** | Writing | Free | Voice to text application that allows you to post to text messages or social media or compose text for writing assignments. iPad and iPhone compatible. | https://itunes.apple.com/us/app/dragon-dictation/id341446764?mt=8 | List Note https://play.google.com/store/apps/details?id=com.khymaera.android.listnotefree&hl=en |

*(Continued)*

| Name | Category | Price | Description | iTunes Preview | Similar Tool for Android |
|------|----------|-------|-------------|----------------|--------------------------|
| **Read2Go** | Literacy | $19.99 | Bookshare is the largest accessible online library for people with print disabilities. Read2Go allows you to search and download titles directly from your iPad, iPhone, or iPod touch. | https://itunes.apple.com/us/app/read2go/id425585903?mt=8 | Go Read (free) https://play.google.com/store/apps/details?id=org.benetech.android&hl=en |
| **Khan Academy** | Learning | Free | Learning videos and interactive practice in mathematics concepts from arithmetic through calculus. Other content area videos include biology, chemistry, physics, economics, and the humanities. iPad, iPhone, or iPod touch. | https://itunes.apple.com/us/app/khan-academy-learn-math-biology/id469863705?mt=8 | Khan Academy https://play.google.com/store/apps/details?id=org.khanacademy.android&hl=en |
| **Study Blue** | Learning | Free | Create and share mobile flashcards, study guides, and quizzes, or choose from the collection of student-authored flashcards on various topics. iPad, iPhone, or iPod touch. | https://itunes.apple.com/us/app/studyblue/id323887414?mt=8 | StudyBlue https://play.google.com/store/apps/details?id=com.studyblue&hl=en |
| **Dictionary.com** | Literacy | Free | Comprehensive dictionary and thesaurus, works online or offline. Includes voice search, audio pronunciation, spelling suggestions, and a translator. iPad, iPhone, or iPod touch. | https://itunes.apple.com/us/app/dictionary.com-dictionary/id308750436?mt=8 | Dictionary.com https://play.google.com/store/apps/details?apps/details? |

| App | Category | Price | Description | iTunes URL | Google Play URL |
|---|---|---|---|---|---|
| **Lumosity** | Brain Training | Free | Attention and memory training. iPad, iPhone, or iPod touch. | https://itunes.apple.com/us/app/lumosity-mobile/id577232024?mt=8&ign-mpt=uo%3D8 | Lumosity https://play.google.com/store/apps/details?id=com.lumoslabs.lumosity |
| **Studious** | Time Management | $0.99 | Intuitive homework planner that reminds you when you are having a test and organizes assignments by class. iPad, iPhone, or iPod touch. | https://itunes.apple.com/us/app/studious/id1002217017?mt=8&ign-mpt=uo%3D8 | Studious (free) https://play.google.com/store/apps/details?id=leslie3141.android.studious&hl=en |
| **Pocket** | Organization | Free | Save Web content like articles and video and view offline in an easy to read format. iPad, iPhone, iPod touch, or Mac. | https://itunes.apple.com/us/app/pocket-save-articles-videos/id309601447?mt=8&ign-mpt=uo%3D8 | Pocket https://play.google.com/store/apps/details?id=com.ideashower.readitlater.pro |
| **Educreations** | Presentation | Free | Interactive whiteboard and screencasting tool. Use to annotate, or explain anything on your iPad. | https://itunes.apple.com/us/app/educreations-interactive-whiteboard/id478617061?mt=8&ign-mpt=uo%3D8 | Lensoo Create (free) https://play.google.com/store/apps/details?id=com.lensoo.create&hl=en |
| **Explain Everything** | Presentation | $3.99 | Similar to Educreations, this app allows users to add video and use a laser pointer. | https://itunes.apple.com/us/app/explain-everything-interactive/id431493086?mt=8 | Explain Everything (free) https://play.google.com/store/apps/details?id=com.morriscooke.explain everything |

## CLOUD-BASED NON-CONTENT SPECIFIC TECHNOLOGY TOOLS

All have a FREE version that allows basic functionality in the classroom.

| Name | Category | Ideas for Classroom Use | Access |
|------|----------|-------------------------|--------|
| Animoto | Creativity | Videos, digital storytelling | https://animoto.com |
| Toondoo | Creativity | Illustrate vocabulary words, tell a story with cartoons | http://www.toondoo.com |
| Soundcloud | Creativity | Create and host podcasts | https://soundcloud.com |
| WeVideo | Creativity | Videos, digital storytelling | https://www.wevideo.com |
| Storybird | Creativity | Creative writing and narrations | http://storybird.com |
| Google Drive | Collaboration | Word processing, spreadsheet, slide presentation, chat with others simultaneously, cloud storage | https://www.google.com/drive |
| Padlet | Collaboration | Brainstorming, categorizing | https://padlet.com |
| Wikispaces | Collaboration | Add content, personalize information | http://www.wikispaces.com |
| TitanPad | Collaboration | Brainstorming, backchannel | https://titanpad.com |
| Google Hangouts | Collaboration | Real-time video and audio interaction | https://hangouts.google.com |
| Edmodo | Communication | Secure social network for schools | https://www.edmodo.com |
| Remind | Communication | Texting program that masks real phone number | https://www.remind.com |
| Popplet | Communication | Brainstorming, mind-mapping | http://popplet.com |
| WordPress | Communication | Blog | https://wordpress.com |
| Twiducate | Communication | Secure micro-blogging system (similar to Twitter, except for education) | https://voicethread.com |

| Name | Category | Ideas for Classroom Use | Access |
|---|---|---|---|
| VoiceThread | Communication | Record narration | https://voicethread.com |
| Edublogs | Communication | Secure blogging platform for education | http://edublogs.org |
| TimeToast | Critical Thinking and/or Problem Solving | Use to create timelines, can also be used without dates for sequencing | http://www.timetoast.com |
| Web Search Engines | Critical Thinking and/or Problem Solving | Use to conduct research and explore solutions | https://www.google.com http://www.bing.com |
| Cacoo | Critical Thinking and/or Problem Solving | Organizational and mindtool | https://cacoo.com |
| Tiddlywiki | Critical Thinking and/or Problem Solving | Non-linear organizer for text, images, sound, video | http://tiddlywiki.com |
| Piktochart | Critical Thinking and/or Problem Solving | Infographic maker to prepare visual data and reference charts | http://piktochart.com/piktochart-infographics |
| SymbalooEDU | Critical Thinking and/or Problem Solving | Visual display of social bookmarks with keywords | http://www.symbalooedu.com |
| PowToon | Presentation Tools | Create animated videos and presentations | http://www.powtoon.com |
| Prezi | Presentation Tools | Non-linear presentation tool | https://prezi.com |
| EMaze | Presentation Tools | Presentation templates include 3D images and video backgrounds | https://www.emaze.com |
| Voki | Presentation Tools | Create speaking avatars for presentations | http://www.voki.com |

# REFERENCES

Asher-Schapiro, A., & Hermeling, A. (2013). Racing the iPad in k12 education. *District Administration, 49*(4), 70–73.

Cheung, A. C., & Slavin, R. E. (2013). The effectiveness of educational technology applications for enhancing mathematics achievement in K–12 classrooms: A meta-analysis. *Educational Research Review, 9*, 88–113.

Christensen, C. M., Horn, M. B., & Johnson, C. W. (2008). *Disrupting class: How disruptive innovation will change the way the world learns* (Vol. 98). New York, NY: McGraw-Hill.

Davies, R., & West, R. (2014). *Handbook of research on educational communications and technology*. New York, NY: Springer.

Desai, T., Chow, K., Mumford, L., Hotze, F., & Chau, T. (2014). Implementing an iPad-based alternative communication device for a student with cerebral palsy and autism in the classroom via an access technology delivery protocol. *Computers and Education, 79*, 148–158.

Ertmer, P. A. (2005). Teacher pedagogical beliefs: The final frontier in our quest for technology integration? *Educational Technology Research and Development, 53*(4), 25–39.

Fernandez-Lopez, A., Rodriguez-Fortiz, M. J., Rodriguez-Almendros, M. L., & Martinez-Segura, M. J. (2013). Mobile learning technology based on iOS devices to support students with special education needs. *Computers and Education, 6*, 177–190.

Ferriter, B. (2012). *Are kids really motivated by technology?* Retrieved from http://smartblogs.com/education/2012/08/17/are-kids-really-motivated-technology

Gray, T., Silver-Pacuilla, H., Brann, A., Overton, C., & Reynolds, R. (2011). Converging trends in educational and assistive technology. In T. Gray & H. Silver-Pacuilla (Eds.), *Breakthrough teaching and learning* (pp. 5–24). New York, NY: Springer.

Halverson, R., & Smith, A. (2009). How new technologies have (and have not) changed teaching and learning in schools. *Journal of Computing in Teacher Education, 26*(2), 49–54.

Hicks, A., & Graber, A. (2010). Shifting paradigms: Teaching, learning, and Web 2.0. *Reference Services Review, 38*(4), 621–633.

Individuals with Disabilities Education Improvement Act of 2004, 20 U.S.C. § 1400 *et seq* (2004).

Johnson, L., Adams Becker, S., Estrada, V., & Freeman, A. (2014). *Horizon report: 2014 K–12 edition*. Retrieved from http://www.editlib.org/p/147472/

Kaplan, A. M., & Haenlein, M. (2010). Users of the world, unite! The challenges and opportunities of social media. *Business Horizons, 53*(1), 59–68.

Lietsala, K., & Sirkkunen, E. (2008). *Social media: Introduction to the tools and processes of participatory economy*. Tampere, Finland: Tampere University Press.

Meyer, A., Rose, D., & Gordon, D. (2014). *Universal Design for Learning: Theory and practice*. Wakefield, MA: CAST.

O'Malley, P., Lewis, M. B., Donehower, C., & Stone, D. (2014). Effectiveness of using iPads to increase academic task completion by students with autism. *Universal Journal of Educational Research, 2*(1), 90–97.

Papert, S. (1980). Teaching children thinking. *Contemporary Issues in Technology and Teacher Education, 5*(3/4), 353–365.

Peterson-Karlan, G. R. (2015). Assistive technology instruction within a continuously evolving technology environment. *Quarterly Review of Distance Education, 16*(2), 61–76.

Schaffhauser, D. (2013). The surprising ways BYOD, flipped classrooms, and 1-to-1 are being used in the special ed classroom. *T H E Journal.* Retrieved from https://thejournal.com/articles/2013/06/04/the-surprising-ways-byod-flipped-classrooms-and-1-to-1-are-being-used-in-the-special-ed-classroom.aspx

Speak Up. (2011). *How today's educators are advancing a new vision in teaching and learning.* Retrieved from http://www.tomorrow.org/speakup/speakup_data_findings.html#infographics

Stoner, J. B., Angell, M. E., & Bailey, R. L. (2010). Implementing augmentative and alternative communication in inclusive educational settings: A case study. *AAC: Augmentative and Alternative Communication, 26*(2), 122–135.

Strong, R., Silver, H., & Robinson, A. (1995). Strengthening student engagement. *Educational Leadership, 53*(1), 8–12.

U.S. Department of Education. (2010). *Transforming American education: Learning powered by technology. National Education Technology Plan 2010.* Washington, DC: Office of Educational Technology. Retrieved from http://files.eric.gov/fulltext/ED512681.pdf

## WEBSITES TO KEEP UP WITH TECH TRENDS

➡ National Center on Accessible Materials: http://aem.cast.org

➡ Educause http://www.educause.edu

➡ Center on Technology and Disability: http://www.ctdinstitute.org

➡ Horizon Report: https://www.nmc.org/nmc-horizon

## APPS WE LOVE

➡ Jing

➡ Kahoot

➡ SMORE

➡ Google Docs

➡ Study Stack

# SECTION II

## *What Really Works With Instruction*

# 6

# *Culturally Responsive Teaching to Support All Learners*

Jacqueline Rodriguez
*The College of William & Mary*

Stacey E. Hardin
*Illinois State University*

Let's be frank. Mastering culturally responsive teaching (CRT) is as important and as challenging as mastering content area instruction. Educators spend years learning the most effective methods to teach students about content. We should be devoting the same amount of energy during those years to learning how to teach content to diverse exceptional learners in a culturally competent and responsive manner. Hey, aren't we all diverse and exceptional in one way or another? We should be learning how to employ our student's cultural capital to learn content in ways that make sense and engage every learner in the classroom.

# WHAT *IS* CULTURALLY RESPONSIVE TEACHING?

Of the many definitions for CRT, we've been most excited and most invested in Geneva Gay's (2002) working definition, which is defined as "using the cultural characteristics, experiences, and perspectives of ethnically diverse students as conduits for teaching them more effectively" (p. 1). What does that boil down to for us as educators? Our charge is to learn our students to such a degree that we can identify their strengths and leverage those strengths in our teaching. We also recognize that they are culturally rich (Moll, Amanti, Neff, & Gonzalez, 1992), and in turn, we can then teach our students how to capitalize on their experiences, their backgrounds, their cultural knowledge, their will, and their grit to be purposeful in making decisions about their future. Empower them!

Many educators would call this differentiation. What's the difference? CRT certainly includes differentiation for all learners. The added element is that culturally responsive teachers are thinking about and planning around their student's academic and cultural backgrounds when differentiating instruction in order to invest the learner in the lesson, make the lesson more realistic, and apply the lesson to real-world outcomes. When you think of CRT, we want you to consider it as you would the chassis of a car. It is the framework around which everything else is built. In keeping with this analogy, we want you to include differentiation as one highly regarded evidence-based practice that augments your driving experience. Thus, while CRT coordinates the instructional practices in your classroom, differentiation is one method you can use to navigate that instruction.

Why does this matter so much to educators who work with exceptional students? More students with exceptionalities are being included in the general education classroom for standards-based instruction with their peers than ever before in the history of our system of education (Kena et al., 2015). These students are being included in greater volume and with greater percentages of time in the general education classroom. They come to the classroom with individualized education programs (IEPs) that are implemented by general educators often with the support of special educators or English language learner (ELL) coaches, and in many cases through a shared in-class collaboration called co-teaching.

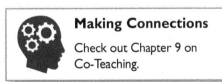

**Making Connections**

Check out Chapter 9 on Co-Teaching.

Now that we've established that more and more students with exceptionalities are receiving their instruction in the least restrictive environment with their IEPs as navigation guides (Kena et al., 2015), we can ask the question again: Why does this matter so much? In the past, special educators provided the majority of instruction to students with exceptionalities, which resulted in them being the only ones with in-depth knowledge of those learners. Now that we've included more special learners in the general education environment, it's imperative that all educators, whether you're in a co-taught classroom or you're the only educator in an inclusive classroom, know and understand how the richness of your students' cultural and linguistic diversity impacts their exceptional needs and access to your instruction. We know you don't have time to learn the specific details of each student's background, especially if you teach secondary and may have 150 students, but read on to learn why you want to engage with each student to get to know him or her beyond the seating arrangement and his or her grades in your class—especially your students who have disabilities *and* come from a diverse background!

## WHAT THE EXPERTS HAVE TO SAY ABOUT CULTURALLY RESPONSIVE TEACHING

When we talk about culture, we are talking about values, traditions, languages, symbols, beliefs, and attitudes, as well as the impact of these concepts on one's life perspective. For example, Gay (2002) identified three areas of culture that influence students' learning: (1) their sense of community, (2) their sense of adult authority toward children, and (3) gender roles in their culture and how those roles generalize to the classrooms. Cultural attitudes toward these concepts constitute a myriad of perspectives that a teacher must spend time uncovering.

**Key Concepts**

Your three heavy hitters in CRT?

- Sense of community
- Sense of adult authority toward children
- Gender roles and how they generalize to the classroom

Ladson-Billings (1995) instructs us to uncover these culturally based perspectives through meaningful interactions with our students' families. Interactions with families can take various forms from in-person dialogue to phone conversations to home visits. Each of these interactions requires preparation. The first rule in family communication has always been to make the initial interaction a positive one where the teacher is introducing himself or herself and providing a complimentary anecdote about the student. The CRT experts challenge you to go the extra mile (Klingner et al., 2005). Get to know your families on a deeper level by asking them to discuss what their hopes, goals, and interests are for their children (Townsend, 2000). No time for 150 phone calls—or even 30? Consider sending home a survey with all students or at least those students you feel you need to know better to help teach them effectively. While it is important to introduce ways in which you will communicate with families, it is equally as important to find out how families would like to communicate with you. Language barriers and cultural attitudes toward communicating with authority figures are just a couple of culturally based nuances you must consider. Home visits have been heralded as a means to become more deeply involved in your students' education. However, we caution you to take the appropriate steps ahead of time before showing up on someone's doorstep. A home is a personal place of security, and different cultures value that space as independent from the school and the system of education. A home visit is by invitation only!

**Making Connections**

Check out Chapter 19 on School-to-Home Collaboration.

Culture, however, is not the only key to being a culturally responsive teacher. As Matias (2013) puts it, CRT "is a process for living racial justice" (p. 78). As educators, we are deeply rooted in the ideologies of social justice, equality in teaching, and access to highly effective teachers for our students. As such, we must also be willing to reflect on our own actions toward our students. Recognizing and accepting our own bias is emotionally taxing and requires a lot of humility, but it is, nevertheless, absolutely required (Domnwachukwu, 2010).

Disproportionality is also a real issue to consider (Losen & Orfield, 2002). Of the innumerable studies conducted over the decades, we know that students from culturally diverse backgrounds continue to be disproportionately represented in special needs education (e.g., Artiles, Harry, Reschly, & Chinn, 2002; Hosp & Reschly, 2004). Whether overrepresented or underrepresented, students with disabilities are often misidentified. When risk ratios indicate that students from a culturally diverse group are 2.5 times more likely to be identified with a severe and profound disability or an emotional disability, there is absolute cause for concern (Kena et al., 2015). These examples are not extreme; they are reality. Experts agree that one factor contributing to over- and underidentification of students from diverse backgrounds into special education is the contrasting cultural backgrounds of the teacher and the cultures represented in their classrooms (Klingner et al., 2005; Losen & Orfield, 2002).

**Making Connections**

Check out Chapter 15 on English Language Learners.

More than 80% of teachers in American public schools are non-Hispanic White, while students from diverse backgrounds account for 46% of our student population (National Center for Education Statistics, 2013). With that said, even teachers of diverse backgrounds are often teaching students from different cultural backgrounds. This incongruent match of diversity in our classrooms often creates a divide between the student, the teacher, and even the student's peers. The divide, however, does not need to be a forgone conclusion in our classrooms. Through authentic discussions, culturally responsive content lessons, activities that include students' backgrounds and interests, and deliberate purposeful classroom management, the differences between the culture of the teacher and the culture of the student can be acknowledged, integrated into the classroom, and even celebrated. It is important to recognize that every person in the classroom brings unique and valuable cultural capital to the table!

We've framed the next section around purposeful teaching. Given the imperative to reflect in order to grow, we'd like you to be considerate of your own culture and your own bias by keeping the following questions in mind as you learn more about purposeful CRT: (a) How can we reach out to students from diverse exceptional backgrounds as members ourselves of other cultures? (b) How can we as educators advocate for students with disabilities when they are in inclusive classrooms with nondisabled peers? And (c) how can we continue to grow in our own teaching as our experiences, positive and negative, shape our perspectives and our priorities?

## Purposeful Teaching

All teachers want to invest learners with truly engaging material. One of the missteps we often have in attempting to craft culturally responsive lessons is in being teacher-centered and not student-centered when it comes to developing engaging material. Instead of asking *how* you can motivate a learner, first ask yourself *what* motivates a learner (Wlodkowski & Ginsberg, 1995). Tie concepts to what students are invested in. The more practical you can make the material, the more you open students up to aligning the lesson to their lives and then believing in the utility of learning (Ladson-Billings, 1995). Practical applications can be demonstrated in crafting real-world products. The CRT approach is a method of bringing forth the silenced voices of our history (Matias, 2013). We do not shield students from the past; rather we discuss the ethnic groups, contextualizing the decisions made, and bring forth multiple perspectives for a comprehensive examination of history (Gay, 2002).

Education is supposed to address students' academic and social-emotional well-being. Once we've determined that the content of our lesson plan is culturally relevant, we want to ensure that students are invested in learning the material in an environment that is conducive to trying and failing and persisting again. We should have high expectations for all our students, including those with identified special needs. For students with exceptionalities of diverse backgrounds, though, we want to stress how important it is to go beyond internally hosting positive dispositions toward your students and encourage you to start externalizing those expectations. We want you to verbally encourage your students by saying things like,

"You are ready for this exam. You've studied the material. You've put forth intense effort. You are prepared." By providing affirmative statements to students about how you, as their teacher, believe in their ability, you can alleviate what studies have been telling us for years in the research: that being solo or one of a few students from diverse backgrounds in class can negatively impact self-efficacy. This, in turn, negatively impacts the performance of students from diverse backgrounds, especially those who are invested in school and want to succeed (Steele, 2010).

Affirming your student's self-worth is no small task. Students who feel respected by their teacher leaders are more likely to accept guidance and mentoring. How can teachers demonstrate and garner respect from their students? First, we encourage you to get to know your students, their cultural backgrounds, and their personal expectations. This is a vital exercise in our classrooms currently, where cultural and linguistic diversity in our student populations is not a trend but a norm in our schools. It is to your advantage to consider where your students are from and examine what cultural norms guide the expectations for students in those locales.

In every culture, creating a welcoming classroom atmosphere grounded in respect begins with the behavior management system. Make sure that rules of the classroom have purpose. What exactly do we mean by *purpose*? The principles behind each rule should be grounded in practical utility intended to support students academically, socially, and in their postsecondary futures. Students need to understand and be able to explain why the rules in the classroom exist, as well as explain how the consequences are aligned with those rules. Equally important is the application of expectations, rules, and consequences. We highly encourage all educators to use

**Making Connections**

Check out Chapter 8 on Positive Behavior Supports.

positive behavioral supports (Sugai et al., 2000), which are research driven and capitalize on strengths. Positive reinforcement of productive academic and social behavior builds a functional classroom filled with engaged, driven students.

Student grouping should be purposeful (Howard, Sugarman, Perdomo, & Adger, 2005). Think through how you want your students to collaborate with their peers during each segment of a lesson. Be discerning when forming student groups. It's simple to count off or to use nominal forms of segregating students into groups. There is a time and place for benign grouping such as alphabetical clusters or by birth month. However, with an increasingly diverse community of learners in our schools, use caution when implementing "traditional grouping" methods like gender or arbitrary high achieving and low achieving student pairs. Peer coaching and feedback is a highly valued method to increase understanding during instruction; be thoughtful in how you create the pairs.

# NOT THERE YET! THE ROAD TO CRT IS CLUTTERED WITH STOP SIGNS

The following are a list of stop signs en route to becoming culturally responsive. As educators, we understand the imperative to be lifelong learners. So, check yourself with the following stop signs, and if you find yourself breezing by one, pause and take note. We can all be more responsive to our students!

**Teachers, STOP doing this:**

✗ **STOP assuming you are the expert.** Yes, we know you are the expert in your content area or in teaching, but when we consider our students, *don't* ever assume you are the expert on their cultural backgrounds. You are learning your students, and there is something new to learn every day. Parents and guardians are great resources to learn more about their children, treat them as such! Keep parents and guardians involved, as well as previous teachers and related service providers, to learn more about your students. At the end of the day, as teachers, our job is to ensure our students get exactly what they need.

✗ **STOP assuming you have nothing left to learn or unpack.** Our experiences shape us. Each new experience frames our perspective and influences our priorities. When we learn more about our students, we are better teachers. When we disregard what we learn, we are not. So continuously reflecting on each experience with a student and a family is an imperative.

✗ **STOP disconnecting yourself from teaching the whole child.** As students progress through K–12 education, teachers begin to make the content the center of instruction instead of keeping the student at the center of instruction. Once teachers make this transition, they have disconnected themselves from teaching the whole child and have focused only on the content. This is not CRT! We must continue to keep our students at the center of instruction to ensure they have the best possible opportunities to learn and grasp the concepts we are teaching.

✗ **STOP assuming that everyone has common knowledge of a subject matter topic.** Exposure to different concepts is often based on a family's cultural background. These differences impact all students but can be particularly salient to students who have immigrated to the United States and students who have moved to new locations within the United States. For example, some students will have experienced a hurricane and others an earthquake. Similarly, some students may have moved from a region where they experienced four seasons and others may have only experienced two. Just because your students are now in a U.S. classroom does not ensure their understanding of a democratic government or concepts germane to the community in which you are teaching. Inversely, some students will understand the concept of a totalitarian regime having had a lived experience, while others will need to be taught the concept entirely. Be cautious to survey your class before beginning instruction to include enough pre-teaching of concepts that are not universally understood.

✗ **STOP using deficit based thinking.** Creating low expectations for students because you are empathizing with their lower socioeconomic background, difficult childhood, lack of parental involvement, or other ancillary challenges they bring with them from home perpetuates those challenges in the classroom. Instead, recognize that challenges exist and troubleshoot those challenges to ensure students have access to the curriculum. Keep your expectations for all learners, even your diverse learners with exceptionalities, high!

✗ **STOP feeling like you are in this alone!** Your colleagues and peers within your school and at other schools are a community to tap into. Veteran teachers in your school will potentially know the families of the students in your classroom. Administrators will have experience in working collaboratively with students of similar backgrounds and families in your community. Often, the families of your students are not only willing but are also motivated to share what has worked in the past with their children and goals they have for them in the future.

✗ **STOP being myopic, and start gathering data from various sources.** Let's breakdown our interpretation of what it means when you hear the concept *teach to the whole child*. Teach to the whole child requires learning the whole child. Students are people with multifaceted personalities, a combination of their life experiences, their learned behaviors, their intrinsic and extrinsic motivations, their interests, their strengths and areas of challenge, their hopes, fears, and goals. We may have 30 students or 150 students; so how can we see all our students for who they are, what they bring to the table, and what experiences have influenced them? Examine other sources of information such as previous teachers, personal records, patterns in their behavior, and so on. Spend time during lunch, recess, appropriate transitions, before school, or after school with your students. We must recognize the details in their attitudes, their scholarly contributions, and their academic struggles.

✗ **STOP excluding important personnel from major decisions.** Of course there are key personnel who are required to be at the table when making decisions about your student's well-being, but don't leave out the mentor, leader, or collaborator in the student's life. For example, when your student goes to see a coach for mentorship because he or she feels aligned to the coach, that coach should be a part of the multidisciplinary team of stakeholders that collaborates on the student's IEP, as well as other school-related decision making. Invite everyone who knows the student to collaborate! Stakeholders are people meant to advocate and collaborate for the student's well-being. Don't be afraid to have them at the table alongside you.

✗ **STOP teaching superficially.** This is a multifaceted problem in our schools. Often our instruction includes the teaching of history, the realities of revolution, war, enslavement, epidemics, and a plethora of topics that can be polarizing. To curb any sense of disenfranchisement by our students, it is our responsibility to deliver the factual, authentic history of our society, their society. How can you deliver such content in an authentic manner and not come off as superficial? BE PREPARED. Don't assume you know the background from a cursory search online or a review of the textbook. This is where your students play a large role in your delivery of authentic content. When you are introducing a subject, do so at least a week or more in advance. Task your students with doing the preliminary research on the subject matter, each student taking a different lens and providing their information to the class in the form of on op-ed or news talking points. Your students' practical engagement in the topic will also translate into more time saved for you to teach the skills and concepts required in your standards.

✗ **STOP griping about your students with other adults.** You're frustrated, and you see a friend and colleague in the teacher's lounge. It's natural to want to vent. However, we have to be careful about that. We know words have meaning, but we sometimes forget that they have power. Remember that students are people who are equally as impacted by interpersonal interactions as you are throughout the day. Treat them as you would like a colleague to treat you—with respect, humility, and generosity.

✗ **STOP holding grudges.** We all have moments when a student's behavior impacts us negatively. If you only think about that negative interaction with your student, you will inevitably hold a grudge that moves beyond the professional and moves into the personal. When that happens, that student's education is impacted by your bias. Be cautious when responding to students with whom you've had less than positive previous experiences and remember that everyone deserves second chances. Um . . . and sometimes fifth and 20th chances!

✗ **STOP testing out new concepts without first vetting them with your colleagues.** This applies to us all, but be especially careful when you are a new teacher and when you are a teacher new to urban schools with a high density of culturally diverse students. The best strategies to support students from culturally and linguistically diverse backgrounds are the ones supported by research and experience.

✗ **STOP making assumptions about families' participation before you have met, interacted, and supported their dynamic engagement in the classroom.** This includes assuming that your families are too busy working hard for their children to be participatory in school. Yes, your student's families may very well be working and unable to participate in traditional activities in your classroom, but why not provide them with untraditional opportunities to participate? Donating items to the classroom (maybe even from their jobs), hosting synchronous interview sessions with families who are unable to come to school, creating a private YouTube channel to host informational videos about what parents, guardians, siblings, and extended family members do in the workplace. These are just a few out of the ordinary options you can recommend to families, but they only scratch the surface! Volunteering time is wonderful, but for parents who do not have the time to volunteer, allow them to volunteer their ideas, their cultural capital, and even material resources, and acknowledge those donations each and every time to the entire class.

## GO  READY, SET, GO!

The following list of bullet points are your green lights. Start implementing these suggestions in your classrooms and you'll be modeling CRT for your colleagues. Always remember: You are your students' best and most effective advocate!

**Teachers, DO this:**

✔ **LEARN about your students.** Your students will present an array of diverse backgrounds. Their backgrounds can be used to enhance student learning. You could have a 30 second "Share-Out" every day from a different student in which he or she tells the class something about his or her culture. Find a way to learn more about the diverse faces present in your classroom.

✔ **KNOW who *you* are.** Understand your own culture. Often, we enter the classroom not realizing that each and every one of us is multicultural! Culture embodies race, gender, religion, sexual orientation, and so much more. Take a step back to recognize what your culture is so that you are more sensitive to multiculturalism in the classroom.

✔ **CREATE a warm and inviting atmosphere.** Students love a classroom where they see people on the walls who resemble what they see in the mirror. But let's not stop there! We must relate and connect role models to the subject matter being taught to help students understand the importance and relevance of the content. A warm and inviting atmosphere also encompasses the tone of the classroom. Make your students feel comfortable with asking questions, answering questions, and participating in discussions.

✔ **FIND out more about your students.** In the beginning of the school year, take every opportunity to have formal and informal conversations with your students. This will create a community grounded in effective communication and respect among students. Have short surveys, ask a new, specific question to the whole class daily, or have students engage in a universally designed project that focuses on a topic or hobby they are interested in outside of school. By knowing their interests you will be able to build your lesson plans around what is important to them! When you get the rare chance to have those personal discussions, before school, during transition time, or after school, take full advantage. You will learn so much about your students, and they will view you as a stakeholder in their life.

 **Plugged In**

Want to find helpful surveys?

- www.teacherspayteachers.com
- www.educatorstechnology.com
- http://www.livebinders.com

✔ **MAKE initial family contact as soon as the school year begins or as soon as a new student enters your classroom.** Students are mostly influenced by their parents or guardians. Parents and guardians should also be viewed as the experts of their children. As teachers, we want to use this expertise to enhance instruction as well as begin to build rapport with family members to keep them involved in their child's education. Initial contact is key to starting a positive relationship between school and home.

✔ **ATTEND events your students are involved in outside the school environment.** When your students invite you to attend their activities or community events, it's an opportunity to see and learn more about their world. This may be for a bar/bat mitzvah, quinceañera, basketball game, or dinosaur presentation. Treat the invitation with the respect it absolutely deserves. Be on time. Be attentive. Say hello and introduce yourself to your student's family. Sure, you're making a connection with your student, but more importantly, you are demonstrating your interest in his or her long-term well-being.

✔ **ADDRESS misconceptions and stereotypes among students in the classroom.** Many misconceptions and stereotypes have negative connotations associated with them that do not make our students feel welcomed or safe. We can always turn these moments into teaching and learning moments to unpack and combat stereotypes and misconceptions. We promise, this will definitely enhance your instruction, and students will learn so much from these teaching and learning moments.

✔ **TIE the concepts you teach to real life *and* to the students in your classroom.** In the 21st century classroom, we hear the advice "connect your concepts to real life" so often. But let's not forget to relate the concepts to the interests of students in your classroom. Yes, this means your lesson plans will have to change each year depending on the students you have in your classroom. You will be presented with different students and cultures every year and the interests of each child will not be the same. The examples you use and the way you keep students engaged will have to change to fit the students you currently teach, but they will also constantly add to your teaching toolbox. The next time you have a student who is Cambodian, you may already know elements of his culture to help welcome him!

✔ **LEAD with generosity of spirit.** We want you to always think positively first. Assume the best of intentions. Not all expectations are universally understood, so when things go awry, engage by listening, thereby opening the door for students and families to teach you about their understanding of the situation.

✔ **START thinking of your students from a strengths-based approach.** Everyone has strengths (yes, even that student who drives you insane). When we consider the ways in which we are meant to support students, it is easy to immediately take note of their weaknesses. Deficit thinking, though, has been proven to perpetuate stereotypes and causes students to question their place in school, which in turn is demoralizing and lowers self-efficacy. Framing the unique cultural and linguistic backgrounds that students bring with them as strengths allows you as their teacher to incorporate those strengths in your teaching. This demonstrates to students their value in the classroom. For example, a student who is responsible for younger siblings has a high degree of leadership, strategic thinking, and problem-solving skills. We often see teachers lower their expectations for these students because they appear tired in class or are nonparticipatory. Instead of assuming these students can't keep up because of their home life, recognize the strengths they have cultivated and employ those strengths when asking for students to lead group discussions or class debates.

✔ **GATHER helpful information diplomatically.** We often provide surveys to our students and their families at the beginning of the school year to learn about who our students are and what they find important; however, make sure your informational sheets are culturally responsive. Whenever possible, deliver the surveys in the person's primary language. (We know that's not always possible, but check around to see if there is a faculty or staff member who might help you out with this.) Also, be cognizant that some information will not be divulged on paper and will require more consistent interactions with the student and their families to build trust and mutual rapport.

✔ **BELIEVE in high expectations for everyone.** To do this, you must first believe that your students deserve a high quality education, even when they are pushing your behavior management system to the very last rung on the ladder. Don't let difficult behavior make you stop believing they are deserving. Think about it. If you were in a foreign country and constantly given material you didn't understand, would you smile sweetly all the time? Or might you give up—or act out—or try to hide? Find a way to connect on their level. Figure out what they are good at, what they love, and where their skills are just being masked by cultural differences or a disability—and then leverage the heck out of those things!

## INTEREST INVENTORY

Name: _____ Name you prefer: _____

Language(s) spoken at home: _____

Who do you live with? _____

_____

Have you ever lived somewhere else or traveled to another country? Where?

_____

_____

Favorites . . .

Book: _____ Movie: _____

School Subject: _____ Food: _____

Musical Artist: _____ TV Show: _____

What organizations, teams, or clubs are you a part of? _____

_____

Who do you admire and why? _____

_____

What are you an expert on? _____

What do you wish you knew more about? _____

_____

What are your goals after high school? _____

_____

What would be the title of a movie about your life? _____

If you had $10, what would you do with it? _____

What else do you think I should know about you? _____

_____

_____

## RESILIENCY CHART

Your name: _____

| List a major life challenge/adversity you have gone through. | List all your personal qualities (internal characteristics) that helped you make it through the adversity—rack your brain, ask people who know you well, list as many as you can. (Be as specific as possible.): |
| --- | --- |
| | List the environmental supports that helped you as well: Any person, organization, place, activity, and so on that assisted you. |

1. When people bounce back from adversity, one main reason is that the strengths (protective factors) on the right-hand side of this chart pull them to a resilient outcome.
   - How did your protective factors (written above on the right-hand side of your resiliency chart) help propel you through your adversity?
   - How did going through this adversity foster (or force) your positive growth (i.e., ways you became a better, stronger, or wiser person)?
   - Write down the individual protective factors listed in the chart that are most natural for you (i.e., which ones do you use most frequently)?
   - Identify a personal problem or challenge you are facing. How can you use your individual protective factors shown in the chart above to help you overcome, learn, and grow from this situation?

2. Recall the earliest time in your life you can remember using one or more of your protective factors. What are some early protective factors you can remember using?
   - How old were you at the time, and what was the situation?
   - How does this memory give you clues to your resilient core?

3. Adding to your individual factors: Resiliency research is in its infancy, only a few decades old. Researchers are continuing to explore other personal characteristics that facilitate resiliency.
   - What other personal characteristics within yourself or others can you add to the boxed list of individual protective factors?
   - How do you think these characteristics increase resiliency (i.e., what is your rationale for adding them to the list)?

4. Select one personal protective factor from the boxed list (or from additional factors you have listed) to strengthen.
   - Which one have you chosen?
   - How can you strengthen it? (Use your best ideas, or research how to develop this characteristic, and/or ask others you respect for their ideas.)

*Source:* Adapted from Henderson, N., & Milstein, M. (2003). *Resiliency in schools: Making it happen for students and educators.* Thousand Oaks, CA: Corwin.

# REFERENCES

Artiles, A. J., Harry, B., Reschly, D. J., & Chinn, P. C. (2002). Over-identification of students of color in special education: A critical overview. *Multicultural Perspectives, 4*(1), 3–10.

Domnwachukwu, C. S. (2010). *An introduction to multicultural education from theory to practice.* Lanham, MD: Rowman & Littlefield.

Gay, G. (2002). Preparing for culturally responsive teaching. *Journal of Teacher Education, 53*(2), 106–116.

Henderson, N., & Milstein, M. (2003). *Resiliency in schools: Making it happen for students and educators.* Thousand Oaks, CA: Corwin.

Hosp, J. L., & Reschly, D. J. (2004). Disproportionate representation of minority students in special education: Academic, demographic, and economic predictors. *Exceptional Children, 70*(2), 185–199.

Howard, E., Sugarman, J., Perdomo, M., & Adger, C. T. (2005). *The two way immersion toolkit.* Providence, RI: Education Alliance at Brown University.

Kena, G., Musu-Gillette, L., Robinson, J., Wang, X., Rathbun, A., Zhang, J., . . . Dunlop Velez, E. (2015). *The condition of education 2015* (NCES 2015–144). Washington, DC: U.S. Department of Education, National Center for Education Statistics.

Klingner, J. K., Artiles, A. J., Kozleski, E., Harry, B., Zion, S., Tate, W., . . . Riley, D. (2005). Addressing the disproportionate representation of culturally and linguistically diverse students in special education through culturally responsive educational systems. *Education Policy Analysis Archives, 13*(38), 1–43.

Ladson-Billings, G. (1995). But that's just good teaching! The case for culturally relevant pedagogy. *Theory into Practice, 34*(3), 159–165.

Losen, D. J., & Orfield, G. (Eds.). (2002). *Racial inequity in special education.* Cambridge, MA: Harvard Education Press.

Matias, C. (2013). Check yo'self before you wreck yo'self and our kids: Counterstories from culturally responsive white teachers. *Interdisciplinary Journal of Teaching and Learning, 3*(2), 68–82.

Moll, L. C., Amanti, C., Neff, D., & Gonzalez, N. (1992). Funds of knowledge for teaching: Using a qualitative approach to connect homes and classrooms. *Theory into Practice, 31*(2), 132–141.

National Center for Education Statistics. (2013). Characteristics of public and private elementary and secondary school teachers in the United States: Results from the 2011–12 schools and staffing survey (NCES 2013–314). Washington, DC: Author.

Steele, C. (2010). *Whistling Vivaldi: How stereotypes affect us and what we can do.* New York, NY: W.W. Norton.

Sugai, G., Horner, R. H., Dunlap, G., Hieneman, M., Lewis, T., Nelson, C. M., . . . Ruef, M. (2000). Applying positive behavior support and functional behavioral assessment in schools. *Journal of Positive Behavior Interventions, 2*(3), 131–143.

Townsend, B. L. (2000). The disproportionate discipline of African American learners: Reducing school suspensions, and expulsions. *Exceptional Children, 66*(3), 381–391.

Wlodkowski, R. J., & Ginsberg, M. B. (1995). A framework for culturally responsive teaching. *Educational Leadership, 53*(1), 17–21.

# ADDITIONAL RECOMMENDED READING ON CULTURALLY RESPONSIVE TEACHING

Brown-Jeffy, S., & Cooper, J. E. (2012). Toward a conceptual framework of culturally relevant pedagogy: An overview of the conceptual and theoretical literature. *Teacher Education Quarterly, 38*(1), 65–84.

Gay, G. (2010). *Culturally responsive teaching: Theory, research, and practice.* New York, NY: Teachers College Press.

Hudley, A. C., & Mallinson, C. (2010). *Understanding English language variation in U.S. schools.* New York, NY: Teachers College Press.

Ladson-Billings, G. (1995). Toward a theory of culturally relevant pedagogy. *American Educational Research Journal, 32*(3), 465–491.

Ladson-Billings, G. (2001). *Crossing over to Canaan: The journey of new teachers in diverse classrooms.* San Francisco, CA: Jossey-Bass.

# TOP FIVE WEBSITES TO SUPPORT CULTURALLY RESPONSIVE TEACHING

➡ http://www.tolerance.org/supplement/being-culturally-responsive

➡ http://www.nea.org/home/16723.htm

➡ http://www.brown.edu/academics/education-alliance/teaching-diverse-learners/strategies-0/culturally-responsive-teaching-0

➡ http://iris.peabody.vanderbilt.edu/module/clde/

➡ http://steinhardt.nyu.edu/metrocenter/center/technical_assistance/program/disproportionality

# APPS WE LOVE

➡ One Globe Kids

➡ Remind: Keep in Touch with Parents

➡ Touchable Earth

➡ Educreation

➡ Kids Planet Discovery

➡ Culture Compass

# 7

---

# *Thanks for the Memories*

## *Brain–Based Learning at Its Best*

### Horacio Sanchez
*President / CEO, Resiliency Inc.*

## INCREASE MEMORY, INCREASE SUCCESS

What if I told you that you could significantly improve the life success of any exceptional learner by simply improving your expertise in one area? Would you? Well . . . you can! The area in which you need to increase your expertise is *memory*. The ability to help students create new memories is not only important to academic success but also to life success. There are three compelling reasons why every educator should become versed in how the brain develops memories. First, knowing how to provide memorable instruction will improve the academic performance of all students—our students with disabilities, those who are English language learners (ELLs) or gifted, our twice-exceptional learners, and even typically developing students. Second, teaching students strategies for improving their own memory will increase their ability to make better life choices. Third, students' ability to retain information is an issue across a wide range of special needs; enhancing retention will assist in multiple areas of the student's life. Knowing more about brain-based learning, and specifically how it improves memory, will help you as an educator do a better job with all your students.

## HOW TO MAKE A SHORT-TERM MEMORY

A basic premise of learning is that memories must be created. If you are unable to remember what you have learned, how can that information be validated or applied? To know more, we need to look to the brain. Learning begins in the hippocampus, where short-term memories are created. Although every teacher wants to get key information into their students' short-term memory, they are often unaware of how the hippocampus selects the limited information that enters short-term memory. If the information does not enter short-term memory, it has no opportunity to become a long-term memory. So let's do a mini-lesson on memory and the brain: Welcome to "Short-Term Memory 101."

Nothing enters short-term memory unless it is focused on. Therefore, teachers who are adept at getting students' attention stand a better chance of helping them create a short-term memory. The hippocampus is a novelty seeker. Information, experiences, actions, or items that are exciting and new usually draw the attention of the hippocampus. However, once you get its attention, you have to know how to keep it. So how do you do this? Well, it's helpful to know that the hippocampus does not like language. Think about that! Humans were on the face of the earth thousands, if not millions, of years prior to the inception of language (Johanson & Edgar, 1996). One of the primary roles of the hippocampus then and now is to process senses. All senses are processed by the hippocampus through slightly different pathways in the brain, and different processes mean different routes of recall. A short-term memory is more likely to be remembered if it has stimulated more than one sense simultaneously. For example, your husband proposed to you at your favorite restaurant shortly after the meal arrived at the table, while a local cover band was performing Elton John's, "Your Song." It is 20 years later, and you can still trigger that specific memory whenever you smell the same dish you ate that evening, hear the song that was playing, or even see him in that silly sports coat he was wearing that is now a little too snug.

Therefore, when teaching new information, adding a visual cue, physical movement, touch, smell, or even a rhythmic pattern can increase the probability that the hippocampus can bring back the associated information because it can be recalled in more than one way. Too many teachers add in cutesy items because they think they are addressing different learning styles; in fact, there is absolutely no empirical data to support learning styles—but there is plenty to support

**Plugged In**

Want to learn more about memory? Check out these great videos!

- Eleanor Maguire: The Neuroscience of Memory: https://youtu.be/gdzm NwTLakg
- Peter Doolittle: How your "working memory" makes sense of the world: https:// youtu.be/UWKvpFZJwcE

brain-based learning (Herrmann, Raybeck, & Gutman, 1992; Siegel & Bryson, 2011).

Stimulating the senses helps the hippocampus, but the fact remains that it still does not like processing language. Reducing language into manageable chunks helps. Many students are taught that Christopher Columbus made four trips across the Atlantic Ocean from Spain: in 1492, 1493, 1498, and 1502. A strategy that can help students access the detailed information on this topic is to identify a key fact (chunk) that they can easily recall. The recalling of the key fact enables the brain to begin to open related memory files. Therefore, it is always a good idea to have a chunk of information that can be easily remembered related to a new section of learning. For me it was, "Columbus sailed the ocean blue in 1492." Although this is only one fact, it accomplished two goals: (a) it helped me remember an important date, as well as (b) provided me with a small chunk of information that helped me access the other detailed information. Once one memory file was opened, it enabled the other information I retained on Christopher Columbus to be accessed that I could not recall as easily.

**Making Connections**

Check out Chapter 4 on Instructional Strategies and Universal Design for Learning.

However, one of the most important methods for creating a short-term memory is repetition. The problem is that pacing guides allow little time for repetition and too many students do not engage in enough homework to produce automation (effortless recall). In addition, more advanced concepts cannot be grasped until the related foundational information is automated. For example, the brains of many students struggling with advanced concepts are working too hard to recall basic related information. Those students who are special learners may not only be grappling with the advanced content; they also may be trying to understand the language, the context, and the assignment requirements. The hippocampus prioritizes information that is heard repeatedly, even if it is not interested in the data. Many individuals turn on the television as a backdrop of white noise while they engage in other activities. However, most people can recite the commercials they have heard repeatedly. Commercials do a better job of appealing to the hippocampus than most classroom teachers today, because they have the opportunity for frequent repetition. There are other aspects of commercials that teachers can learn from in an effort to appeal to the hippocampus. Consider these elements: Many commercials play music that sparks the attention of the hippocampus and influences heartrate by the beats per measure. If the product wants you excited, it speeds up beats per measure; if it wants you calmer, it slows it down. What can you do? Create a soundtrack to your lessons. Commercials employ visuals to aid and increase the speed of learning about the merchandise, and most products utilize a logo representing the brand. What can you do? Include visuals and even logos to help trigger the recall of key information. The commercial communicates a lot of information in a short period of time, but to make sure you can retrieve the information, it reduces the message to a catch phrase. Then the commercials play repeatedly to gain subconscious importance in the hippocampus. Once a commercial has aired a sufficient amount of times, commercials edit out large sections of content because they are confident you will remember most of the associated information. You may not have the luxury of constantly repeating yourself, but you can identify catch phrases to repeat and review; you can also help students boil down a lot of content to the most salient parts to retain. Ultimately, teachers can learn a lot from those marketing gurus. In fact, when it comes to brain-based instruction, commercials know how to "just do it" and are confident that their advertising strategy will succeed because they are "the ultimate driving machine."

Okay, so let's move into long-term memory. How do we get students to retain information for longer than just the next day or the most recent test? The process of the brain utilized to convert a short-term memory to long-term memory is the repetition that occurs while we sleep. You're probably starting to notice that repetition is really key to memory. The hippocampus repeats information through a process called *synaptic consolidation*, a rapid procedure occurring within minutes to hours. Once synaptic consolidation is complete, then the long-term consolidation process begins, which can take several weeks. During this time, the memory becomes independent of the hippocampus by transferring to the cerebral cortex. Luckily for us, there is a technique that educators can use to help students make a long-term memory faster. Connect to what they know! Have students associate the new information into an existing framework of knowledge. The assimilation of the new information into a well-established framework of knowledge expedites permanence. For example, every adult who has developed a certain level of expertise in any area has noticed that so many things they encounter in life relate to their area of expertise. That happens because the more you know about a topic, the more connections you observe. Thus, if new information can be connected to information that the student is already knowledgeable about, it is easier for the brain to maintain a new memory. A great strategy is to poll students at the beginning of the year to discover the activities they spend the most time doing. When students spend a lot of time on particular activities, they have already created rich networks in their brains related to those activities to which can easily be connected. Once you synthesize students' responses, you will usually find a few activities that most students have in common, including your students with exceptionalities. When introducing new challenging information, attempt to connect the lesson to those activities students know the most about. This is especially critical for special learners who may not be as adept at making the connections automatically as their typically developing peers may be.

# MEMORY IS NOT ABOUT THE PAST BUT ABOUT THE FUTURE

During every significant decision we face, our brains consciously and subconsciously bring back relevant past information to help us make better decisions in the present. Students who struggle with emotional regulation utilize a larger number of brain regions when performing memory tasks, which makes recall more taxing (Mensebach et al., 2009). Inefficient recall has both behavioral and academic implications. Students whose brains do not efficiently bring back pertinent information are prone to making the same mistakes. Haven't we all had students to whom we have repeatedly given the same instruction, advice, or warnings? As frustration builds, we find ourselves talking to them faster and louder (as if that is going to help). Knowing more about how the brain works can help put all this in perspective. One concrete strategy you can employ is to improve students' memory. When relevant data is not recalled quickly enough, emotions elevate and the risk for impulsive behaviors increase. In addition, these same students are more likely to act out to avoid learning, because from a young age, the act of learning and remembering has been frustrating. When the brain works harder performing a simple task, then more challenging tasks produce anxiety and irritation. Success is reinforced in the brain by a chemical called dopamine. Every time we get something right, dopamine is triggered, motivating us to repeat the action. On the other hand, failure secretes hormones associated with a lack of motivation. Think of it this way, would you be motivated to engage in an activity if you were certain you will fail? Students won't either. It is not surprising then that a pattern of avoidance and inappropriate behavior often accompanies many emotional and learning disorders.

**Making Connections**

Check out Chapter 12 on Emotional and Behavioral Disorders.

This brings us back to why brain-based learning is so important. The more we know about how the brain works, the more we can target our strategies to our exceptional learners. The great news is that every strategy that helps the special learner also improves the performance of all students. For example, all teachers should teach specific strategies for improving recall. It is important not only to introduce these strategies, but to also provide ample opportunities for students to practice them until they become more proficient. It is helpful to let students know that initially the strategies might be a little frustrating, but in time, they will be easier and make them more productive students. If we do this from elementary through secondary, students will become better at recall over time and identify strategies that help them learn best. At the end of this chapter are just a few example strategies to improve memory. With exposure and practice, you can help students identify which memory strategies work best for them. The key is *practice*!

# IMPROVE MEMORY—IMPROVE LIFE SUCCESS

The greatest predictor of not only academic success, but also of life success, is self-regulation (Blair, 2002). Blair has long advocated that schools should emphasize the teaching of self-control and self-regulation, because it has been found to be the greatest predictor of academic success. Yes, even more than reading, writing, and math! Clearly then, we teachers need to know how the brain develops self-regulation skills. The ability to exercise self-regulation is dependent on the development of the prefrontal cortex to the point that it can exert control over the limbic system (primitive brain) (Munakata et al., 2011). The prefrontal cortex can be developed by enhanced focus and improved memory. Helping students develop self-control during the primary grades changes the trajectory of their entire academic experience. How do we help students develop self-regulation skills? To do this, we need to provide students with three things: predictable environments, positive social interactions, and learning (which begins with focus and memory). That's doable, right? Definitely. In fact, you can read Chapter 6 on Culturally Responsive Teaching and Chapter 8 on Positive Behavior Supports for strategies on the first two. This chapter continues to provide information on enhancing focus and memory through brain-based learning.

**Key Concepts**

Want to develop self-regulation skills in your students? Be sure to provide:

- A predictable environment
- Positive social interactions
- Learning that emphasizes focus and memory strategies

There might be no better example of how improving memory increases life success than the research conducted by Ullman and Pullman (2015). They determined that by simply improving declarative memory (i.e., memory of facts or events), the brain is better able to compensate for a wide range of social, behavioral, and cognitive deficits associated with multiple neurodevelopmental disorders. These researchers studied students with diverse impairments in five common conditions: autism spectrum disorder, obsessive-compulsive disorder (OCD), Tourette's syndrome, dyslexia, and developmental language disorder (Ullman & Pullman, 2015). In spite of the disorders being so diverse, they found that improving declarative memory also promoted healthier brain functions in areas not associated with memory. If improving memory increases the opportunities for life success in students with a range of disabilities, it can certainly be an effective strategy in every classroom regardless of student profiles.

**Making Connections**

Check out Chapter 11 on Learning Disabilities and Chapter 13 on Autism Spectrum Disorder.

## APPLYING BRAIN-BASED LEARNING TO THE CLASSROOM

For you to become proficient in providing instruction, you need to become versed in how the brain learns. It's as simple as that. The ability to provide instruction that is more likely to be remembered significantly improves the future success of any student, those with and without special needs. The days of separating behavior and learning should come to an end. Teachers need to know more about how the act of learning transforms the brain and how it strengthens the prefrontal cortex to exercise control over the limbic system (self-regulation). But we also need to remember that learning begins with small steps, getting information into short-term memory to achieve long-term memory. It also requires the identification of foundational information that will enable abstract thinking and higher-level goals to be achieved. I know there are days we'd all like to jump right into the advanced, interesting stuff in our subject, but there is a real brain-based purpose for scaffolding, repetition, and connecting new content with previously learned material.

Another wonderful fact concerning the human brain is that learning is its own reward. That's not just a nice platitude; it's true! Once students experience success in learning, dopamine (a chemical that plays a huge role in reward-motivated behavior) secretes in the nucleus accumbens (a part of the brain that plays a significant role in the cognitive processing of motivation, pleasure, and reward, among other things). It is dopamine that creates habits. This increase in dopamine motivates students to want to learn more. You've seen that, haven't you? The student who was loath to engage in your class has a moment of success and that leads to him or her trying a bit more? We know it can work the other way as well, unfortunately. Just as success builds success, so too can failure lead to students who stop trying. That's why it is so important that we create lessons that are designed to help students succeed. Lessons learned and remembered help actually transform the brain. This transformation helps students increase and improve self-control and discipline; in turn, this improvement of self-regulation offers increased success both in school and life. Wow. All that just by knowing how the brain works and creating lessons geared to help students better retain information!

## BAD CHOICES RELATED TO MEMORY, LEARNING, AND THE BRAIN

Teachers:

&#10007; **STOP thinking that everything in a curriculum is of equal value.** Some information is foundational and should be reviewed frequently. We just learned that we cannot get everything into short-term memory, so choose wisely how to spend your instructional time.

✗ **STOP placing emphasis on higher-level thinking objectives without having a system of review in place for related foundational learning.** When the brain struggles with foundational information, advanced concepts will be difficult to obtain. For example, a student may struggle to understand a number line because his or her brain is working too hard to remember number values. If the information is something that the student will have to consistently utilize, then you need to put strategies in place for that student to engage in brief reviews of the foundational elements. When automation of those core elements occurs in the brain, many of the advanced related concepts that the student has been exposed to will click.

✗ **STOP lecturing without stimulating any of the other senses.** The initial function of the hippocampus was to process senses and not language. The hippocampus struggles with language retention. Think about your lesson. Do you have visuals? Will students be moving or touching or smelling anything? Is there a video or soundtrack you can incorporate to enhance the lesson?

✗ **AVOID transitioning into the lesson too quickly after students return to the classroom.** Often, students who lack self-regulation also struggle with making transitions. To better adjust to change, the brain prefers something that is familiar, like a ritual. Transition rituals should either reinforce a positive message, help students get ready to learn, or build a bridge to the lesson. Avoid rituals that are boring; a worksheet does not a good ritual make. Warm-ups, bell-ringers, homework reviews, and short discussions all serve to bring a student's attention to the class without starting immediately with new content.

✗ **STOP talking in the same tone of voice throughout the lesson.** Every brain has preferred tonalities that need to be stimulated every 10 minutes (Wilkins, Hodges, Laurienti, Steen, & Burdette, 2014). Also, no one wants to hear a monotone or even the same voice for an hour on end. Let students talk to one another, even teach the class at times, or interject a new voice periodically by the use of videos or music. Co-teaching can also serve to provide a different voice or frame of reference.

**Making Connections**

Check out Chapter 9 on Co-Teaching.

✗ **STOP having students learn everything in the same position and location in the classroom.** The brain registers the location and the position at the time something is learned. Having students always seated and in the same location for everything learned does not help the brain distinguish one lesson from another. This is a wonderful opportunity to condition yourself to consistently incorporate movement into the lesson. Another added benefit is that the part of the brain that engages in problem solving also is enhanced by movement (Thomas & Lleras, 2009).

Administrators:

✗ **STOP perceiving that those classrooms in which students are standing, moving, or singing are not engaged in learning.** These activities help the brain remember and comprehend as long as there is still structure and order to the activities. In fact, many struggling learners actually require movement to keep attention and focus on the lesson at hand. So if a room looks chaotic, take a few minutes to see if perhaps it is indeed an "organized chaos" designed to engage and improve instruction.

✗ **STOP thinking that maintaining a certain pace in the curriculum is equivalent to meeting state standards and better test performance.** Too often, teachers try to zip through their curriculum to "cover it all." In curriculum that builds off of the prior lesson, moving too quickly can compromise future learning. The best teachers are the ones who use regular progress monitoring and are constantly checking that their students are comprehending before moving on to the next level of understanding and complexity.

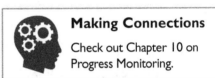

**Making Connections**

Check out Chapter 10 on Progress Monitoring.

✗ **STOP allowing too many distractions during instructional time.** Students who struggle to focus have a difficult time filtering out distractions. Remember, the hippocampus has to be able to engage and focus for information to make it into short-term memory. Therefore, every announcement, bell, guest, phone call, and hallway transition reduces learning. As the administrator, you have the power to change the culture of your school to limit these annoyances.

✗ **STOP believing a conversation is an effective intervention.** The brain learns better by seeing and practicing, so encourage your teachers to show students what they want and then have the students demonstrate the skills back to them. Work to students' strengths.

✗ **STOP using loud bells to trigger transitions.** Loud bells trigger the startle response in the amygdala (the part of the brain that controls emotions), which slows activity in the cortex and hampers the learning process. Yes, it gets everyone's attention, but do you really think they aren't already aware that it is almost time to go to lunch? Instead, use a quieter or less startling way to announce transition times.

✗ **STOP perceiving school climate as separate from academic achievement.** For all students, a positive school climate promotes homeostasis. Homeostasis is when the brain is in a state of chemical balance. When homeostasis is achieved, a student can maximize their cognitive and emotional capacity. Thus, a positive school climate actually allows students' brains to maximize behavior and academic performance. Who knew?

## STRATEGIES FOR MAXIMIZING MEMORY, LEARNING, AND BRAIN PERFORMANCE

Teachers, DO this:

✔ **EMPHASIZE self-regulation.** Remember the three things the brain requires to promote self-regulation: predictable environments, positive social interactions, and learning. These three things calm the amygdala. Do a check: Are you certain each of your students would say they have all three? Why don't you ask them?

✔ **INCORPORATE the body when teaching abstract concepts.** Doing so is the premise for *embodied cognition*. Embodied cognition is defined as the body subconsciously aiding us to comprehend a new abstract concept. For example, people all over the world lean two millimeters back when they think about the past and two millimeters forward when they think about the future (Miles, Karpinska, Lumsden, & Macrae, 2010). This helps explain how researchers were able to improve math comprehension of students by incorporating gestures when introducing new math strategies (Skipper, Goldin-Meadow, Nusbaum, & Small, 2009). So find ways to involve the body in learning and you'll be creating embodied cognition!

✔ **INCREASE the speed of the review session.** . . . But only once students begin to demonstrate better recall of key information. Increasing speed promotes myelination, which helps memories to be recalled more efficiently. Myelination is the process by which a layer of myelin forms around the axons, allowing nerve cells to transmit information faster and to perform more complex brain functions. So start slow but then add games and quick recall reviews once the students are starting to "get it."

✔ **ATTEMPT to make certain that the material on the first test is information that students are confident they know and understand.** Dopamine secretes whenever an individual gets an answer correct. (That's a good thing!) Dopamine creates a craving for additional correct answers (Puig & Miller, 2012). Wrong answers produce a loss of motivation. Thus, it is in your best interest to help students find success in your class early on. It will make them want to continue that habit.

✔ **ESTABLISH consistent rituals in the classroom.** Being in a predictable environment helps further the development of the prefrontal cortex, thereby improving self-regulation (Leon-Carrion, García-Orza, & Pérez-Santamaría, 2004). In addition, predictable environments promote homeostasis, which aids in better behavior and learning. Plus, as I'm sure you know, many students with special needs don't do well with unexpected transitions and will crave rituals and consistency.

✔ **INCORPORATE focus drills.** One of the unexpected outcomes of increased interaction with technology is the reduction of focus (Ophir, Nass, & Wagner, 2009). However, focus is essential for learning and is one of the key methods for increasing self-regulation. A simple way of understanding focus drills is to remember games you played as a child that forced you to stay on task, like the game "Concentration." There are so many websites with exercises that improve memory so use some of those to design quick activities for students to improve focus and memory. Make it fun and get other teachers to do it, too, then you can share ideas.

 **Plugged In**

Check out these websites that help you strengthen your brain and help with focus, attention, and memory:
- www.luminosity.com
- www.fitbrains.com

✔ **IDENTIFY the minimal amount of information that must be automated for students to be successful in the standard curriculum.** Look at the higher-level thinking goals of the curriculum, then identify the concepts that must be taught to achieve those advanced goals. Once higher-level thinking goals and advanced concepts are identified, ask what information students will need to use consistently to learn the concepts and meet the advanced goal. The most utilized information needs to be reviewed in quick sessions throughout the year to achieve automation. Remember, the brain cannot comprehend advanced concepts until foundational information has reached a level of automation.

## Administrators, DO this:

✔ **DEVELOP your commercial for success.** Repeat a positive message in the form of a catch phrase that tells students that they are all capable of being successful at school as long as they make the effort. Over time, the brain does not distinguish if a message is said a hundred times by a hundred different people or by one person. The brain tends to be subconsciously influenced by repeated messages (Weaver, Garcia, Schwarz, & Miller, 2007). We want students to believe they can succeed; tell them they can. Repeatedly.

✔ **SUPPORT the use of manipulatives, visuals, music, and experiential learning activities in your school.** Each of these activities helps the hippocampus comprehend and remember. Your teachers are not just having fun; they are helping students retain information. The *having fun* part is an added bonus!

✔ **INSTITUTE a schoolwide social skills program.** Social skills training that leads to better social interaction between students helps promote the development of the prefrontal cortex, which in turn advances self-control and academic achievement. Need to learn more about social skills? Check out Dean's (2015) chapters in the *What Really Works in Elementary/Secondary Schools* series.

✔ **ENCOURAGE teachers to dedicate time to do brief focus drills with students.** Many students are struggling to learn because the constant interaction with technology is diminishing their ability to focus (Pea et al., 2012). Technology often promotes multitasking. However, staying on task is a predictor of school success (McClelland, Morrison, & Holmes, 2000). If students lack the capacity to remain on task, it is counterproductive to constantly remind them and eventually discipline them. Instead, have teachers increase students' capacity to remain on task by improving their focus skills. Help teachers recognize that this will not be wasted instructional time.

✔ **FOCUS on teaching and practicing transitions between classes.** The increase in stimuli during transitions causes students with chemical imbalance to become impulsive. Did you know that the brain has to process less stimuli in a classroom than during hallway transitions? The increase in stimuli is one of the major reasons impulsive behaviors increase during these unstructured times. The more predictable the transition, the lower the level of chemical arousal. Remember, the amygdala is calmed by familiar patterns. This is as important at the secondary level as it is at the primary level.

✔ **PROVIDE professional development opportunities to learn more about the brain.** This chapter has focused primarily on the brain and memory, but that is just scratching the surface. Bringing in presenters who can help teachers understand how the brain works and impacts learning can also help reinforce best practices in instruction that will help all students, including those who are exceptional learners.

## STRATEGIES TO HELP WITH MEMORY

**Mnemonic Devices**

Mnemonics are patterns of letters, ideas, or associations that assist in remembering something. For example, "**P**lease **E**xcuse **M**y **D**ear **A**unt **S**ally" as a way to remember the order of operations in math (**P**arentheses, **E**xponents, **M**ultiplication, **D**ivision, **A**ddition, **S**ubtraction). These can also take the form of key words, peg words, visual connections, and memory "tricks."

**Location, Location, Location**

Have the student place a memory in a familiar location that can be easily pictured in his or her mind. This is a great strategy for learners who do well with visual aids. The student can then trigger the memory by merely picturing the location.

**Tell Me a Story**

Put information into a story format. For example, taking a list of vocabulary words:

**Minute:** a period of time equal to sixty seconds; infinitely small

**Accord:** concurrence of opinion

**Evident:** clearly revealed to the mind or the senses or judgment

**Intend:** have in mind as a purpose

**Issue:** some situation or event that is thought about

**Concern:** something that interests you because it is important

**Commit:** perform an act, usually with a negative connotation

**Approach:** move toward

And creating a story from them:

Standing in front of the judge for one **minute** felt like a lifetime. The jury had reached one **accord** quickly and it was **evident** that they **intended** to convict him for murder. The only **issue** that **concerned** him now was whether they thought he intended to **commit** murder. The last words he remembered hearing were, "Please **approach** the bench."

## BRAIN-BASED TEACHING ELEMENTS

*Use the following guidelines to develop brain-based strategies that support the lesson that is being taught.*

**Get students' attention**

- Novelty
- Interesting activity

**Identify a key fact that should be recalled quickly**

- Reduce to chunk (catch phrase)
- Associate with a visual (logo, symbol, or simple picture)
- Think of a gesture students can do when saying the catch phrase
- Establish when it will be reviewed and how many times it will be reviewed

**Abstract concepts (embodied cognition—get the body involved)**

- Utilize movement, touch, rhythmic pattern, or an interactive activity
- Stimulate senses simultaneously whenever possible (Are there opportunities to incorporate music, touch, smell, movement?)

**Higher-level thinking goal (brain putting things together)**

- Design an activity that guides students to put key facts and concepts learned together to meet the higher-level thinking goal

# REFERENCES

Blair, C. (2002). School readiness: Integrating cognition and emotion in a neurobiological conceptionalization of children's functioning at school entry. *American Psychologist, 57*(2), 111–127.

Dean, M. (2015). Superb social skills instruction: What really works in social skills in the elementary/secondary classroom. In W. W. Murawski & K. L. Scott (Eds.), *What really works in elementary/secondary education* (pp. 303–321). Thousand Oaks, CA: Corwin.

Herrmann, D. J., Raybeck, D., & Gutman, D. (1992). *Improving student memory.* Toronto, Canada: Hogrefe & Huber.

Johanson, D. C., & Edgar, B. (1996). *From Lucy to language.* New York, NY: Simon & Schuster.

Leon-Carrion, J., García-Orza, J., & Pérez-Santamaría, F. J. (2004). Development of the inhibitory component of the executive functions in children and adolescents. *International Journal of Neuroscience, 114*(10), 1291–1311.

McClelland, M. M., Morrison, F. J., & Holmes, D. L. (2000). Children at risk for early academic problems: The role of learning-related social skills. *Early Childhood Research Quarterly, 15*(3), 307–329.

Mensebach, C., Beblo, T., Driessen, M., Wingenfeld, K., Mertens, M., Rullkoetter, N., . . . Woermann, F. G. (2009). Neural correlates of episodic and semantic memory retrieval in borderline personality disorder: An fMRI study. *Psychiatry Research: Neuroimaging, 171*(2), 94–105.

Miles, L. K., Karpinska, K., Lumsden, J., & Macrae, C. N. (2010). The meandering mind: Vection and mental time travel. *PLoS ONE, 5*(5), e10825.

Munakata, Y., Herd, S. A., Chatham, C. H., Depue, B. E., Banich, M. T., & O'Reilly, R. C. (2011). A unified framework for inhibitory control. *Trends in Cognitive Sciences, 15*, 453–459.

Ophir, E., Nass, C. I., & Wagner, A. D. (2009). Cognitive control in media multitaskers. *PNAS, 106*(37), 15583–15587.

Pea, R., Nass, C., Meheula, L., Rance, M., Kumar, A., Bamford, H., . . . Zhou, M. (2012). Paper media use, face-to-face communication, media multitasking, and social well-being among 8 to 12 year old girls. *Developmental Psychology, 48*(2), 327–336.

Puig, M. V., & Miller, E. K. (2012). The role of prefrontal dopamine D1 receptors in the neural mechanisms of associative learning. *Neuron, 74*(5), 874–886.

Siegel, D. J., & Bryson, T. P. (2011). *The whole-brain child: 12 revolutionary strategies to nurture your child's developing mind.* New York, NY: Bantam Books.

Skipper, J. I., Goldin-Meadow, S., Nusbaum, H. C., & Small, S. L. (2009). Gestures orchestrate brain networks for language understanding. *Current Biology, 19*(8), 661–667.

Thomas, L. E., & Lleras, A. (2009). Swinging into thought: Directed movement guides insight in problem solving. *Psychonomic Bulletin and Review, 16*(4), 719–723.

Ullman, M. T., & Pullman, M. Y. (2015). Adapt and overcome: Can a single brain system compensate for autism, dyslexia and OCD? *Scientific American Mind, 51*, 24–25.

Weaver, K., Garcia, M. S., Schwarz, N., & Miller, T. D. (2007). Inferring the popularity of an opinion from its familiarity: A repetitive voice can sound like a chorus. *Journal of Personality and Social Psychology, 92*(5), 821–833.

Wilkins, R., Hodges, D., Laurienti, P., Steen, M., & Burdette, J. (2014). Network science and the effects of music preference on functional brain connectivity: From Beethoven to Eminem. *Nature Scientific Reports, 4*(6130).

 ## ADDITIONAL RECOMMENDED READING

Bunge, S. A., & Zelazo, P. D. (2006). A brain-based account of the development of rule use in childhood. *Current Directions in Psychological Science, 15*, 118–121.

Ho, Y.-C., Cheung, M.-C., & Chan, A. S. (2003). Music training improves verbal but not visual memory: Cross-sectional and longitudinal explorations in children. *Neuropsychology, 17*(3), 439–450.

Sanchez, H. (2016). *The education revolution: How to apply brain science to improve instruction and school climate.* Thousand Oaks, CA: Corwin.

Sanchez, H. (2016, May 13). 3 keys to academic success [Web log]. Retrieved from http://corwin-connect.com/2016/05/3-keys-academic-success/

Upson, S. (2014). The science of memory. *Scientific American Mind, 25*(3).

 ## TOP FIVE WEBSITES TO SUPPORT BRAIN-BASED LEARNING

➡ https://youtu.be/gdzmNwTLakg

➡ https://youtu.be/UWKvpFZJwcE

➡ http://www.fitbrains.com

➡ http://ankisrs.net

➡ http://www.luminosity.com

 ## APPS WE LOVE

➡ MindGames

➡ Elevate

➡ Memorado

➡ Epic Win

➡ Forest: Stay Focused

# 8

# Positive Behavior Intervention and Supports in the Inclusive Classroom

Jennifer D. Walker
*University of Mary Washington*

Brittany L. Hott
*Texas A&M University–Commerce*

## WHAT ARE POSITIVE BEHAVIORAL SUPPORTS?

Kids misbehave. They talk out of turn, sleep in class, push each other, and get out of their seats without permission. Some students even take it to another level—have a screaming fit, teach *you* new curse words, or throw chairs. Whatever the level, negative behaviors can be a major issue in the typical classroom.

Educators may find themselves . . . let's say, challenged . . . by the academic, behavioral, and social needs of all students, including those receiving special education services. Schools across the country are responding to the range of needs of all students by using a continuum of supports in a three-tiered model of support. Though those tiers can also help with academic and social needs, this chapter focuses on behavior. Positive behavioral interventions and supports (sometimes referred to PBIS but most often referred to as PBS, which is the acronym we'll use throughout this chapter) is a systems approach for creating a positive social culture and developing individualized behavioral supports. Interventions are developed and implemented as a team-based approach and continuously monitored for intervention effectiveness.

PBS includes three tiers of intervention, varying in intensity and individualization. Challenging behaviors may be addressed at the primary (universal), secondary (small group), or tertiary (individual) level. These supports may include schoolwide, classwide, and/or individual interventions, but all are used to improve the social and academic success of all students.

**Key Concepts**

PBS includes three tiers of intervention, varying in intensity and individualization.

In Tier 1 of the PBS model, all students in a school are supported with proactive, universal behavior management strategies. Strategies at this tier include positively stated schoolwide procedures and expectations, reinforcement, and instructional techniques that minimize disruption. These strategies are taught systematically in both classroom and nonclassroom settings (e.g., gym, hallways, cafeteria). If Tier 1 strategies are in place, approximately 80% of all students respond to the Tier 1 level of support (Fairbanks, Sugai, Guardino, & Lathrop, 2007). Eighty percent is good, but certainly not enough if that means that 20% of your kids are out of control!

Tier 2 supports address the behavioral needs of approximately 15% to 20% of the school population. The students targeted at Tier 2 may not respond to Tier 1 strategies and may or may not be identified as needing special education services. This is a small group of students who inconsistently follow rules or who know the rules but continue to test boundaries.

Students who are unresponsive to Tiers 1 or 2 level supports require more intensive interventions in Tier 3. Fewer than 5% of students typically fall into the Tier 3 level of supports in a PBS framework (Fairbanks et al., 2007). Often these students will receive special education services and will need individualized interventions, such as functional behavior assessments (FBA) and behavior intervention plans (BIP). One to five percent doesn't seem like much, but if you are the teacher who is having to deal with major behaviors, you know this tier is critical!

## PRACTICAL ISSUES AND SUPPORTING RESEARCH

Is it worth it to have all these tiers? Research would say yes. In fact, schools that consistently implement Tier 1 PBS interventions and supports report a decrease in office discipline referrals (Bradshaw, Mitchell, & Leaf, 2010) and an increase in positive interactions between teachers and students. Further, tiered supports are associated with academic achievement (Horner et al., 2009) and improved perceptions of school health and safety.

Tier 1 strategies may include increasing the opportunities to respond, integrating technology into instruction (Hott & Walker, 2012), peer tutoring (Hott, Walker, & Sahni, 2012), and self-monitoring (Hott, Walker, & Brigham, 2014; Hott & Weiser, 2013).

At Tier 2, PBS reduces off-task behavior and behavioral issues that result in office referrals (Hawken, MacLeod, & Rawlings, 2007). The supports for students who need Tier 2 level assistance may include small group social skills instruction, a check-in/check-out (CICO) arrangement, or targeted academic support, just to name a few. These supports should be combined with Tier 1 supports and should not replace universal strategies. This means that, in addition to the rules and structure established for all, some students need more. Doesn't this sound like what all teachers do—just in a more structured, systematic way?

For example, in the CICO program, students have a set of weekly goals that are tied to schoolwide behavioral expectations. Using these goals, students begin and end each day by checking in with an adult at school. Students are given encouragement, verbal praise, and reinforcement during CICO sessions. During the school day, students using CICO goals receive teacher feedback. The goals and feedback from teachers is also communicated with parents as a way to make connections with all members of the student's team. The CICO program has been shown to reduce office discipline referrals with all disability areas (Hawken & Horner, 2003).

So when do you need to implement Tier 3? Use Tier 3 interventions when behaviors persist despite universal interventions such as a safe and positive environment, positive relationships, engaging instruction, clear expectations, effective procedures and structure, and teaching, modeling, and reinforcing desired behaviors. Tier 3 supports focus on the individualization of interventions that can reduce specific emotional and behavioral issues.

Tier 3 supports may include an FBA and BIP to address individualized student behavioral challenges. An FBA is an assessment that describes a targeted behavior and identifies environmental antecedents that maintain that behavior. The FBA is used to develop a plan for teaching replacement behaviors while reducing the frequency or severity of the targeted problematic behavior. Okay, in laymen's terms, we want you to define the behavior really clearly; to be able to say what happens before, during, and after the behavior

**Plugged In**

Need more info on FBAs and BIPs? Check out www.specialeducationguide.com and www.pbis.org.

happens; to decide why the child is doing the behavior; and to figure out a different behavior the child can do that makes you and him or her happy. That's it. Of course, it's never quite that easy; there is a process, however, that helps us do all this.

The FBA process should begin with a team approach and an operationally defined behavior of concern. Data on this behavior could take the form of observations, interviews, and document analysis. Data should be collected across settings, staff members, and times of day to provide a complete picture of student behavior. Antecedents and consequences should be noted in an effort to identify functions of behavior. The most common functions of behaviors are attention, escape, control, tangible items, and sensory stimulation (i.e., it just feels good).

Teams must work together to identify and teach replacement behaviors that serve the same function as the behavior of concern. An effective replacement behavior is one that is stated positively and is incompatible with the behavior of concern so the two cannot happen simultaneously. For example, if a student is seeking attention from peers by making noises during class, the team must develop a positive way for the student to gain attention that is not distracting or disruptive (e.g., reading to the class).

After completing an FBA, a BIP is developed. The BIP uses a step-by-step process to outline changes to the antecedents, consequences, and replacement behaviors. Remember, you are not creating one of these for every kid in your class who talks out of turn; a BIP is reserved for only that 1% to 5% of the population who really needs something intensive. The goal of the BIP is to address the targeted behavior through skill instruction, reinforcement, setting changes, and interventions. When individualized behavioral interventions are based on functions of behavior, the result is significant behavior change. But this isn't a situation in which you just want to try something one time and pray it works; stubborn behaviors require consistent intervention!

It is important to remember that the BIP is a working document that should be revisited as often as needed. For students with more challenging behaviors, these reviews may occur at a preset interval (such as monthly or even biweekly) until the behavior is under control. The BIP serves as an individualized plan that works for a student within the PBS model.

We now have our overarching model for PBS. What does this actually look like in terms of what teachers and administrators should or shouldn't do to make it work? The following strategies are our top suggestions and warnings to improve all behaviors within a school setting.

## THINGS NOT TO DO IN A PBS SCHOOL!

**Teachers:**

✗ **STOP assuming that all students know how to execute desirable behaviors.** Some students haven't been taught how to take turns, respect property, or speak respectfully. Students need to be explicitly taught how to perform these behaviors and how to generalize across school settings. They may need step-by-step instruction, scaffolding, or a task analysis to learn these behaviors. A great resource is the National Professional Development Center on

**Making Connections**

Check out Chapter 13 on Autism Spectrum Disorder.

Autism Spectrum Disorder (http://autismpdc.fpg.unc.edu/sites/autismpdc.fpg.unc.edu/files/TaskAnalyis_Steps_0.pdf) for more information.

✗ **STOP telling students what behaviors they *aren't* doing correctly and focus on what they *are* doing correctly.** Positive and frequent reinforcement should be used to shape and increase desired behaviors. Try to ignore minor behavioral infractions and praise positive behaviors. We know from research that punishment just doesn't work in the long run.

✗ **STOP collecting data without analysis.** While data collection is a necessary first step, it must be analyzed to determine whether interventions are effective and if adjustments need to be made. It is great that you are using ClassDoJo or another app to manage class behavior, but just collecting data for the sake of collection doesn't change behavior. Analysis, adjustment, and interventions change behavior!

✗ **STOP moving through tiers of support before giving interventions a chance to work and impact behavioral change.** While a behavior plan for a student might be brilliant, it takes time to change behavior. Since behaviors serve a purpose, it is often difficult for students to see the value of doing something differently, especially if another behavior has worked so well for them for so long. Don't give up! Just like us, students need time to make behavioral changes. If a student isn't responsive right away, remember that it takes time for behavior to start to change . . . for everyone! Including your most difficult students.

✗ **STOP thinking that PBS can be developed without a commitment.** With support, schools require 2 to 3 years to effectively establish schoolwide discipline systems. These systems require developing a PBS team, pinpointing areas of need by analyzing behavioral data, developing a small number of schoolwide expectations, and identifying what these expectations and procedures look like across the school setting. And that's just the planning! Then everyone must work together to disseminate these expectations so that staff and students alike know the expectations and procedures. Check out the forms provided on the PBS website to monitor progress at the school level and make adjustments as needed.

✗ **STOP working in isolation when addressing behavioral challenges.** Teams should plan, design, and implement FBAs and BIPs together. When one or two members of a team are absent, valuable information about students remains unshared. Without a team approach, individual members may be overwhelmed with responsibilities and requirements.

✗ **STOP generating BIPs that don't include a replacement behavior to address the same function of the problematic behavior.** Just saying that a student will stop doing a behavior doesn't work. Teams must work together to identify and teach replacement behaviors that serve the same function as the behavior of concern. Behavior change will likely not occur if the replacement behavior doesn't match the function. If Edon needs attention, give it to him—just on your terms, not his!

Administrators:

✗ **STOP assuming that PBS will run itself once implemented.** Although staff may be trained during initial implementation, there will need to be additional training and checks for fidelity (whether the interventions are implemented as designed) over time. Giving staff time to work together to identify needs and assess for effectiveness will promote the success of PBS.

✗ **STOP viewing PBS as a special education initiative.** PBS is a system of supports for each and every student in the entire school. All members of the community are involved—parents, teachers, secretaries, custodians, bus drivers, and cafeteria monitors. Everyone plays a critical role!

**Plugged In**

Graph meaningful data with sites like ChartDog: http://www.interventioncentral.org/teacher-resources/graph-maker-free-online.

✗ **STOP holding only the special education teacher accountable for all the data collection.** Provide data collection training for teachers and staff. Check out some examples of data collection options and a list of apps for data collection at the end of the chapter. Use Google Docs to collect data together with a team. Then graph the data so the whole team can see progress.

✗ **STOP punishing students without providing interventions, instruction, and support.** Silent lunch, removals from class, and suspensions all take away opportunities to learn academic and desirable social skills. Instead, plan proactively, get to the function of the behavior, and teach students new skills. Once students start practicing new skills, praise and reinforce their behavior.

✗ **STOP allowing teams to wait until a series of suspensions result in the requirement of a BIP.** When problems requiring an individual level of support are identified, be proactive. Provide support to complete a comprehensive FBA and effective BIP. Since every state and school jurisdiction has their own FBA and BIP documentation forms, it is imperative that school staff understand how to complete the process.

✗ **STOP assuming that everything costs money.** Free or low-cost incentives may be best. Remember, getting to eat lunch with the principal is a major incentive in many elementary schools, while a positive call home works wonders at the secondary level!

✗ **STOP displaying or overlooking behaviors that violate the school rules.** Don't cut the lunch line, chew gum, or talk loudly during a fire drill and remind your teachers to do the same. Remember to model the behaviors we want everyone to display.

## STRATEGIES FOR PBS SUCCESS

Teachers, DO this:

✔ **DO put settingwide supports in place.** Supports should include: (a) a clear PBS purpose statement, (b) positively stated schoolwide expectations, (c) procedures for teaching expectations, (d) a continuum of reinforcement, and (e) a continuum of consequences. See the end of the chapter for examples of these supports.

✔ **ALIGN expectations, procedures, and reinforcements across the school and within individual classrooms.** Using an expectation and procedure matrix in classrooms unifies the process and reduces confusion for students as they move across school settings. For reference, see the example matrix at the end of this chapter.

✔ **ENSURE that universal strategies are in place for all students, regardless of their disability or least restrictive environment.** All settings should include positive environments, positive relationships, engaging instruction, clear expectations, effective procedures and structure, and the teaching, modeling, and reinforcing of desired behaviors. Note that this does not mean that every student will receive the same consequence for the first or second infraction; a student with an emotional or behavior disability may very well have an individualized education program indicating different consequences. However, that student needs to know what the expectations are and needs to be taught the desired behaviors.

✔ **DO deliberately select staff-student pairings for CICO supports.** Students should feel supported and encouraged by the adult they are paired with for CICO. Staff should offer verbal praise (e.g., "You followed directions today, that's excellent work!") and other means of reinforcement (high fives, singing the praises of the student to another adult, notes of praise). The adult should be consistent and adhere to predetermined schedules for CICO meetings.

✔ **ALLOW 6 to 8 weeks of consistent implementation to determine student responsiveness to CICO.** Students should be given ample opportunity for success before moving to a Tier 3 intervention. Check out our CICO model at the end of the chapter.

✔ **DO triangulate data collection when developing an FBA.** Collect data across settings, staff, days, and times of day. Consider the setting events in which the problematic behavior is most and least likely to occur. A setting event is the location, activity, time of day, and day of the week that the behavior occurs. This is important because where and when the behavior occurs can provide important information about why the student may be engaging in the behavior. If Soon is only refusing to work in algebra, and sometimes in chemistry, it might be that he is struggling with his math skills. If Nicola's behavioral challenges escalate on Mondays and during the first hour of the day, it might be that she has difficulty transitioning from home to school. Take note of the behavior's intensity, duration, and frequency to garner a complete profile of the data. Be sure to ask for help and support!

✔ **FOCUS on one behavior at a time and define the behavior clearly when developing an FBA.** The behavior should pass the "stranger test," meaning it is clear and defined enough that during an observation a stranger would know exactly what the behavior looks and sounds like. We call it MOO—measurable, observable, and objective. This behavior should also be used for data collection purposes across settings. Still not clear? We've provided an example at the end of the chapter.

✔ **DEVELOP a system for reinforcement, praise, and rewards.** Within the PBS framework, focus on opportunities to praise and acknowledge positive student behavior. Outside of planned reinforcement or reward assemblies that acknowledge students, staff should "catch them being good" as much as possible during day-to-day interactions. Give out high-fives, thumbs up, and smiles. They are free and encouraging!

✔ **PROVIDE a range of reinforcement options and schedules.** Consider intermittent and continuous reinforcement, tailored to school, classroom, and individual needs. A variety of social, tangible, and activity-based reinforcements should be used to support desired behaviors. Need ideas? Check out the list of reinforcements we've provided at the end of the chapter. To get even better ideas, ask your students what reinforcements are . . . well, reinforcing.

✔ **PLAN for nonresponders.** This includes *refusers* and may include alternate interventions, modified plans to include academics, or more individualized supports. Consider adaptations such as function-based reinforcements and addressing Tier 2 level setting events. If you find yourself at a loss for what to do next, ask yourself the questions at the end of the chapter. Also, check out our Top Five Websites. Help is just a click away! There are a TON of forms and resources to support students who do not respond to the typical interventions.

✔ **COMMUNICATE with parents and families.** Families should be involved and aware of PBS expectations and procedures as well as individualized plans. In particular, parents or guardians should be part of the CICO and FBA and/or BIP process. Schools should not only share behavioral concerns but also behavioral successes. Schools can share PBS information by posting it to the school or class website, sending home information about expectations for the week, month, or semester on an information sheet or newsletter, and by sending home positive postcards for students who are following PBS expectations and procedures.

✔ **REMEMBER to stay positive!** There is always something great about every kid! It may take some looking, but it's our job to find it.

**Administrators:**

✔ **REMIND teachers that change takes time.** Students who need Tier 2 and Tier 3 supports will require individualized supports to decrease behaviors of concern. Progress may be slow. For example, when Jason perceives an assignment as too difficult or requiring too much time, he loudly curses to express his frustration. Cursing will not stop immediately. It took time to learn all those curse words! It will take even more time to break the habit.

✔ **FOCUS on PBS program buy-in from staff, particularly when teachers are working with more challenging students in Tiers 2 and 3.** All staff should understand the benefits of PBS and the processes that make tiered interventions successful. This will also ensure that expectations for procedures are consistently upheld so behaviors that are expected in Classroom A are also expected in Classroom B. For students with behavioral challenges, consistency across settings is a critical component in shaping desirable behavior

**Plugged In**

Need to be inspired? A collection of inspirational videos can be found at https://www.pbis.org/swpbs_videos/pbs_video-discovering_swpbs.aspx.

and reinforcing behavior change. If a school team begins to question whether PBS is still worth it, take some time to share PBS success stories.

✔ **DO maintain consistency despite issues that may arise because of behavioral challenges.** Although some students may have interfering behaviors, it is important that PBS is implemented consistently and with fidelity. Remember that students who receive Tier 3 supports need individualized interventions to be successful. Fair is not always equal! We know it's tough in a school of many students; however, a few extra minutes to ensure interventions are implemented with fidelity and CICO plans and BIPs are in place avoids loss of instructional time, mounds of paperwork documenting behavioral incidents, your time, and your sanity! If just one teacher in a team isn't following through, it is difficult to hold students accountable given the inconsistencies.

✔ **PROVIDE ongoing training and professional development to staff.** All faculty should be trained on PBS and should have a solid understanding of their roles and responsibilities under the PBS framework and tiers of intervention. Often a PBS committee can help address challenges with training, implementation, and evaluation. Be sure to review our Top Five Websites for ideas on professional development and training to support *all* personnel.

✔ **DO consider assigning a CICO program coordinator.** A coordinator can help with selecting students, communicating with staff and parents, creating CICO reports, monitoring feedback and reinforcement, and making data-based decisions. Some schools ask the 504 coordinator, assistant principal, or school counselor to take on the CICO coordinator role.

✔ **INVOLVE parents and families.** Consider sharing the PBS model with the PTA, boosters club, and band. Share the positive results and areas where growth is needed. Post success to your school website. Invite support staff and parents to recognition ceremonies. Celebrate progress and recognize achievement!

## TIERED STRATEGIES AND INTERVENTIONS

More information on Tier 1 and Tier 2 strategies are available in Hott, B. L., Isbell, L., & Walker, J. (2015). Positive Behavioral Supports: Strategies for elementary educators. In W. W. Murawski & K. L. Scott (Eds.), *What really works in elementary education* (pp. 122–139). Thousand Oaks, CA: Corwin.

**Tier 3 Strategies (impacts 1%–5% of students)**

- Conduct a Functional Behavior Assessment (FBA)
  - Identify and define the behavior of concern
  - Collect data across settings and time to establish a baseline
  - Determine the antecedents and maintaining consequences of the behavior
  - Determine the function of the behavior
  - Generate a hypothesis "*When presented with* **x**, *Jeremie engages in* **y** *behavior to get* **z**."
  - Test out the hypothesis by removing the antecedents or consequences

- Conduct a Behavior Intervention Plan (BIP)
  - Determine a replacement behavior that will serve the same function as the existing behavior
  - Develop a plan to teach replacement skills
  - Incorporate new responses to behaviors
  - Outline a schedule for reinforcement
  - Collect data and monitor progress

- Consider developing a behavior contract
  - Use a team approach to develop a contract and get team buy-in
  - Target a behavior to change
  - Collect baseline data
  - Meet with the student to discuss a plan for change and get student buy-in
  - Solicit student input on a desired activity, tangible item, or reward
  - Use baseline data to set a realistic goal to earn a reward
  - Design the contract. Need ideas? https://www.freebehaviorcontracts.com/downloads.php
  - Be consistent and persistent with monitoring the behavior contract
  - Reward the student as soon as the goal has been reached
  - Honor the contract

- Focus on parent training and collaboration
  - Conduct sessions on functional analysis that can be done at home
  - Invite parents to FBA and BIP meetings
  - Solicit parent support for data collection at home
  - Keep a daily communication log

- Explore alternatives to suspension and expulsion
  - Develop modules to teach new behaviors
  - Create a menu of options that allow for restitution
  - Use a problem-solving model to meet with students one to one
  - Remove privileges (or earn them again)
  - Utilize community service activities as an alternative

- Use evidenced-based interventions
  - Visit the What Works Clearinghouse at http://ies.ed.gov/ncee/wwc/findwhatworks.aspx to explore what works

---

*Source:* Adapted from Hott, B. L., Isbell, L., & Walker, J. (2015). Positive Behavioral Supports: Strategies for elementary educators. In W. W. Murawski & K. L. Scott (Eds.), *What really works in elementary education* (pp. 122–139). Thousand Oaks, CA: Corwin.

## DATA COLLECTION APPS

| App | Description |
|---|---|
| **Tally Counters** | Tally behaviors using a frequency count. |
| **Quantifier** | Collect a range of numerical data and plot the information over preselected time ranges. |
| **ClassDojo** | Monitor individual predetermined positive and negative classroom behaviors. Summarize and graph behavior. |
| **Percentally Pro** | Enter goals for individual students; collect data on corrections, prompting, accuracy, or elapsed time. Analyze data. |
| **Class Gather** | Collect data using a timer, counter, or checklist. Create scales to record degrees of behaviors. |

# SETTINGWIDE SUPPORT EXAMPLES

**A clear PBS purpose statement**
- To develop student achievement by utilizing proactive behavioral and academic support systems
- Build capacity to teach behaviors, make data-based decisions, and promote family and community involvement in academic and behavior change

**Positively stated schoolwide expectations**
- Responsibility (I do what is expected of me), On-task (I use my time wisely), Attitude (I act positively in my school environment), and Respect (I treat everyone with respect)
- Be Caring (follow instructions the first time), Be a Thinker (come to class prepared), Be Safe (keep hands and feet to yourself)

**Procedures for teaching expectations**
- Direct instruction to include defining the expectation, using examples and nonexamples, guided practice following expectations, role-play, feedback, and reinforcement
- Explain and model what responsibility, being on-task, or respect looks like across settings (cafeteria, hallways, bathrooms, bus)

**Continuum of reinforcement**
- Verbal praise, nontangible reinforcements, tangible reinforcements, and no cost to low cost
- Activity-based, social, and tangible reinforcements
- Immediate, delayed, or intermittent reinforcement

**Continuum of consequences**
- May include: nonverbal warning, verbal warning, modification (change of seat), problem solving, parent contact, behavior module
- May include: whole group reminder, individual reminder, one-to-one conference with teacher, parent contact, problem solving during lunch

## CHECK-IN/CHECK-OUT (CICO) MODEL

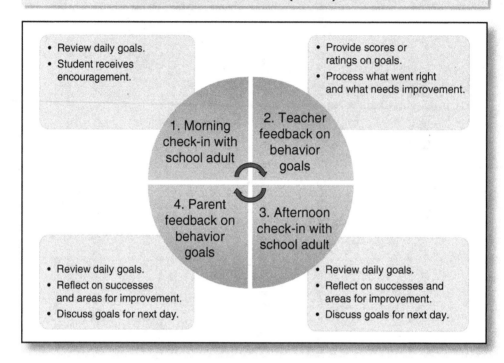

- Review daily goals.
- Student receives encouragement.

- Provide scores or ratings on goals.
- Process what went right and what needs improvement.

1. Morning check-in with school adult

2. Teacher feedback on behavior goals

4. Parent feedback on behavior goals

3. Afternoon check-in with school adult

- Review daily goals.
- Reflect on successes and areas for improvement.
- Discuss goals for next day.

- Review daily goals.
- Reflect on successes and areas for improvement.
- Discuss goals for next day.

## CHECK-IN/CHECK-OUT (CICO) DAILY REPORT EXAMPLES

### Pleasantville Elementary School Pirates (ARG!)

Student Name: _____   Check-in/Check-out with: _____

Date: _____

*Have each teacher throughout the day share how well you are following the Pirate Way!*

☺: Great job     ☺ Good/ okay job     ☹: Needs improvement

| | Acting Safely | | | Respectful Behavior | | | Get Ready to Learn | | | Total | Initials |
|---|---|---|---|---|---|---|---|---|---|---|---|
| Morning work | ☺ | ☺ | ☹ | ☺ | ☺ | ☹ | ☺ | ☺ | ☹ | | |
| Reading | ☺ | ☺ | ☹ | ☺ | ☺ | ☹ | ☺ | ☺ | ☹ | | |
| Math | ☺ | ☺ | ☹ | ☺ | ☺ | ☹ | ☺ | ☺ | ☹ | | |
| Specials | ☺ | ☺ | ☹ | ☺ | ☺ | ☹ | ☺ | ☺ | ☹ | | |
| Lunch | ☺ | ☺ | ☹ | ☺ | ☺ | ☹ | ☺ | ☺ | ☹ | | |
| Social Studies | ☺ | ☺ | ☹ | ☺ | ☺ | ☹ | ☺ | ☺ | ☹ | | |
| Recess | ☺ | ☺ | ☹ | ☺ | ☺ | ☹ | ☺ | ☺ | ☹ | | |
| Science | ☺ | ☺ | ☹ | ☺ | ☺ | ☹ | ☺ | ☺ | ☹ | | |
| Total Daily Points | ☺ = _____ | | | ☺ = _____ | | | ☹ = _____ | | | | |

Goal: 19 ☺

### Blundell High School Hornets

Student Name: _____   Check-in/Check-out with: _____

Date: _____

2 points: Without teacher reminders   1 point: Needed 2 or 3 reminders   0 points: Over 3 reminders

| | Be Respectful Keep hands, feet to self | | | Be Responsible Bring materials to class | | | Be Reliable Participate in class | | | Notes Place * if student recognized need for additional supports | Initials |
|---|---|---|---|---|---|---|---|---|---|---|---|
| 1st block | 2 | 1 | 0 | 2 | 1 | 0 | 2 | 1 | 0 | | |
| 2nd block | 2 | 1 | 0 | 2 | 1 | 0 | 2 | 1 | 0 | | |
| 3rd block | 2 | 1 | 0 | 2 | 1 | 0 | 2 | 1 | 0 | | |
| 4th block | 2 | 1 | 0 | 2 | 1 | 0 | 2 | 1 | 0 | | |
| Lunch | 2 | 1 | 0 | 2 | 1 | 0 | 2 | 1 | 0 | | |
| 5th block | 2 | 1 | 0 | 2 | 1 | 0 | 2 | 1 | 0 | | |
| 6th block | 2 | 1 | 0 | 2 | 1 | 0 | 2 | 1 | 0 | | |

Total Daily Points: _____

Goal: 80% of points or 34 points

## STRATEGIES FOR ADDRESSING DIFFICULT BEHAVIOR

| Behavior description (Instead of this . . .) | Measurable, Observable, Objective (MOO) behavior definition (Try this . . .) | Strategies to address behavior based on individually identified function of the behavior |
|---|---|---|
| Martin is aggressive. | When provided with an assignment that he perceives as difficult, Martin hits peers and staff with open and clenched hands and kicks with his feet. | *Function: Escape difficult work*<br>• Identify what's difficult for him<br>• Talk to him before giving work<br>• Embed difficult work between easy work<br>• Give a break before and during difficult work<br>• Have paraprofessional work with him on difficult work |
| Mace is disruptive. | During instruction, Mace calls out answers and information unrelated to the topic of discussion without raising her hand. | *Function: Attention from peers*<br>• Provide opportunities for peer attention (help with roll call in the morning, incorporate peer tutoring/group work)<br>• Praise Mace for raising her hand and waiting to be called on<br>• Provide more praise for being on topic |
| Sara is off task. | During carpet time, Sara does not make eye contact or face the speaker. She does not remain seated in an upright position and attempts to engage peers in conversation. | *Function: Power and control*<br>• Provide opportunities for Sara to lead the class to the carpet<br>• Create a self-monitoring chart and discuss Sara's progress individually after each carpet time<br>• When ready, assign Sara to help monitor class behavior during carpet time; remind Sara that she sets the tone as a helper and needs to demonstrate self-control<br>• Allow Sara to earn the opportunity to lead the book discussion during carpet time |
| Molly is annoying. | During lessons, Molly engages in one or more of the following behaviors: taps pencil on desk, chair, or other object; repeatedly kicks the legs of desks; moves chair side to side causing the legs of the chair to scrape across the floor. | *Function: Sensory*<br>• Provide walk breaks<br>• Consider use of Silly Putty or stress ball to allow for movement<br>• Provide sensory cushion in the desk seat to allow Molly to wiggle without making noise or creating a safety issue |

## CONSIDERATIONS FOR NONRESPONDERS

| Ask yourself: | If the answer is no, then: |
|---|---|
| Do I have a relationship with this student? | Take some time to meet with the student. Make sure they understand your concerns and desire to help them. Ask them for their perspective on the behavior. Start with "What do you want me to know about you?" and include "How can I best help you?" |
| Do I know what motivates this student? | |
| Does this student know she or he can trust me to help them? | |
| Do I have a positive attitude about this student? | While we may be frustrated with a student's behavior, it is important to remain positive and optimistic. Behavior can change! If students feel like their teachers dislike them, they certainly aren't going to make strides to do things differently. |
| Have I reached out to the parents? | Seek information from parents about their child. They know them best. Find out what motivates your student and what works at home. Ask parents what they think you should know about their child. |
| Do I know how this student is doing in other classes? | Perhaps there is a specific reason a student isn't responding to you. Maybe they don't feel competent in your subject area, maybe there are peers in the room who create anxiety, maybe they hate mornings. Talk with your peers, brainstorm, and troubleshoot. |
| Have I determined the function of the student's behavior? | If you don't know the function of a behavior, you can't change it. Even though we may not want to give a student power or control, if that is the reason they are misbehaving, we have to figure out a way to give the student some power and control in a controlled way. |
| Have I tried to teach this student new skills? | If a student can't read, we plan interventions and teach them letters, sounds, and words. When a student can't behave in a specific way, we need to approach them the same way we would approach a nonreader. We need to teach new skills. Plan a lesson on behavior just as you would for academics. Include a motivational hook, guided and independent practice, and an assessment. |
| Have I given interventions a chance to work? | Although there are certainly some exceptions, like safety, interventions should be implemented over several weeks and progress should be monitored. While it might be easy to want to give up and find another alternative placement for a student, it's our job to adhere to an intervention with fidelity and allow change to occur. |
| Am I at the end of my rope? | That's okay! Keep trying! Keep communicating with the student, your team, the parents, your administration, and outside agencies. Keep it up! You are making a difference. |

# REFERENCES

Bradshaw, C., Mitchell, M. M., & Leaf, P. J. (2010). Examining the effects of school-wide positive behavior interventions and supports on student outcomes: Results from a randomized controlled effectiveness trial in elementary school. *Journal of Positive Behavior Interventions, 12,* 133–148.

Fairbanks, S., Sugai, G., Guardino, D., & Lathrop, M. (2007). Response to intervention: Examining classroom behavior support in second grade. *Exceptional Children, 73,* 288–310.

Hawken, L. S., & Horner, R. H. (2003). Evaluation of a targeted intervention within a schoolwide system of behavior support. *Journal of Behavioral Education, 12,* 225–240.

Hawken, L. S., MacLeod, K. S., & Rawlings, L. (2007). Effects of the behavior education program on office discipline referrals of elementary school students. *Journal of Positive Behavior Interventions, 9,* 94–101.

Horner, R. H., Sugai, G., Smolkowski, K., Eber, L., Nakasato, J., Todd, A., & Esperanza, J. (2009). A randomized, wait list controlled effectiveness trial assessing school-wide positive behavior support in elementary schools. *Journal of Positive Behavior Interventions, 11,* 133–144.

Hott, B. L., & Walker, J. D. (2012). Five tips to increase student participation in the secondary classroom. *Learning Disabilities Forum.* Retrieved from http://www.cldinternational.org/Publications/LdForum.asp

Hott, B. L., & Weiser, B. L. (2013). *Incorporating self-monitoring procedures to support content area learning.* International Webinar sponsored by the International Council for Learning Disabilities. Materials available from http://members.cldinternational.org/civicrm/event/info?reset=1&id=3

Hott, B. L., Isbell, L., & Walker, J. (2015). Positive Behavioral Supports: Strategies for elementary educators. In W. W. Murawski & K. L. Scott (Eds.), *What really works in elementary education* (pp. 122–139). Thousand Oaks, CA: Corwin.

Hott, B. L., Walker, J. D., & Brigham, F. J. (2014). Implementing self-management strategies in the secondary classroom. In A. Cohan & A. Honingsfeld (Eds.), *Breaking the mold of classroom management: What educators should know and do to enable student success* (pp. 19–26). Lanham, MD: R & L Education.

Hott, B. L., Walker, J. D., & Sahni, J. (2012). International Council for Learning Disabilities InfoSheet: Peer tutoring. Retrieved from https://www.cldinternational.org/InfoSheets/PeerTutoring.asp

# ADDITIONAL RECOMMENDED READING ON PBS

Allington, R. L. (2011). *What really matters in response to intervention: Research-based designs.* Upper Saddle River, NJ: Pearson.

Honingsfeld, A., & Cohan, A. (2014). *Breaking the mold of classroom management.* Lanham, MD: Rowman & Littlefield Education.

Hott, B. L., & Limberg, D. (2015). Positive behavioral supports: Strategies for secondary educators. In W. W. Murawski & K. L. Scott (Eds.), *What really works in secondary education* (pp. 120–136). Thousand Oaks, CA: Corwin.

Walker, J. D., & Hott, B. L. (in press). Response to Intervention (RTI). In S. B. Mertens, M. M. Caskey, & N. Flowers (Eds.), *The encyclopedia of middle level education.* Charlotte, NC: Information Age.

## TOP FIVE WEBSITES TO SUPPORT POSITIVE BEHAVIOR SUPPORTS

➡ www.pbis.org/school
➡ www.swis.org
➡ www.rtinetwork.org/learn/behavior-supports/schoolwidebehavior
➡ www.pbisnetwork.org/resources
➡ www.iris.peabody.vanderbilt.edu/module/fba

## APPS WE LOVE

➡ Numbers
➡ TeacherKit
➡ Super Duper Data Tracker
➡ D.A.T.A.
➡ Behavior Tracker Pro

# 9

# *Beyond Just "Playing Nicely"*

## *Collaboration and Co-Teaching*

Amy Kramer

*Bowling Green State University*

Wendy W. Murawski

*California State University, Northridge*

## CO-TEACHING: ESSENTIAL ELEMENTS

If we could start and end our chapter by saying "just play nicely with one another," we would. Unfortunately, however, collaboration and co-teaching simply aren't that easy. Today's educators are faced with the daunting task of identifying and planning for quality instruction for all their students, including those who are exceptional learners. Sifting through all the options and strategies that will result in the best educational experience for students with special needs can be an overwhelming task. This is especially true if teachers have to face this task alone. The National Center for Education Statistics reported that the number of students with disabilities who spend 80% or more of their time in general education classrooms has almost doubled in the past two decades, comprising 61% of the total population of identified students with disabilities in 2011 (U.S. Department of Education, 2013). The antiquated mindset of placing a student with a disability in a separate classroom, without consideration for his or her unique abilities, is a thing of the past. The forecast predicts that inclusive services for students with special needs is not a trend or a phase; rather, it is an approach to education that is grounded in the moral and ethical obligations we have to provide all students with a quality educational experience. It's simply good practice.

So where do co-teaching and collaboration come into all this? Our job as educators is to make sure we are fulfilling what legislation already supports and what we know to be the best option for students. "Inclusive education is both the vision and practice of welcoming, valuing, empowering, and supporting the diverse academic, social/emotional, language, and communication learning of all students in shared environments . . ." (Villa & Thousand, 2016, p. 18). We recognize that this can be much easier said than done however. How do you do what you know to be right when it's also challenging and a lot of work? You share the load! Co-teaching has been, and continues to be, a dominant way to support the demands of teaching students with diverse needs in an inclusive setting (Murawski, 2009). Today, schools are all over the map in terms of how progressive they are with the implementation of a collaborative or co-taught model. While it is true that some schools are more advanced in their practice than others, it is also true that co-teaching is a service delivery option that requires detailed attention to many facets. When implemented with fidelity (yes, that's the catch), co-teaching has the power to fully support an inclusive environment. A collaborative support system, flexible instructional approaches, and data-driven decisions are an integral part of what makes co-teaching work. All these things are possible when two teachers work together and are committed to the process *and* when there is administrative support.

**Key Concepts**

The three required components of true co-teaching?

- Co-planning
- Co-instruction
- Co-assessment

Let us clarify the difference between co-teaching and collaboration because they are not synonymous terms. Collaboration is when adults share a common goal; they communicate regarding how to attain that goal, as well as share resources and responsibilities as they work toward goal attainment. Teachers can collaborate on projects, on problem solving about a student or situation, or even on lessons, but it doesn't mean that they are necessarily co-teaching. Co-teaching means that two credentialed educators *co-plan, co-instruct, and co-assess* a single group of students with diverse needs (Murawski, 2010). For purposes of inclusive education, these two educators are most typically a general education teacher and a special education teacher. Lack of fidelity or commitment, unwillingness to collaborate or share control, and an uncertainty of what co-teaching is can lead to confusion, frustration, and faulty implementation (Friend, Cook, Hurley-Chamberlain, & Shamberger, 2010). When this happens, the students will not reap the greatest benefits that co-teaching can provide—and let's face it, teachers will be unhappy too.

## CO-TEACHING: RESEARCH AND PRACTICE

Successful co-teaching has its roots in collaboration. Teacher preparation programs and the professional development opportunities teachers are provided often don't address critical teacher dispositions and the need for effective collaborative skills (Brinkmann & Twiford, 2012). This means that teachers are at a disadvantage when they embark on their first co-teaching experience. They may have been taught how to teach math or teach students with disabilities, but have they been taught how to effectively communicate, problem solve, and collaborate with others? Without effective collaboration, co-teaching is most likely to flounder. Let's face it, just putting two adults in the same room doesn't mean they will get along or even agree on what's best for their students. Co-teaching should always begin with professional development so everyone knows what to expect (Murawski & Bernhardt, 2015). This will help set the stage for this highly collaborative professional journey. Job embedded professional development is also recommended to provide ongoing support (Shaffer & Thomas-Brown, 2015). High quality professional development is a way for each co-teacher to know what is expected of them, how they can establish parity as a teacher team, and how they can optimize their individual roles to best meet the diverse needs of their learners. In addition, this type of professional development can benefit teachers who may not yet be co-teaching or who only co-teach for part of their day and just "collaborate" or "give or receive support" for the rest of it. Skills in collaboration are necessary for all these roles.

Just placing students with special needs into a general education setting does not facilitate the *special* in specialized instruction (Conderman & Hedin, 2014; King-Sears & Bowman-Kruhm, 2011). While the notion that placement in the general education classroom does offer a gateway for access to the general education content, it does not guarantee anything beyond that unless the professionals who are charged with planning and executing the lessons take initiative. Marilyn Friend (2016) describes how co-teachers need to focus their attention on the specialized part of instruction. She called this Co-teaching 2.0. This means going beyond just sharing a classroom to connecting lessons to students' individualized education programs (IEPs), teaching within the students' areas of need, changing the content (if necessary), providing unique modes of delivery or methodology, conducting progress monitoring, and implementing specialized techniques for learning that other learners do not necessarily need. Essentially, co-teachers need to ensure that specially designed instruction (SDI) is occurring daily in their shared class. Don't worry! You have a partner, and the two of you will be doing all this together.

Research points to numerous reported benefits of co-teaching. Teachers feel that the academic and social needs of the students they serve, with and without disabilities, are better met in a co-taught class than a non–co-taught class (Strogilos & Avramidis, 2016). Like any other skill in teaching, however, co-teaching needs to be cultivated. Perfection cannot be expected at the onset. In fact, you will want to set a 3- to 5-year goal for yourself. Include reasonable action steps and strategies to achieve your goal. As in any close relationship—and co-teaching is described as a "professional marriage" (Murawski, 2009) so that's definitely a close relationship—there will be conflict. Recognizing and discussing this as a team to figure out how conflict will be resolved, can help minimize frustrations later on. Communication is quintessential to both collaboration and co-teaching. When implemented with fidelity, co-teaching has the potential to foster an environment that can help students flourish.

Initially, co-teachers will need to think about three things that will help them in their endeavors. Wendy Murawski (2009) emphasized that co-teaching requires three activities to be considered "true" co-teaching: *co-planning, co-instructing, and co-assessing*. Each of these areas is discussed to facilitate the understanding of what successful co-teachers do.

### Co-Planning

The research on co-teaching is clear that co-planning is necessary for true co-teaching to occur; it is equally clear that co-planning is often lacking between teachers and that, even when that time is provided, it is not always used well (Howard & Potts, 2009; Murawski, 2012). A staple at the onset of any co-teaching relationship is to acknowledge that co-planning needs to occur and then to establish when common planning time will take place and what it will look like. Finding time to collaborate can be difficult. Teachers are busy, and time during the day is a precious commodity. Support from building administration is critical to ensure co-planning time has been allocated for co-teachers (Murawski, 2012; Scruggs, Mastropieri, & McDuffie, 2007). Having difficulty putting common planning periods into the master schedule? There are a plethora of options for providing co-planning time for the administrator willing to be creative; these include using substitute teachers, providing stipends, using "specials" (e.g., art, PE, music), reallocating duties, using PLC time, and more (Murawski & Dieker, 2012).

Uninterrupted co-planning time cannot be emphasized enough. Phone calls, meetings, grading papers, and even socializing will have to wait for another time (Murawski, 2012). Co-planning is a sacred time that needs to be prioritized so each teacher can bring his or her unique expertise into the planning process to allow teachers to be proactive rather than reactive. Typically, the general education teacher brings the knowledge of the curriculum, pacing, and classroom management while the special education teacher brings knowledge of specialized instruction for students with disabilities, data collection, and learning for mastery (Conderman & Hedin, 2014; Friend et al., 2010). This is the time when special educators can help their colleagues proactively create universally designed lessons that include specially designed instruction and differentiation.

Given that time is limited, co-teachers need to be intentional about what will be covered during their co-planning sessions. An agenda will help the planning stay on topic. The "What/How/Who" approach described by Murawski (2012) will help narrow the focus and make planning time more efficient. At the end of this chapter, we've included a helpful table tent that you can laminate and use when planning to help you remember the various approaches. Don't forget to consider how to differentiate the "content (what you teach and what students learn), the process (how students think about or make sense of ideas and information), and/or the product (how students show what they know)" (Tomlinson, 1995, p. 45). Differentiating the instruction for all students may seem insurmountable with one teacher; however, now that there are two expert teachers, differentiating is easier to tackle! Planning that is focused on data-driven decisions, access to the curriculum, and differentiation will result in instruction that meets each child where they are and takes them further than what one teacher can do alone.

## Co-Instructing

When instruction is being delivered to students, it is important that both teachers have an active role in the lesson. Parity (a.k.a. equality) must be established on a relational level between co-teachers and clearly evident to students. When one teacher's role is reduced to that of an assistant or helper, students become aware of the power differential and therefore struggle to see both teachers as an equal (Embury & Kroeger, 2012). Parity is important because it leads to greater trust between the students and the two teachers in the classroom. This type of respect between partners will open communication and dialogue that will naturally allow for more active engagement by both adults.

To engage more learners and help address diverse student needs, co-teachers should vary the instructional approaches as often as possible and make sure both of you are actively engaged whenever you are together. The five instructional approaches first suggested by Bauwens, Hourcade, and Friend (1989) offer strategies to help teachers reduce the student-to-teacher ratio and/or provide a deeper level of assistance to those who need it the most. Three of the five co-teaching approaches allow for smaller instructional groups (i.e., Parallel, Station, Alternative). When small, flexible student groups are used in the classroom, there are ample benefits for students and adults alike (Reid, 2002).

This is the kind of regrouping we want to see in all classes—at the elementary, middle, and high school levels! Currently, there is not enough small group instruction at the secondary level (Murawski, 2009), but using co-teaching approaches that regroup students can help ensure that teachers are able to deliver high-level content, without watering it down, to a diverse range of learners. Yes, there will be short moments of organized chaos as students transition between groups, but embrace them. Kids of all ages need those brain breaks!

As the different approaches are used and small groups are planned, co-teachers need to make sure that the groups are fluid and data driven. If special education students are consistently grouped, for example, with the other students who struggle, then a stigma starts to be associated with that group and defeats the purpose of an inclusive classroom. When teachers constantly mix up the group arrangements, students accept this as normal and quickly realize that groups are formed for any number of reasons (Ford, 2005). These flexible and fluid groups require both teachers to be active and present in the classroom for the duration of the lesson. This means that special educators should not be regularly pulled from their co-teaching setting to serve as substitute teachers, attend emergency meetings, meet with parents, and so forth (Murawski & Dieker, 2012).

## Co-Assessing

Why co-assess? To collect data, of course. Data truly drives a strong co-taught classroom. There are four times when co-teachers should be discussing assessments; (1) as co-teaching pairs are beginning their journey, (2) before a unit of study, (3) during instruction, and (4) after instruction (Conderman & Hedin, 2012). As co-teaching teams are being formed, it is important for them to openly share their assessment philosophy. Because every teacher comes to a co-teaching

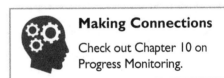

**Making Connections**

Check out Chapter 10 on Progress Monitoring.

situation with different experiences and backgrounds, having a conversation about assessment beliefs is important to prevent future frustration or issues. For example, co-teachers should consider using the questions below as a starting point for quality discussions around co-assessing:

- Should homework be graded? If so, how often?
- What assessments should be included in the gradebook?
- Should feedback be provided to students on everything we collect? How should we provide this feedback? Written? Verbal?
- Who is going to grade what assessments? Will we take turns, or is there something that each of us will always "own"?
- When and how should we keep parents informed of their child's progress?

- What assessments, if any, need to be modified, adapted, or enriched for specific students?
- How are we documenting assessment information for IEPs?
- How can we ensure that we are regularly providing multiple means of expression for students to show what they've learned?
- When, how, and how often should we assess ourselves and our co-teaching relationship? How should we communicate to one another our feelings?

Co-assessing can provide opportunities for teachers to understand what students already know about a topic before it is taught. This will give you a better start at grouping students and differentiating instruction. Often, teachers report feeling guilty about not giving their higher-level learners as much attention as the ones who struggle. When preassessment is used to determine what students already know about a topic, then co-teachers can work together to provide meaningful learning experiences for the high-level student instead of forcing them to sit through material they already know. When teachers use strategies such as compacting the curriculum to move beyond what the curriculum requires or project-based learning to have students collaborate, the students are learning critical skills that will help challenge them and extend their learning (Galvan & Coronado, 2014; Hughes & Murawski, 2001; Reis & Renzulli, 1992). These strategies can help English language learners, gifted learners, twice-exceptional students, students with disabilities, and peers without identified exceptional needs.

**Making Connections**

Check out Chapter 15 on English Language Learners and Chapter 17 on Twice-Exceptional Learners.

Preassessments not only benefit students who struggle, but also can be used to gain a holistic picture of the entire class so everyone benefits.

During instruction, co-teachers should utilize formative assessments. *Formative assessments* are defined as "a planned process that uses assessments to inform changes in instruction or learning" (Popham, 2008, p. 17). Using formative assessments to adjust ongoing instruction fits in nicely with the co-teaching instructional approaches. As data trends emerge, co-teachers are able to use flexible groups to pre-teach, reinforce, or enrich the content that was or will be taught. When teachers use data formatively to drive instruction, student achievement goes up (Conderman & Hedin, 2012). However, imagine how much easier it will be to create assessments, give assessments, analyze data, and plan the next step of instruction when you have two people! Not to mention the fact that now you have a partner to help you *meet* all the diverse needs the data just showed you.

Assessing your own developing relationship is important, too. Take time to discuss what is working for you both and what is not. Dieker's (2015) co-teaching lesson planner is an excellent resource because it has regular questions throughout the planner that teams are asked to respond to with one another. Proactively considering what might be your pet peeves or areas of concern is a smart move for any team—new or veteran. Teacher teams were once optional, utilized only by those who were outgoing and had a knack for getting along with others. Collaboration among educators is no longer an option; it is an essential part of educating children (Cramer & Stivers, 2007). But even the least "touchy feely" teacher can collaborate and have a healthy and collaborative relationship with a co-teacher. Our bulleted points give you some suggestions to consider as you embark on your co-teaching experience.

 ## CO-TEACHING PITFALLS

✗ **STOP calling it co-teaching unless you are able to co-plan, co-instruct, and co-assess on a regular basis.** If these three components are not happening, then you cannot claim that you are truly co-teaching. What we often see is co-existing. Two teachers are sharing a room, but one acts more like an aide because there has been no proactive planning of instruction.

✗ **STOP using the words "my students" and "your students."** These need to be omitted from your vocabulary if you are co-teaching. It is not about students who are receiving special education services versus the rest of the class. As co-teachers, both of you now "own" all the students.

✗ **STOP breaking up the grading.** In many situations, we see the special education teacher grading for the students with an IEP and the general education teacher doing the rest of the grading. This results in another mine-yours situation, which we want to avoid. Instead, share grading and be sure you both have input in student grades.

✗ **STOP the "parallel play."** It may seem easy to just each take a group and do your own thing. However, if time has not been set aside to work out mutual ownership of the classroom, pooled resources, and finding common ground on basic classroom rules and procedures, you will have a much more challenging school year as co-teachers. Take the time to get to know each other and to establish a truly shared environment.

✗ **STOP complaining.** Don't assume your administrators know what you need as co-teachers to be successful. Reach out to them and schedule a meeting to discuss what is working well and what needs you may have. Many administrators have no prior experience with co-teaching, so they won't know what you need or what to expect. Don't wait for them to come to see you; take initiative and invite them in to see a co-taught lesson or to listen in on your co-planning sessions!

✗ **STOP recreating the wheel.** Co-teaching isn't new, and honestly, your issues are probably not unique. Rather than trying to come up with a whole new game plan for finding time to plan, go online and see what other teachers are doing. Rather than spending hours designing a co-taught lesson, see if others have already created one on your topic. There is a free lesson plan template and example lessons on the 2 TEACH LLC website.

**Plugged In**

For resources on co-teaching and co-planning, see the 2 TEACH website at www.2TeachLLC.com.

### Administrators:

✗ **STOP switching partners constantly.** The longer co-teachers can stay together, the easier and more effective the service delivery becomes (Murawski & Dieker, 2012). Both teachers begin to blend their expertise over time. If you change teachers frequently, they don't have time to learn the content, the strategies, or one another. Try to keep teams together for a few years!

✗ **STOP pulling the special educator out to be a substitute teacher.** We get it. You have a class with no substitute teacher and you see another class with two teachers in it. As tempting as this may be, you need to avoid using a co-teacher as a sub. First of all, the students who have been identified as needing co-teaching are depending on the quality instruction from both their teachers. Second, they are legally entitled to that service if it has been written in their IEP. Third, you are negatively impacting the consistency and trust between co-teachers if one can't be depended on to be there. Be creative, find another way to cover that class.

✗ **STOP putting too many students with special needs in the same class.** On average, no more than 25% to 30% of the class should be comprised of students identified as needing special services (Murawski & Dieker, 2012; Villa & Thousand, 2016). This is considered closer to what is called *natural proportion* of individuals with disabilities in society. Keeping to this percentage will not only include sufficient students with exceptional needs to warrant a full-time co-teacher, but it will also prevent teacher burnout by not creating a de facto special education class.

✗ **STOP assessing co-taught classes the same way you assessed solo-taught classes.** They are different and should be assessed as such. Standard observation and walk-through tools won't be geared to pick up the activities in which both teachers are engaged (or should be).

Use the co-teaching core competencies to see how well your teams are doing. Assess both teachers simultaneously so you are judging the team as a unit, not as independent teachers.

**Plugged In**

Check out the Co-teaching Core Competencies at www.coteachsolutions.com.

## STRATEGIES FOR SUCCESS

✔ **PLAN before the school year starts.** Set aside time to work out expectations and come to common agreements on things such as classroom management, grading, and roles and responsibilities. Remember, co-teaching is like a marriage (Murawski, 2009). Once you get "engaged," it's all about the planning!

✔ **BE CONSISTENT.** Start and end the class period together. If one teacher is often late or absent, students will begin to consider the other adult as the "real" teacher. Plus, how much time would you want to spend planning a great lesson with someone if you weren't sure they'd even show up for it?

✔ **PROVIDE instruction for all students in the same space.** Pull out instruction should be minimal, and if it is necessary, students who leave the class should be a heterogeneous group to prevent any stigma. For example, if you want to offer reading a test aloud, offer it to anyone in the class who feels they would benefit.

✔ **HOLD meeting times sacred.** You need to meet with your partner. Seriously, you *need* to. You might be a veteran teacher, but in sharing a class you are going to need to collaborate to plan instruction, collect and analyze data from assessments, and divide responsibilities for classroom duties. Co-planning sessions can easily be "eaten up" by phone calls, parent meetings, IEP paperwork, and other "urgent" issues. We know those are important, but meeting with your partner is, too. Hold your designated co-planning sessions sacred to ensure you are providing the best instruction for students.

✔ **COLLABORATE to analyze data and make instructional decisions based on assessments.** Look at your data to help you determine flexible grouping, how to address IEP goals, how to differentiate the assessments used to allow more student choice, and so on. Be strategic. It's perfectly fine to have times when you divide and conquer (e.g., "I'll do Monday's grading if you do Tuesday's."), but be sure to share results and discuss *why* students did or did not do well.

✔ **MIX it up!** There are five co-teaching approaches and myriad ways to combine them. Utilize the variety of co-teaching instructional approaches to maximize the benefits for students. One approach does not fit all, nor does it fit a particular disability type, grade level, or subject. Think about which approach or approaches work best for tomorrow's lesson, given the student group you have, their needs, their cultures and backgrounds, and the objective of the lesson.

**Making Connections**

Check out Chapter 6 on Culturally Responsive Teaching.

✔ **DEMONSTRATE your parity.** How can you do that? Make sure that both teachers have equal "face time" with the students, both names are on the door, both names are on parent communications, both teachers are present at open house, and both teachers have a desk in the room. Don't have room for two teacher desks? Clear out some drawers in the one desk that is there. No one likes to feel displaced; make sure that, at least during the time you are together, you both feel that the space you are in is both of yours.

✔ **ASK YOURSELVES the essential question for co-teaching.** How is what the two of you "are doing together *substantively different* and *better for students* than what one teacher would do alone" (Murawski & Spencer, 2011, p. 96)? This question can be used as a formative assessment for each co-teaching pair to reflect and discuss how they can continually work together to provide the best educational opportunities for students. It is also appropriate for administrators to ask when coming in to observe co-teaching in action.

✔ **KEEP an open line of communication!** You know what they say: The most important component of any good marriage is communication. Identify and address any problems or conflicts with each other promptly and professionally. To adequately serve the students in your co-taught class, co-teachers need to take care of their relationship first. If you two are bickering or feeling poorly about your relationship, it will come across to your students. If need be, go talk to a colleague whom you both respect and ask him or her to play marriage counselor for you!

✔ **BE STRATEGIC about how you will spend your time together.** If you are not co-teaching and are only able to work with a colleague for a short amount of time daily or weekly, consider how that time is best spent. "Facilitated support" is when you and your colleague choose if you will spend your time co-planning *or* co-instructing *or* co-assessing (Murawski & Dieker, 2012). If you can't do full-blown co-teaching, facilitated support at least allows you both to proactively know how you will collaborate when you are together; this is much better than doing a quick "pop-in" or "drive-by," which rarely tends to benefit students or teachers!

## Administrators:

- ✔ **READ up on co-teaching.** Throwing two people together in the same class simply isn't sufficient. You need to know the difference between consultation, collaboration, in-class support, and co-teaching. Not every teacher will be able to co-teach; nor will they be able to co-teach with multiple partners. Set up your teams carefully and with as much teacher input as possible.

- ✔ **SCHEDULE strategically.** If inclusion is a priority for you (and it should be!), then you will need to rethink the way you do your master schedule. This means ensuring that special educators are clustered by grade or subject so they are not too spread out, that general educators do not have too many different partners, that classes do not have more than 25% to 30% of the class with special needs, that co-teachers have rooms near one another when possible, and so on. To learn more about how to set up a strong schedule for co-teaching, read *Leading the Co-Teaching Dance: Leadership Strategies to Enhance Team Outcomes* by Murawski and Dieker (2012).

- ✔ **GIVE THEM TIME.** Teachers need common planning time in their regular schedule to meet and plan together. This can be done through shared planning periods, stipends for planning time, the use of substitute teachers, professional learning communities (PLCs), communities of practice (CoP), and more. In addition to planning time, teachers also need time to gel as a team. Too often, co-teaching teams are broken up after just a semester or year; this simply doesn't allow them to build their skills in working with diverse learners.

- ✔ **SUPPORT continuous improvement.** All teams can improve. Using the Collaborative Teaching Improvement Model of Excellence (CTIME), you can help teachers self-identify where they would like to improve first (Murawski & Lochner, in press). Teachers then use a microteaching process to work on that particular area, getting feedback from peers and using videotape to see themselves. This helps increase buy-in, focus instruction, reduce overwhelmedness and burnout, and provide opportunities for self-reflection. The CTIME process is described more fully in *No Fail Co-Teaching* by Murawski and Lochner (in press).

## CO-PLANNING TABLE TENT

**Directions**: Photocopy this page and cut out the tent. Copy it onto colored paper and laminate it. Fold it in half and make a table tent. Sit the table tent on the table as you and your partner plan, to help you remember the co-teaching approaches and the What/How/Who planning strategy.

**Efficient and Effective Co-Planning: What/How/Who Approach**
Murawski, W. W. (2012). Ten tips for using co-planning time more efficiently. *TEACHING Exceptional Children, 44*(4), 8–15.

1. **WHAT:** What is the content that needs to be taught? What are the big ideas and essential questions for all, most, and some to learn?

2. **HOW:** How can we use UDL strategies to teach it (i.e., multiple means of representation, engagement, and expression)? How long is the lesson? Which co-teaching approach/es will best meet the needs of the learners and the lesson? How will we assess learning?

3. **WHO:** Who might still struggle even after we create a universally designed lesson? Who might need additional differentiation? Who will do what in creating and implementing the lesson?

. . . . . . . . . . . . . . . . . . . . . . . . . . . . . .   fold   . . . . . . . . . . . . . . . . . . . . . . . . . . . .

### 5 Co-Teaching Approaches
Bauwens, J., Hourcade, J., & Friend, M. (1989). Cooperative teaching: A model for general and special education integration. *Remedial and Special Education, 35*(4), 19–24; Murawski, W. W. (2010). *Collaborative teaching in elementary schools: Making the co-teaching marriage work!* Thousand Oaks, CA: Corwin.

- **One Teach-One Support:** One teacher leads instruction, while the other actively supports learning through questioning, data collection, monitoring, proximity control, and so on.
- **Parallel Teaching:** Both teachers divide the class in half. They can teach the same content in the same way, same content in different ways, or teach different content altogether.
- **Station Teaching:** Teachers divide the class into three or more small groups. Groups rotate around with different activities. Teachers can man a station or supervise multiple groups.
- **Alternative Teaching:** Teachers divide the class into a large group and a small group. The groups can be for re-teaching, pre-teaching, or enrichment.
- **Team Teaching:** Both teachers share the stage for modeling, debating, roleplaying, and the like.

## CO-TEACHING CORE COMPETENCIES

1.2  Ask fors: Co-Instruction: Evidence of Differentiation

1.6  It is difficult to tell students with special needs from the general education students.

1.8  Co-teachers phrase questions and statements so that it is obvious that all students in the class are included.

1.9  Students' conversations evidence a sense of community including peers with disabilities and from diverse backgrounds.

2.7  Both teachers engage in appropriate behavior management strategies as needed and are consistent in their approach to behavior management.

3.7  Differentiated content and strategies, based on formative assessment are used to meet the range of learning needs.

4.5  Two or more professionals working together in the same physical space.

5.7  A variety of instructional approaches (five co-teaching approaches) are used, include regrouping students.

5.9  Communication (both verbal and nonverbal) between co-teachers is clear and positive.

6.1  Ask fors: Evidence of Co-Assessment

7.2  Ask fors: Evidence of Co-Planning

8.1  Ask fors: Evidence of Co-Instruction: Grouping

8.5  Ask fors: Evidence of Co-Instruction: Parity

8.6  During instruction, both teachers assist students with and without disabilities.

8.8  Class instruction and activities proactively promote multiple modes of representation, engagement and expression (Universal Design for Learning [UDL]).

8.13 Technology (to include Assistive Technology) is used to enhance accessibility and learning.

8.16 Co-teachers ask questions at a variety of levels to meet *all* students' needs (basic recall to higher order thinking).

9.5  Class environment demonstrates parity and collaboration (both names on board, sharing materials, and space).

9.6  The class moves smoothly with evidence of co-planning and communication between co-teachers.

9.10 Co-teachers use language ("we"; "our") that demonstrates true collaboration and shared responsibility.

11.3 It is difficult to tell the specialist from the general educator.

11.6 Both teachers begin and end class together and remain in the room the entire time.

*Source:* Murawski, W. W., & Lochner, W. W. (2016). Co-teaching core competencies. Winnetka, CA: 2 TEACH LLC. Retrieved from www.coteachsolutions.com

# REFERENCES

Bauwens, J., Hourcade, J., & Friend, M. (1989). Cooperative teaching: A model for general and special education integration. *Remedial and Special Education, 35*(4), 19–24.

Brinkmann, J., & Twiford, T. (2012). Voices from the field: Skill sets needed for effective collaboration and co-teaching. *International Journal of Educational Leadership Preparation, 7*(3), 1–13.

Conderman, G., & Hedin, L. (2012). Purposeful assessment practices for co-teachers. *TEACHING Exceptional Children, 44*(4), 18–27.

Conderman, G., & Hedin, L. R. (2014). Co-teaching with strategy instruction. *Intervention in School and Clinic, 49*(3), 156–163.

Cramer, S., & Stivers, J. (2007). Don't give up! Practical strategies for challenging collaborations. *TEACHING Exceptional Children, 39*(6), 6–11.

Dieker, L. (2015). *The co-planner: Two professionals + one plan for co-teaching* (4th ed.). Whitefish Bay, WI: Knowledge by Design.

Embury, D. C., & Kroeger, S. D. (2012). Let's ask the kids: Consumer constructions of co-teaching. *International Journal of Special Education, 27*(2), 102–112.

Ford, M. P. (2005). *Differentiation through flexible grouping: Successfully reaching all readers.* Naperville, IL: Learning Point Associates.

Friend, M. (2016). Welcome to co-teaching 2.0. *Educational Leadership, 73*(4), 16.

Friend, M., Cook, L., Hurley-Chamberlain, D., & Shamberger, C. (2010). Co-teaching: An illustration of the complexity of collaboration in special education. *Journal of Educational and Psychological Consultation, 20*(1), 9–27.

Galvan, M. E., & Coronado, J. M. (2014). Problem-based and project-based learning: Promoting differentiated instruction. *National Teacher Education Journal, 7*(4), 39–42.

Howard, L., & Potts, E. A. (2009). Using co-planning time: Strategies for a successful co-teaching marriage. *TEACHING Exceptional Children Plus, 5*(4), 2–12.

Hughes, C. E., & Murawski, W. W. (2001). Lessons from another field: Applying co-teaching strategies to gifted education. *Gifted Child Quarterly, 45*(3), 195–204.

King-Sears, M. E., & Bowman-Kruhm, M. (2011). Specialized reading instruction for adolescents with learning disabilities: What special education co-teachers say. *Learning Disabilities Research & Practice, 26*(3), 172–184.

Murawski, W. W. (2009). *Collaborative teaching in secondary schools: Making the co-teaching marriage work!* Thousand Oaks, CA: Corwin.

Murawski, W. W. (2010). *Collaborative teaching in elementary schools: Making the co-teaching marriage work!* Thousand Oaks, CA: Corwin.

Murawski, W. W. (2012). Ten tips for using co-planning time more efficiently. *TEACHING Exceptional Children, 44*(4), 8–15.

Murawski, W. W., & Bernhardt, P. (2015). An administrator's guide to co-teaching. *Educational Leadership, 73*(4), 30–34.

Murawski, W. W., & Dieker, L. (2012). *Leading the co-teaching dance: Leadership strategies to enhance team outcomes.* Arlington, VA: Council for Exceptional Children.

Murawski, W. W., & Lochner, W. W. (2016). Co-teaching core competencies. Winnetka, CA: 2 TEACH LLC. Retrieved from www.coteachsolutions.com

Murawski, W. W., & Lochner, W. W. (in press). *No fail co-teaching: A data-driven continuous improvement model.* Arlington, VA: Association for Supervision and Curriculum Development.

Murawski, W. W., & Spencer, S. (2011). *Collaborate, communicate, and differentiate! How to increase student learning in today's diverse schools.* Thousand Oaks, CA: Corwin.

Popham, W. J. (2008). Formative assessment: Seven stepping-stones to success. *Principal Leadership, 9*(1), 16–20.

Reid, J. (2002). *Managing small-group learning.* Newton, Australia: Primary English Teaching Association.

Reis, S. M., & Renzulli, J. S. (1992). Using curriculum compacting to challenge the above-average. *Educational Leadership, 50*(2), 51–57.

Scruggs, T. E., Mastropieri, M. A., & McDuffie, K. A. (2007). Co-teaching in inclusive classrooms: A metasynthesis of qualitative research. *Exceptional Children, 73*(4), 392–416.

Shaffer, L., & Thomas-Brown, K. (2015). Enhancing teacher competency through co-teaching and embedded professional development. *Journal of Education and Training Studies, 3*(3), 117–125.

Strogilos, V., & Avramidis, E. (2016). Teaching experiences of students with special educational needs in co-taught and non–co-taught classes. *Journal of Research in Special Educational Needs, 16*(1), 24–33.

Tomlinson, C. A. (1995). *How to differentiate instruction in mixed-ability classrooms.* Alexandria, VA: Association for Supervision and Curriculum Development.

U.S. Department of Education. (2013). Office of Special Education Programs, Individuals with Disabilities Act (IDEA) database. Retrieved from http://nces.ed.gov/programs/digest/d13/tables/dt13_204.60.asp

Villa, R., & Thousand, J. (2016). *The inclusive education checklist: A self-assessment of best practices.* Naples, FL: Dude.

# ADDITIONAL RECOMMENDED READING

Friend, M., Embury, D. C., & Clarke, L. (2015). Co-teaching versus apprentice teaching: An analysis of similarities and differences. *Teacher Education and Special Education, 38*(2), 79–87.

Murawski, W. W., & Dieker, L. A. (2008). 50 ways to keep your co-teacher. *TEACHING Exceptional Children, 40*(4), 40–48.

Murawski, W. W., & Lochner, W. W. (2011). Observing co-teaching: What to ask for, look for, and listen for. *Intervention in School and Clinic, 46*(3), 174–183.

Pratt, S. M. (2014). Building mentorships: How administrators can support co-teachers in mentoring and coaching each other. *Research to Practice: K–12 Scholarship Journal, 4*, 33–39.

Reilly, M. (2015). Saying what you mean without being mean. *Educational Leadership, 73*(4), 36.

Simpson, J. F., Thurston, R. J., & James, L. E. (2014). Exploring personality differences of teachers for co-teaching. *Journal of Instructional Psychology, 41*(4), 100–105.

## TOP FIVE WEBSITES TO SUPPORT CO-TEACHING AND COLLABORATION

➡ www.2TeachLLC.com

➡ www.marilynfriend.com

➡ www.coteachsolutions.com

➡ http://www.mrfunkyteacher.com/teachers/co-teaching

➡ http://education.wm.edu/centers/ttac/resources/articles/consultcollab orate/coteachingmovingbeyond/index.php

## THE APPS WE LOVE

➡ Edmodo

➡ gTasks

➡ Minute

➡ GroupMe

➡ Personality Quiz

# 10

# *Progress Monitoring*

## *Your Classroom Itinerary*

Kyena E. Cornelius and Kimberly M. Johnson-Harris
*Minnesota State University, Mankato*

## IF IT'S FRIDAY, THIS MUST BE ROME

The running joke of any organized tour goes something like, "Well, if today is Friday, this must be Rome." Name any day of the week and any famous city, the joke still applies. It is as if the travelers are so tired and over-whelmed that they do not even recognize the famous landmarks of their location. A look out of the train window would reveal the beauty of the Swiss Alps, perhaps a glimpse of the Matterhorn in the distance could tell the weary travelers they have not quite made it into Italy. However, the itinerary says it is time to be in Rome, so therefore they *must* be in Rome, right? Unfortunately, Rome is still a day's ride away. But how would the travelers know if they did not examine the progression of the trip, take note of the time spent at each stop, and record each landmark along the way?

If the final destination is Rome and we must be there by Friday, how do we make that happen? How do we plan and monitor our trip to make sure we are in our final destination by the time we need to be there? Does the tour guide decide to get back on track by skipping Milan or Venice?

Maybe, but the professional tour guide plans before the trip begins, makes adjustments based on detours or longer layovers, and recalculates travel time based on weather and other obstacles. With a plan, conscious progress monitoring, and correction when necessary, travelers will not need to skip beautiful sights along the way.

As a teacher, you are the tour guide and your students' individualized education program (IEP) goals are the final destination. You must track students' progress, examine their stops along the way, and record each celebration they experience. Otherwise, you will never know where your young travelers are along their journey or the estimated time of arrival at the destination. In addition to being a good idea, progress monitoring is a legal requirement of the IEP. Unfortunately, it is also the component of the IEP that is most likely to be out of compliance (Etscheidt, 2006). Many IEP teams do not develop practical plans for monitoring progress toward IEP goals. This is typically left to teacher discretion, but teachers do not always know how to collect meaningful data. That is about to change. We are going to share tools you can use to measure student growth. Our purpose is to help you develop a system to help students with disabilities, some of the neediest travelers, appreciate all the beautiful landmarks and arrive at their final destination on schedule.

## EXACTLY WHAT IS PROGRESS MONITORING?

Progress monitoring is the "collection of data that is used to determine the impact of instruction and intervention over a short period of time" (Salvia, Ysseldyke, & Bolt, 2010, p. 423). Progress monitoring takes many forms depending on the content being taught and the purpose for collecting the data. Curriculum-based measurement (CBM) and formative assessment are two forms of progress monitoring that capture student growth. Each looks slightly different in practice in terms of timing, delivery, data collection procedures, and information to be gleaned. We briefly explain both.

Research suggests that outcomes for students with disabilities are improved when "students' instructional gaps are identified, progress relative to these gaps is monitored, and explicit and intensive intervention is provided" (Vaughn & Linan-Thompson, 2003, p. 145). Identifying students' gaps and monitoring their progress toward the end goal is not only a legal requirement, it is also logical (Hosp & Ardoin, 2008). Progress monitoring tools should capture data that is specific enough to (a) evidence instructional progress (Yell & Drasgow, 2007), (b) inform strategies and teaching methods (Hojnoski, Gischlar, & Missall, 2009), and (c) ensure that specialized instruction is meaningful and beneficial (Etscheidt, 2006; Yell & Drasgow, 2007).

Using progress monitoring to measure student growth must also be intentional. The best way to ensure that progress monitoring happens is to embed it into lesson planning. Whether you are using CBM to measure improvement of basic skills (Deno, 2003) or measuring a variety of skills through formative assessment (Conderman & Hedin, 2012), you must be deliberate in your efforts to gather data. So how do you know which to use? Let's review.

**Key Concepts**

Your major concepts in progress monitoring?

- Curriculum-based measurements (CBM)
- Formative assessments

**Curriculum-based measurement.** While the term *progress monitoring* is often used synonymously with CBM, they are not one and the same. Curriculum-based measurements are quick tests that are used to measure student progress toward specific content knowledge (Stecker, Lembke, Foegen, 2008) and basic skills (Deno, 2003) that should be mastered by the end of the school year. These short tests are generally administered weekly and take less than 5 minutes. Results are graphed and teachers can monitor IEP progress in one visual display. For example, a teacher could use the Dynamic Indicators of Basic Early Literacy Skills (DIBELS) CBM, to measure student progress on phonological awareness and reading fluency. While the information gleaned from CBM data does allow for the teacher to change the course of instruction from week to week, it does not provide information necessary for the teacher to change the course of instruction mid-lesson or for the lesson that will be taught tomorrow.

**Formative assessment.** Summative and formative assessments are both vital to evaluating student learning. "Formative assessment is assessment used *for* student learning while summative assessment is assessment *of* student learning" (Blanks, 2015, p. 217). When using these terms for students with disabilities, think of the annual IEP meeting where evidence of IEP progress is provided to parents as summative assessment. Formative assessments are used as a means to measure progress throughout the year. Formative assessments can be administered before, during, or after a learning segment or unit of instruction (Conderman & Hedin, 2012). Before a learning segment, a formative assessment can be administered to provide the teacher with information related to students' prior learning and life experience. It can also provide information related to maintenance of previously taught skills. When kids say "we learned this already," a formative assessment would let you know if that is true. Formative assessments can be administered during a learning segment to provide the teacher with on-the-spot information related to whether learners have acquired specific skills targeted in the IEP (Alexandrin, 2003). Naturally, they can also let you know how students are doing with the general education content, but since our focus is on students with special needs, we want to be sure you are not forgetting to address their IEP goals and objectives. When formative assessment is used at the conclusion of a lesson, teachers are again able to collect data on students' progress. Formative assessments administered after a learning segment also provide the teacher with information related to students' metacognitive skills (i.e., students' awareness of their own learning process) and executive functioning skills (i.e., students' ability to plan and persevere through a task; Black & Wiliam, 2009). For example, a teacher could give a formative assessment that asks students to explain the process they used to solve a problem or the strategy they used to complete a task. Many students with disabilities need to be explicitly taught these skills; measuring them regularly informs teachers of the progress being made.

Accurate progress monitoring helps ensure that interventions or strategies being implemented are responsive to students' needs (Vaughn & Linan-Thompson, 2003). Based on the data collected, you will know whether you should alter materials, adjust student groupings, increase or decrease time spent on tasks, and/or change motivational strategies (Stecker et al., 2008). We think that would be helpful for any teacher, don't you? The first step is to make a plan to collect data that informs your instructional decisions. By choosing the proper tools (see Your Travel Brochures at the end of the chapter) and using them over time, you will have enough evidence to support your reports of student progress. Remember, the IEP is the heart of a student's special education program and the law requires both general and special education teachers to monitor and report progress on IEP goals and objectives regularly (Yell & Drasgow, 2007). When progress on IEP goals is not monitored, the IEP is rendered useless.

## HOW TO AVOID DERAILMENT

Teachers:

✗ **STOP using the terms** *progress monitoring* **and** *CBM* **interchangeably.** Progress monitoring is a collection of data that informs instructional decision-making and IEP progress. CBMs are content specific, quick tests used to measure student progress in basic skills such as math, reading, writing, and spelling. Think about it this way, a resort is a hotel, but not every hotel is a resort; CBM is a form of progress monitoring, but not every form of progress monitoring is a CBM.

✗ **STOP ignoring IEP goals and objectives in the planning process.** IEP goals and objectives should be a major point of consideration when planning instruction, not just the general education content. Remember that students with disabilities are supposed to also have specially designed instruction; how have you worked that into your lesson plan? If that seems overwhelming, consider co-teaching!

**Making Connections**

Check out Chapter 9 on Co-Teaching.

✗ **STOP using summative assessments and/or standardized tests as the only progress monitoring tools.** Summative assessments and standardized tests do not provide the teacher with the necessary information to capture the students' subtle changes over time related to IEP goals.

✗ **STOP thinking CBM is the *only* way to monitor progress.** Using *both* CBM and formative assessments provides a well-rounded understanding of student progress and timely instructional adjustments.

✗ **STOP thinking the assessment *is* the intervention.** A CBM or formative assessment is not instructive. Neither moves student learning forward. These assessments are done to provide the teacher with necessary information to make instructional decisions.

✗ **STOP only using "thumbs up/thumbs down" or merely asking, "Do you understand" to gauge student learning.** These quick checks may not yield true information. Students with disabilities often respond in tandem with nondisabled peer role models.

✗ **STOP evaluating progress based on feelings or perceptions of student understanding.** Teachers are quite intuitive when it comes to their students, but IEP goal progress must be based on defensible data. Too many teachers go to IEP meetings and respond to the questions of progress with "Um . . . yes, sure. I think he can do that."

✗ **STOP ignoring progress monitoring data that should inform instructional decisions.** If we are going to take the time to collect progress monitoring data, we should also take the time to analyze the data and use the information to make appropriate instructional adjustments.

Administrators:

✗ **STOP expecting all teachers and/or teaching teams (e.g., grade level, content area) to do the same thing, on the same day, in the same way.** Specialized instruction that is meaningful and beneficial will look different from one classroom to another. Inclusive classes require individualization.

✗ **STOP relying on student grades and district benchmark scores to measure student progress.** Although students with disabilities are working toward grade-level expectations, their progress is also measured based on IEP goals. Share data with the community on how students are improving behaviorally and socially as well.

**Making Connections**

Check out Chapter 19 on School-to-Home Collaboration.

# HOW TO STAY ON TRACK

**Teachers:**

✔ **USE IEP goals and objectives in the planning process.** IEP goals and objectives must be targeted immediately, intensively, and purposefully. Plan instruction to address them and monitor progress toward them. By co-planning, special and general educators are each able to bring in their expertise. As the general educator ensures the content focus, the special educator can ensure the specially designed instruction that also addresses IEP goals.

✔ **CREATE meaningful progress monitoring strategies/activities and write them into your lesson plan.** Progress monitoring should be quick and easy to administer so it does not take time away from instruction, sensitive to change to detect day-to-day differences, and educationally meaningful so that we are measuring what the IEP team determined was important. For example, if a teacher is planning a writing lesson about adding three supporting details to paragraphs, she would write in her unguided practice portion of the lesson plan to check the number of supporting details in each students' paragraph. If Sean, Alex, and Kiersten each only have one supporting detail, the teacher would be alerted that she should provide some additional instruction for these students before the next lesson.

✔ **CREATE meaningful data collection tools.** Data collection tools should be easy to use, capture patterns of growth and regression, and track progress on IEP goals and objectives. Data collection tools should also be representative of overall skills and sub-skills/discrete skills (e.g., a checklist might include correct words per minute and specific targeted word families). See the websites at the end of this chapter for numerous resources. There are also ready-to-use formative assessment templates in the article, *Formative Assessment Made Easy: Templates for Collecting Daily Data in Inclusive Classrooms* (Cornelius, 2013).

**Plugged In**

Get templates and strategies from the Regional Special Education Technical Assistance Support Center, the Center on Response to Intervention, and The IRIS Center. All websites are listed at the end of this chapter.

✔ **USE assessment data to inform instructional planning.** Reflect on formative assessment data and adjust tomorrow's instructional plan based on student progress or lack of progress. For example, when you notice that a couple of students missed a concept, plan a small group activity just for them. You can reteach and clarify the missed concept while the rest of the class completes the warm-up activity. This does not require a lot of extra planning. You probably have that back-up explanation already to go, and the materials are still available from today's class. Furthermore, since you are going to do this during the warm-up activity, it does not take away instructional time from the class and gives you a window for direct instruction.

✔ **INTERPRET assessment data to alter instructional delivery.** Consider the following questions and make just-in-time adjustments as you move through your lesson. Have these questions written down and within reach until they become part of your routine.

- Do I need to provide a clearer description and/or demonstration to help students understand the goals of the lesson?
- Do I need to provide more models (e.g., examples and nonexamples)?
- Do I need to provide more opportunities for practice?
- Do I need to provide different materials?
- Have I addressed potential barriers to understanding?
- Have I addressed potential barriers to demonstration of knowledge and understanding?
- Do I need to provide more specific feedback and correction?
- Do I need to connect more to prior knowledge/experience?

✔ **USE portable data collection methods for monitoring progress on behavioral goals.**

- Wear an apron with clothespins attached to the pocket. When a behavior is observed, place a clothespin in a pocket. Count the clothespins in the pocket at the end of the class period and mark progress on your graph.
- Use a clicker attached to your pants pocket. When a behavior is observed, click the clicker once. At the end of the day, the total on your clicker is the total to be graphed.
- Cut a strip of paper about an inch wide. Draw lines to divide the strip into three or four sections and write students' names in each section. Tape the strip of paper around your wrist, and you are ready to mark a tally each time a behavior is observed—all you need is a pen or pencil.
- Move paperclips from one pocket to another when you observe a behavior.

✔ **USE apps available for your mobile devices.** These apps also allow you to generate printed reports that monitor student progress.

- Class Dojo helps monitor behavior and build classroom communities. This app also allows you to communicate instantly with parents. You can record student progress on behavioral goals to include, but not limited to, staying on task, perseverance, and turning in assignments.

- Poll Everywhere can be used for warm-up activities, during instruction check-ins, quizzes, and exit tickets. This tool allows you to design content specific questions and engage students while you are monitoring their progress. Secondary students especially love the fact that they get to use their cell phones to text in answers. Why not use the technology they depend on for their learning, too?

## YOUR TRAVEL BROCHURES: FORMATIVE ASSESSMENTS YOU CAN USE

**Before Instruction**

- **Anticipation guide:** Students respond in writing to two or three questions about the topic.
- **Warm-ups:** Students complete two or three problems related to the previously taught skills.
- **Pretests:** Students complete a short quiz that directly assesses skills to be taught.

**During Instruction**

- **Class discussions:** The teacher facilitates a discussion that allows her to determine whether students understand key concepts.
- **Response cards:** The teacher asks specific questions and students hold up cards with preprinted responses such as yes or no or A, B, C to show the teacher and/or class their answers.
- **Dry-erase boards:** During the lesson, the teacher asks students to perform specific tasks such as solve a math problem or spell a word correctly. Students perform the task and hold up the individual dry-erase board.

**After Instruction**

- **Exit slips:** Students respond in writing to one or two questions about the topic covered in class or about their evaluation of their own learning.
- **Drafts of writing assignments:** Review what students completed and monitor for either quantity (e.g., number of words, sections completed) or quality (e.g., content accuracy or mechanics).
- **Progress on projects:** As students wrap up their work for the day, they can self-report on their progress. Did they meet today's goal? What will they do first next time? After this is completed, monitor actual progress compared to student reported progress as well as check for quantity and/or quality.

## IEP GOAL MONITORING OPTIONS

- **Comprehensive collection sheet with discrete skills:** This tool can be used during daily reading instruction. As you are planning, review the passages students will read as part of the lesson. Then look to see how many words are in each passage that will be read and fill that space in before class begins, list the sight words in each passage and the targeted word family groups. As students are reading, you can write in the number of errors, check the sight words they read correctly, circle the word family words they read, and count the number of times the student attempted to self-correct their errors.

- **Lesson plan template that embeds IEP goals and data collection:** Purposefully incorporate IEP goals and objectives into your lesson plans. Then purposefully capture the number of opportunities students had to engage with the goal or objective as well as the successful occurrences right on your lesson plan template. This will allow you to collect evidence of student progress and also reflect on missed goals for future lessons. We've included a lesson plan template at the end of the chapter.

- **Daily tracking sheet:** Create this tool while you are lesson planning, after you have determined the number of prompts on a warm-up, guided practice response activities, and exit slips. Have the day's data right at your fingertips to help you gauge student understanding and progress. Make sure to leave room for anecdotal notes that you may miss or forget if you wait until the end of the day to write down.

- **Data sticky notes:** Use sticky notes to collect data. Jot down quick notes about what you observe students doing. During the day you can keep them on a clipboard and then transfer them to cards or student folders. Post-it even helps you organize various goals and contents by providing notepads in several color choices.

- **File folders:** When collecting data, you may need to also collect student work samples for evidence of progress. By using file folders to write down notes while observing students work, you have a great way to document progress and file away student work samples all in one easy step.

## COMPREHENSIVE COLLECTION SHEET WITH DISCRETE SKILLS: EXAMPLE

| Student | Number of Words in Passage | Errors | Sight Words | Word Family Groups | Attempts to Self-Correct |
|---|---|---|---|---|---|
| Curtis | 50 | 16 | Away ✓<br>After ✗<br>There ✓ | "ap"<br>ⓒap, nap, nap | // |
| Julia | 45 | 8 | There ✗<br>Said ✓<br>Where ✗ | "ap"<br>nap, ⓛap, ⓣap | //// |
| Noah | 50 | 4 | Away ✓<br>Said ✗<br>What ✓ | "ap"<br>ⓒap, ⓝap, tap | //// |

# COMPREHENSIVE COLLECTION SHEET WITH DISCRETE SKILLS: BLANK

| Student | Number of Words in Passage | Errors | Sight Words | Word Family Groups | Attempts to Self-Correct |
|---------|---------------------------|--------|-------------|--------------------|--------------------------|
|         |                           |        |             |                    |                          |
|         |                           |        |             |                    |                          |
|         |                           |        |             |                    |                          |

# LESSON PLAN TEMPLATE THAT EMBEDS IEP GOALS AND DATA COLLECTION

Subject: _____  Lesson Objective: _____

Content Standard:

Related IEP Goal/Objective:

Essential Question:

Prerequisite Skills/Key Vocabulary:

| Instructional Plan | Modifications/Accommodations | Materials |
|---|---|---|
| | | |

| Student | Targeted Skill/Objective | Attempts/Opportunities | Successful Occurrences |
|---|---|---|---|
| | | | |
| | | | |
| | | | |
| | | | |

# DAILY TRACKING SHEET: EXAMPLE

| Student | Math: Solving for "x" | | | | | | | | | | | | | | | English | | | | | | | | | | |
| --- | --- | --- | --- | --- | --- | --- | --- | --- | --- | --- | --- | --- | --- | --- | --- | --- | --- | --- | --- | --- | --- | --- | --- | --- | --- |
| | Warm-Up Inverse Operations | | | | | Response Card Practice Problems | | | | Exit Ticket Order of Operations | | | | | | Warm-Up | | | | | Writing Probe Transition Sentences | | | | Essay Progress |
| | 1 | 2 | 3 | 4 | 5 | 1 | 2 | 3 | 4 | P | E | M | D | A | S | 1 | 2 | 3 | 4 | 5 | 1 | 2 | 3 | 4 | Next Step |
| Curtis | | ✓ | ✓ | ✓ | ✓ | ✓ | ✓ | ✓ | | ✓ | ✓ | ✓ | ✓ | ✓ | ✓ | ✓ | ✓ | ✓ | ✓ | ✓ | ✓ | ✓ | | ✓ | Start body |
| Julia | ✓ | | ✓ | | | | ✓ | ✓ | | ✓ | | ✓ | ✓ | ✓ | ✓ | ✓ | ✓ | ✓ | ✓ | ✓ | ✓ | | ✓ | ✓ | Finish intro |
| Noah | | ✓ | ✓ | ✓ | ✓ | ✓ | ✓ | | | ✓ | | ✓ | ✓ | ✓ | ✓ | ✓ | ✓ | ✓ | ✓ | ✓ | ✓ | | | ✓ | Start body |
| Caity | ✓ | ✓ | ✓ | ✓ | ✓ | ✓ | ✓ | | | ✓ | | | ✓ | ✓ | ✓ | ✓ | ✓ | ✓ | ✓ | ✓ | ✓ | ✓ | | ✓ | Start conclusion |
| Colin | ✓ | ✓ | ✓ | ✓ | ✓ | ✓ | | | | ✓ | | ✓ | ✓ | | ✓ | ✓ | ✓ | ✓ | ✓ | ✓ | ✓ | | ✓ | ✓ | Finish body |

**Notes:** Julia subtracts rather than divides for the inverse operation of multiplication.

All students missed the problem with the exponent. Reviewed exponents.

Use exponents in tomorrow's warm-up.

# DAILY TRACKING SHEET: BLANK

| Student | Subject: | | | | | | | | | | | | | | | | | | | | | | Subject: | | | | | | | | | |
|---|---|---|---|---|---|---|---|---|---|---|---|---|---|---|---|---|---|---|---|---|---|---|---|---|---|---|---|---|---|---|---|---|
| | 1 | 2 | 3 | 4 | 5 | 1 | 2 | 3 | 4 | 1 | 2 | 3 | 4 | 5 | 6 | 1 | 2 | 3 | 4 | 5 | 1 | 2 | 3 | 4 | 1 | 2 | 3 | 4 | 5 | | | |
| | | | | | | | | | | | | | | | | | | | | | | | | | | | | | | | | |
| | | | | | | | | | | | | | | | | | | | | | | | | | | | | | | | | |
| | | | | | | | | | | | | | | | | | | | | | | | | | | | | | | | | |
| | | | | | | | | | | | | | | | | | | | | | | | | | | | | | | | | |
| Notes: | | | | | | | | | | | | | | | | | | | | | | | | | | | | | | | | |

# REFERENCES

Alexandrin, J. R. (2003). Using continuous, constructive, classroom evaluations. *TEACHING Exceptional Children, 36*(1), 52–57.

Black, P., & Wiliam, D. (2009). Developing the theory of formative assessment. *Educational Assessment, Evaluation, and Accountability, 21*, 5–31.

Blanks, B. (2015). Amazing assessment. In W. W. Murawski & K. L. Scott (Eds.), *What really works in secondary education* (pp. 216–231). Thousand Oaks, CA: Corwin.

Conderman, G., & Hedin, L. (2012). Classroom assessments that inform instruction. *Kappa Delta Pi Record, 48*, 162–168.

Cornelius, K. E. (2013). Formative assessment made easy: Templates for collecting daily data in inclusive classrooms. *TEACHING Exceptional Children, 45*(5), 14–21.

Deno, S. L. (2003). Developments in curriculum-based measurement. *The Journal of Special Education, 37*, 184–192.

Etscheidt, S. K. (2006). Progress monitoring: Legal issues and recommendations for IEP teams. *TEACHING Exceptional Children, 38*(3), 56–60.

Hojnoski, R. L., Gischlar, K. L., & Missall, K. N. (2009). Improving child outcomes with data-based decision making: Collecting data. *Young Exceptional Children, 12*(3), 32–44.

Hosp, J. L., & Ardoin, S. P. (2008). Assessment for instructional planning. *Assessment for Effective Intervention, 33*(2), 69–77.

Salvia, J., Ysseldyke, J., & Bolt, S. (2010). *Assessment in special and inclusive education*. Belmont, CA: Wadsworth.

Stecker, P. M., Lembke, E. S., & Foegen, A. (2008). Using progress-monitoring data to improve instructional decision making. *Preventing School Failure: Alternative Education for Children and Youth, 52*(2), 48–58.

Vaughn, S., & Linan-Thompson, S. (2003). What is special about special education for students with learning disabilities? *The Journal of Special Education, 37*, 140–147.

Yell, M. L., & Drasgow, E. (2007). The Individuals with Disabilities Education Improvement Act of 2004 and the 2006 regulations: Implications for assessment: Introduction to the special series. *Assessment for Effective Intervention, 32*, 194–201.

# ADDITIONAL RECOMMENDED READING

Burns, M. K., & Parker, D. C. (2014). *Curriculum-based assessment for instructional design: Using data to individualize instruction*. New York, NY: Guilford Press.

Hosp, M. K., Hosp, J. L., & Howell, K. W. (2007). *The ABCs of CBM: A practical guide to curriculum-based measurement*. New York, NY: Guilford Press.

Nagro, S. A., Hooks, S., Fraser, D. W., & Cornelius, K. E. (2016). Whole-group response strategies to promote student engagement in inclusive classrooms. *TEACHING Exceptional Children, 48*, 243–249.

## TOP FIVE WEBSITES TO SUPPORT PROGRESS MONITORING

➡ http://iris.peabody.vanderbilt.edu/iris-resource-locator/?term=assessment

➡ http://www.rti4success.org/essential-components-rti/progress-monitoring

➡ http://www.p12.nysed.gov/specialed/techassist/rsetasc/home.html

➡ http://www.onsetasc.org/resources.cfm?subpage=831879&adminActivate=1

➡ http://trackstudentlearning.weebly.com/apps.html

## APPS WE LOVE

➡ iDoceo

➡ TeacherKit

➡ Super Duper Data Tracker

➡ Classkick

➡ Stick Pick

➡ ClassDojo

➡ Poll Everywhere

# SECTION III

## *What Really Works With Special Populations*

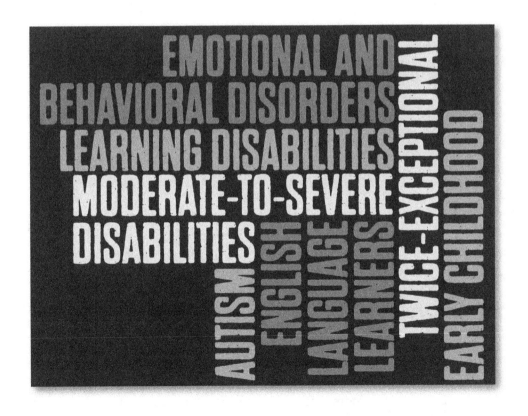

# 11

## Addressing the *"Invisible Disability"*

### Supporting Students With Learning Disabilities

Janet Josephson
*Millersville University*

Anne Brawand
*Kutztown University*

Ruby L. Owiny
*Trinity International University*

## STRATEGIES TO SUPPORT STUDENTS WITH LEARNING DISABILITIES: WHO ARE THESE STUDENTS AND WHAT ARE THEIR NEEDS?

Students with learning disabilities (LD) are a heterogeneous group. Like all students, they have their own unique strengths and areas for development. However, it can often be difficult for these students to meet their potential in the classroom setting due to their "invisible" disability. Over 67% of students with LD spent 80% or more of the school day in the general education classroom in the 2013–2014 school year (U.S. Department of Education, 2015). The recent trends toward inclusion are a major factor in the prevalence of students with LD in general education classes today. Whether instruction is delivered in a general education setting or special education resource room, teachers must plan for "high-quality, intensive instruction" to promote high levels of learning (McLeskey & Waldron, 2011). That's what all teachers strive for though, isn't it? So what makes this difficult or different?

Many students with LD exhibit difficulties in the area of memory and general strategy use, literacy and communication, specific processes and strategies associated with mathematical problems, and motivation and affect (Bryant & Bryant, 2008). Yes, just about everything we as teachers need our students to have to succeed! The high-quality, intensive instruction discussed by McLeskey and Waldron (2011) encourages the provision of instruction that has a strong research base and is more intense than what is typically delivered in a general education classroom. While considering what high-quality, intensive instruction is most appropriate for students, it is equally important to examine students' individual needs when determining what strategies to implement. No two children with LD are alike. Some of you may be thinking, "Whoa! I'm supposed to up my game in intensity and quality, while also individualizing for each student?" Afraid so. But we'll give you strategies on how to do so effectively and efficiently.

So how *do* you meet the needs of students with LD? A key factor in meeting their needs is the implementation of evidence-based practices (EBPs). The use of EBPs is required by the Individuals with Disabilities Education Act (IDEA) and the Elementary and Secondary Education Act (ESEA) as these strategies have been shown to improve outcomes for students with disabilities in high-quality research trials (Torres, Farley, & Cook, 2014). There are several user-friendly online tools that allow teachers to search by grade level and learner characteristic or concern. You can learn more about implementing EBPs by visiting the top websites listed at the end of this chapter. There's a strategy for that!

### Strategies for Developing Memory

Students with LD can be quite forgetful due to short or long-term memory issues. Mnemonics are a set of memory strategies that come in various forms and have been successfully implemented with students with poor memory skills. They can be used across all subject areas. Three commonly applied mnemonic strategies include letter strategies, keyword strategies, and pegword strategies (Mastropieri, & Scruggs, 2014; Uberti, Scruggs, & Mastropieri, 2003).

Letter strategies include acrostics and acronyms. Maybe you recall how FOIL once helped you recall the process for multiplying two binomials in algebra class (first, outside, inside, last). Likewise, maybe the word

HOMES helped you recall the names of the five Great Lakes (Huron, Ontario, Michigan, Erie, Superior).

Keyword strategies are another form of mnemonics that can assist students with LD. Keyword strategies can be especially helpful in assisting students as they learn new vocabulary words. For example, in a science class, the word *ranidae* is the scientific term for frogs. To recall this word, the teacher displays a picture of a frog enjoying the rain (Mastropieri & Scruggs, 2014). The connection between the word *ranidae* and the image of the frog's rainy day can be easily retrieved on a later assessment of vocabulary.

Mathematics keyword strategies are also known as *pegwords*. These help students recall lists and facts (Kleinheksel & Summy, 2003). Pegwords are rhyming words that are linked to numbers (Schumaker, Bulgren, Deshler, & Lenz, 1998). Pegwords can assist students in recalling lists of items, or even math facts. For example, the number two is represented by the pegword *shoe*, while the number five is represented by the pegword *hive*, and the number ten is represented by the pegword *hen*. A student may use these pegwords to recall that $2 \times 5 = 10$ by creating a story in which she steps on a *hive* (5) with her *shoe* (2) and a *hen* (10) pops out of the hive. Although this may seem like a complicated strategy, there is lots of research to suggest its success with students with LD (Mastropieri & Scruggs, 2000).

## Strategies for Developing Visual Processing

Visual processing occurs when the eyes communicate what they see to the brain. Some students with LD have weaknesses in this eye-to-brain communication leading to visual processing disorders. Students may see written symbols incorrectly or have difficulty demonstrating spatial awareness (Hinkley & Smith, 2011). Strategies for developing students' visual processing include using a reading tracker device to help students read line by line in a book, offering audio versions of reading activities when available, providing paper with raised lines for kinesthetic feedback during writing, and breaking down visual-intensive activities into smaller increments of time. For a student with a visual processing deficit, you may want to provide cloze procedure notes rather than having him or her copy notes from the board (Steele, 2008).

## Strategies for Developing Auditory Processing

Students with auditory processing difficulties have trouble processing the information taken in aurally (through their ears). They may have trouble identifying differences between sounds, sequencing sounds during oral communication, or following verbal instructions. So what can you do to help? Supplement oral information with visual supports such as pictures and written instructions. Slow down your speech and use concise directions. Break down multiple-step directions and introduce them one at a time. Do not get frustrated when students don't follow directions or seem to have misunderstood you; they may truly not have processed everything you asked of them. Avoid a lot of straight lecture (Jalongo, 1991). We believe many of your students, not just those for whom auditory processing is a difficulty, would thank you for that!

### Strategies for Developing Metacognition and Self-Regulation

Have you ever encountered a student who has read an entire book, only to not recall any main ideas from the book? Students with LD may lack the ability to monitor their own thinking process, also known as *metacognition*. The student you are thinking of hasn't developed skills such as monitoring their comprehension as they read. You can help this student, however, by teaching a skill known as *self-monitoring* (Jitendra, Hoppes, & Xin, 2000). In self-monitoring, students evaluate their performance against a criterion and reinforcement is provided if necessary. For example, after reading a few paragraphs in a text, Sylvia records the main idea in a notebook to ensure comprehension (Boulware-Gooden, Carreker, Thornhill, & Joshi, 2007). You can have self-monitoring help with behavior challenges also. For example, Gustavo keeps a baseball counter on his desk, and every time he calls out an answer he gets a strike; whereas, when he remembers to raise his hand he gets a ball.

## I NEED MORE STRATEGIES. WHAT CAN I USE?

**Graphic organizers.** Graphic organizers can be employed to target deficits in memory characteristic to students with LD. Ciullo and Reutebuch (2013) conducted a literature review that examined interventions utilizing computer-based graphic organizers for students with LD. Researchers found that content acquisition interventions were effective and promising advances were evident in the area of writing. In addition, studies with the most effectiveness incorporated explicit instruction, guided practice, and feedback to support learning. Providing explicit instruction in the use of graphic organizers may assist students with LD to comprehend reading concepts or to study for assessments (Boon, Burke, Fore, & Spencer, 2006). And lucky you, there are tons of graphic organizers already created for you and available on the web for an array of contents, grade levels, and needs!

**Key Concepts**

Your three heavy hitters in working with students with LD?

- Graphic organizers
- Cognitive strategy instruction
- Mnemonics

**Cognitive instruction.** Students with LD can practice cognitive instruction to improve the ability to process information through the use of strategies. Cognitive strategy instruction has demonstrated improvements in verbalization of both problem representation and solution for students with and without LD (Montague, Krawec, Enders, & Dietz, 2014). Cognitive instruction is a strategy for problem solving consisting of modeling self-questioning by thinking aloud, providing prompts, and providing corrective feedback (Montague et al., 2014). Cognitive instruction is verbally sharing with the students how teachers are making a decision by bringing in what they are thinking, talking out loud, making mistakes, and/or modeling corrections. Other examples of cognitive instruction may include components such as reading the problem, making a drawing, and performing the operation.

Montague, Enders, and Dietz (2011) studied the effectiveness of a research-based cognitive strategy instructional program designed to improve problem solving (*Solve It!*) in both inclusive general education and intensive eighth-grade mathematics classes. Overall, students who received *Solve It!* instruction had higher improvement in math problem solving over the school year than students in the control group who received typical classroom instruction. The intervention was equally successful across all ability levels, including students with LD, low-achieving students, and average-achieving students. This study was replicated with seventh-grade students resulting in similar effects over the school year as the students who received the same cognitive strategy instructional intervention showed significantly greater growth than the comparison group (Montague et al., 2014). This kind of strategy is critical for students with LD, but the research shows it helps peers without disabilities, too, so it is perfect for inclusive classes!

Krawec et al. (2013) also implemented the *Solve It!* intervention for average-achieving students as well as for students with LD in seventh and eighth grades. Across ability levels, results indicated that students who received the *Solve It!* intervention used significantly more strategies than students in the control group, and students with LD also had a higher increase from pretest to posttest than the control group. Although it may require additional time for students to learn, cognitive strategy instruction is a beneficial way to help students with LD and their nondisabled peers remember a process.

 **Making Connections**

Check out Chapter 1 on Mathematics.

**Mnemonics.** The use of mnemonics is an effective instructional strategy to improve the learning and retention of material for students with LD (Mastropieri & Scruggs, 2014). Did you learn "Every good boy does fine" EGBDF for your fingering in music? Or "ROY G BIV" as a mnemonic for the colors of the rainbow (red, orange, yellow, green, blue, indigo, violet)? These are mnemonics and are designed to support learning, not slow it down. Students have been successful using keyword method mnemonics to enhance learning of both concrete and abstract vocabulary as measured by recall and comprehension tests (Mastropieri, Scruggs, & Fulk, 1990). In another teacher application of the mnemonics strategy comparing students with and without LD, students with LD performed to the same level of achievement as students without disabilities (Uberti et al., 2003). Mnemonics is a strategy that helps both students with and without LD remember the meaning of vocabulary words and comprehend both fictional and informational text in the classroom.

## STOP! COLLABORATE AND LISTEN!

Teachers:

- ✗ **STOP being a doormat.** Sitting back and taking an inactive role won't help students make progress. Depending on the needs of students, you will often find yourself collaborating with other teachers. Practice good communication skills with your colleagues (see Sileo, 2011) to enhance educational programming for students with disabilities across instructional settings.

- ✗ **STOP only using what's "cool" with your students.** Students with LD have difficulty reaching their potential. Pinterest certainly has a lot of cute games and activities for students, but where is the research that these activities have been shown to produce positive outcomes for students with LD?

- ✗ **STOP keeping secrets!** Be sure to share your techniques, strategies, and ideas with general education teachers. When you consult with other teachers, you are adding to their toolbox of strategies to use when the students are in general education.

- ✗ **STOP giving all students with LD the same accommodations.** Why does every student's individualized education program (IEP) state that they will be pulled out for small group testing or have tests read to them? They don't all need that; in fact, many hate to be pulled and read to! Do updated assessments to ascertain if these accommodations really do benefit the student or are just rewritten into the IEP each year out of habit.

- ✗ **STOP being territorial.** Turfism is out; collaboration is in! Special education teachers will want to collaborate with general education colleagues for a number of reasons. Their job isn't to check up on you or report on your teaching. Instead, they're in your classes to support your teaching. In some cases, special education teachers may co-teach with you, while in other cases they may want to consult with you to problem solve in a collaborative way. Capitalize on each other's strengths and training to meet this goal.

✘ **STOP referring to students as "my students" and "your students."** We're in this for one reason: to engage learners and move them forward. These are "our" students, and we both have skills and insight that can benefit all of the students in the classroom.

✘ **STOP watering down the content.** Students with LD can demonstrate their potential. Watering down content lowers the bar for these students, and they'll know that you expect less from them. Use evidence-based practice to meet their learning needs without lowering expectations. You'll likely find that *all* your students benefit!

✘ **STOP feeling like you have to do the same thing for *all* students.** Students with LD look just like everyone else in the classroom, but they require different tools and approaches to be successful. Other students may not understand why Jojo earns a break after 15 minutes of instruction while the others continue on with their academics. Realize that your other students do not need these frequent breaks and that it is okay to continue on.

✘ **STOP getting frustrated by the inconsistency of students with LD.** On Monday, they've completely grasped a concept, and by Tuesday they've forgotten it completely. They are not trying to frustrate you; this inconsistency is a hallmark of a learning disability and it is more frustrating for you than for them. Be patient. Use strategies. Support their learning.

Administrators:

✘ **STOP allowing a divide-and-conquer approach to teaching students with disabilities.** Teachers in your building are on the same team, and they are the team you lead. As team members, they need to collaborate to meet the complex needs of each student. Encourage your teachers to celebrate the diverse set of skills each brings to the table. Help your teachers learn how to marry those bodies of knowledge and experience together to benefit all students. Develop your team as one with one goal—to effectively meet student needs through working together and sharing ideas.

**Making Connections**

Check out Chapter 9 on Co-Teaching.

## STRATEGIES FOR SUCCESS SECTION

GO

**Teachers, DO this:**

✔ **USE evidence-based practices.** Identify evidence-based practices that will allow these students the opportunity to show their potential. Evidence-based practices are a *must* for students with LD. Using what has been shown to work will increase student learning. Examples of evidence-based practices are provided throughout this chapter. Choose one that meets the needs of your students to get started. Add more into your instruction as you get comfortable.

✔ **WORK with one another for improved inclusion.** Attend team planning sessions to become aware of important upcoming events, curricular emphases, and teacher concerns. If you can't attend planning sessions, arrange another form of regularly scheduled communication. Many teachers love to use Google Docs, WeChat, and Slack for communication.

**Plugged In**

2 TEACH offers example co-taught lessons and a free lesson plan template for co-teachers at www.2TeachLLC.com.

✔ **IMPLEMENT letter strategies, such as acrostics and acronyms.** An example of an acrostic is "Never **e**at **s**hredded **w**heat." The underlined letters remind the student of the first letter of each cardinal direction in clockwise order; north, east, south, west. An example of an acronym mnemonic for treating a sprain would be RICE. The letters in this word remind us of the steps for treating a sprain: **R**est the injured area, **I**ce it, **C**ompress with a wrap, and **E**levate the injured area. Students with LD often struggle with memory tasks, and this strategy has been shown to be effective.

✔ **TEACH the keyword strategy for recalling new vocabulary words.** For example, to remember the term *ratatouille*, the student may think of a rat who has a tattoo of this delicious vegetable dish. When students are asked to recall the meaning of ratatouille, the image of the tattooed rat comes to mind and the student makes the connection to this popular cuisine. Though many students without LD are able to come up with their own memory strategies, students with LD often need to be provided suggestions; doing so frequently will help them learn how to create their own in the future.

✔ **MATCH the strategy to the student needs.** Strategies should not be universally applied. Instead of thinking about the student's disability category, look at the specific needs and characteristics of the student, and identify the strategy that best meets his or her need. It's likely you'll find that the strategies you identify to meet the needs of students with LD will meet needs of many of your students! It's a win-win!

**Plugged In**

Do2Learn (http://www .do2learn.com) is a great resource for identifying strategies that are not only easy to implement, but also are helpful to your students' learning.

✔ **TEACH pegwords in mathematics.** Pegwords are keywords for mathematics. For example, the pegword for the number eight is *gate*. To help a student remember that a spider has eight legs, a picture card could be produced with a spider on a gate. Pegwords can also assist students in the upper grades. In a science class, students may learn about the various classes of levers. Create a picture of a rake leaning against a tree (the pegword for number three) to help recall a rake as a third-class lever. A list of pegwords is provided at the end of this chapter.

✔ **TEACH self-monitoring skills.** Encourage students to pay attention to individual mastery of content and recognize when they hit a bump on the road to learning. Provide lots of formative assessment opportunities that allow students to evaluate their level of understanding and prepare for upcoming assessments. For example, students can apply the *cover, copy,* and *compare* strategy to identify spelling words that still need to be learned, practice with flashcards to assess proficiency of basic math facts by keeping track of those missed, and/or use a timer to regulate number of words read per minute to measure reading fluency.

✔ **COMMUNICATE with your IEP team members.** If you have an immediate concern about a student, don't wait until an IEP meeting. Talk to one another (e.g., general education teacher, speech, occupational or physical therapist, family member) now to seek some resolution.

✔ **ASK for help!** Special education teachers and general education teachers have unique and complementary skill sets. Ask for help identifying strategies that you can implement to support your students. Commit to use strategies that are proven to work!

✔ **TEACH about invisible disabilities.** Unlike other disabilities, LD are somewhat invisible. It may seem unfair to some students that Jessie gets a sticker each time she shares an answer aloud in the classroom. By educating students about LD, we can teach them that *fair* does not always mean *equal*. There are many wonderful examples of children's literature that discuss disabilities in an engaging manner that will capture your students' attention.

✔ **MAKE A HABIT of including supports for visual and auditory processing into your everyday lessons.** *All* students will benefit when you can provide visual and auditory supports when giving instructions. Break up your longer tasks into shorter, more manageable tasks for students. Make an effort to deliver instructions in a succinct manner. Break videos into short parts and summarize sections. Use color coding with notes. Ask students to repeat back instructions to you in their own words. Model note taking, and have some students use a cloze procedure where they only have to fill in keywords. Consider how a graphic organizer can supplement instruction while helping *all* students organize their thinking across many subject areas.

✔ **DESIGN lessons with Universal Design for Learning principles in mind.** Universal design for learning (UDL) is a set of principles for instructional planning that give all individuals equal opportunity

**Making Connections**

Check out Chapter 4 on Instructional Strategies and Universal Design for Learning.

to learn. Consider how you can provide multiple means for student engagement, presentation of content, and demonstration of learning. When you develop lessons with UDL principles in mind, you are taking a proactive approach to teaching and learning!

✔ **ENCOURAGE transferability.** If students have practiced a self-monitoring skill in a special education setting, encourage them to apply it to the general education setting. Communicate with one another to learn what is being taught in self-contained or specialized settings and how those skills can transfer to the general education classroom. Implementing checklists, goal setting, and collaborating with other teachers promote the generalization of students' self-monitoring skills to other academic settings (Korinek & deFur, 2016).

## Administrators, DO this:

✔ **EDUCATE the whole school on the definition of a learning disability.** Emphasize on a regular basis to your faculty that students learn differently and that sometimes they need additional strategies to perform to their ability. For example, calculator use might be permissible for some students with memory deficits trying to recall basic facts when solving equations. This will hopefully alleviate any bullying for students requiring certain tools to learn. Faculty will also be more effective accommodating students who become frustrated with academics and act out once they fully understand characteristics of a student with LD.

✔ **IDENTIFY strengths and interests from all students.** When administration has a system in place to inform teachers of student capabilities as well as areas of need, faculty can leverage strengths to support areas of weakness. All too often schools target the needs of students to improve assessment scores when knowing individual interests and abilities are essential to help students obtain goals. Highlight the strengths of students with LD whenever possible.

✔ **BUILD your team strategically.** Carefully select teams of general education teachers and special education teachers and specialists who work effectively together. Hire team players and those committed to the inclusion of all students and to teaching to high standards.

✔ **PROMOTE relationship building among and between teams.** Create schedules for mutual planning time for general education teachers and special education teachers. Identify teacher strengths and share successes. Help teachers use peer mentoring and collaboration strategies to encourage one another. Consider creating a schoolwide newsletter on strategies and have teachers share their best practices for helping all students, including students with LD.

✔ **DEDICATE TIME at faculty meetings and through professional development activities to co-teaching, collaboration, and other topics like UDL that promote full inclusion and high achievement for all students.** Rather than a one-time presentation on a topic, set up professional development that builds in mentoring, in-class observations, and continuous improvement. The CTIME process (Collaborative Teaching Improvement Model of Excellence) is an example of a process for supporting co-teaching that uses microteaching, continuous improvement, corrective action plans, teacher buy-in, and the Plan-Do-Study-Act procedure to help ensure "no fail co-teaching" (Murawski & Lochner, in press).

✔ **CREATE a culture of inclusion in your building.** Promote the inclusion of all students in your building. Intentionally seek to promote our students vs. yours or mine. For example, have an "On a Roll" student recognition board, instead of merely an "Honor Roll" that focuses on academic grades. Highlight individual growth rather than overall achievement scores. Bring in speakers and plays that describe LD and help students understand differences. Include students with LD in cross-grade reading buddy programs, where they can be leaders to younger students within the school. Provide service-learning opportunities for students with and without LD to encourage learning and friendships that transcend the academic setting.

✔ **REMEMBER the whole team of both general educators and special educators.** Promote teamwork among your general educators and special educators. Remember they are on the same team with you and desire for all students to achieve. Sometimes achievement requires a different pathway for students with LD. Be sure to ask your special educators if something different is needed to meet standards of achievement.

## VOCABULARY WORDS, KEYWORDS, DEFINITIONS, AND ILLUSTRATIONS

| Vocabulary Word | Keyword | Definition | Illustration |
|---|---|---|---|
| Ionosphere | atmosphere | A layer of Earth's atmosphere | Atmosphere, with ionosphere |
| Airborne | air | Carried by air | Things in the air, carried by air |
| Abandon | band | To leave | A band where people have left |
| Extraterrestrial | ET | From outside of Earth | ET outside of Earth |
| Daze | maze | In a state of confusion | In a state of confusion, thinking about a maze |
| Specimens | inspect | Part of a sample to study | A sample to study, being inspected |
| Fjords | board | A body of water | A board on a body of water |
| Jettisoned | jet | Throw overboard | A jet throwing something overboard |
| Aloft | leaf | High up in the sky | A leaf high up in the sky |
| Vegetal | vegetable | Made up of vegetables | Vegetables, made of vegetables |

*Source:* Uberti, H. Z., Scruggs, T. F., & Mastropieri, M. A. (2003). Keywords make the difference! Mnemonic instruction in inclusive classrooms. *TEACHING Exceptional Children, 35*(3), 56–61.

## TEACHER PROCEDURES FOR SELECTING VOCABULARY AND DEVELOPING MATERIALS

1. Carefully examine the class reading materials.

2. Identify important and challenging vocabulary words.

3. Make a list of those words and their definitions.

| Vocabulary Word | Definition |
|---|---|
| Aloft | High up in the sky |
| Specimen | Part of a sample to be studied |
| Daze | In a state of confusion |
| Abandon | To leave behind |

4. Examine each vocabulary word that will be challenging and recode that word to an acoustically similar, but concrete and familiar word or what we call a keyword or cue word. For example, "leaf" sounds like "aloft."

5. Take that keyword and relate it in an interactive picture with the to-be-remembered information. In this case, a leaf floating high up in the sky.

6. Use clipart and make the picture.

**aloft — leaf**
– High up in the sky

7. Think up some relevant story for your target student population. In this case, something like the following:

Here is a new way to help you remember the definition of some vocabulary words. When you hear the word "aloft," think of the keyword "leaf." Leaf sounds like aloft, and it is easily pictured. What is the keyword for aloft? "Leaf." Correct! Now remember this picture of a leaf high up in the sky. When I ask you what aloft means, first think of the keyword that sounds like aloft. In this case it is what? Right, leaf. Now think back to the picture with the leaf in it and think about what was happening in that picture. Right, a leaf was high up in the sky. That should help you with the definition of aloft, which is what? Correct, high up in the sky.

8. Remember, when using the keyword method:

- First, learn the keyword.
- Second, remember the picture of the keyword and the definition doing something together.
- Third, when asked the definition, think of the keyword and what was happening in that picture then retrieve the definition.

*Source:* Adapted from Uberti, H. Z., Scruggs, T. F., & Mastropieri, M. A. (2003). Keywords make the difference! Mnemonic instruction in inclusive classrooms. *TEACHING Exceptional Children, 35*(3), 56–61.

*Images source:* clipart.com

## EVIDENCE-BASED PRACTICES FOR STUDENTS WITH LD ORGANIZED BY SUBJECT AREA

| Cross-Subject | • **Peer-assisted learning strategies (PALS)** is a structured peer-tutoring program in which students are meaningfully paired to play the role of tutor and tutee.<br>• **Direct instruction** is a student-centered approach to teaching in which the pacing of the lesson is quick and provides multiple opportunities for students to participate and receive feedback.<br>• **Cue cards** help students learn and remember steps for academic or behavioral skills (i.e., steps for decoding a word, steps to solving a story problem, strategies for calming down). Students can monitor their own progress with cue cards and develop greater independence leading to self-regulation. |
|---|---|
| Literacy | • **Dialogic reading** involves an adult and a child sharing a book-reading experience. Through dialog, the child and adult alternate roles and the child learns to become the storyteller.<br>• **Teaching strategies for planning, revising, and editing** is an effective practice for developing students' writing proficiency.<br>• Additional activities such as **sentence combining** and **providing models of excellent writing** can support students as writers. |
| Mathematics | • Teach students how to create **visual representations** to support their understanding of the mathematical process.<br>• Encourage the use of **multiple strategies for solving problems.**<br>• Teach students how to **break word problems into manageable steps** for solving. |
| Behavior | • The inclusion of **social skills training** for students with behavioral difficulties is an evidence-based practice aimed at improving student behavior. The What Works Clearinghouse has reviewed several specific social skills curricula (http://ies.ed.gov/ncee/wwc).<br>• Schoolwide **positive behavioral interventions and supports (PBIS)** has been the focus of much recent research. This flexible tiered system provides students with increasingly individualized support. PBIS implementation can vary by school (www.pbis.org). |

## ACCOMMODATIONS AND MODIFICATIONS

| **Modifications** | |
|---|---|
| *Modifications change the expectation for students by either lessening the learning expectations of the student or decreasing the amount of work completed or content learned.* | |
| General classroom modifications | • Reduce the number of items to complete so the student is only doing the least difficult problems<br>• Work on foundational skills that build to the content that other students are working on<br>• Lower the degree for mastery (for example, from 80% accuracy to 60% accuracy) |
| **Accommodations** | |
| *Accommodations don't change the content or the outcome for students. Accommodations simply increase access to the content for students.* | |
| General classroom accommodations | • Provide students with audiobooks or digital print instead of traditional textbooks<br>• Provide review sheets for exams and quizzes<br>• Pre-teach vocabulary that is important for comprehension of a lesson |
| Accommodations to materials | • Permit writing assignments to be completed on computer<br>• Use of raised line paper or a pencil grip |
| Accommodations to teaching methods | • Provide instruction that includes multiple means of representation (visual, auditory, kinesthetic, and tactile)<br>• Record lessons for students to review later<br>• Allow students to work with a partner during practice |
| Health and behavioral accommodations | • Provide frequent breaks<br>• Consider preferential seating options<br>• Provide checklists of daily tasks to complete<br>• Use personal behavior charts or contracts |

# REFERENCES

Boon, R. T., Burke, M. D., Fore, C., & Spencer, V. G. (2006). The impact of cognitive organizers and technology-based practices on student success in secondary social studies classrooms. *Journal of Special Education Technology, 21,* 5–15.

Boulware-Gooden, R., Carreker, S., Thornhill, A., & Joshi, R. M. (2007). Instruction of metacognitive strategies enhances reading comprehension and vocabulary achievement of third-grade students. *The Reading Teacher, 61,* 70–77.

Bryant, B. R., & Bryant, D. P. (2008). Introduction to the special series: Mathematics and learning disabilities. *Learning Disability Quarterly, 31,* 3–10.

Ciullo, S., & Reutebuch, C. (2013). Computer-based graphic organizers for students with LD: A systematic review of literature. *Learning Disabilities Research & Practice, 28,* 196–210.

Hinkley, S., & Smith, P. (2011). Evidence for familial link in visual processing disorders. *Optometry and Vision Development, 42*(1), 25–35.

Jalongo, M. R. (1991). *Strategies for developing children's listening skills.* Bloomington, IN: Phi Delta Kappa Educational Foundation.

Jitendra, A. K., Hoppes, M. K., & Xin, Y. P. (2000). Enhancing main idea comprehension for students with learning problems: The role of a summarization strategy and self-monitoring instruction. *The Journal of Special Education, 34*(3), 127–139.

Kleinheksel, K. A., & Summy, S. E. (2003). Enhancing student learning and social behavior through mnemonic strategies. *TEACHING Exceptional Children, 36*(2), 30–35.

Korinek, L., & deFur, S. H. (2016). Supporting student self-regulation to access the general education curriculum. *TEACHING Exceptional Children, 48,* 232–242.

Krawec, J. K., Huang, J., Montague, M., Kressler, B., & Melia de Alba, A. (2013). The effects of cognitive strategy instruction on knowledge of math problem-solving processes of middle school students with learning disabilities. *Learning Disability Quarterly, 36,* 80–92.

Mastropieri, M. A., & Scruggs, T. E. (2000). *The inclusive classroom: Strategies for effective instruction.* Upper Saddle River, NJ: Prentice-Hall.

Mastropieri, M. A., & Scruggs, T. E. (2014). *The inclusive classroom: Strategies for effective differentiated instruction.* Upper Saddle River, NJ: Pearson Education.

Mastropieri, M. A., Scruggs, T. E., & Fulk, B. J. M. (1990). Teaching abstract vocabulary with the keyword method: Effects on recall and comprehension. *Journal of Learning Disabilities, 23,* 92–96.

McLeskey, J., & Waldron, N. L. (2011). Educational programs for elementary students with learning disabilities: Can they be both effective and inclusive? *Learning Disabilities Research & Practice, 26*(1), 48–57.

Montague, M., Krawec, J., Enders, C., & Dietz, S. (2014). The effects of cognitive strategy instruction on math problem solving of middle-school students of varying ability. *Journal of Educational Psychology, 106,* 469–481.

Montague, M., Enders, C., & Dietz, S. (2011). Effects of cognitive strategy instruction on math problem solving of middle school students with learning disabilities. *Learning Disability Quarterly, 34,* 262–272.

Murawski, W. W., & Lochner, W. W. (in press). *No fail co-teaching: A data-driven continuous improvement model.* Alexandria, VA: Association for Supervision and Curriculum Development.

Schumaker, J. B., Bulgren, J. A., Deshler, D. D., & Lenz, B. K. (1998). *The recall enhancement routine*. Lawrence, KS: University of Kansas.

Sileo, J. M. (2011). Co-teaching: Getting to know your partner. *TEACHING Exceptional Children, 43*, 32–38.

Steele, M. M. (2008). Helping students with learning disabilities succeed. *Science Teacher, 75*(3), 38–42.

Torres, C., Farley, C. A., & Cook, B. G. (2014). A special educator's guide to successfully implementing evidence-based practices. *TEACHING Exceptional Children, 47*(2), 85–93.

U.S. Department of Education, Office of Special Education Programs. (2015). Individuals with Disabilities Education Act (IDEA) database. Retrieved from http://www2.ed.gov/programs/osepidea/618-data/state-level-data-files/index.html#bcc

Uberti, H. Z., Scruggs, T. F., & Mastropieri, M. A. (2003). Keywords make the difference! Mnemonic instruction in inclusive classrooms. *TEACHING Exceptional Children, 35*(3), 56–61.

## ADDITIONAL RECOMMENDED READING ON STRATEGIES FOR STUDENTS WITH LEARNING DISABILITIES

Martin, L. (2009). *Strategies for teaching students with learning disabilities*. Thousand Oaks, CA: Corwin.

Mastropieri, M. A., & Scruggs, T. E. (1998). Enhancing school success with mnemonic strategies. *Intervention in School and Clinic, 33*(4), 201.

Mastropieri, M. A., Sweda, J., & Scruggs, T. E. (2000). Putting mnemonic strategies to work in an inclusive classroom. *Learning Disabilities Research & Practice, 15*(2), 69–74.

## WEBSITES TO SUPPORT STUDENTS WITH LEARNING DISABILITIES

➡ www.lessonbuilder.cast.org

➡ http://teachingld.org

➡ www.bestevidence.org

➡ http://ies.ed.gov/ncee/wwc

➡ http://www.ldonline.org

➡ http://www.intensiveintervention.org/chart/instructional-intervention-tools

## APPS WE LOVE

➡ Remind

➡ Tally Counter

➡ Kahoot!

➡ ShowMe

➡ Quizlet

# 12

# *Search for the Miracle Cure*

## *Working With Students With Emotional and Behavioral Disorders*

Brittany L. Hott
*Texas A&M University–Commerce*

Jennifer D. Walker
*University of Mary Washington*

Audrey Robinson
*Texas A&M University–Commerce*

Lesli Raymond
*Texas A&M University–Commerce*

## EDUCATING (NOT JUST WRANGLING) KIDS WITH EBD

Did you flip right to this chapter? Are you eager to learn the secrets to working with students who have emotional and behavioral disorders (EBD)?

Are you tired of trying to teach, only to feel like you've spent the whole day trying—and failing—to manage your classroom? Well, you are not alone! That said, while we will provide you with much of what really works with this population, we have to also admit at the start that kids are different and there is no "silver bullet" or "miracle cure." Wait! Don't close the chapter. Focus on the fact that we said we do indeed have strategies—evidence-based techniques that have been shown to work with this difficult population. Read on. We just might have the perfect technique to help your particular situation.

According to the Individuals with Disabilities Education Act (IDEA, 2004), students are eligible for special education services under the emotional disturbance (ED) category if they exhibit one or more of the following characteristics over a sustained period of time and to a marked degree that adversely affect performance: (a) inability to learn not explained by other factors (e.g., intellectual, sensory, or health), (b) inability to have interpersonal peer relationships, (c) inappropriate behavior or feelings under normal circumstances, (d) pervasive mood of depression or unhappiness, or (e) tendency to develop physical symptoms or fears. The IDEA definition for ED also includes schizophrenia but does not apply to children who are socially maladjusted, unless it is determined that they also qualify for ED through other means. The federal definition for emotional disturbance has not significantly changed since its inception, and this lack of change remains problematic. Since the passage of the initial special education legislation, PL 94-142 in 1975, only two changes to the emotional disturbance classification have occurred across reauthorizations. These changes are (a) the development of autism spectrum disorder as a distinct disability category separate from emotional disturbance, and (b) the 1997 change in category from "serious emotional disturbance" to "emotional disturbance" (Gargiulo, 2012).

Today there continues to be a debate over the terminology, classification, and service provisions for this population. Compounding these issues are differences among state and neighboring locality's definitions. While most schools use the federal term ED, researchers and professional organizations use emotional or behavioral disorders or emotional or behavioral disability (EBD). This distinction—using EBD instead of ED—allows for the fact that many of the students with this label primarily manifest a behavioral difficulty over an emotional one. EBD incorporates both and more accurately describes this population of students.

The good news is that outcomes for students with EBD can be significantly improved with evidence-based strategies and interventions. What can you do, you ask? No problem. Your specialized instruction should include quality academic instruction, interventions, and positive behavioral supports.

## ACADEMIC AND BEHAVIORAL INTERVENTIONS

First and foremost, it is important to ensure that students are set up for success. Positive behavioral interventions and supports (PBIS) include tiered procedures to ensure that all students have access to a safe and productive learning environment (Lane, Oakes, & Menzies, 2014). These supports include developing schoolwide rules and classroom procedures that fit within the school rules (Bradshaw, Koth, Bevans, Ialongo, & Leaf, 2008) and a system of supports for students needing more instruction and support. One of the most important

**Key Concepts**

Want to know why a behavior is occurring? Your five functions of behavior are

- Attention
- Escape/avoidance
- Power/control
- Sensory
- Tangible

supports for students with EBD is a functional behavior assessment (FBA) and behavior intervention plan (BIP). It is best to have a team of specialists (e.g., school psychologist, administrator, counselor, special education teacher, general education teacher, school nurse) work collaboratively to develop a FBA. The team should have skills to assess a child needing interventions and work collaboratively to determine the function of a behavior. Then the team should develop ideas for more acceptable replacement behaviors serving the same function (Scott et al., 2004). The student should be included to the fullest extent possible. When developing an FBA, it is important to remember that most behaviors can be attributed to five functions: (a) attention, (b) escape or avoidance, (c) power and control, (d) sensory, or (e) obtainment of something (Lee, Vostal, Lylo, & Hua, 2011). The goal of the FBA team is to clearly define or *operationalize* the problematic behavior(s) and then systematically determine the frequency and duration of the behavior(s) through data collection and triangulation. Triangulation just means that you have multiple sources agreeing that there is a problem and what it looks like. Acceptable replacement behaviors can then be recommended. After an FBA is complete, a formal plan is drafted addressing each of the student's needs with the goal of reducing problematic behaviors while increasing positive, replacement behaviors.

Similar to the process for developing an FBA, a team should work collaboratively to develop a BIP that addresses areas of need including instruction and supports. Measureable goals and methods for measuring progress are clearly outlined (Hott, Walker, & Brigham, 2014). The FBA and BIP should be viewed as working documents that are consistently and systematically reviewed to continue to meet the student's needs. While the focus is on preventative and instructional measures, it may be appropriate to also include an individualized crisis plan. A BIP is part of the individualized education program (IEP); therefore, parents, and most important the student, should be supported in taking active roles in the development of a quality BIP. We know, so many procedures, forms, and steps, and so little time. No worries; there are great resources available for collecting data and making decisions to support all students.

In addition to schoolwide PBIS, simple classroom practices may result in significant behavioral and academic improvements for students with EBD. These practices can be done individually with students with EBD or in a whole-class setting. A few of these strategies include opportunities to respond (OTR), peer tutoring, and self-monitoring.

An OTR occurs each time a student is provided with an instructional stimulus (Farkis, Belfiore, & Skinner, 1997). Examples of OTRs include reading passages, oral or electronic questions, or math calculation problems. To be successful, each student needs four to six OTR per minute when learning new material and eight to 12 responses per minute during independent practice portions of lessons (Scheuermann & Hall, 2011). However, these figures may be an underestimate of the number of OTR needed to support students with EBD. Wondering how you can possible work in so many opportunities to respond when you have a class of 30 to 40 students? We get it! It can be difficult to ensure that each student receives the ideal OTR, so we suggest strategies like choral responding, preprinted cards, response cards, electronic clickers, or a variety of free online tools that let students respond frequently. And hey! We know that frequent student engagement and participation is key for all students, which means it won't just be your one student with EBD who is benefitting!

**Making Connections**

Check out Chapter 4 on Instructional Strategies and Universal Design for Learning.

Peer tutoring is another option to support students with EBD as they practice social and academic skills. While there are a number of ways that peer tutoring groups can be created, reciprocal peer tutoring is one option to support students with EBD (Hott, Alshreed, & Henry, 2014). Other peer tutoring configurations and suggestions for planning can be found on the Peer Tutoring form at the end of this chapter.

Self-monitoring allows a student to track his or her academic or behavioral progress (Hott & Walker, 2012). This shifts the responsibility from the teacher to the student while allowing the student to see his or her progress. This is an important skill for students with EBD since self-monitoring and self-control may be areas of concern. We know what you are thinking: "*My student would never be able to monitor her own behavior! She's too busy being defiant or acting out.*" And yet we've seen this strategy successfully used with a variety of students. You may need to pair it with intrinsic and extrinsic rewards at first, but you'll be surprised how well it can work.

Praise is another evidence-based practice to support students with EBD. Praise statements can be provided through a variety of formats. These include whole-class or individual praise statements, quiet praise, loud praise, verbal praise, written praise, peer praise, teacher praise–the list is endless. Research indicates that

**Making Connections**

Check out Chapter 8 on Positive Behavior Supports.

as long as the praise is specific and there is high rate of positive to negatives, it is effective (Shora & Hott, 2016). For students with EBD, who may have experienced high rates of failure or have poor school experiences, praise is a way to positively bring attention to student success. We know that inappropriate behaviors seem to be the most critical. They are always the ones that seem to get in the way of your instruction and the other students' learning. However, in addition to interventions to support behavioral progress, academic interventions are desperately needed. Students with EBD often miss significant amounts of class time due to behavior. It is not uncommon to see a series of removals during the early elementary years. While this chapter is too brief to include a comprehensive overview, check out the resources section for a list of syntheses that can provide a detailed summary of interventions available.

## THINGS TO IMMEDIATELY STOP DOING . . . UNLESS YOU WANT THE PROBLEM TO CONTINUE

Teachers:

- ✗ **STOP assuming that behavioral interventions will improve academic outcomes.** Many students with EBD also have coexisting learning difficulties that behavioral interventions do not address. Provide academic interventions that are structured and systematic, that include regular review of previously learned concepts, and that involve repeated and varied opportunities for practice.

- ✗ **STOP providing instructional tasks that aren't at the student's instructional level.** Students will never reach their full academic potential if they are never challenged to do so. Providing only "easy" tasks because you're afraid of a student's reaction to more challenging material isn't doing the student any favors. Know your students' instructional levels for every subject area. Instructional activities should include a balanced mixture of problems at their instructional level to ensure they experience success and problems that are more challenging to ensure their academic growth.

- ✗ **STOP starting with restrictive placements.** Special education placements for students should start out in the *least* restrictive environment. Yes, we know you and your colleagues cringe at the thought of the student with severe behavior challenges in a class with 35 other kids. But hey! One "typical" student saying "Dude, that's so not cool" is way more powerful than 32 behavioral goals. More restrictive placements can be gradually introduced, if gathered data warrants the change and shows that needs are not being met in the current placement. Until then though, err on the side of having students in the typical general education classroom.

✗ **STOP working in isolation.** Ask for help. There are many individuals with expertise who are available to provide support. This includes families! Parents often know what works, what doesn't, and what triggers behaviors. Using a collaborative approach can shape goals, objectives, and interventions by eliminating the bias of individuals.

**Making Connections**

Check out Chapter 10 on Progress Monitoring.

✗ **STOP making decisions without data.** Data are needed to show change. There is no way to know if supports and interventions are successful without it. Thoughts and feelings about whether goals and objectives have been met can be misleading. Data driven decisions are in the best interest of the student and provide accurate, objective information.

## Administrators:

✗ **STOP blaming the student.** Placing blame on the student is detrimental to the relationship and shames the student. There are many factors that contribute to EBD outside of the control of the student. Finding someone to blame—whether the student, parents, the environment—does not help the situation. Instead, extend empathy to the student and work collaboratively with mutual respect to create a plan. All behavior serves a purpose.

✗ **STOP suspensions without interventions.** Suspension does not lead to improved behavior (Bowman-Perrott et al., 2011). Students with EBD need increased opportunities to see appropriate social skills being modeled and to practice those social skills; this can't happen if they aren't in school! Before moving to a suspension, ensure that evidence-based behavioral interventions are in place for the student and interventions are being carried out with fidelity. If they are and they are not working, try to figure out a new plan!

✗ **STOP leaving IEP meetings.** You're busy. There are so many other things you could be doing. Unfortunately however, the message you send to teachers, parents, and students when you leave an IEP meeting is: "This isn't important." Stay for the entire meeting. Be engaged, offer support, and be available to answer questions before, during, and after the meeting.

✗ **STOP the negativity.** A simple language transformation from negative to positive statements makes a difference when supporting students and teachers. For example, changing from "don't run in the halls" to "walk in the halls" frames the expectation positively. Model the language that you want your faculty and staff to use.

# STRATEGIES FOR SUCCESS WITH EBD LEARNERS

**Teachers, DO this:**

- ✔ **GIVE each kid what he or she needs.** One-size-fits-all interventions are ineffective. Tailor a plan, with the help of educators, parents, and the student, to fit the student's specific needs. It is okay, encouraged even, to provide different supports for students based on their needs.

- ✔ **BUILD a relationship.** Students respond better to educators who are invested in them. Educators who have quality relationships with students have fewer discipline problems. A relationship can be founded on three core components: (1) empathy—considering the student's unique experience and environment; (2) acceptance—taking in the good and bad, starting fresh each day, where all behaviors are understood, but not all behaviors are condoned; and (3) being genuine and caring.

- ✔ **ALLOW students to experience frustration and failure within a positive support system.** Walking on eggshells and insulating students from all triggers, stressors, and failures denies the student the opportunity to learn how to manage negative situations and emotions. The real world is fraught with frustrations, disappointments, and failure. Students need practice coping with such circumstances in a healthy way within a positive support system to build in the skills necessary to handle the circumstances. Give students a place to cool down when upset, process and discuss frustrating and upsetting situations, and create plans for future events. Encourage students to role-play alternative responses and develop a strategy for handling challenging situations (deep breathing, counting by 5s, visualizing a prize or accomplishment they desire).

- ✔ **SET clearly defined limits.** Landreth (2012) created the three-step ACT limit setting model, which is used in parent training groups and in play therapy. It is also effective in education settings. The ACT name is an acronym for the steps: (a) **A**cknowledge the feeling, (b) **C**ommunicate the limit, and (c) **T**arget an alternative. For example, if a student is refusing to transition from reading to math, say, "You'd like to continue to finish reading, and the time now is for math. You can continue your reading assignment when you finish the math, at lunch, or at home."

- ✔ **REMEMBER all behavior serves a purpose.** A student is not engaging in a behavior without a specific reason. Perhaps the student is looking for power, control, and/or attention? To help students with EBD develop new behaviors and skills, analyze the function of the behavior first. If a student is throwing paper balls to get attention from peers, recognize this function as a need first. Then create opportunities for students to get attention from peers in a way that is not disruptive. This could include answering predetermined questions in class, coming to the front of the class as a helper, or earning a short time to share a story at the end of class.

✔ **RECOGNIZE that no one wins in a power struggle.** Students who want power and control in the classroom may attempt to engage in power struggles with teachers and staff. Unfortunately, when teachers engage in power struggles, no one wins. It is best to remain matter of fact about expectations and keep your emotions at bay.

✔ **USE universal preventative strategies in your classroom.** Universal preventative strategies are sometimes called *good teaching*. It's key to make sure that things like procedures, expectations, and rules are in place. Use proximity and move around your classroom. Practice "withitness," and know what is going on in all parts of your classroom. Set up zones in your classroom and teach your students how to use materials and navigate through lessons. A student with EBD thrives in a structured environment—as do most other students.

✔ **GIVE frequent, specific, and genuine praise.** Let students know when they are doing something well, whether behaviorally or academically. Resist the temptation to say things like "good job" or "you're correct." Be specific when giving praise. For example, "The way you solved that math problem was impressive. I noticed you planned out your problem-solving steps and it helped you arrive at the correct answer" is more specific than "great work." It is important to praise students not just for getting the correct answer, but also for the work they put in along the way.

**Plugged In**

Check out great SRS resources at https://getkahoot.com and http://www.socrative.com. An online resource for creating response cards is https://www.plickers.com.

✔ **PROVIDE students with multiple opportunities to respond.** Increased opportunity to respond (OTR) results in improved academic performance for students with EBD (Vannest, Temple-Harvey, & Mason, 2009). Student response systems (SRS) are one way to increase OTR, and are available at little to no cost. The use of response cards is another technique that results in increased participation by students with EBD (Blood, 2010).

✔ **BUILD ways for students to engage in a risk-free environment.** Use choral responding or response cards. Choral responding involves the teacher posing a question and students responding in unison. Preprinted response cards can be easily made with sticky notes. If a classroom set is desired, index cards including "yes" and "no" or "true" and "false" on opposite sides can be laminated and kept for repeated use. Multiple choice (A/B/C/D) can be created by using multiple cards. Another option is to use write-on response cards. Even better? Purchase shower board at a local hardware store, cut into 8.5 × 11-in. sheets, and students have their own personal white board!

✔ **TEACH students to self-monitor.** While providing support, have the student create an academic or behavioral goal. Using a timer or reminder, teach the student to record his or her progress on paper or using computer software. Show students how their efforts are making changes in their academics and behaviors. Students love to see graphs of their progress going up, up, up!

✔ **INCORPORATE peer-mediated instructional activities.** Pair students with EBD with students who demonstrate strong interpersonal skills and work habits while taking individual personalities and differences into account. This will also provide your students with increased opportunities to practice social skills and will allow you to individualize instructional activities. To avoid frustration, only use peer tutoring as a review or reinforcement of previously learned material, not as a way to introduce new content. To ensure success, model each step of the instructional method you want the students to use and then watch them practice it while providing corrective feedback.

✔ **COLLECT data to inform decision making about interventions and behaviors.** There are many simple, easy ways to collect data. For behaviors that require frequency counts, consider using a sticky note. Place a sticky note on the back of your name tag, clip board, or desk. Whatever place is easiest for you. Simply tally each time you need to count a behavior such a cursing, blurting out, getting out of seat, or refusing to complete assignments. Do you have several students who need to be monitored? Use different colored sticky notes or fold a larger sticky note into three columns. Better yet, teach students to use the sticky note to record their own behavior. Don't like the idea of using pen and paper? Simply move a penny or paper clip from your right pocket to your left pocket and count after class!

✔ **REMEMBER the behavior plan is a working document.** Students with EBD experience difficulty with managing emotions and behavior. When an incident occurs, follow the plan in place. We know it sounds simple, *but* it works. Each student is an individual, and the function of his or her behavior is unique and may change over time. For example, John may yell out to gain attention and Kate may yell out to obtain power and control of a situation. Remember function and try to provide an alternative. If a strategy works, write it down and share. The BIP is a working document. If the strategies are no longer working, then it is time to meet as a team.

## Administrators, DO this:

✔ **FACILITATE professional development opportunities for the entire school** including bus drivers, custodians, cafeteria staff, office staff, and school nurses. It is important that all staff members who interact with students with EBD are adequately trained to understand their characteristics and behaviors. Ensure a plan of action is in place if a behavioral situation arises and an administrator or other credentialed personnel is not present or available.

✔ **PARTICIPATE in professional development.** It is important for you to stay informed about current best practices in teaching students with EBD. This will allow you to provide useful guidance and feedback to your teachers. Invite teachers of students with EBD to attend professional development, workshops, or conferences with you.

✔ **SHOW that you support, appreciate, and trust teachers.** Make frequent visits to classrooms. Listen to teachers' suggestions and trust them to make decisions that are in the best interest of their students. Allow teachers to visit other classrooms, including special education classrooms, and support their attendance at workshops, even if it means the students will have a substitute teacher.

✔ **RECOGNIZE that families of students with EBD face many challenges.** Be supportive and seek resources to assist families. Encourage interagency collaboration. Parents need resources, too! Consider sharing about *PACER*, a funded parent resource center that focuses on support and advocacy for families; Ed Gov's *Parent Landing*, the U.S. Department of Education's (2015) resources site for parents; and *Parent Center Hub*, an easy place to go to understand list of terms and strategies for students with EBD.

**Plugged In**

Looking for organizations that help parents?

- http://www.pacer.org
- http://www2.ed.gov/parents/landing.jhtml
- http://www.parentcenter-hub.org/repository/emotionaldisturbance

✔ **SEE challenges as teachable moments.** Model the skills that you want students to demonstrate. Using a calm tone, explain a rationale for why a particular skill is needed, and allow opportunities to practice. This will go a long way in preventing behavioral incidents from escalating.

## ADDITIONAL RECOMMENDED READING ON EMOTIONAL/BEHAVIORAL DISORDERS

**Resources to Assist With
Functional Behavior Assessment (FBA) Development**

| Resource | Citation | Summary |
|---|---|---|
| Technical Assistance Document: Virginia Department of Education FBA Guidelines | http://www.doe.virginia.gov/ support/student_conduct/ fba_guidelines.pdf | Provides a basic overview of the FBA process |
| Book: Applied Behavior Analysis for Teachers | Alberto, P. A., & Troutman, A. C. (2013). *Applied behavior analysis for teachers* (9th ed.). Upper Saddle River, NJ: Prentice Hall. | Shares data collection procedures in a simple, direct manner |
| Data Collection Forms and Tools: PBIS.org | https://www.pbis.org/ evaluation | Illustrates how to use a variety of implementation tools to support FBA development |
| Online Training: Center for Effective Training and Practice | http://cecp.air.org/fba/ default.asp | Provides online training and materials for FBA development |
| Online Training: IRIS Center | http://iris.peabody.vanderbilt .edu/module/fba/ | Delivers online training, materials, and resources for FBA |

*(Continued)*

(Continued)

## Resources to Assist With Behavior Intervention Planning (BIP)

| Resource | Citation | Summary |
|---|---|---|
| Book: Managing Problem Behaviors | Kauffman, J. M., & Brigham, F. J. (2009). *Working with troubled children*. Verona, WI: Attainment. | User-friendly resource for parents, support personnel, and teachers that shares empirically validated strategies for students with complex behavioral challenges |
| Technical Assistance Document: VDOE Guidelines for Handing Behaviors During Emergencies | http://www.doe.virginia.gov/support/student_conduct/guidelines_managing_behaviors_emergency.pdf | Provides strategies for challenging behaviors during emergency situations; addresses use of physical restraint and seclusion |
| Technical Assistance: Behavior Intervention Planning Tool | http://www.interventioncentral.org/tools/behavior-intervention-planner | Provides a step-by-step guide to drafting a BIP; links to other research based sites that provide additional resources and information |
| Book: Tools to Develop BIPs | Lane, K. L., & Beebe-Frankenberger, M. (2004). *School-based interventions: The tools you need to succeed*. Boston, MA: Allyn & Bacon. | Shares forms that can be used to develop goals and collect data; emphasizes instruction and treatment fidelity |
| Online Training: IRIS Center | http://iris.peabody.vanderbilt.edu/module/bi2/ | Training modules that provide step by step instruction and resources to develop comprehensive BIPs |
| Book: Behavior Intervention Strategies | Lane, K. L., Menzies, H., Bruhn, A., & Crnobori, M. (2011). *Managing challenging behaviors in schools: Research-based strategies that work*. New York, NY: Guilford Press. | Shares practical strategies and numerous consumables to assist with behavior management at the classroom and individual levels |

**Resources to Support Academic Needs of Students With EBD**

| Resource | Citation | Summary |
|---|---|---|
| Article: Synthesis of Writing Interventions | Sreckovic, M. A., Common, E. A., Knowles, M., & Lane, K. L. (2014). A review of self-regulated strategy development for writing for students with EBD. *Behavioral Disorders, 39,* 56–77. | Provides a summary of research on the use of self-regulated strategy development (SRSD) use in providing writing instruction for students with EBD |
| Article: Synthesis of Math Interventions | Templeton, T. N., Neel, R. S., & Blood, E. (2008). Meta-analysis of math interventions for students with emotional and behavioral disorders. *Journal of Emotional and Behavioral Disorders, 16*(4), 226–239. | Shares a synthesis of math interventions for elementary and secondary students with EBD |
| Article: Synthesis of Reading Interventions | Vaughn, S., Levy, S., Coleman, M., & Bos, C. S. (2002). Reading instruction for students with LD and EBD: A synthesis of observation studies. *The Journal of Special Education, 36*(1), 2–13. | Reports outcomes of reading studies for students with EBD and LD |
| Article: Synthesis of Academic Interventions | Wehby, J. H., Lane, K. L., & Falk, K. B. (2003). Academic instruction for students with emotional and behavioral disorders. *Journal of Emotional and Behavioral Disorders, 11*(4), 194–197. | Provides a synthesis of available academic interventions for elementary and secondary students with EBD |

## HOW I'M FEELING TODAY

| Feeling | A little     1  2  3  4  5  6  7  8  9  10     A lot | |
|---|---|---|
| Sad | 1  2  3  4  5  6  7  8  9  10 | |
| | Gloomy | Devastated |
| Mad | 1  2  3  4  5  6  7  8  9  10 | |
| | Frustrated | Furious |
| Happy | 1  2  3  4  5  6  7  8  9  10 | |
| | Glad | Ecstatic |
| Scared | 1  2  3  4  5  6  7  8  9  10 | |
| | Nervous | Horrified |

I felt (sad, mad, happy, scared) _____ when:

_____

Things I did when I felt (sad, mad, happy, scared) _____

_____

Next time to help myself I can try _____

_____

_____

*Image sources:* iStock/Kir_Prime and iStock/SuslO

## OPPORTUNITY TO RESPOND (OTR) TRACKING FORM

**Directions:** Ask a colleague or assistant to observe the OTR for a student, group of students, or class. Simply provide a tally mark for each interval and then calculate the rate of OTR by dividing the number of OTRs by the class time. You may also calculate the number of correct responses by dividing the number of correct OTRs by class time or percentage correct of the OTRs provided.

Student(s): _____ Date: _____

Class: _____ Subject: _____

Start Time: _____ Finish Time: _____

Finish Time – Start Time × 60 = Total Observation Time: _____

Types of OTR: _____

OTR (enter tally mark)

OTR / Time = _____ Rate of OTR

OTR / Correct Responses = _____ Accuracy

OTR / Responses = _____ Fluency

Notes and Goals for Next Observation: _____

_____

_____

_____

## PEER TUTORING PLANNING FORM

Peer Tutoring Configuration

_____ Same Age Tutoring

_____ Cross Age Tutoring

_____ Classwide Peer Tutoring

_____ Peer Assisted Learning Strategies (PALS)

_____ Reciprocal Peer Tutoring

> Want to learn more about each of these tutoring options? See http://www
> .council-for-learning-disabilities.org/peer-tutoring-flexible-peer-mediated-
> strategy-that-involves-students-serving-as-academic-tutors to select a model.

Skill: _____

Class Roster—*List students from highest performing (Student 1) to lowest performing (Student 2) on the skill selected.*

| Partner 1 | Partner 2 |
|-----------|-----------|
| 1. | 6. |
| 2. | 7. |
| 3. | 8. |
| 4. | 9. |
| 5. | 10. |

List changes to groups due to student dynamics or individual needs:

_____

_____

Peer Tutoring Teams—*It is often fun to have students select their team name.*

| Team Name | Partner 1 | Partner 2 |
|-----------|-----------|-----------|
|  |  |  |
|  |  |  |
|  |  |  |
|  |  |  |
|  |  |  |

# REFERENCES

Blood, E. (2010). Effects of student response systems on participation and learning of students with emotional and behavioral disorders. *Behavioral Disorders, 38,* 214–228.

Bowman-Perrott, L., Benz, M. R., Hsu, H. Y., Kwok, O. M., Eisterhold, L. A., & Zhang, D. (2011). Patterns and predictors of disciplinary exclusion over time: An analysis of the SEELS national data set. *Journal of Emotional and Behavioral Disorders, 21*(2), 83–96.

Bradshaw, C. P., Koth, C. W., Bevans, K. B., Ialongo, N., & Leaf, P. J. (2008). The impact of school-wide positive behavioral interventions and supports (PBIS) on the organizational health of elementary schools. *School Psychology Quarterly, 23*(4), 462.

Farkis, M. A., Belfiore, P. J., & Skinner, C. H. (1997). The effects of response repetitions on sight word acquisition for students with mild disabilities. *Journal of Behavioral Education, 7*(3), 307–324.

Gargiulo, R. M. (2012). *Special education in contemporary society: An introduction to exceptionality.* Thousand Oaks, CA: Sage.

Hott, B. L., & Walker, J. D. (2012). Five tips to increase student participation in the secondary classroom. *Learning Disabilities Forum.* Retrieved from http://www.cldinternational.org/Publications/LdForum.asp

Hott, B. L., Alresheed, F. M., & Henry, H. R. (2014). Effects of peer tutoring interventions for students with autism spectrum disorder: A meta-synthesis. *The Journal of Special Education and Rehabilitation, 15,* 109–121.

Hott, B. L., Walker, J. D., & Brigham, F. J. (2014). Implementing self-management strategies in the secondary classroom. In A. Cohan & A. Honingsfeld (Eds.), *Breaking the mold of classroom management: What educators should know and do to enable student success* (pp. 19–26). Lanham, MD: R & L Education.

Individuals with Disabilities Education Act. 20 U.S.C. 1401 *et seq.* (2004).

Landreth, G. L. (2012). *Play therapy: The art of the relationship* (2nd ed.). New York, NY: Brunner-Routledge.

Lane, K. L., Oakes, W. P., & Menzies, H. M. (2014). Comprehensive, integrated, three-tiered models of prevention: Why does my school—and district—need an integrated approach to meet students' academic, behavioral, and social needs? *Preventing School Failure: Alternative Education for Children and Youth, 58*(3), 121–128.

Lee, D. L., Vostal, B., Lylo, B., & Hua, Y. (2011). Collecting behavioral data in general education settings: A primer for behavioral data collection. *Beyond Behavior, 20,* 22–30.

Scheuermann, B. K., & Hall, J. A. (2011). *Positive behavioral supports for the classroom.* Boston, MA: Pearson Higher Ed.

Scott, T. M., Bucalos, A., Liaupsin, C., Nelson, C. M., Jolivette, K., & DeShea, L. (2004). Using functional behavior assessment in general education settings: Making a case for effectiveness and efficiency. *Behavioral Disorders, 24,* 89–201.

Shora, N., & Hott, B. L. (2016). A job well done: Five tips for effective use of praise. *New Teacher Advocate, 37,* 4–5.

U.S. Department of Education, National Center for Education Statistics. (2015). *Digest of Education Statistics, 2013* (NCES 2015–011), Chapter 2.

Vannest, K. J., Temple-Harvey, K. K., & Mason, B. A. (2009). Adequate yearly progress for students with emotional and behavioral disorders through research-based practices. *Preventing School Failure*, 53(2), 73–83.

## TOP FIVE WEBSITES TO SUPPORT STUDENTS WITH EBD

➡ http://www.ccbd.net/home

➡ http://www.parentcenterhub.org/topics/orgbehavior

➡ https://www.pbis.org/resource/320/school-based-wraparound-for-students-with-emotional-and-behavioral-challenges

➡ https://www.teachervision.com/classroom-management/teaching-methods-and-management/26200.html

➡ http://www.swiftschools.org

## APPS WE LOVE

➡ iRewardChart

➡ SymTrend

➡ ClassDojo

➡ Hero K12

➡ LiveSchool Teacher

# 13

## Addressing the Autism Spectrum Disorder "Epidemic" in Education

Claire E. Hughes
*Canterbury Christ Church University, England*

Lynnette M. Henderson
*Vanderbilt Kennedy Center*

## AUTISM SPECTRUM DISORDER: IT'S A SPECTRUM

Fairly or unfairly, students with autism spectrum disorder (ASD) are often known for their meltdowns, tantrums, and otherwise difficult behavior in a classroom. Students with ASD may have limited energy and resilience and reach their level of tolerance without the capability to meet the demands of the task or the environment. The only options of communication they may perceive are a meltdown, a shutdown, or a complete withdrawal. Because the access to appropriate responses can be so different from person to person, or even within the same person under different circumstances, we refer to ASD as a *spectrum* because it can vary so widely.

Complying with the learning expectations in a typical classroom places many physical and cognitive demands on the student with ASD. This disability, though often invisible, requires a "prosthetic" to replace what is missing for the student. Because of the differences in the development and brains of students with ASD, what students with ASD need is a prosthetic *environment*. As teachers, we have significant control of one of our primary teaching tools—the environment—and thus the ability to adapt it to meet the needs of students with ASD. Students need the classroom to provide them with what they cannot easily access on their own: structure, predictability, communication supports, social supports, and emotional regulation (Brown & Brown, 2015). The more we can structure a supportive environment, the less likely a student is to experience these infamous meltdowns, shutdowns, or complete withdrawals.

## WHAT WE KNOW FROM THE RESEARCH

*So what is autism spectrum disorder and what is this I hear about an "epidemic"?*

Autism spectrum disorder is a developmental and neurobiological disability. That means that (a) it affects the way a person develops and (b) it is rooted in biological brain differences. When we think about that in children, we think about the way their physical bodies and muscles develop, their development in the way they learn, think, interact with people, see, and hear—all those things are part of development. Developmental disability means that some part of that development is not tracking along in the way we would expect. It's not in sync with typical development, or with the rest of the child's own development.

It's also developmental because it changes over time with the child. What we look for to diagnose ASD is very different in a child than in an adult. ASD produces challenges over the whole lifespan. The challenges that come with ASD grow up with that child, and there are certain things that will always be hard for a person with ASD, because the challenges will stay with them throughout their lifespan. People with ASD do improve and will continue to improve throughout life. A study by Fein and associates (2013) found that with early intervention and intensive work, some children were able to lose the ASD label, although they did not lose all the ASD characteristics. You may not always be able to see that they are struggling, but that struggle is the difference between what comes naturally and what comes with effort.

ASD is also a neurobiological disorder because it is based in the brain. It's not a decision, it's not a mental health disorder, it's not meanness or orneriness or bad parenting; it's a difference that is based in the brain that affects many parts of the body. ASD is a *spectrum disorder*. It can range from very mild to severe and can look very different in an introvert or an extrovert, in a boy or a girl, or in a 3-year-old or a 30-year-old.

### Labeling

*Autism spectrum disorder* is a relatively new label—certainly not as old as visible disabilities, such as blindness or deafness, and other intellectual delays. Originating in the 1940s by Leo Kanner (1943), *autism* was a label used for children with unusual fixations, speech patterns, and social issues. In May 2013, the American Psychiatric Association (2013) updated the *Diagnostic and Statistical Manual* (*DSM-V*) to create one category of ASD with a severity of impact scale. Previously, there were three types of ASDs: autistic disorder, Asperger syndrome, and pervasive development disorder-not otherwise specified (PDD-NOS). The change in the manual came about because it was discovered that the diagnoses are *not* reliably different. Whether a person got the diagnosis of autistic disorder, PDD-NOS, or Asperger's did not depend on what their characteristics were; *it depended more on who gave the person the label.* These old terms may still be comfortable for people who are using them.

### Autism Spectrum Disorder "Epidemic"

Autism spectrum disorder currently has a prevalence rate of 1 in 68 (Centers for Disease Control and Prevention [CDC], 2016) and is 4.5 times more prevalent in boys. There are no racial, ethnic, or social boundaries to the condition. All developmental disabilities are on the rise, not just ASD. The rise of ASD can be attributed to (a) better understanding of ASD as a spectrum, (b) more awareness and diagnostic testing availability, (c) some diagnostic crossover since some children who used to be classified as having speech and language issues or cognitive or intellectual disabilities are now classified as having ASD, and (d) the possible increase in some environmental triggers (Hansen, Schendel, & Parner, 2014). It has been clearly established by the scientific community—over and over again—that vaccines do not cause ASD (CDC, 2015). It is very difficult to sort out these various causes because our world has changed quite a bit over the time in which these numbers have risen. You could take almost any common factor of modern life and it would correlate with the rise in ASD. Take the number of cable channels, the percentage of flip flops worn as regular shoes, the number of YouTube videos in the world, or the number of remote controls in the average house—any of these will show a positive and strong correlation with the rise of ASD in the world, but these factors have *no bearing* on causing ASD. Correlation does not necessarily imply causation. What we do know is that there is no single known cause. Research is pointing toward ASD, multiple types of ASD that arise from different causes related to the complexity of the gene environment interaction. There are many genes already identified that may lead to an increased risk for ASD, as well as links to environmental and neurobiological triggers that seem to result in observed abnormalities

**Key Concepts**

What's causing the rise in ASD? It might be:
- Better understanding of ASD
- More awareness and assessment
- Diagnostic crossover
- Increase in environmental triggers

in brain structure and connectivity (Chen, Peñagarikano, Belgard, Swarup, & Geschwind, 2015). See the figure at the end of the chapter called A Behaviorally Based Diagnosis for examples of some of these biomarkers of brain differences. The ASD diagnosis is based on a set of behavioral observations. The two circles in the center of the figure represent the behavioral differences upon which the *DSM-V* diagnosis is based. The surrounding circles are other aspects of ASD that are often comorbid, which means happening at the same time, and can impact the student and their learning and behavior in your classroom. Be wary of sensationalist science about causation and getting into conversations about causation. As an educator, your job is to deal with the student in your classroom and their learning needs, whatever the cause.

## Core ASD Symptom: Impaired Social Communication

Social communication deficits can be thought of as a *lack of interest* in being social and in communicating with anyone. These deficits in social interest are the faulty foundation upon which the delayed social and communication *skills* are shakily balanced. People with ASD have difficulty or struggle with these tasks. It's usually not a matter of "can't do;" it's a matter of "comes with effort." Take for example, developing peer relationships. For some reason, it is often easier for a child with ASD to be friendly with and interact with adults than it is with other children. Often, we as adults know how to help conversation in a way that children haven't learned how to do yet. Social deficits can also be found in how children with ASD respond to social or situational cues or facial expressions. Social cues can be difficult. Most people are familiar with "the teacher look." While it may work with almost everyone else, children with ASD may not respond to the "You're in trouble" face. Not responding to that face may seem disrespectful to the teacher, but rather than a lack of respect, the child with ASD most likely simply does not recognize that social cue and facial expression.

Another social difference that we see with people with autism spectrum disorder is that they have difficulty being motivated by social reinforcement. Even in babies, we can see differences in social interest and skill; very young babies will be fascinated by faces and will find them rewarding. Babies at risk for ASD may not love the game peekaboo because the only thing appealing about it is the social reinforcement. The same reward system rules apply for older children. Social reinforcement of "Cool clothes!" may or may not appeal to them. They may not care what everyone else wears. It may matter more whether they are comfortable. They can easily get the label of *weird* because they do not appear to know or care about social norms. We have to be careful about understanding particular individuals and how they feel about social motivation and reward. As a complicating factor in social awareness, individuals with ASD often have issues with "theory of mind" or understanding what another person might be thinking (Baron-Cohen, 1997). They tend to be very egocentric and don't understand or appear to care what other people think or what other people think about them.

### Core ASD Symptom: Restricted, Repetitive Behaviors

As an integral part of the definition, students with ASD will all have a form of a restricted or repetitive behavior. These may be more physical in younger students (e.g., lining up objects or spinning wheels) and can change to more restricted interests and activities as the child develops cognitively. The need for repetition is often expressed in the need for predictable events (Wong et al., 2015), and students can become distressed by new activities or changes in routines. This springs from a lack of control and information in their lives. People with ASD do not get all the information typically developing people get from the environment about what is going to happen next by watching others or overhearing conversations. It often seems to them as if decisions are made without them and changes in activity and routine come out of nowhere, because the signs that everyone else was reading were too subtle for them to read. Transitions between activities are particularly challenging for students with ASD because they often miss the cues that signal that change is coming, or they become anxious about the upcoming demands that are going to be asked of them.

**Making Connections**

Check out Chapter 8 on Positive Behavior Supports.

Added to this are the differences in the ways in which students with ASD experience the sensory world. Some of the neurobiological differences include hearing and sight differences that may make individuals sensitive to extremes of light and sound (Cascio, Woynaroski, Baranek, & Wallace, 2016). As a conscious or unconscious self-protection measure, persons with ASD may try to avoid sensory experiences they find to be aversive; these could be sounds (like echoing, large cavernous loud places or bright places, a particular voice or babies' cries), visual (like fluorescent lights), or tactile (like particular textures of fabric or food). These attempts to avoid negative sensory experiences are often the root of behavioral issues (Cascio et al., 2016). On the other hand, there are also sensory experiences that can be very soothing and serve to reduce anxiety and calm the mind or release body tension. Repeated body movements are often used in this way. Sometimes referred to as *stimming*, they are not that different from typical behaviors. Rocking chairs and swings were invented because human beings find that motion comforting. Watch a group of excited girls greet one another and there will be plenty of jumping and flapping to go along with the squealing. The difference is context. It is important to remember that the stim is serving a purpose for the person with ASD, and any energy or cognitive load that they are spending on suppressing the stimming behavior is not available for learning anything else.

Restricted interests can also be an unusual attachment to objects or an attachment to an unusual object because of its shape, texture, or smell. Parents of children with ASD will emphasize how strong these attachments can be (Hughes, 2010). Family stories may describe how the family would not dare leave home without the object and how they would make sure to have three spares in the closet just in case! Educators may want to minimize these attachments or perseverations, but rather than trying to force a different object or focus area, why not instead embrace the item or topic and make it part of the curriculum?

## Other Associated Issues: Intellectual, Medical, Attentional

The picture one sees of the student with ASD will of course be impacted by the student's intellectual ability, which can fall within the full range, just like any other child. Not every child with ASD will have intellectual disability or language impairment, but because language is a social-communication task and measuring intelligence is a social-communication task, it is likely that the student's deficits in social communication will affect their performance in these areas. For early talkers, these difficulties may not show up until the demands of social communication become more complex in middle school with the addition of local and group-specific slang, sarcasm, idioms, and figurative language or the need for abstractions in the classroom.

The medical and behavioral issues associated with ASD are important to address for students who exhibit those symptoms, because if left untreated, they can interfere significantly with a student's success in the classroom. Some of these issues include epilepsy, fragile X, and sleep issues. Did you know that 40% of people with ASD have insomnia (Allik, Larrson, & Smedge, 2006)? Tummy troubles, such as chronic constipation, and mental health issues are also common. Depression is more likely to show up in young adulthood, and anxiety seems to be present in *many* people with ASD (Henderson, Moseley, Peltz, & Blumberg, 2015). For many persons on the spectrum who are not verbal or conversational, conveying the extent and placement of pain and other body pain can prevent them from obtaining timely medical treatment. Thus, behavioral changes, such as outbursts, withdrawal, or self-injury, may be their only way of communicating pain and discomfort.

Attentional and cognitive skills also vary widely in students with ASD (Wong et al., 2015). Some may have attention deficit hyperactivity disorder (ADHD), while others may have excellent (even hyper) focus. As more and more students with ASD are receiving high-quality early intervention, we are seeing their initial difficulties with social interest and motivation ameliorated enough to no longer affect their ability to learn in school. Don't think that every child with ASD will avoid eye contact or flap their hands. In fact, through elementary school, some students with ASD may appear as if they have only specific learning disabilities (e.g., reading, math, or language processing), but then as they enter middle school, with its higher social and communicative requirements, and as puberty begins to rewire the brain, ASD reasserts its social communication difficulties. At these higher levels of cognitive demand, difficulties with executive function and other processing disorders can become quite apparent. When a student with ASD is under a heightened cognitive load, you are going to be able to see them struggle more with their ASD. The increased cognitive load makes the work of "faking normal" more difficult.

Each of the characteristics we've discussed (attention, personality, intellectual ability, medical, and physical Issues) will impact the student's social communication and will be expressed in each student in his or her own unique way. Each of these characteristics can be thought of as the elements of a kaleidoscope around the central issues of social communication and restricted, repetitive behaviors. Something changes (e.g., the student starts sleeping better), and CLICK, you have a new picture of the student with ASD! The intervention you have been implementing works, and the student has better language and is using that language to ask questions! CLICK! The questions aren't appropriate. New intervention needed. CLICK!

It is worth noting that the usual sources of research-based practices (e.g., What Works Clearinghouse, Best Evidence Encyclopedia, and the Promising Practice Network) did not contain as much information for classroom teachers to use with students with ASD as we would expect. So where can you find good strategies beyond this chapter? You will find excellent information in the chapters on ASD in the other titles in this series: *What Really Works in Elementary Education* (Murawski & Scott, 2015a) and *What Really Works in Secondary Education* (Murawski & Scott, 2015b). Stellar sources of research-based information can also be found at the National Professional Development Center on ASD (NPDC on ASD), the Frank Porter Graham Center (Wong et al., 2014), the National Autism Center (NAC), National Standards Project (Randolph, 2015), the Ohio Center for Autism and Low Incidence, the Indiana Resource Center for Autism, and TRIAD at the Vanderbilt Kennedy Center.

**Plugged In**

Great resources for ASD information:

- www.fpg.unc.edu
- https://www.autismspeaks .org/science/professional- development-resources
- www.ocali.org
- https://www.iidc.indiana .edu/pages/irca
- http://vkc.mc.vanderbilt .edu/vkc/triad

## STOP TALKING! STOP, LOOK, AND LISTEN . . .

Teachers:

- ✗ **STOP taking behavior personally.** The way a student with ASD interacts with you may not have anything to do with you. If they are having a tantrum, it may because of something that happened 2 hours earlier and a simple question was more than they could handle at that point. They are not acting *that way* to get back at you or to ruin your day. Because of theory of mind deficits, they are probably not capable of taking your viewpoint enough to know how something will affect you.

**Making Connections**

Check out Chapter 12 on Emotional and Behavioral Disorders.

✗ **STOP reinforcing behavior.** If a student is having a meltdown and you are yelling at her, allowing her to escape, insisting that she look at you, or doing anything that allows her to be successful in accomplishing the function of their behavior, you are reinforcing it. Understand the process of escalation (Colvin & Sugai, 1989).

✗ **STOP asking only open-ended questions.** "What do you think . . . ?" may be too open-ended for students with ASD to process without some prompting. Give an answer with two choices instead as an accommodation. You'll find this may also be helpful for students with other disabilities and language needs. Even, "How are you today?" can be stressful when a child with ASD doesn't know the "correct answer" of "Fine." Providing a list of emoji faces to point at would be a better way to use visual images rather than phrases that require the use of additional language. Check out page 220 in Chapter 12 to see an example.

✗ **STOP talking so much.** When students with ASD are beginning to stress out, the torrent of language that a teacher provides can be overwhelming. When you see the student beginning to shut down, get down on their level (stop looming!) and use visuals to draw the student's attention. The higher the stress, the fewer words you should use.

✗ **STOP insisting on eye contact.** When you insist on eye contact, you are often forcing the student to choose between comprehension and eye contact. Often, they can process language better when they are not forced to look someone in the eye. Looking someone in the eye can be tremendously overwhelming and anxiety producing. Because this is often perceived as a lack of attention or disrespect, you can teach some students to look at the bridge of the nose or the edge of the eye rather than directly into someone's eyes. Another strategy might be to do a "hit and look away," where the student glances at the person talking and then looks away to process the information. These are also useful skills for other students in the class whose home culture may not reinforce looking adults in the eye.

✗ **STOP bullying . . . yours and theirs.** If you see other students bullying the child with ASD in your classroom and school, stop it immediately. However, be careful that your own high standards don't become a form of bullying to students who are neurodiverse (van Roekel & Scholte, 2010). There are many ways to be smart and demonstrate intelligence and learning. Who is displaying rigid and repetitive behaviors if you can't be flexible enough to try something different?

Administrators:

✘ **STOP assuming that students with ASD need to be in one classroom.** Students with ASD fall along a wide spectrum of abilities and can even be gifted. Many can be amazing mimics, and being around typical peers can help them tremendously with their social behaviors. On the other hand, some students with ASD need a more struc-

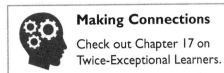

**Making Connections**

Check out Chapter 17 on Twice-Exceptional Learners.

tured environment to learn. It is best to look at each student individually and make decisions based on the characteristics of the child, not the label.

✘ **STOP using restraint as a resort to major behavioral issues.** Many states are enacting laws restricting the use of restraint, and it is highly recommended that your staff learn alternatives. There are strategies such as SCARED (Safe, Calm, Affirmation, Routine, Empathy, Develop Strategies) (Lipsky & Richards, 2009) that have been found to be effective in handling and not escalating behavioral issues. Have your staff learn them. We've included a helpful table at the end of the chapter to help you share the strategy with others.

✘ **STOP trying to solve behavior problems with traditional approaches.** It would be a good idea to have a specialist or someone trained in behavior interventions to do a functional behavioral assessment for a student with ASD because the functions of the behavior aren't as immediately obvious as they may be for other students. Often, behavior for students with ASD is very complex, and it takes someone with significant training to look for the clues. If you attempt to punish a child with ASD for *having* ASD, you are teaching them nothing.

## WHAT TO DO WITH STUDENTS WITH ASD

Teachers:

✔ **ASK parents or caregivers if they would like to have their child referred to as an "autistic student" or a "student with ASD."** The neurodiversity movement is stating that ASD is part of that child's identity; using the phrase "autistic child" is designed to recognize the differences, while not belittling the person. To them, a "child with ASD" is as awkward as saying a "child with left-handedness," or a "child with Irishness" (Sinclair, 1999). When one identifies a child as "the Irish child," the Irishness is part of their identity. However, some families and the special education field in general still support "person-first language" in which the child is emphasized, not the condition. Due to the variety of perspectives on this important issue of language, it is best to ask and respect the answer.

✔ **RESPECT the family's schedule and demands as they try to captain their ASD team.** There are so many other professionals with whom parents of children with ASD have to interact. Their child may be seeing a nutritionist, a speech therapist, a behavioral specialist, a specialty dentist, occupational therapist, physical therapist, developmental optometrist, and the list continues. They may ask you to document or chart behaviors, to refrain from offering gluten products, or to use specific electronic tools in instruction. If it is within your capacity to do so without disrupting the education of your classroom, please try to do your part on the team. Often, parents will be getting contradictory directions from various specialists. If you are seen as a team member to help this child, you can help them navigate the varying paths of treatment. Show them that you are on their side (Henderson & Hughes, 2011).

**Making Connections**

Check out Chapter 19 on School-to-Home Collaboration.

✔ **UNDERSTAND the grief cycle.** An angry family member may not be angry at you; they might be angry because all the children their child's age are getting drivers' licenses and they are grieving or re-grieving their child's disability diagnosis. They may not be showing up for meetings because they are depressed. They may be demanding answers you don't have. Keep trying. Keep providing information. Keep taking data and sharing it with them.

✔ **START conversations with the student and provide him or her with sentence starters.** Asking questions is not always helpful because the student with ASD may not be able to process the question and then find answers. A teacher who asks a student "Today, do you feel happy or sad?" is allowing time for the student to select an appropriate response and reducing the cognitive load needed to find an appropriate answer.

✔ **ENCOURAGE scripting and its intentional cousin, the Social Story** (Gray, 2010). Scripts are how a student with ASD finds comfort, releases stress, and communicates with others. Scripting can be snippets that the student picked up from television, movies, or conversations, and often appear to be unrelated to the topic at hand. It is worth noting that sometimes scripts may contain inappropriate language or be from an activity typically favored by younger children. Teachers have to understand the purpose for the script and support the child to use a different script rather than being punitive. Social stories can also help prepare a student for a new situation or help teach a new or replacement behavior, which can be helpful at any age.

✔ **RESPECT the stim.** Every student with ASD will have a repetitive behavior of some kind. This behavior soothes an anxiety-riddled emotional state, reduces cognitive load, or serves some function for the student. Stims can be repetitive questions that the student knows the answer to, physical movements, or a form of obsession. It does not work to tell the student to stop because the stim itself is fulfilling a need. Unless the student is hurting himself or herself or others, the stim needs to be accommodated. The student will give up the stim when the anxiety level is reduced or he or she finds something else to stim on. Replacement of the stim with an approximation (e.g., pen clicking, hair twirling, foot jiggling) that they can take into adulthood may be worth your time if it can meet the students' needs and also allow them and their classmates to learn more effectively. Check out the PDQ Model for Anxiety Reduction at the end of this chapter and use it to help your own anxious students!

**Making Connections**

How should a student with ASD receive services? Check out Chapter 18 on Legal Issues to learn the difference between a 504 Plan and an IEP.

✔ **EMPHASIZE and LABEL your own happy expressions.** "This is my happy face! This is me looking proud of you!" Students with ASD often cannot read positive body expressions, and so they do not perceive the positive feedback you are trying to provide them. You need to label and emphasize the expressions and the tone that is meant to convey positive responses without *over*emphasizing the volume or pitch of your voice.

✔ **PRESUME COMPETENCE.** Even if students are nonverbal and appear to be in a world of their own, you have to assume that they are processing what is around them (Soraya, 2014). There are so many stories of teachers who acted or said inappropriate things in front of a student they assumed to be oblivious, only learning later that the student was able to retain and recall that experience. There are numerous examples of nonverbal students with ASD who have been able to learn to type and communicate (Zurcher, 2013). Always presume that the student is competent and that your job is to find a way for the student to demonstrate his or her capability.

✔ **ALLOW movement in the classroom.** Exercise is one of the cheapest, easiest, and most effective methods for helping students with ASD focus and gain control over themselves.

✔ **DETERMINE the function of a behavior.** All behavior is either to get something like social attention, a favored sensory experience, a preferred item, control, or to get away from something. Finding out what that *something* is that is triggering behavior is key to helping modify the environment. Too often teachers think a student is avoiding the content area, when it might be something sensory or even a certain other student.

✔ **FIND replacement behaviors.** When a student with ASD is behaving inappropriately rather than just telling them to stop, it is important to teach them something else to do. The behavior the student is exhibiting might be the only one that the student sees as an option in the circumstances. Your job is to teach that another behavior will get the results that he or she is looking for.

✔ **USE visuals. And repetitive patterns.** Because language can be so difficult for a student with ASD to process, it is important to use alternative methods of instruction. The use of pictures, graphic organizers, and clear, step-by-step repetitive instructions (e.g., First we do . . ., second, we do . . ., last, we do . . . .) reduces the cognitive load needed for a student with ASD to process the language demands.

✔ **BE EXPLICIT.** Adam, a student with ASD, had to be taught personal space distances. He learned that "acquaintances are the distance of a whole arm. Friends are the distance from the elbow to the hand. Secrets and very close family members are a hands-distance away." When he met you, he would ask if you were an acquaintance, a close friend, or a family member so that he could adjust the appropriate distance to talk to you. Such social cues did not come naturally to him and had to be explicitly taught.

✔ **SCHEDULE. And schedule again. And make it visual.** Students with ASD do not do well with surprises. They want to be aware of what is coming up. There are so many great visual schedules available on the Internet; check out some of our recommended websites at the end of the chapter to find some that might work for your students. That surprise game or activity or fun visitor is frequently going to create stress and anxiety in the student with ASD. Since life is not always on schedule, teaching the student a script or a story of what to say or do when there is a change can also provide a structure where there is a deviation. Unscheduled events, such as having a substitute teacher, can trigger anxiety and inappropriate behaviors, unless there is a schedule for an unscheduled event provided.

## Administrators:

✔ **SET THE TONE.** Model how you think your teachers should act around children with special needs. Listen to parents. Go to training about the characteristics and needs of students with ASD. Be sensitive in your language.

✔ **PROVIDE "Safe Places" around the school where a stressed-out child can go.** If these are known and supervised places, a child can take a break with the understanding that the location will be safe from intrusion and behavioral expectations.

✔ **HAVE SAFETY PROCEDURES in place and practiced by your staff.** Often, students with ASD may wander, which means that you will need to have a system to keep children accounted for. There have been several terrible cases of students with ASD who wandered off because they were unescorted and unobserved and were killed or hurt. Similarly, if you call the police, please be sure that you provide them with information about how to handle the student; too often, police can misunderstand certain actions and make decisions that can end disastrously. An excellent resource is called "BE SAFE The Movie" (Iland, 2013), which teaches individuals with ASD how to interact with police.

**Plugged In**

Help teach students how to appropriately interact with police by watching "BE SAFE The Movie" at www.besafethemovie.com.

## A BEHAVIORALLY BASED DIAGNOSIS

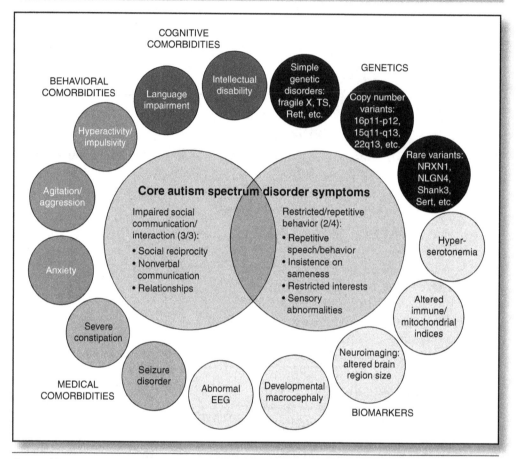

*Source:* Veenstra-VanderWeele, J., & Blakely, R. D. (2011). Networking in autism: Leveraging genetic, biomarker and model system findins in the search for new treatments. *Neuropsychopharmacology Reviews, 37,* 196–212. Reprinted with permission from Macmillan Publishers Ltd: Nature Publishing Group.

## AVOID ESCALATING BEHAVIOR!

| | What It Stands For | What It Looks Like in the Classroom/Hallway/ Lunchroom/School Yard | What Teachers/ Adults Can Do |
|---|---|---|---|
| **S** | Safe | | |
| **C** | Calm | | |
| **A** | Affirmation | | |
| **R** | Routine | | |
| **E** | Empathy | | |
| **D** | Develop strategies | | |

*Source:* Adapted from Lipsky, J., & Richards, W. (2009). *Managing meltdowns: Using the S.C.A.R.E.D. calming technique with children and adults with autism.* London, England: Jessica Kingsley.

## A RUBRIC FOR EVALUATING AN IDEAL INTERVENTION FOR STUDENTS WITH ASD

| | |
|---|---|
| **I** | Does it address the student's need in the most **INCLUSIVE**, least **INTRUSIVE** way possible? |
| **D** | Does it **DEAL** with the antecedents and consequences of the behavior you would like to change? |
| **E** | Does it focus first on changing the **ENVIRONMENT** (which is in our control) before requiring change from the student? |
| **A** | If the student continued the behaviors suggested by this intervention into **ADULTHOOD,** would that be **ACCEPTABLE**? |
| **L** | Will this intervention take time away from **LEARNING** for you or the student or the class? If yes, set a time in advance that you consider to be a reasonable tradeoff period. |

## PDQ MODEL FOR ANXIETY REDUCTION

### Picture: BRAINS

- **Brain:** My brain has a lot of parts to it.
- **Racing:** I can feel my brain beginning to race.
- **Anxious:** I have chemicals in the middle of my brain that are taking over and stopping it all from working. They operate like a fire does.
- **Identify:** I am feeling anxious right now.
- **Need:** I need to take action.
- **Strategies:** I have strategies that can help the chemicals deflate like a balloon.

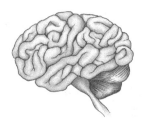

### Do: BODIES

- **Breathe:** 15 breaths. Count them. This helps deflate the balloon of chemicals.
- **Organize:** Organize your breathing. Breathe into the tops of your lungs, the chest, and your diaphragm. Let out the breaths from the diaphragm, the chest, and then the top of your lungs. Blow out the chemicals. Breathe for 2 minutes.
- **Drink:** Drink some water. Feel the water going down. Imagine it putting out the fire of anxiety in your head.
- **Identify** a place to go: If the chemicals aren't deflating quickly, you can go to a safe place in the room. But you don't have to go.
- **Explore** the other parts of your brain as they start to work: *I can breathe away the anxiety. I can feel the rest of my brain working. I have control.* If you don't, breathe again.
- **Sense** the chemicals going out: *Things will be okay, now. I can do this.*

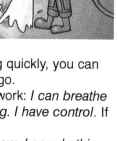

### Question: HANDS

- **How** *am I doing now?*
- **Ask:** *What is the teacher asking me to do?*
- **Next:** *What do I need to do next?*
- **Do:** *I can do this, or I can ask for help.*
- **Strategies:** *I have strategies for dealing with this, and I can use them again. The chemicals will not win.*

*Images source:* clipart.com

## REFERENCES

Allik, H., Larrson, J.-O., & Smedge, H. (2006). Insomnia in school-aged children with Asperger syndrome or high-functioning autism. *BioMed Central Psychiatry, 6*, 18.

American Psychiatric Association. (2013). *Diagnostic and statistical manual of mental disorders: DSM-5*. Washington, DC: American Psychiatric Association.

Baron-Cohen, S. (1997). *Mindblindness: An essay on autism and theory of mind*. Boston, MA: MIT Press.

Brown, C., & Brown, M. (2015). Teaching autism students in inclusive classrooms. Retrieved from http://www.child-autism-parent-cafe.com/autism-students-in-inclusive-classrooms.html

Cascio, C. J., Woynaroski, T., Baranek, G. T., & Wallace, M. T. (2016). Toward an interdisciplinary approach to understanding sensory function in autism spectrum disorder. *Autism Research*. doi:10.1002/aur.1612

Centers for Disease Control and Prevention. (2015). *Vaccines do not cause autism*. Retrieved from http://www.cdc.gov/vaccinesafety/concerns/autism.html

Centers for Disease Control and Prevention. (2016). *Autism spectrum disorder: Data and statistics*. Retrieved from http://www.cdc.gov/ncbddd/autism/data.html

Chen, J. A., Peñagarikano, O., Belgard, T. G., Swarup, V., & Geschwind, D. H. (2015). The emerging picture of autism spectrum disorder: genetics and pathology. *Annual Review of Pathology, 10*, 111–144.

Colvin, G., & Sugai, G. (1989). *Responding to non-responders: Managing escalations*. Retrieved from https://www.pbis.org/common/cms/files/pbisresources/gsescalations1107.ppt

Fein, D., Barton, M., Elgsti, I.-M., Kelley, E., Naigles, L., Schultz, R. T., . . . Tyson, K. (2013). Optimal outcome in individuals with a history of autism. *Journal of Child Psychology and Psychiatry, 54*, 195–205.

Gray, C. (2010). *The new social story book: Over 150 social stories that teach everyday social skills to children with autism or Asperger's syndrome, and their peers* (2nd ed.). Arlington, TX: Future Horizons.

Hansen, S. N., Schendel, D. E., & Parner, E. T. (2014). Explaining the increase in the prevalence of autism spectrum disorder: The proportion attributable to changes in reporting practices. *JAMA Pediatrics, 169*(1), 56–62.

Henderson, L., & Hughes, C. E. (2011, March). *Autism IEPs: Factors involved in the parental and professional satisfaction of the IEP process*. Annual Gatlinburg Conference, San Antonio, TX.

Henderson, L. M., Mosely, A., Peltz, A., & Blumberg, S. (2015). *Autism orientation professional presentation*. Nashville, TN: Autism Tennessee.

Hughes, C. E. (2010). *Children with high functioning autism: A parent's guide*. Austin, TX: Prufrock Press.

Iland, E. (2013). *Be safe the movie*. Retrieved from https://besafethemovie.com

Kanner, L. (1943). Autistic disturbances of affective contact. *Nervous Child, 2*, 217–250.

Lipsky, J., & Richards, W. (2009). *Managing meltdowns: Using the S.C.A.R.E.D calming technique with children and adults with autism*. London, England: Jessica Kingsley.

Murawski, W. W., & Scott, K. L. (Eds.). (2015a). *What really works in elementary education*. Thousand Oaks, CA: Corwin.

Murawski, W. W., & Scott, K. L. (Eds.). (2015b). *What really works in secondary education*. Thousand Oaks, CA: Corwin.

Randolph, M. A. (2015). *Findings and conclusions: National standards project, phase 2*. Randolph, MA: National Autism Center.

Sinclair, J. (1999). Why I dislike person-first language. Retrieved from http://www.cafemom.com/journals/read/436505

Soraya, L. (2014). Acceptance, empathy, and presuming competence. Psychology Today: Asperger's Diary. Retrieved from https://www.psychologytoday.com/blog/aspergers-diary/201401/acceptance-empathy-and-presuming-competence

van Roekel, E., & Scholte, R. H. J. (2010). Bullying among adolescents with autism spectrum disorder: Prevalence and perception. *Journal of Autism and Developmental Disorders, 40*(1), 63–73.

Veenstra-VanderWeele, J., & Blakely, R. D. (2011). Networking in autism: Leveraging genetic, biomarker and model system findins in the search for new treatments. *Neuropsychopharmacology Reviews, 37*, 196–212.

Wong, C., Odom, S. L., Hume, K., Cox, A. W., Fettig, A., Kucharczyk, S., . . . Schultz, T. R. (2014). *Evidence-based practices for children, youth, and young adults with autism spectrum disorder*. Chapel Hill: University of North Carolina, Frank Porter Graham Child Development Institute, Autism Evidence-Based Practice Review Group. Retrieved from http://fpg.unc.edu/sites/fpg.unc.edu/files/resources/reports-and-policy-briefs/2014-EBP-Report.pdf

Zurcher, A. (2013). Presume competence: What does that mean, exactly? *Emmas Hope Book: Online blog*. Retrieved from https://emmashopebook.com/2013/03/07/presume-competence-what-does-that-mean-exactly/

 ## ADDITIONAL RECOMMENDED READING ON ASD

A Diary of a Mom blog. Retrieved from www.adiaryofamom.com

Des Roches-Rosa, S., & Myers, J. B. (2011). *Thinking person's guide to autism*. Deadwood SD: Deadwood.

Grandin, T. (1996). *Thinking in pictures: And other reports from my life with autism*. New York, NY: Vintage.

Silberman, S. (2015). *Neurotribes: The legacy of autism and the future of neurodiversity*. New York, NY: Avery.

Tammet, D. (2006). *Born on a blue day: Inside the extraordinary mind of an autistic savant*. New York, NY: Free Press.

## TOP FIVE WEBSITES TO SUPPORT LEARNERS WITH ASD

➡ http://www.nationalautismcenter.org

➡ http://afirm.fpg.unc.edu/node/137

➡ http://www.ocali.org/center/autism

➡ https://www.iidc.indiana.edu/pages/irca

➡ http://vkc.mc.vanderbilt.edu/VKC/triad

➡ http://www.ideapartnership.org/using-tools/learning-together/collections
   .html?id=1592:autism-spectrum-disorder-collection-tools&catid=383:autism-
   spectrum-disorder-asd

## GREAT SITES TO FIND APPS TO SUPPORT LEARNERS WITH ASD

➡ https://www.autismspeaks.org/autism-apps

➡ http://www.parenting.com/gallery/autism-apps

➡ http://www.thinkingautismguide.com/p/resources.html

## APPS WE LOVE

➡ AutiPlan PictoPlanner

➡ Autism Learning Games: Camp Discovery

➡ Proloquo2Go: AAC In Your Pocket

➡ ProxTalker App

➡ Choiceworks

➡ Routinely

# 14

# Teaching Students With Moderate-to-Severe Disabilities

*You've Got This!*

Dawn W. Fraser
*Kennedy Krieger Institute*

## WHO ARE THESE KIDS?

You've seen a list of the students who will be in your sixth-grade classroom this year. In addition to four children identified as gifted and three children who are English language learners, you learn that you will have three children with learning disabilities, two children with attention deficit hyperactivity disorder (ADHD), one child with an emotional disability (ED), two children with autism spectrum disorder (ASD), and one child with intellectual disability (ID). At first you shake your head—how is this possible? Even learning that some of those students are twice-exceptional (i.e., students who are both gifted and have a disability) doesn't make this easier. Working with a special educator, you learn that most of your students have what is known as *mild-to-moderate* disabilities, while others have *moderate-to-severe* disabilities. How will you know the difference? What will you need to do differently? Can students with significant disabilities even be in your class?

Slow down and take a deep breath. You've got this. Students are students and, though some may have needs more profound than others, the good news is that there is help! This chapter will help you understand who the students are who fall under the category of having moderate-to-severe disabilities. For example, all the students in the opening vignette may or may not fall into this classification. All those students may or may not need significant academic, behavioral, communication, and social supports to succeed in school. So who are these kids?

The scope of students with moderate-to-severe disabilities falls both across and within disability categories. In fact, the terms *moderate* and *severe* are included in the definitions of both high-incidence and low-incidence disabilities. That means that something like a learning disability (high incidence) or Down Syndrome (low incidence) could each be a mild, moderate, or severe disability, depending on the student's needs. While it may seem as though the label of *severe disability* would be easier to define, experts in the field disagree. Individuals with severe disabilities are often categorized, usually in at least two areas, as having large deficits that require extensive and consistent support (Reschly, 1996). However, some researchers limit the category of severe disabilities even further to include only those individuals with moderate-to-profound intellectual impairment who also demonstrate severe communication deficits (Downing & MacFarland, 2010). If you are thinking that adding the term *moderate disabilities* will only make things more confusing, you are right! Including moderate disabilities in the continuum only makes the defining parameters more blurred because the term *moderate* is often used to describe both disability categories: *mild to moderate* and *moderate to severe*.

 **Making Connections**

Check out Chapter 13 on Autism Spectrum Disorder.

While ID has traditionally been categorized by severity levels, most other disability categories lack a distinct separation between severity types. For example, ASD, ED, and LD all include a wide range of severity levels, ranging from mild to severe. The revised diagnostic criteria in the fifth edition of the *Diagnostic and Statistical Manual of Mental Disorders* (DSM-V) may make determining severity levels within ASD easier because individuals diagnosed using the criteria within the current manual will receive two distinct severity specifiers: one in the area of social communication and one in the area of restricted, repetitive behaviors (Level 1: Requiring Support; Level 2: Requiring Substantial Support; Level 3: Requiring Very Substantial Support). ASD diagnoses will also include specifiers indicating the presence or absence of intellectual impairment and/or language impairment (American Psychiatric Association, 2013). Unfortunately, other disabilities don't include these specifiers. Without a distinction within the diagnostic criteria for other disabilities, it will remain difficult for experts in the field to reach a consensus on a clear definition of the category *moderate-to-severe disabilities*.

Without a clear definition, it is challenging to estimate the prevalence of students who fall under the category of moderate-to-severe disabilities. One method is to use the least restrictive environment (LRE) categories as listed on a student's individualized education program (IEP), because every public school in the United States is required to report this statistic under the Individuals with Disabilities Education Act (IDEA, 2004). Historically, students with severe disabilities, when afforded educational opportunities, received services in a separate school for students with disabilities, a separate residential facility, or in a home-bound/hospital placement. During the 2013–2014 school year, 3.6% of students age 6 to 21 years served under IDEA, Part B, were placed in one of those LRE categories (U.S. Department of Education, 2015). By this point, you are probably wondering how this number is impacted by the fact that students with disabilities, including those with severe disabilities, are increasingly being provided services in general education classrooms. Students who are included in the general education setting fall into one of three LRE categories based on the percentage of the school day spent within the general education classroom (less than 40% of the school day, between 40% and 79% of the school day, and 80% or more of the school day). So if you add the percentage of students who were in a typical general education classroom for less than 40% of the school day, the number rises to 17.4%. But wait! What about the students who fall into the category of moderate disabilities? As you have probably guessed, these students are typically placed in the general education classroom between 40% and 79% of the school day, causing the prevalence to rise again, more than doubling the previous statistic, to 36.8% of all students age 6 to 21 years served under Part B of IDEA during the 2013–2014 school year (U.S. Department of Education, 2015). As you have already figured out though, while LRE statistics are easily accessible, this method encompasses significant flaws. The biggest flaw lies in the assumption that IEP teams base placement decisions on severity level alone. Unfortunately, numerous extraneous variables factor into placement decisions such as cost, program availability, individual interpretations of the law, and parental requests. Just think about the student who is minimally verbal and non-ambulatory whose parents insist he be in a general education class all day long, or the student with a learning disability whose family would prefer he be in a small special education setting for instruction. Looking only at the placement of students no longer helps us know who they are or what they need!

It is not just educators who tend to promote inclusive practices for students. Legal authorities also continue to emphasize access to the general education environment for all students, as evidenced by the Every Student Succeeds Act (ESSA) signed into law in December 2015, replacing No Child Left Behind (NCLB, 2002). As ESSA mandates high academic standards for all students to ensure preparation for success in college and careers (The White House, 2015), the requirement for grade level standards to be included on every student's IEP, regardless of disability severity, continues. This has really impacted how students with moderate-to-severe disabilities are taught. This emphasis on academic standards can result in the neglect of other parts of the law pertaining specifically to students with severe disabilities, such as the requirement for special education services to be designed to meet the student's unique needs and prepare them for further education, employment, and independent living (IDEA, 2004). How can we be sure we are meeting the unique academic, behavioral, communication, social, and functional needs of students with moderate-to-severe disabilities?

## THE RESEARCH BEHIND THE STRATEGIES

As students with moderate-to-severe disabilities often need more intense supports and specialized instruction as compared to students with mild disabilities, evidence-based practices (EBPs) significantly differ between these two groups of students. Due to the unique, multifaceted characteristics of students *within* the category of moderate-to-severe disabilities, experts in the field even take it a step further, recommending that educators use EBPs that address disability-specific needs to provide intensive, explicit instruction within the broader general education curriculum (Brownell, Sindelar, Kiely, & Danielson, 2010). As the prevalence of ASD continues to rise, researchers have spent a considerable amount of time analyzing studies in an effort to identify EBPs specific to students with this diagnosis.

Two different organizations have conducted comprehensive analyses of the research to identify EBPs for students with ASD. The National Professional Development Center on ASD (NPDC on ASD) identified 27 EBPs (Wong et al., 2013) and the National Autism Center (NAC) identified 14 established treatments in the second phase of the National Standards Project (NAC, 2015). For a comprehensive list of EBPs for students with moderate-to-severe disabilities see the table Evidence-Based Practices for Students With Moderate-to-Severe Disabilities at the end of this chapter. While the NPDC on ASD focused on individual interventions, the NAC clustered individual strategies together into intervention classes (Wong et al., 2013). All 14 established treatments identified by the NAC overlap with 23 of the 27 EBPs identified by the NPDC on ASD. The remaining four EBPs identified by the NPDC on ASD were identified as emerging interventions by the NAC.

Other researchers have conducted literature reviews that focused on identifying EBPs specific to students with ID. Courtade, Test, and Cook (2015) identified eight EBPs within the professional literature for teaching academic skills to students with severe ID. In addition, Courtade and colleagues (2015) reviewed the 63 EBPs identified by the National Secondary Transition Technical Assistance Center (NSTTAC) related to secondary transitions for students with disabilities. By examining participant characteristics within the original research studies, the authors were able to link 16 of the 63 practices to students with severe ID. However, many of the EBPs were supported by only a single study that often involved fewer than five participants diagnosed with severe ID (Courtade et al., 2015). Hudson, Browder, and Wood (2013) conducted a research review that focused on EBPs related to academic learning for students with moderate-to-severe ID in general education settings. These authors identified only one EBP, embedded instruction trials using constant time delay, within the literature (Hudson et al., 2013).

**Making Connections**

Check out Chapter 4 on Instructional Strategies and Universal Design for Learning.

## WHAT *STUDENTS* HAVE TO SAY ABOUT INCLUDING PEERS WITH MODERATE-TO-SEVERE DISABILITIES IN GENERAL EDUCATION CLASSROOMS

You take out your class list again, feeling more prepared, as your initial shock has subsided. But now you only have more questions! How will your typically developing students feel about sitting next to a peer who can't talk but communicates using an iPad instead? What about the instructional aide assigned to work with one of your students; how will you introduce this extra adult to the rest of the class? How much information should you share about the students' needs? What happens if one of the students has an emotional outburst and starts hitting classmates? How can you include the students who are reading 3 years below grade level without calling attention to their deficits? Let's look to the students for answers!

Understanding the perspectives of students, both with and without disabilities, who have experienced inclusion can provide valuable insight into making inclusion work—for *everyone*. Luckily, researchers have already tackled this daunting feat for you! To examine the factors that contribute to the success of inclusion for all students, including those with moderate and severe disabilities, researchers conducted focus groups with students (both with and without disabilities) who attended elementary and middle schools that were recognized as exemplars for schoolwide inclusive practices for all students, from typically developing to those with severe disabilities (Shogren et al., 2015). Shogren and colleagues (2015) identified three major factors that attributed to the schools' success with inclusion: (1) a positive school culture that promoted a sense of belonging, (2) a collaborative school climate that emphasized similarities over differences, and (3) the implementation of evidence-based practices that focused on individualized instruction where

**Key Concepts**

Your three factors for successful inclusion?
- Positive school culture
- Collaborative climate
- Implementation of evidence-based practices that focus on individualized instruction

all students were given what they needed to succeed. Typically developing students often expressed that they played an important role in helping students with disabilities, including those falling in the category of severe disabilities (Shogren et al., 2015).

Students with severe disabilities attending these elementary and middle schools were also observed (Kurth, Lyon, & Shogren, 2015). It is important to note that although these students represented the full gamut of inclusive services and support levels provided by the school, only students who had experienced success in the general education classroom were included in the observations. The practices that most often emerged as successful in supporting students with severe disabilities in inclusive schools involved active student participation across a variety of teaching arrangements, the use of co-teaching models, and instructional leadership.

Additionally, staff were frequently observed engaging in both formal (e.g., data sharing and planning) and informal (e.g., briefly sharing student progress during instructional periods) collaborative activities (Kurth et al., 2015). Now that you know what some

**Making Connections**

Check out Chapter 9 on Co-Teaching.

of the key research says, let's take a closer look at the dos and don'ts when working with students with moderate-to-severe disabilities.

## DEMONSTRATE CAUTION BY AVOIDING THESE COMMON MISTAKES!

Teachers:

- ✗ **STOP judging a student's cognitive ability based solely on their communication skills.** Cognitive ability is only one of the many factors that can impact a student's method of, and ability to, communicate. For example, a student with Cerebral Palsy may lack the motor skills necessary to communicate verbally and gesturally, but when given an augmentative and alternative communication

(AAC) device controlled through eye gaze, it may be difficult to get the student to *stop* communicating!

✘ **STOP talking about students in front of them.** Receptive language abilities typically exceed expressive language abilities. In other words, just because a student may not have the ability to *tell* someone what you said, *does not* mean they do not *understand* what you said.

✘ **STOP telling the student no repeatedly throughout their day.** Consider how you would feel if someone consistently told you *no* every time you tried to do something. My guess is you would be quick to stop trying altogether, not to mention the lack of self-confidence and self-esteem that would be sure to follow.

✘ **STOP having the adult supporting the student place demand after demand on the student throughout the entire school day.** Imagine if you went to work and for 6 to 7 hours straight you had someone with you telling you what to do. I bet you would quit within a day! Instead, provide the student with short, frequent independent breaks with a preferred activity without adult direction. The student probably wants a break from the adult just as much as the adult probably wants a break from the student!

✘ **STOP expecting paraprofessionals to just know what to do.** Paraprofessionals shouldn't have to figure out what to do with a student; they need support and guidance. In addition, too many paraeducators are seen just standing around, waiting to be given directions. Provide clear, explicit directions, and enable them to be the classroom help you and the students deserve!

✘ **STOP limiting your contact with parents to reporting only the negatives.** Parents are people too, and they need to hear the positives just like everyone else. There's a good chance that all their contacts with school personnel to date have only involved negative things (e.g., James doesn't pay attention, Sheryl is reading below grade level, Camilla can't stay in her seat). Celebrate the small steps and make a parent's day by surprising them with a positive phone call or handwritten note! A little effort on your part will go a long way in establishing a positive home-school relationship.

**Making Connections**

Check out Chapter 19 on School-to-Home Collaboration.

✘ **STOP limiting the work presented to students to activities that far exceed their ability level.** Just like anyone else, these students need to feel successful. Once again, imagine a day at work where you were only presented with tasks that you did not understand and were just too difficult. How would you feel about yourself?

What motivation would you have to continue to get out of bed and go to work every morning?

✗ **STOP making assumptions about why you think a student is doing something or how you think the student is feeling.** Use only objective measures to analyze observable behaviors to determine why a student is doing something or how a student may be feeling. For example, you may be inclined to make the assumption that your student who receives free and reduced meals constantly screams because she is hungry. What if, however, she is screaming because she is in excruciating pain, but as a result of her disability, she lacks the communication skills to tell you? Due to your assumptions, her severe pain would not be addressed and could continue to worsen. Unless a student specifically says, "I am frustrated!" you cannot assume they are frustrated. You can, however, report observable behaviors such as, "He always breaks his pencil in half during extended writing assignments."

✗ **STOP assuming that *inclusion* refers only to a student's physical presence in the general education classroom.** Special education is not a *place*. Rather, inclusion means that students with special needs (a) are included as valued members of the school community, (b) belong to the school community and are accepted by others, (c) participate actively in the academic and social community, and (d) are given supports that afford them the opportunity to succeed (McLeskey, Rosenberg, & Westling, 2013).

Administrators:

✗ **STOP misinterpreting the law (IDEA) to mean that every student *must* be included in the general education classroom.** IDEA states that students with disabilities should be included in the general education classroom to the "maximum extent possible," not that *all* students with disabilities are required to be in the general education classroom for the entire school day. It is critical that students with disabilities have their needs met, so work as a team to consider all factors before making placement decisions.

## SAFE TO PROCEED—USE THESE STRATEGIES FOR SUCCESS!

Teachers:

✔ **INCORPORATE visual supports to increase comprehension and promote appropriate behavior.** A picture is worth a thousand words, so go ahead, pair words with pictures throughout your classroom. This can be helpful even for your fluent readers because as the saying goes, a lot more information can be gained by glancing at a picture when compared to glancing at a well-written paragraph. This is especially true for those students who have difficulty with impulse control! Visual supports are frequently used to promote positive behavior by increasing predictability through daily visual schedules and providing visual reminders of the rules.

✔ **USE manipulatives to incorporate hands-on learning opportunities.** Students with moderate-to-severe disabilities often learn best by doing things repeatedly. First, using manipulatives, model what you want the student to do. Then give the students the manipulatives to provide them with multiple opportunities to practice the skills and concepts. Finally, allow the students to demonstrate what they learned using the manipulatives!

✔ **INCORPORATE technology whenever possible.** Students today, even those with severe disabilities, are digital natives and excel when it comes to technology. Using technology can open doors for all students by increasing motivation, engagement, and predictability, as well as helping facilitate social and communication skills.

**Making Connections**

Check out Chapter 5 on Using Technology and Assistive Technology.

✔ **CONSIDER low-tech options first.** Low-tech options—that is, those that don't require a power source (e.g., Velcro)—are often much more cost-effective than purchasing high-tech tools from specially designed catalogues, and are more time-efficient than waiting for a special item to be shipped. For example, give a student a closed binder to write on if you don't have a slant board and then use a rug lock to keep it in place. Provide graph paper to help students who have difficulty aligning math problems. Place Wikki Stix on paper to provide a visual and tactile stationary boundary to help students write or color within designated areas. Check out the table Low-Tech Options Using Dollar Store Finds at the end of this chapter for specific ideas.

**Plugged In**

Want free modules on how to collect data and make data-based decisions? Check out East Carolina University's MAST website at http://mast.ecu.edu.

✔ **COLLECT and ANALYZE data frequently across all areas—academics, behavior, communication, and independence—and USE the data for planning and making decisions.** Not only is data-based decision making promoted by law, research continuously demonstrates positive student outcomes when implemented correctly. Data collection alone is not sufficient; it's what you *do* with the data that makes a difference.

✔ **PROVIDE appropriate wait time.** Students with moderate-to-severe disabilities often require more time to process information, so giving students an extra 3 to 5 seconds to come up with an answer makes a big difference. Time yourself a few times so you know what 3 to 5 seconds feels like. Since those seconds seem to take forever, and as teachers, we know that every second is valuable, give Darrell his question and tell him you will come back to him for his answer. Then ask two more students additional questions before returning to Darrell for his answer.

✔ **PROVIDE choice-making opportunities throughout the day to promote self-determination skills.** For example, give students the choice between two different writing utensils or allow students to choose the order in which they solve their math problems. Either way, the student is still completing the required tasks, but now they have a sense of empowerment, which often heads off behavior issues—a winning situation for all!

✔ **PROVIDE explicit social skills instruction and support opportunities to practice newly learned skills in the natural environment.** If students with moderate-to-severe disabilities were able to learn through observation alone, they would not *have* social skill deficits in the first place! They

**Plugged In**

Access free modules on social skills instruction from the National Professional Development Center on Autism Spectrum Disorder at http://afirm.fpg.unc.edu/afirm-modules.

need to be *taught* those social skills. The good news is that many of their peers will benefit from practicing or learning social skills along with them!

✔ **PROMOTE frequent home-school communication.** This becomes especially important when working with students with limited communication. Provide families with alternatives to asking their child, "How was your day at school?" by sending home daily communication regarding what the students did in school that day. Having this information allows parents to ask more specific questions and provide prompting if needed, in order to increase the likelihood their child can share information regarding his or her school day. Use the PROSE checklist at the end of this chapter to improve written communication between home and school (Nagro, 2015).

✔ **USE applied behavior analysis (ABA) principles to promote appropriate student behavior and decrease inappropriate behavior.** A student does not have to understand the principles of ABA for the strategies to be effective. Effective educators implement more behavioral strategies rooted in ABA than they even know! Not familiar with ABA? Most school districts have behavioral specialists on staff—just ask!

✔ **COMPLETE a functional behavior assessment (FBA) to identify the function of an inappropriate behavior.** To effectively decrease inappropriate behaviors, you must identify the function that the behavior serves the student. All behavior serves as communication. Is Carla hitting adults to escape demands? Is Dylan yelling at his peers to gain their attention? To accurately identify the function of a behavior, you must collect the appropriate data.

**Making Connections**

Check out Chapter 8 on Positive Behavior Supports and Chapter 12 on Emotional and Behavioral Disorders.

✔ **TEACH appropriate replacement behaviors.** Once you have identified the function of a student's inappropriate behavior, you can begin to teach him or her more appropriate ways to communicate his or her wants and needs. Make sure the strategies you are teaching the student are easily accessible across environments. For example, you identified that Jamal is flipping his desk over to escape work demands. Although Jamal communicates verbally, when his behaviors are escalated, he has difficulty verbally expressing his wants and needs. So you provide him with a break card and a help card so he can easily request both, even when he is feeling overwhelmed. You teach Jamal how and when to use the cards. Next period, Jamal goes next door for science and no longer has access to the cards. What do you think he will do when he wants to escape a demand? If you are visualizing an overturned desk, give yourself a gold star! The key then is to teach appropriate replacement behaviors, and then help students generalize them!

✔ **INCORPORATE a student's augmentative and alternative communication (AAC) device into every aspect of the day.** When you don't, you are essentially taking away the student's *voice.* Don't spend a lot of time programming the device with specific academic language and content; instead, use what's already programmed on the device by asking yes-no questions and providing multiple choice options for answering questions using letter or number keys. Think about it: What percentage of your free time do *you* spend talking about academic topics? Which is more meaningful to you: being understood by others and conversing with peers or sitting in a class passively listening to instruction? Which will have a greater impact on the student's quality of life: reciting facts or being able to interact with a variety of people in a meaningful way?

## Administrators, DO this:

✔ **PROVIDE co-teachers with sufficient time to plan together.** Research shows that co-planning is a key component to successful co-teaching. When working with students with significant disabilities, these educators need to communicate and plan proactively. Too often, general and special educators have limited to no common planning time due to scheduling difficulties. Make this a priority when scheduling!

✔ **ALLOW teachers to write realistic student learning objectives.** Students often receive special education services because they have demonstrated a lack of progress when provided with traditional teaching methods. Just as special educators are required to write attainable IEP goals for students, teachers should be able to write attainable student learning objectives as well. Is it realistic to expect students reading 3 years below grade level to be reading on grade level within 1 year's time?

✔ **SEEK OUT knowledge of special education practices and don't be afraid to rely on the expertise of others.** Educators would rather hear, "I don't know, let me look into that" as opposed to being provided a random answer immediately. Pretending to know everything is not beneficial for anyone—students, teachers, or administrators. Educators recognize the multitude of knowledge administrators are required to have to effectively do their job and understand that a comprehensive knowledge of special education does not fall into this category, nor do we expect this. However, educators, just like anyone else, appreciate honesty.

## EVIDENCE-BASED PRACTICES FOR STUDENTS WITH MODERATE-TO-SEVERE DISABILITIES

| Evidence-Based Practice (EBP) | Wong et al. (2013) | NAC (2015) | Courtade, Test, & Cook (2015) |
|---|---|---|---|
| Antecedent-Based Intervention | ✓ | ✓ | |
| Cognitive Behavioral Intervention | ✓ | ✓ | |
| Community-Based Instruction | | ✓ | NSTTAC |
| Differential Reinforcement of Alternative, Incompatible, or Other Behavior (DRA/I/O) | ✓ | ✓ | |
| Discrete Trial Teaching (DTT) | ✓ | ✓ | ✓ |
| Exercise | ✓ | ** | |
| Extinction | ✓ | ✓ | |
| Functional Behavior Assessment (FBA) | ✓ | ✓ | |
| Functional Communication Training (FCT) | ✓ | ** | |
| Functional Use | | | ✓ |
| In Vivo Instruction | | | ✓ |
| Modeling | ✓ | ✓ | |
| Naturalistic Intervention | ✓ | ✓ | |
| One-More-Than Strategy (money skills) | | | NSTTAC |
| Opportunities to Respond | | | ✓ |
| Parent-Implemented Intervention | ✓ | ✓ | |
| Peer-Mediated Instruction and Intervention | ✓ | ✓ | |
| Picture Exchange Communication System (PECS) | ✓ | ** | |
| Pivotal Response Training (PRT) | ✓ | ✓ | |
| Prompting | ✓ | ✓ | ✓ |
| Reinforcement | ✓ | ✓ | |
| Response Interruption/Redirection (RIRD) | ✓ | ✓ | |
| Scripting | ✓ | ✓ | |
| Self-Determined Learning Model of Instruction | | | NSTTAC |
| Self-Directed IEP | | | NSTTAC |
| Self-Management | ✓ | ✓ | NSTTAC |
| Self-Monitoring | | ✓ | NSTTAC |

| Evidence-Based Practice (EBP) | Wong et al. (2013) | NAC (2015) | Courtade, Test, & Cook (2015) |
|---|---|---|---|
| Simulations | | | NSTTAC |
| Social Narratives | ✓ | ✓ | |
| Social Skills Training | ✓ | ✓ | |
| Structured Play Group | ✓ | ✓ | |
| Systematic Instruction | | | ✓ |
| Task Analysis | ✓ | ✓ | |
| Technology-Aided Instruction and Intervention | ✓ | ** | |
| Time Delay | ✓ | ✓ | |
| Video Modeling | ✓ | ✓ | NSTTAC |
| Visual Supports | ✓ | ✓ | ✓ |
| Whose Future Is It Anyway? | | | NSTTAC |

*Notes:*

✓ Indicates the practice was identified by the corresponding group.

** Indicates the practice was identified as an emerging intervention by the corresponding organization.

NSTTAC = EBPs identified by the National Secondary Transition Technical Assistance Center then linked to students with severe ID by the corresponding group.

## LOW-TECH OPTIONS USING DOLLAR STORE FINDS

| Items | Uses |
| --- | --- |
| Cookie sheets | Magnetic boards for use with magnetic letters, numbers, and so on; the edges help keep the items on the sheet |
| Clothespins | Matching activities, fine motor skills practice, hold paper in place while students write by clipping it to the front cover of a heavy book |
| Color transparent rulers | Help students keep their place when reading |
| Picture frames | Eye gaze frames |
| Plastic kids ring | Affix to the button on a computer mouse to help students with motor difficulties keep their finger and hand in place |
| Popsicle sticks | Tape one to each page of a book so they stick out from the book when closed to help students with motor difficulties turn the pages independently |
| Knit gloves | Help students avoid accidental hits when using touch screens by having them wear a glove with the index finger removed |
| Silly Putty, Koosh Balls, stretchy toys, squishy balls | Helps students focus and concentrate by providing them with a quiet, nondisruptive way to move while staying in their seat |

## PROSE STRATEGY

Use **PROSE** to improve written communication between home and school (Nagro, 2015):

**P** = Improving Print
**R** = Improving Readability
**O** = Improving Organization
**S** = Improving Structure
**E** = Improving Ease of Reading

| | |
|---|---|
| **P** | **Print**<br>☐ All one font<br>☐ Consistent font size throughout<br>☐ Running text is medium font (e.g. 12-point font)<br>☐ Sentence case print rather than all capitals or italics<br>☐ Selective use of highlighting or bold print to draw attention rather than to decorate |
| **R** | **Readability**<br>☐ Reading level is ideally fifth grade but no higher than eighth grade<br>☐ Multisyllabic words are limited so most words are one or two syllables<br>☐ Sentences are 10–15 words ideally but no more than 25 words<br>☐ Longer sentences are broken into several shorter sentences<br>☐ Prepositional phrases are limited to shorten sentence length |
| **O** | **Organization**<br>☐ Predictable left-to-right, top-to-bottom layout<br>☐ Headings guide the reader and are set apart from running text<br>☐ Diagrams (lists, tables, charts, and graphs) are set apart from the running text<br>☐ Diagrams (lists, tables, charts, and graphs) are simple (no more than 15 labels and 75 items)<br>☐ Diagrams (lists, tables, charts, and graphs) are labeled and self-explanatory |
| **S** | **Structure**<br>☐ Ideally one page or broken into sections<br>☐ Page numbers are provided for documents longer than one page<br>☐ Balance white space so that text is not overly dense<br>☐ Images and figures supplement the content rather than serve as decoration |
| **E** | **Ease**<br>☐ Written in the active voice (passive sentences close to 0%)<br>☐ Pronouns replaced by the original nouns so sentences have no more than one pronoun<br>☐ Terms written out rather than using acronyms unless the acronym is widely known to parents outside the education field (e.g., name of the school)<br>☐ Real-world examples are included when possible |

*Source*: Nagro, S. N. (2015). PROSE checklist: Strategies for improving school-to-home written communication. *TEACHING Exceptional Children, 47*(5), 256–263.

# REFERENCES

American Psychiatric Association. (2013). *Diagnostic and statistical manual of mental disorders* (5th ed.). Arlington, VA: American Psychiatric Publishing.

Brownell, M. T., Sindelar, P. T., Kiely, M. T., & Danielson, L. C. (2010). Special education teacher quality and preparation: Exposing foundations, constructing a new model. *Exceptional Children, 76*(3), 357–377.

Courtade, G. R., Test, D. W., & Cook, B. G. (2015). Evidence-based practices for learners with severe intellectual disability. *Research and Practice for Persons with Severe Disabilities, 39*(4), 305–318.

Downing, J. E., & MacFarland, S. (2010). Severe disabilities (Education and individuals with severe disabilities: Promising practices). In J. H. Stone & M. Blouin (Eds.), *International encyclopedia of rehabilitation*. Retrieved from http://cirrie.buffalo.edu/encyclopedia/en/article/114/#s9

Hudson, M. E., Browder, D. M., & Wood, L. A. (2013). Review of experimental research on academic learning by students with moderate and severe intellectual disability in general education. *Research and Practice for Persons with Severe Disabilities, 38*(1), 17–29.

Individuals with Disabilities Education Act (IDEA). 20 U.S.C. § 1400 *et seq.* (2004). Retrieved from http://idea.ed.gov/download/statute.html

Kurth, J. A., Lyon, K. J., & Shogren, K. A. (2015). Supporting students with severe disabilities in inclusive schools: A descriptive account from schools implementing inclusive practices. *Research and Practice for Persons with Severe Disabilities, 40*(4), 261–274.

McLeskey, J. M., Rosenberg, M. S., & Westling, D. L. (2013). *Inclusion: Effective practices for all students* (2nd ed.). Boston, MA: Pearson.

Nagro, S. N. (2015). PROSE checklist: Strategies for improving school-to-home written communication. *TEACHING Exceptional Children, 47*(5), 256–263.

National Autism Center (NAC). (2015). *Findings and conclusions: National standards project, phase 2*. Randolph, MA: Author.

No Child Left Behind (NCLB) Act of 2001, 20 U.S.C. 70 § 6301 *et seq.* (2002). Retrieved from http://www2.ed.gov/policy/elsec/leg/esea02/107-110.pdf

Reschly, D. J. (1996). Identification and assessment of students with disabilities. *The Future of Children, 6*(1), 40–53.

Shogren, K. A., Gross, J. M. S., Forber-Pratt, A. J., Francis, G. L., Satter, A. L., Blue-Banning, M., & Hill, C. (2015). The perspectives of students with and without disabilities on inclusive schools. *Research and Practice for Persons with Severe Disabilities, 40*(4), 243–260.

U.S. Department of Education, Office of Special Education Programs. (2015). *Individuals with Disabilities Education Act (IDEA) database*. Retrieved from http://nces.ed.gov/programs/digest/d15/tables/dt15_204.60.asp?current=yes

The White House, Office of the Press Secretary. (2015). Fact sheet: Congress acts to fix No Child Left Behind [press release]. Retrieved from https://www.whitehouse.gov/the-press-office/2015/12/03/fact-sheet-congress-acts-fix-no-child-left-behind

Wong, C., Odom, S. L., Hume, K. Cox, A. W., Fettig, A., Kucharczyk, S., . . . Schultz, T. R. (2013). *Evidence-based practices for children, youth, and young adults with autism spectrum disorder*. Chapel Hill: The University of North Carolina, Frank Porter Graham Child Development Institute, Autism Evidence-Based Practice Review Group.

## ADDITIONAL RECOMMENDED READING

Alberto, P. A., & Troutman, A. C. (2013). *Applied behavior analysis for teachers* (9th ed.). Upper Saddle River, NJ: Pearson.

Collins, B. C., Karl, J., Riggs, L., Galloway, C. C., & Hager, K. D. (2010). Teaching core content with real-life applications to secondary students with moderate and severe disabilities. *TEACHING Exceptional Children, 43*(1), 52–59.

Fraser, D. W. (2013). 5 Tips for creating independent activities aligned with the common core state standards. *TEACHING Exceptional Children, 45*(6), 6–15.

McConnell, M. E., Cox, C. J., Thomas, D. D., & Hilvitz, P. B. (2001). *Functional behavioral assessment*. Denver, CO: Love.

Sundberg, M. L., & Partington, J. W. (1998). *Teaching language to children with autism or other developmental disabilities*. Concord, CA: AVB Press.

## TOP FIVE WEBSITES TO SUPPORT STUDENTS WITH MODERATE-TO-SEVERE DISABILITIES

➡ Technology Toolkit for UDL in All Classrooms: http://udltechtoolkit.wikispaces.com

➡ TEACCH Autism Program: https://www.teacch.com

➡ Tech4Learning: http://www.tech4learning.com

➡ Online Classroom Timers: http://www.online-stopwatch.com/classroom-timers

➡ AAC and Other Technology Simplified: http://lburkhart.com/main.htm

## APPS WE LOVE

➡ iCommunicate

➡ iPrompts

➡ iModeling

➡ Endless Reader

➡ Endless Numbers

# 15

*English Language
Learners With
Disabilities*

*Best Practices*

Brenda L. Barrio
*Washington State University*

Pamela K. Peak
*University of North Texas*

Wendy W. Murawski
*California State University, Northridge*

It's another rainy and cool morning at Wilson School. Mrs. Rodriguez is getting her classroom ready for the day to begin, but while drinking some of her favorite coffee, she thinks about her recent struggles to properly teach and accommodate her diverse learners. In a class of 25, five of her students receive special education services due to their learning disabilities, speech impairments, and autism spectrum disorder. Seven additional students receive English language support with only one instructional class per week due to the shortage of personnel in the district. To make matters more complicated, out of these seven students, three of them speak languages other than Spanish (one speaks Russian, another Vietnamese, and the third speaks Somali), and two of them are also identified as having a disability! Although Mrs. Rodriguez earned a teaching certification in English as a Second Language (ESL) over 2 years ago, her resources, knowledge, and skills are fairly limited. Sipping her coffee, she wonders, "What quick strategies can I immediately implement to assist my English language learners? Can they also be used with students with disabilities?" Luckily for Mrs. Rodriguez, a list of dos and don'ts are provided in this chapter, following some background about English language learners (ELLs) with and without disabilities.

## UNDERSTANDING ELLs

Mrs. Rodriguez's situation is not uncommon. Many of us work in classes with high numbers of ELLs, individuals with disabilities, and a combination of the two. In some states like California, Texas, and New York, ELLs account for more than 15% to 20% of the K–12 population and numbers are rising exponentially in all states (National Center for Education Statistics, 2015). The increased number of linguistically diverse students in the United States has brought a positive increase in diversity, talent, and experiences to our schools. With it, changes and challenges to the education framework have also increased. Because of the national trend toward inclusive practices and collaboration, exceptional learners are more frequently taught in the general education classroom than in the pull-out models of the past (Murawski, 2010). This applies to ELL students with and without disabilities. This means that typical classroom teachers are now responsible for teaching their grade-level content, while also incorporating language instruction and any necessary adaptations for students with disabilities. So how can we do that?

First, we give up or start from scratch. There are many strong approaches for working with ELLs. For example, sheltered instruction is the content-based instructional model most often used to address the needs of English learners (Collier, 2015a). Sheltered instruction essentially requires teachers to use clear, simple English language and a variety of scaffolding strategies to provide input in the particular content area. There are many different types of sheltered instruction, to include Content-Based Instruction (CBI), Sheltered Instruction Observation Protocol (SIOP), and Specially Designed Academic Instruction in English (SDAIE). Collier (2015a) writes that "regardless of the approach used, the key premise remains the same for all—teachers must integrate language and content in a meaningful way" (p. 254). Clearly, this makes sense and remains an important goal for teachers. But what happens when those second—or sometimes third or fourth—language learners also have a concomitant disability? That's where this chapter comes in!

To start, we take a moment to discuss who these students are and identify some of the issues that can be faced when working with students who are ELLs and have a disability. Then of course, we jump right into identifying what really works with this population. We tell you right off that many of the strategies used when working with students who are ELLs are also strong choices when working with students with disabilities. The key is to know your students and to be able to recognize the etiology of the learning difficulty: Is it due to a language barrier or a true disability or both?

## DISABILITY OR LANGUAGE BARRIER?

It turns out that determining whether a learning difficulty is due to a language barrier or a true disability is not that easy to do. In fact, language difficulties are often confused with disabilities, resulting in a mislabeling or misidentification of the real need. How does this happen? Don't we know the difference? You would think by now we would, but we continue to use standardized assessments in special education to identify students with disabilities, without having clearly determined how to differentiate learning difficulties when the student is an English learner. In fact, many assessments used to diagnose students with disabilities show different biases toward individuals from other cultural backgrounds and for whom English is the second language. Historically, these biases have led to the misidentification of ELL students for special education services (Sullivan, 2011).

The problem, however, does not just lie in the test itself; it also lies in *how* the test is given. In some cases, the assessments' procedures, administration, and formatting have proven to be unreliable and invalid when trying to differentiate between disability and language difference (Abedi 2004, 2006; MacSwan & Rolstad, 2006). In addition, ELLs' confusion based on their language barrier can negatively impact their appropriate academic responses, leading to wrongful identification as having a disability. In short, a student might be struggling academically because of a disability or might simply be struggling because of his or her lack of English proficiency. Unless we can assess accurately, all we see is the struggle. We know what you are thinking—why don't we just test the student in his or her native language? Good question. Certainly, assessment in a native language is a preferable (and even recommended) practice. But how many psychologists and diagnosticians work in your district who speak Cantonese, Farsi, Swiss German, Russian, and Urdu? Not only would they need to speak the language, but they would also have to have appropriate training on how to administer the assessments in that language. Therefore, though bilingual or nonverbal assessments may be available in the district, personnel may not be professionally trained to administer the assessment or the school district may not have the resources to provide the assessment in a student's native language (Artiles, Kozleski, Trent, Osher, & Ortiz, 2010).

The result of not being able to adequately and accurately assess ELL students for special education services has led to something called *disproportionality*. The disproportionate representation of culturally and linguistically diverse students (e.g., ELLs) in special education has been a recurring concern within the United States for years (Artiles et al., 2010). Disproportionate representation in this situation refers to the unequal representation of students within special education who are ELLs compared to those students who speak English as a first language (Artiles et al., 2010). More than 4.6 million students in the United States are considered to be ELLs and clearly qualify as special learners regarding their language needs, but about 500,000 of those students currently receive services in special education (U.S. Department of Education, 2014) as well!

ELLs are overrepresented in special education, especially in the category of learning disabilities (Harry & Klingner, 2006). The disproportionate representation of ELL students in the category of learning disabilities can be attributed to many factors, including the subjectivity of the referral process itself. Think about it. It can take 7 to 10 years to become proficient in academic English (Fernandez & Inserra, 2013). During that time, students are interacting with numerous teachers and continuing to miss out on

 **Making Connections**

Check out Chapter 11 on Learning Disabilities.

critical instruction since they do not yet possess the ability to comprehend the complex content. Until fairly recently, the definition of a learning disability was when a discrepancy existed between ability and achievement. Doesn't that seem to fit with many students who are ELLs? They have typical-to-strong ability in their native language, but when it comes to their achievement in the classroom, they are failing. Many are referred for special education and, based on numbers, a large (and disproportionate) number of them are being identified as needing special education services (Harry & Klingner, 2006).

Disproportionality works the other way as well. Did you know that ELLs are actually the least likely group to be identified gifted services (DeNisco, 2016)? Yes, ELL students are rarely identified as being gifted and talented and even less so as twice exceptional (gifted with a disability). Given that being an ELL is a special need (as is being gifted and having a disability), perhaps students who share all three of these characteristics are thrice-exceptional? There is clearly a major issue of inequity if too few English learners are identified for gifted programs and too many are identified for special education!

So how do you know if you should refer a student for special education assessment? We know that you don't want to jump the gun and misidentify a student, but at the same time, if an ELL student is struggling academically, you also don't want to deny him or her services that may help. Alba Ortiz, a guru on working with ELLs with special needs, reminds us that there are four components to a recommendation for a comprehensive individual assessment. Each recommendation needs to indicate that (1) the child is in a positive school climate, (2) the teacher has used instructional strategies known to be effective for English learners, (3) neither clinical teaching nor interventions recommended by a school assistance team resolved the problem, and (4) other general education alternatives also proved unsuccessful (Ortiz, 1997). The main question we should be asking is whether the problem is related to language or if it reflects a cognitive difficulty. "The general guideline is that if a student is making academic progress at about the same rate as other ELL students from similar backgrounds (students who share similar linguistic, cultural, educational, or refugee experiences), then the student probably does not have special education needs. Rather, he/she may just need more time and language support as a result of having to process so much new information" (Robertson, n.d., p. 1). If, despite all efforts to individualize and meet specific learning needs, students continue to struggle, they most likely do indeed have a disability.

**Key Concepts**

Prior to referring for special education, be sure the ELL has been exposed to:

- A positive school climate
- Instructional strategies appropriate for ELL
- Interventions recommended by a school team
- Additional general education alternatives

## TEACHING ENGLISH LANGUAGE LEARNERS WITH DISABILITIES

Let's say we've solved the issue of disability versus language difference. (Wouldn't that be nice?) Unfortunately, we are not out of the woods yet. "English language learners who need special education services are further disadvantaged by the shortage of special educators who are trained to address their language- and disability-related needs simultaneously" (Ortiz, n.d.). Now, add to the mix that both ELLs and students with disabilities are increasingly taught in the typical general education classroom. This means that we have classroom teachers who are also stymied and wondering what to do! What can be done?

First of all, know that there is hope. Many of the sheltered English strategies are similar to strategies that are frequently used in special education. These are often the types of strategies that, when shared with general educators, are seen as "great ideas for everyone!" What this means is that, although some of these techniques are *critical* for special learners, such as ELLs with disabilities, they are going to also be well received in a general education class.

Let's start by considering how to approach instruction to a student who (a) doesn't have the language and (b) would struggle regardless due to a learning disability. It's important to recognize that *"comprehension precedes production"* (Collier, 2015a, p. 256, emphasis in original). If students' anxiety is raised by an expectation that they will actively participate daily, have to read aloud, or be constantly lectured at in a language they do not understand, they will shut down. Echevarria, Vogt, and Short (2008) remind us that it is the teachers' job to provide *comprehensible input* to students. We need to think about the vocabulary we are using, the information we are writing on the board, and the questions we are asking. Have we differentiated this for our various students?

Next, determine the cognitive demand you are placing on students and the context in which you are expecting them to meet that demand. Cummins's (1991) Model of Academic Language helps teachers identify the context for learning that they are creating, while concurrently assessing the cognitive demand the task places on the student. His framework (which is described in *What Really Works in Elementary and Secondary Education;* Collier, 2015a, 2015b) emphasizes that, though most teachers' lectures would be considered low context/high demand, the

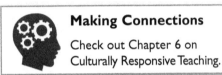

**Making Connections**

Check out Chapter 6 on Culturally Responsive Teaching.

most effective instruction for ELLs, including those with disabilities, would be in high context/high cognitive demand. Historically, teachers who work with students with disabilities tend to have lower expectations of their students (Cameron & Cook, 2013), and teachers who work with ELL students have the same lower expectations (Reeves, 2006). We need to turn that around! Thus, it is critical that teachers learn how to provide high cognitive demand to these learners, while still addressing their need for context. How do you establish a strong context that matches your students' backgrounds, cultures, strengths, and skills? The best way to do that is to use culturally responsive teaching (CRT). CRT is a way to respect students' diverse backgrounds, build them into the curriculum, and use their unique experiences to help instruction rather than detract from it. Since there is an excellent chapter on CRT in this text, we refer you to Chapter 6 to learn more.

Finally, teachers of students who are ELLs *and* have disabilities need to really focus on building literacy skills. Cummins's (1991) seminal work on ELLs found that "the concepts and skills that students acquire in their first language will transfer to their second language *within the right instructional context*" (Collier, 2015b, p. 257). There is the emphasis on context again! Regardless of what grade or content you teach, the key to working with these learners is to find out what they can already do. Use strategies to build on their strengths and the skills they already have. These strategies include cognitive (graphic organizers, thinking maps, strategic note taking), social-affective (groupwork, peer-assisted learning strategies), and metalinguistic (self-awareness and self-determination skills) strategies (Chamot, 1996). This is a perfect example of strategies recommended for second language learners that would be appropriate for individuals with disabilities as well.

We now know that we need to do a better job assessing these students— that it is often difficult to tease out the differences between language-based struggles based on a second language and struggles based on a true disability. We know that we need to create an environment that reduces stress and allows for students to build their comprehension. We know that we should strive for activities that are high cognitive demand and high context, and that literacy is a key aspect of our working with these learners. Let us provide you with a few more things you should know. What follows are our pet peeves (the "Stop doing this" section) and our vital strategies (the "Do this instead" section).

**Making Connections**

Check out Chapter 2 on Literacy and Chapter 3 on Writing Strategies.

## HALT! DETENTE! TAWAQQUF! STOP DOING THESE THINGS!

Teachers:

- ✗ **STOP making assumptions that students who are ELLs have a disability . . . or that they don't.** As stated in our introduction, assessments can be tricky and misleading. Work strategically and closely with diagnosticians, special educators, and ELL coaches to ensure that you have the correct diagnosis.

- ✗ **STOP focusing on deficits.** Given that these individuals struggle with language acquisition *and* a processing disability, it can be difficult at times to recognize strengths. But they're there! Using strengths can help build students' self-esteem and subsequently also serve to improve their areas of deficit. Who wants to always focus on what you're *not* good at?

- ✗ **STOP using the same strategies with all students.** Certainly there are strategies that make good pedagogical sense—such as avoiding too much lecture and using visuals in addition to auditory input. But also remember that kids are unique and have unique needs. Not all ELLs need the same adaptations. Be willing to differentiate!

- ✗ **STOP focusing solely on content.** We know that math and science and social studies are very important, but so are language skills, and they are intricately linked! ELLs will be able to learn the content more easily if you can embed literacy strategies into your instruction. The better they become in literacy, the more they can learn about your subject. Win-win!

✗ **STOP expecting students to produce, produce, produce.** In our outcomes-based educational society, many teachers are very focused on student production. They want to see students writing, talking, and taking tests. We need to remember, however, that students need to feel comfortable and be able to comprehend before they can produce anything. Even babies develop their receptive language before their expressive language; let ELLs with disabilities feel comfortable listening and being more passive before they are expected to actively participate.

✗ **STOP assuming that students need to be provided services in a pull-out capacity.** In many schools, traditional sheltered education has occurred a few times a week in a pull-out or resource classroom. When this happens, students begin to fall further and further behind. Instead, work collaboratively to meet students' needs. The general education classroom teacher, the special educator, and the ELL teacher can co-teach classes or lessons. In this way, all students will benefit from embedded strategies *and* teachers will learn strategies from one another!

**Making Connections**

Check out Chapter 9 on Co-Teaching.

✗ **STOP talking *at* them.** Talk *to* them. And let the rest of their classmates do the same. Create numerous opportunities for peer-to-peer conversations. This type of lower pressure interaction is what will help build students' comprehension and confidence.

✗ **STOP using cutesy games and cooperative learning groups as your only strategy.** Games are fun and engaging, and we are full-blown supporters of bringing fun to the classroom. However, though Pinterest and the Internet are rife with fun activities, you want to be sure the research is supporting your use of strategies with ELLs, with and without disabilities.

✗ **STOP the drill and kill.** We concur that repetition aids retention, but no one likes boring worksheets. In addition, most worksheets lack what Cummins (1991) emphasized as vital for ELLs: high context and high cognitive demand. Students who struggle with language and processing are going to find worksheets antithetical to their learning needs.

## Administrators:

✗ **STOP assuming assessments are valid.** Find out more about how assessments are done in your district and school for individuals who are not native speakers. Ask around. Do you have trained diagnosticians or are special educators who only speak English doing all the assessments, regardless of the student's English language status?

✗ **STOP allowing friends and family to interpret.** Trained interpreters are more than just individuals who speak the language. They understand a school's culture, the special lingo within education, and how to interpret professionally, without adding their own bias. Family and friends will naturally want to add their own input.

**Making Connections**

Check out Chapter 19 on School-to-Home Collaboration.

✗ **STOP forgetting the power of the parent.** Though this holds true for all students, we consider it triply true for those students who are ELLs and have a disability. We need to learn about their backgrounds and what they can tell us about their child's learning history. Your assistance as an administrator can be key in helping teachers gather critical information.

## GEH! ADELANTE! ADHHAB! GO AHEAD WITH THESE INSTEAD!

Teachers, DO this:

✔ **USE valid assessments for determining special education eligibility.** Of course we are supposed to do this. For ELLs, however, this is tricky. Work very hard to ensure that students are tested in both English and their native language to give them an opportunity to show their true knowledge and skills.

✔ **KEEP YOUR EYE OUT for ELLs who are both gifted and receiving special education services.** Just because a student doesn't speak your language and might have a learning disability or attention deficit hyperactivity disorder (ADHD), doesn't mean that he or she isn't also gifted. Be willing to look beyond superficial language or behavioral needs to see if that student might actually be able to cognitively grasp higher-order concepts. The three of us all have doctorates, but if you give us an intelligence test in Farsi, we will all fail miserably! That doesn't mean we have a disability or are unable to participate in high-level conversations if we are given access to the language.

✔ **DO get to know your students!** Focus on students' strengths and abilities rather than weaknesses and/or disabilities. Think about how difficult it must be to struggle not only with a new language, but also with education in general. Learning about students' educational and cultural backgrounds, personal goals and interests, and academic areas of strength will help you motivate, and ultimately *teach*, them.

✔ **UNDERSTAND the challenges that ELLs with disabilities face.** Reading is arduous, writing is problematic, speaking in English is laborious. Given those issues, would you be eager to take a test, answer questions aloud, or be responsible for a section on a group project? The combination of a language barrier and disability may result in the need to work at a slower pace, have additional visuals and checklists, and they may even respond differently to traditional motivators. The more empathy you have, the more you will be willing to recognize these needs as legitimate and deserving of your time and attention.

✔ **IMPLEMENT Universal Design for Learning (UDL) strategies.** Yes, UDL is for everyone and not just ELLs with disabilities, but consider why UDL is so emphasized these days. The whole premise of UDL is to provide multiple means of representation, expression, and engagement. Isn't that exactly what our diverse learners need?

**Making Connections**

Check out Chapter 4 on Instructional Strategies and Universal Design for Learning.

✔ **UTILIZE evidence-based practices from the fields of special education, gifted education, general education, and English as a Second Language.** If someone has done research to say it works with a certain population, feel free to use it with your own students! Keep trying until you find what works. Frequently used strategies include cooperative learning, peer-assisted learning, and the addition of visuals, strategic note taking, explicit instruction, progress monitoring, self-determination, use of primary language, and the use of manipulatives.

✔ **MAKE connections.** Students who are ELLs typically come from another country or from a family who has a different cultural background. Students with disabilities often lack the ability to quickly identify context clues. In both cases, students need teachers to help make concrete connections for them. Thus, the use of books or concepts that have a universal theme will be better suited to teaching these students than a text or article that focuses on the local area or a specific, narrower topic.

✔ **MODEL questioning aloud and chunking when reading.** Reading comprehension will be a critical issue for most ELLs with disabilities. Divide reading passages into chunks, and ask questions frequently to check comprehension. Encourage students to make predictions, and help them piece together information from the reading to form a summary. Each of these tasks may be difficult for a student who is an ELL or a student who has a disability; for the student who has both, they may be overwhelming! Be aware and work with the student at a level that is comfortable.

✔ **USE real-life examples, visual aids, and manipulatives when teaching math.** Again, language is a problem. For ELLs with disabilities, the use of drawings, photographs, or diagrams when teaching about abstract concepts, processing word problems, and building vocabulary will be very helpful.

✔ **HAVE multiple levels of work available.** It may not be possible to teach one-on-one very often. Therefore, you need to be prepared by having different levels of your assignments. Consider your HALO (Murawski, 2010): Does the assignment address your High, Average, Low, and Other student needs? By the way, a student who is ELL and has a disability might cross into many of those categories!

✔ **LINK students' prior knowledge and curriculum.** Again, though appropriate for all students, these strategies will help the ELL with a disability comprehend and process material in a less-threatening manner. These may include: think-pair-share, quick-writes, quick draws, anticipatory charts, class response cards, and word splats.

**Plugged In**

Have students practice their listening skills at Randall's Cyber Listening Lab: www.esl-lab.com.

✔ **IMPROVE listening.** Whenever possible, build in time for ELLs to work on their listening comprehension. This can be done with peers, paraprofessionals, videos, and teachers themselves. Randall's Cyber Listening Lab (www.esl-lab.com) helps students learn to improve their listening comprehension.

✔ **SLOW it down.** The more complex a concept or more unfamiliar the vocabulary, the slower the pace of instruction should be. We recognize you can't slow everything down, and nor should you water your instruction down. But pay close attention to the students in your class. Are you moving so quickly to cover the content that you are not *uncovering* it for many of them?

✔ **EMPOWER students.** Keep in mind that the literature states that teachers tend to have lower expectations for students with disabilities and those who are ELLs (Cameron & Cook, 2013; Reeves, 2006). The students we have been referring to have both. Lowering expectations that much is simply unacceptable. Instead, raise those expectations!

✔ **ENHANCE your own knowledge and skills!** Do you already know a lot about teaching ELLs? Great, learn more about working with students with disabilities. Already a special educator? Fantastic, immerse yourself in instruction about ELLs. There is always more to learn, and ongoing professional development will benefit both you and your students!

**Plugged In**

An excellent place for modules and resources for working with special learners is IRIS. Check them out at http://iris.peabody .vanderbilt.edu/iris-resource-locator.

✔ **FORM authentic and collaborative relationships.** Develop a welcoming demeanor and be willing to work with family members, resource teachers, coaches, specialists, general education teachers, administrators, and community members. Any and all of these individuals might help you provide improved instruction to your special learners. If these students are thrice-exceptional, it may take a village to teach them well!

## Administrators:

✔ **GATHER RESOURCES that will help your faculty assess and instruct ELLs, with and without disabilities.** This may take the form of various standardized assessments, additional paraprofessionals or interpreters, or curriculum adaptations. It may include getting grants to send teachers to professional development or setting up activities wherein families and teachers can interact. Whatever you do, make sure your community can see that you are doing your utmost to support this marginalized population.

✔ **LOOK at the data.** How are ELLs doing at your school? Is there a discrepancy in their achievement from typical learners? What if you look specifically at those ELLs who also receive special education services? Having hard data to analyze will allow you to have meaningful conversations with teachers, as well as see where you need to provide additional supports.

✔ **READ this book!** You may have flipped directly to this chapter because you are struggling specifically with ELLs who have disabilities. But have you noticed how many connections can be made to other chapters? This book is about exceptional learners. ELLs with disabilities cross over into all the other chapters. You can learn great strategies to support them in reading, writing, and math; identify issues with culturally responsive teaching, legal issues, and home-to-school collaboration; and acquire a better understanding of the various disabilities these students may have. As the administrator, you need to lead. Thus, you also need to improve your own personal understanding of working with special learners to include this population of ELLs with disabilities!

## STRATEGIES TO HELP YOUR STUDENTS WHO ARE ENGLISH LANGUAGE LEARNERS AND HAVE DISABILITIES

| Strategy | Explanation |
|---|---|
| Have students answer questions in complete sentences. | When asked, "What are you eating for lunch?", students can respond, "For lunch, I'm eating a hamburger and fries." |
| Use the $R^4$ method: Rephrase, Reason, Reinforce, Rephrase. | For example, "Of the students seeking Class President, who do you think is most qualified?"<br><br>**Rephrase:** Of the students seeking Class President, Alejandro is most qualified.<br><br>**Reason:** I think Alejandro should be nominated Class President because he seeks students' input, encourages student participation, and excels academically.<br><br>**Reinforce:** Since he has been in high school, Alejandro has served as Vice President of the National Honor Society, played two varsity sports, started a new swim club, and completed advanced classes.<br><br>**Rephrase:** So Alejandro is the student who should be voted Class President. |
| Integrate games and songs into lessons to reinforce content by linking humor, music, and repetition. | Allow students to redesign a modern game. For example, they can create a Shakespeare version of Mystery Date. The object of the game is to assemble an outfit by acquiring three matching cards. Students would have to write the directions and create the game pieces in Shakespearean fashion. Think about writing a song demonstrating knowledge of the parts of the cell or legislative branches of government. Inviting students to share a song with the class in their home language can be an effective cross-cultural experience for everyone. |
| Include movement in learning because kinesthetic activity can help students retain information when verbal language is difficult. | Integrate weekly role plays through charades to review main ideas and pantomime to restate critical elements. Create 30-second commercials to advertise past or future content and play Simon Says (touch five nouns, point to three plural words). Movement helps students learn. |

| Strategy | Explanation |
|---|---|
| Pass notes. | Your class can be quite diverse, so meeting individual students' needs while keeping a steady pace can be difficult. Instead of continually interrupting lessons to praise positive behaviors and cue students to appropriate behaviors, pass a note. As you walk around the room, talking and teaching the lesson, simply place a note on the student's desk. Write, "Please turn to page 45. Great job!" or "I liked your comment about the importance of music in your country." These notes can provide immediate feedback, reminders, and praise. |
| Mix it up when reading. | When students struggle with reading, chorally read stories aloud and make audio recordings to include in a center or class library. Use removable sticker dots with auditory feedback prerecorded to direct students' attention to main ideas, supporting details, and other key literary elements. Add sticky notes in the margins of key pages that encourage students to take notes. Encourage students to use accents and pause frequently to ask vocabulary in other languages. |
| Conclude with a consensus. | Remember, learning happens most at the very beginning and very end of lessons, so end strongly. Have each student develop a personal list of the most important facts they learned during the lesson. Have them work together in pairs, trios, small groups, and finally, the entire class, to whittle the list down and negotiate to the one most prominent statement. This will enable students who are ELLs and have a disability to work independently but then to be supported by their peers. In addition, it will help them learn what others think are salient facts, as compared to what they thought. |

*(Continued)*

(Continued)

| Strategy | Explanation |
|---|---|
| Help make connections in fun and different ways. | Give each student an alphabet letter (e.g., magnetic letters, alphabet flashcards), and ask them to identify one word with this letter to summarize the lesson. Share ideas. |
| | Or have each student use one alphabet letter and create one word. Combine three to four students into a small group to write a sentence including all individual words. Students must use all created words, but also may add words to help the sentence make sense. Emphasize that the sentence should link to today's lesson. Share ideas. |
| | Or choose a key word, and have students write the word vertically on their paper. Have them create a word or short phrase from each letter developing an acrostic, summarizing key elements of the lesson. Once again, share ideas. |
| | Or choose two or three random nouns, and write them on the board. Students can brainstorm how the lesson is similar to one or more of the nouns (e.g., the human circulatory system is like a *tree* because one part could be broken). Share ideas. |
| | In each of these situations, students who struggle with language and processing are given multiple ways to make connections and to summarize the lesson. The fact that they share ideas and hear from peers will help them retain that information in multiple ways. |

## HOT LINKS

| Name | Website | Description |
|---|---|---|
| Understood | www.understood.org | Understood is a comprehensive resource for parents of kids with learning and attention issues that provides clear answers, simple tools, and ongoing support. |
| Bookshare | www.bookshare.org | Bookshare is the world's largest accessible digital library for people with print and learning disabilities (such as dyslexia), providing free membership to qualified U.S. schools and students. |
| Crosscultural Developmental Education Services | www.crosscultured.com | CCDES is a company that works with school districts, teachers, and parents, offering technical assistance, professional development, and numerous tools and resources. CCDES specializes in ESL, Limited English Proficient (LEP) and special education issues, as well as an emphasis on parent education and empowerment. |
| LD Online Booklists | www.ldonline.org/kids/books | LD Online includes a number of booklists that feature books for children with learning disabilities or ADHD. Titles include guides for students on learning how to manage a learning disability. |
| Colorin Colorado webcast: ELL students with learning disabilities | www.colorincolorado.org/webcast/English-language-learners-with-disabilities | Featuring bilingual speech pathologist Dr. Elsa Cardenas-Hagan. Includes PowerPoint presentation, discussion questions, and related readings. |
| LD Online: Acquiring English as a Second Language | www.ldonline.org/article/5126 | This article examines "what's normal" when learning a second language and how you can tell when a student has a language-learning disability and when he or she is merely in the normal process of acquiring a second language. |

*(Continued)*

(Continued)

| Name | Website | Description |
|------|---------|-------------|
| The American Speech-Hearing Association's Office of Multicultural Affairs (OMA) | www.asha.org/practice/multicultural | ASHA's Office of Multicultural Affairs (OMA) addresses cultural and linguistic diversity issues related to professionals and persons with communication disorders and differences. |
| The Resource Guide for Serving Refugees with Disabilities | www.refugees.org/wp-content/uploads/2015/12/Serving-Refugees-with-Disabilities.pdf | The Resource Guide is written as a how-to for caseworkers and advocates who serve refugees with disabilities. It is available through the U.S. Committee for Refugees and Immigrants. |

*Source:* Adapted from Robertson, K. (n.d.). *How to address special education needs in the ELL classroom.* Retrieved from http://www.colorincolorado.org/article/how-address-special-education-needs-ell-classroom

# REFERENCES

Abedi, J. (2004). The No Child Left Behind Act and English language learners: Assessment and accountability issues. *Educational Researchers, 33*, 4–14.

Abedi, J. (2006). Psychometric issues in the ELL assessment and special education eligibility. *Teachers College Record, 108*, 2282–2303.

Artiles, A. J., Kozleski, E. B., Trent, S. C., Osher, D., & Ortiz, A. (2010). Justifying and explaining disproportionality, 1968–2008: A critique of underlying views of culture. *Exceptional Children, 76*(3), 279–299.

Cameron, D. L., & Cook, B. (2013). General education teachers' goals and expectations for their included students with mild and severe disabilities. *Education and Training in Autism and Developmental Disabilities, 48*(1), 18–30.

Chamot, A. U. (1996). The Cognitive Academic Language Learning Approach (CALLA): Theoretical framework and instructional applications. In J. E. Alatis (Ed.), *Georgetown University roundtable on languages and linguistics, 1996* (pp. 108–115). Washington, DC: Georgetown University Press.

Collier, S. (2015a). Engaging English language learners. In W. W. Murawski & K. L. Scott (Eds.), *What really works in elementary education* (pp. 253–268). Thousand Oaks, CA: Corwin.

Collier, S. (2015b). Engaging English language learners. In W. W. Murawski & K. L. Scott (Eds.), *What really works in secondary education* (pp. 255–271). Thousand Oaks, CA: Corwin.

Cummins, J. (1991). Language development and academic learning. In L. M. Malave & G. Duquette (Eds.), *Language, culture and cognition* (pp. 161–174). Clevedon, England: Multilingual Matters.

DeNisco, A. (2016). *Gifted ELL students often overlooked*. Retrieved from http://www .districtadministration.com/article/gifted-ell-students-often-overlooked

Echevarria, J., Vogt, M., & Short, D. (2008). *Making content comprehensible for English learners: The SIOP model* (3rd ed.). Needham Heights, MA: Allyn & Bacon.

Fernandez, N., & Inserra, A. (2013). Disproportionate classification of ESL students in U.S. special education. *Electronic Journal for English as a Second Language, 17*(2), 1.

Harry, B., & Klingner, J. K. (2006). *Why are so many minority students in special education?: Understanding race and disability in schools*. New York, NY: Teachers College Press.

McSwan, J., & Rolstad, K. (2006). How language proficiency tests mislead us about ability: Implications for English language learner placement in special education. *Teachers College Record, 108*, 2304–2328.

Murawski, W. W. (2010). *Collaborative teaching in elementary schools: Making the co-teaching marriage work!* Thousand Oaks, CA: Corwin.

National Center for Education Statistics. (2015). *Number and percentage of public school students participating in programs for English language learners, by state: Selected years, 2002–03 through 2012–13*. Washington, DC: Author. Retrieved from https://nces.ed.gov/programs/digest/d14/tables/dt14_204.20.asp

Ortiz, A. A. (1997). Learning disabilities occurring concomitantly with linguistic differences. *Journal of Learning Disabilities, 30*, 321–332.

Ortiz, A. (n.d.). *English language learners with special needs: Effective instructional strategies*. Retrieved from http://www.colorincolorado.org/article/english-language-learners-special-needs-effective-instructional-strategies

Reeves, J. R. (2006). Secondary teacher attitudes toward including English language learners in mainstream classrooms. *Journal of Educational Research, 99*(3), 131–142.

Robertson, K. (n.d.). *How to address special education needs in the ELL classroom*. Retrieved from http://www.colorincolorado.org/article/how-address-special-education-needs-ell-classroom

Sullivan, A. L. (2011). Disproportionality in special education identification and placement of English language learners. *Exceptional Children, 77*(3), 317–334.

U.S. Department of Education. (2014). *Questions and answers regarding inclusion of English learners with disabilities in English language proficiency assessments and Title III annual measurable achievement objectives*. Retrieved from http://www2.ed.gov/policy/speced/guid/idea/memosdcltrs/q-and-a-on-elp-swd.pdf

## ADDITIONAL RECOMMENDED READING

Chu, S.-Y. (2011). Teacher perceptions of their efficacy for special education referral of students from culturally and linguistically diverse backgrounds. *Education, 132*(1), 2–14.

Ortiz, A. A., Robertson, P. M., Wilkinson, C. Y., Liu, Y., McGhee, B. D., & Kushner, M. I. (2011). The role of bilingual education teachers in preventing inappropriate referrals of ELLs to special education: Implications for response to intervention. *Bilingual Research Journal, 34*(3), 316–333.

Shyyan, V., Thurlow, M., & Liu, K. (2005). *Student perceptions of instructional strategies: Voices of English language learners with disabilities. ELLs with Disabilities Report 11*. National Center on Educational Outcomes, University of Minnesota. Retrieved from http://files.eric.ed.gov/fulltext/ED495903.pdf

Sullivan, A. L., A'Vant, E., Baker, J., Chandler, D., Graves, S., McKinney, E., & Sayles, T. (2009). Confronting inequity in special education, Part I: Understanding the problem of disproportionality. *NASP Communiqué, 38*(1), 14–15.

## TOP FIVE WEBSITES TO SUPPORT ELLs

➡ http://www.colorincolorado.org

➡ http://www.eduplace.com/kids/sv/books/content/wordbuilder

➡ http://www.eslfast.com

➡ http://nccc.georgetown.edu/resources/assessments.html

➡ http://www.rti4success.org/related-rti-topics/english-learners

## APPS WE LOVE

➡ English Monstruo

➡ Phrasalstein

➡ Duolingo

➡ Phonetics Focus

➡ VoiceThread

# 16

## *Inclusion as the Context for Early Childhood Special Education*

Zhen Chai

*California State University, Northridge*

Rebecca Lieberman–Betz

*University of Georgia*

## WHAT IS EARLY CHILDHOOD INCLUSION?

By now you know that in 1975, landmark legislation was enacted to provide all children with disabilities access to a public education. Public Law (PL) 94-142 stated that students with disabilities be placed in the least restrictive environment (LRE) and mandated that education for students with disabilities be individualized, free, and appropriate. However, did you know that legislation regulating educational services to children 3 to 5 years of age did not occur until 11 years later with the passage of PL 99-457? Since that time, we have seen additional legislation enacted regulating services for preschool-aged children with disabilities, including the Individuals with Disabilities Education Act (IDEA, 2004), which supports the inclusion of young children with disabilities in the educational settings with their typically developing peers. Given these laws, you would expect that most young children are being taught with their nondisabled peers, wouldn't you? Unfortunately, that isn't the case.

Given that high quality early childhood inclusion (ECI) programs have been found to promote the development of all children whether or not they have a disability (Strain & Bovey, 2011), why is it that by 2013, less than half of preschool children with disabilities were placed in inclusive settings (U.S. Department of Education [USDOE], 2013)? In fact, this number has remained consistent over the past 30 years! What's the holdup, folks? The major challenges to ECI include false beliefs and attitudes toward ECI (e.g., general education teachers consider special education teachers as the primary professionals responsible for young children with disabilities); misunderstanding of policies and legislation (e.g., individualized education program [IEP] team members misinterpret LRE as only occurring within public school settings); and lack of resources (e.g., two teachers are assigned to co-teach without proper training ahead of time) (U.S. Department of Health and Human Services & USDOE, 2015). It's not that we don't know what to do with these students; we do! Current recommended practices by the Division for Early Childhood (DEC, 2014) of the Council for Exceptional Children (CEC) describe a variety of specialized strategies supported by empirical research, which aim to promote the successful inclusion of young children with disabilities in typical classroom and community settings.

ECI doesn't need to take just one form or occur in one place. ECI can happen in any setting; however, simply placing young children with disabilities in general education settings (e.g., public PreK, Head Start, private preschool) is far from sufficient for successful early childhood inclusion (McConnell, 2002). ECI doesn't need to be overwhelming; in fact, we can boil it down to three major things: access, participation, and supports (DEC & National Association for the Education for Young Children, 2009). Easy enough, right? Shouldn't all young children have those three things? *Access* refers to removing the physical and structural barriers of classrooms and other community environments to promote young children with disabilities' engagement in multiple learning opportunities. For starters, make sure there is enough room for children using mobility equipment such as wheelchairs to get around their classroom. *Participation* means that through individualized accommodations, adaptations, and supports, teachers help young children with disabilities actively participate in classroom, family, and community activities, and develop a sense of belonging. For example, make sure the communication device that a

**Key Concepts**

Your three heavy hitters in early childhood inclusion?

- Access
- Participation
- Supports

child uses is programmed with phrases and vocabulary to fit with circle time activities so he or she can initiate and respond to questions along with peers. *Supports* refer to providing supports to personnel who are involved in ECI efforts. Those supports may include procedures and policies that promote ECI (e.g., access to high quality ECI programs within a family's neighborhood), professional development and collaborative opportunities for professionals and families (e.g., attend workshops to learn how to address the needs of culturally diverse families), funding for professional development, and implementation of quality frameworks that assure ECI programs meet the needs of all children and their families (e.g., teachers implement DEC recommended practices).

## WHAT CAN WE DO TO MAKE EARLY CHILDHOOD INCLUSION SUCCESSFUL?

ECI involves practices and approaches that support young children with disabilities including: universal design for learning (UDL), specialized instructional strategies, embedded intervention, the pyramid model (a tiered system to support social emotional development in young children; see what it looks like at the end of this chapter), and family centered practices.

UDL supports young children with disabilities with access to learning and social opportunities by providing multiple means of representation, action and expression, and engagement (Conn-Powers, Cross, Traub, & Hutter-Pishgahi, 2006). To guide development and implementation of inclusive curriculums in early childhood settings, adults incorporating UDL into early childhood classrooms should intentionally plan ahead of time to use different accommodations and modifications to ensure all children can safely access activities and materials, are socially included, and have choices to demonstrate their learning, participation, and competence (Conn-Powers et al., 2006). Professionals also attend to health and safety issues, assessment and evaluation practices, and family involvement (Conn-Powers et al., 2006). UDL can be applied to early childhood activities such as mealtime, center time, and morning meeting (see Chapter 4 on UDL, as well as examples of UDL applications to early childhood at the end of this chapter).

**Making Connections**

Check out Chapter 4 on Instructional Strategies and Universal Design for Learning.

A key element of ECI is the use of naturalistic instructional strategies that address each child's needs. What are those? Well, they include things like following the child's lead, planned forgetfulness, visible but unreachable, piece by piece, parallel/descriptive talk, and time delay (Johnson, Rahn, & Bricker, 2015; see examples at the end of the chapter). Decades of research have provided a growing evidence base of early childhood special education (ECSE) practices incorporating these strategies and targeting skills across domains including pre-academic skills, social-emotional skills, motor skills, social-communication skills, self-help skills, and play skills. Prompting procedures, such as time delay and system of least prompts, have been shown to promote diverse skills in preschoolers with disabilities (e.g., Appelman, Vail, & Lieberman-Betz, 2014). Time delay involves pausing before prompting a child response; system of least prompts uses the least amount of support first to help a child perform a skill (e.g., verbal reminder to wash hands) before moving through a hierarchy of 3 to 4 more intensive prompting strategies, and ending with the most intrusive prompt (e.g., physically moving the child through the hand washing routine). Teachers should use evidence-based instructional strategies in authentic and meaningful ways to provide opportunities to practice the skill across the day, with different people, materials, and settings. A great way to do this is through embedded intervention.

Embedded intervention is a child-initiated, teacher-mediated approach that provides intentional learning opportunities within and across daily routines and activities to address children's individual learning needs. Okay, whoa! What does all that mean? It means that when we notice a child who has an IEP goal targeting use of single words to communicate wants and needs playing with trains, we join the child at the train table (follow the child's lead), narrate her play (descriptive talk), and then hold on to some trains or train-related objects (piece by piece). When the child looks up for an additional piece to build her track, we might pause and look expectantly (time delay), then provide necessary support to elicit the request for "track" or "more" (least to most prompting). Embedded instruction should be used during unplanned activities (such as joining a child at a train table) as well as planned and routine activities (such as center time and meal time). To do this effectively, teachers need to be knowledgeable of children's IEP goals (Johnson et al., 2015). Research shows that embedded intervention has been effective in teaching pre-academic, language, social, and engagement skills to young children with a variety of disabilities in inclusive preschool settings (e.g., Grisham-Brown, Pretti-Frontczak, Hawkins, & Winchell, 2009). Another cool outcome is that once the children learn skills through embedded intervention, they are able to maintain and generalize them (Grisham-Brown et al., 2009). General and special education teachers can support embedded intervention through use of planning tools such as embedding schedules (Johnson et al., 2015) and curriculum webs (Grisham-Brown, Hemmeter, & Pretti-Frontczak, 2005). We've included clear examples of how to use these two tools at the end of the chapter.

Successful ECI programs create physical and social environments that promote social-emotional competence. For example, the Pyramid Model for Promoting Social-Emotional Competence in Young Children

(Fox, Dunlap, Hemmeter, Joseph, & Strain, 2003) is a tiered model that incorporates evidence-based practices to support social-emotional development in young children and prevents and directly addresses challenging behaviors. The first tier incorporates universal practices that include building a safe and supportive learning environment, and establishing positive relationships with children, family, and other professionals. Some recommended practices associated with this tier are having meaningful conversations with children, facilitating their play, implementing a predictable schedule, planning transition, and teaching expectations (Fox, Hemmeter, Snyder, Binder, & Clarke, 2011). The second tier involves preventive practices that focus on teaching friendship skills, emotional literacy, anger management, and social problem solving. Because not every young child learns how to express his or her emotions, control anger, solve conflicts, or develop friendships without intentional instruction, teachers can use games, child literacy, and role play to teach these skills. The third tier is positive behavior support (PBS), which involves using individualized interventions to address severe behavioral problems. PBS requires collaborative teamwork between professionals and family to determine the purpose of challenging behavior, develop individualized behavioral strategies, and teach new skills to replace the challenging behavior (Fox et al., 2011).

**Making Connections**

Check out Chapter 8 on Positive Behavior Supports.

Two fundamental tenets of ECSE involve recognition of the family as the "primary nurturing context" of the child and the importance of strengthening relationships (Odom & Wolery, 2003). We've known for a long time that when parents are involved, the outcomes of interventions are better. As such, family centered practice is a set of principles and beliefs that focus on strengthening family capacity to promote child development and learning (Dunst, Trivette, & Hamby, 2007). In family centered practice, professionals view families as equal partners and the final decision makers for their children, respect and value their choices, and develop interventions based on the strength and uniqueness of the family. For example, professionals jointly develop the child's IEP goals with the family, carefully consider the family's priorities and concerns, are sensitive to the family's needs, understand how culture impacts family decisions, and coach the family to use intervention strategies in their routines to help them increase their competence. Collaborating with families, valuing their contribution to decisions and children's programs, and building relationships among team members are critical for successful inclusion of young children with disabilities.

**Making Connections**

Check out Chapter 19 on School-to-Home Collaboration.

# PRACTICES TO AVOID WHEN WORKING TOWARD SUCCESSFUL ECI

Teachers:

✗ **STOP writing nonfunctional IEP goals and objectives based on standardized assessments.** Stacking five 1-inch cubes is not a functional or meaningful goal for young children, and using standardized assessments that expect children to demonstrate what they know for unfamiliar people using unfamiliar objects does not produce valid or reliable results. Young children are not good test takers! Goals and objectives should be based on authentic assessments conducted in children's natural environments while interacting with familiar people and objects and be functional and meaningful to the child (i.e., promote their independence and participation in typical routines and activities throughout the day).

✗ **STOP blaming challenging behaviors on the child being disobedient.** When young children don't have more appropriate ways to get their needs met, they use challenging behavior to communicate. They may use challenging behaviors to access something (e.g., a desired object, adult attention) or escape a situation they don't like (e.g., circle time, a challenging task). Teachers should conduct a functional behavior assessment in consultation with a behavior specialist before drawing conclusions about why a child is behaving in a certain way and before implementing specific strategies to reduce the behavior.

>  **Plugged In**
>
> Use websites maintained by reputable sources such as the Centers for Disease Control and Prevention, disability-specific organizations (e.g., National Down Syndrome Society, Autism Speaks), and university-affiliated websites (e.g., Autism Focused Intervention Resources and Modules [http://afirm.fpg.unc.edu]).

✗ **STOP using a certain instructional or behavioral strategy just because the teacher next door is using it or because you read about it in a popular magazine or website.** Teachers need to implement systematic procedures with research support to promote young children's learning and development within typical classroom activities. Use valid resources such as peer-reviewed research journals (e.g., *Journal of Early Intervention, Topics in Early Childhood Special Education*) and practitioner journals (e.g., *Young Exceptional Children, TEACHING Exceptional Children*) to gather information about use of evidence-based practices (EBPs) in the classroom. Look into joining professional organizations (e.g., DEC,

NAEYC), which often offer journals geared toward practitioners as part of their membership benefits. Use websites maintained by reputable sources. See the end of the chapter for additional websites to support use of EBPs.

✗ **STOP pulling the child out of the classroom to provide intervention with related service providers.** Teachers should work with other therapists to provide intervention in the classroom within meaningful activities and routines. When children learn an activity with their nondisabled peers, they are far more likely to continue that practice than if they learn it one-on-one in a small room with an adult specialist!

✗ **STOP interpreting embedded/naturalistic practices as nonintentional instruction.** Just because a teacher isn't giving direct instruction on a social skill or behavioral goal doesn't mean he or she isn't teaching it. Providing opportunities to acquire skills requires planning, knowledge of children's goals and objectives, and appropriate instructional strategies to use throughout the day. Be able to explain to parents and other educators what your goals are, how you've set up the classroom to ensure those skills are practiced, and how you are collecting assessment data on goal achievement.

✗ **STOP expecting preschool-age children to just figure out how to interact with one another and navigate early peer relationships.** Young children with disabilities (and often those without) need specific instruction to acquire the skills to initiate social interactions with peers and engage in extended interactions. Teachers should place as much importance on teaching social-emotional skills as pre-academic areas.

### Administrators:

✗ **STOP thinking that inclusion is easy!** High-quality ECI requires a lot of effort and planning from professionals of different disciplines, family, administrators, and the community. It may take a while to get it right, but have patience. Change takes time.

✗ **STOP thinking that co-teaching will happen automatically when you just place two teachers in the same classroom.** Provide professional development ahead of time, provide ongoing coaching and consultation, and allocate time for co-teachers to plan and coordinate to promote successful collaboration. Professional development on co-teaching can also help early childhood educators learn how to observe,

**Making Connections**

Check out Chapter 9 on Co-Teaching.

communicate, and document strategically throughout the day using the various co-teaching approaches.

✗ **STOP thinking that inclusion is more expensive than separated education.** Preschool inclusive programs are no more expensive than traditional noninclusive educational programs for young children with disabilities (Odom et al., 2001). Remember, special education is a service, not a place.

 ## PRACTICES TO SUPPORT EARLY CHILDHOOD INCLUSION

Teachers:

✔ **USE authentic assessment strategies to assess young children's typical functioning in meaningful and routine activities.** Use of direct observation (e.g., observing to collect data on the number and quality of peer initiations during free play), rating scales, interviews, and curriculum-based measures such as the Assessment, Evaluation, and Programming System (AEPS; Bricker, 2002) to observe children in their daily routines interacting with familiar people will provide a more accurate picture of their abilities.

✔ **GRAPH your data to monitor children's progress toward their individualized goals.** It is not sufficient to look at the numbers and claim the child has made some progress because the number changes. Plot your data using Excel or pencil and graph paper for 3 to 5 days right before starting a new instructional strategy and on a regular basis afterward. Visual analysis of graphed data will allow you to detect change or lack of change and patterns in the data to inform decision making. As a bonus, graphed data is very helpful when communicating with parents!

✔ **FIND time to make home visits.** Home visits can provide teachers with insight into family strengths and needs, demonstrate that teachers value the family and care about them, and create opportunities to help families carry over strategies promoting their child's development to the home. If your administration supports home visits, take the opportunity to meet with families where they are most comfortable. Sometimes home visits can cause anxiety for families; therefore, be relaxed yet professional. Start with positives about their child, then ask about the family's perspective on their child's program, their concerns and priorities, and how you can support them in promoting their child's development.

✔ **USE eco-mapping to identify families' current available resources.** The idea of eco-mapping (Hartman, 1978) is based on ecological systems theory (Bronfenbrenner, 1979), which emphasizes the importance of viewing the child and his or her family within their social context. Teachers can use eco-mapping when they first meet a family to facilitate their conversation by identifying resources, supports, and relationships (McCormick, Stricklin, Nowak, & Rous, 2008).

✔ **PROVIDE opportunities for families to be involved in the classroom in multiple ways.** Each family will have their own level of comfort or ability to be involved in their child's program. Don't make assumptions about why a family is or is not engaging with you or their child's program in a particular way. Give families different options to provide information about their child and their priorities and concerns and to participate in class activities.

✔ **USE a variety of active strategies to teach young children friendship skills.** For example, use friendship stories, puppets, role-play, modeling, and prompting to teach turn-taking, giving suggestions, sharing, and giving compliments (Center on the Social and Emotional Foundations for Early Learning, 2006). These friendship skills help young children with disabilities be accepted by their peers and fully participate in inclusive settings (Odom et al., 2006).

✔ **COLLABORATE with family and other professionals.** Form a transdisciplinary team to support ECI, which includes joint planning, role release, and mutual professional development. You're not expected to do it all; don't try to! Ask for help in the areas you need help.

✔ **PROVIDE children time to take their turn in a conversation.** Don't speak over children; give them a chance to initiate and respond to you. Children with communication delays may need some additional time to initiate or take their turn in a conversation. In providing a language-rich environment, we don't want to talk too much and not give children sufficient opportunities to communicate.

✔ **HAVE KNOWLEDGE of the skills needed in kindergarten and support the child in developing those skills to increase success and participation in their next classroom.** To promote successful transitions, we need to have an understanding of important skills that will help children succeed in the next setting. For the transition to kindergarten this does not mean directly teaching pre-academic skills, but it does mean promoting communication, play, and social skills; helping children learn how to follow classroom routines and directions; and teaching children to be as independent as possible in their self-care skills.

Administrators:

- ✔ **BE AWARE of different inclusive options and the continuum of placements including those that are nonpublic.** Understand IDEA's LRE requirements and carefully consider the child's needs and family's concerns and priorities when working with the team to make the placement decision.

**Plugged In**

The Council for Exceptional Children (www.cec.sped.org) is the largest international organization working with individuals with disabilities, their families, and those who work with them.

- ✔ **DEVELOP a vision statement for the school to support the inclusion of young children with various abilities.** Create an inclusive atmosphere and raise community awareness on inclusion. Advocate for inclusion by educating all parents, including those of typical children. Administrators can provide brochures or booklets to disseminate the benefits of inclusive programs for all children in community centers, libraries, and schools, and so on.

- ✔ **PARTICIPATE in professional development regularly.** Get the most up-to-date information on use of DEC Recommended Practices (2014), UDL, collaboration, and assessment. Just go to CEC (www.cec.sped .org) and join the DEC and/or the Council for Administrators of Special Education (CASE). Both will provide you with a plethora of useful resources.

**Making Connections**

Check out Chapter 18 on Legal Issues.

- ✔ **PROVIDE teachers with time to do home visits with children and their families.** Home visits can be an important approach for understanding the concerns and priorities of families, helping caregivers generalize classroom strategies into the home, and promoting caregivers' confidence and competence in supporting their children's development. Administrators can facilitate implementation of home visits by providing teachers with time during the week to visit with families.

## THE TEACHING PYRAMID

A model for supporting social competence and preventing challenging behavior in young children:

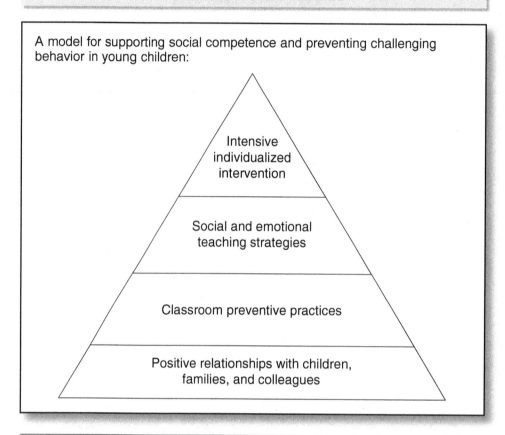

Intensive individualized intervention

Social and emotional teaching strategies

Classroom preventive practices

Positive relationships with children, families, and colleagues

*Source:* Fox, L., Dunlap, G., Hemmeter, M. L., Joseph, G. E., & Strain, P. S. (2003). The teaching pyramid: A model for supporting social competence and preventing challenging behavior in young children. *Young Children, 58,* 49. Copyright © 2003 NAEYC®. Reprinted with permission.

## EXAMPLES OF NATURALISTIC INSTRUCTIONAL STRATEGIES

| Strategies | Examples |
|---|---|
| Following the child's lead | Play and talk about what the child is interested in. |
| Planned forgetfulness | During art, put out all the paint but no paint brushes to see how children respond. |
| Visible but unreachable | Place that favorite toy high up on a shelf where little hands can't reach to see if children will ask you to help them get it down. |
| Piece by piece | Give just a few goldfish crackers at a time during snack to give children an opportunity to ask for more. |
| Parallel/descriptive talk | Narrate the child's actions and experiences so they hear language associated with those activities: "You're painting with the blue paint. You're dipping the brush in the paint and moving the brush from the top of the paper all the way to the bottom." |
| Time delay | Pause briefly during a routine or activity to prompt a response from the child. For example, while blowing bubbles, pause and look expectantly before blowing the next bubble to see if children will ask you for more. |

*Source:* Created based on practices highlighted in Johnson, J. J., Rahn, N. L., & Bricker, D. (2015). *An activity-based approach to intervention* (4th ed.). Baltimore, MD: Brookes.

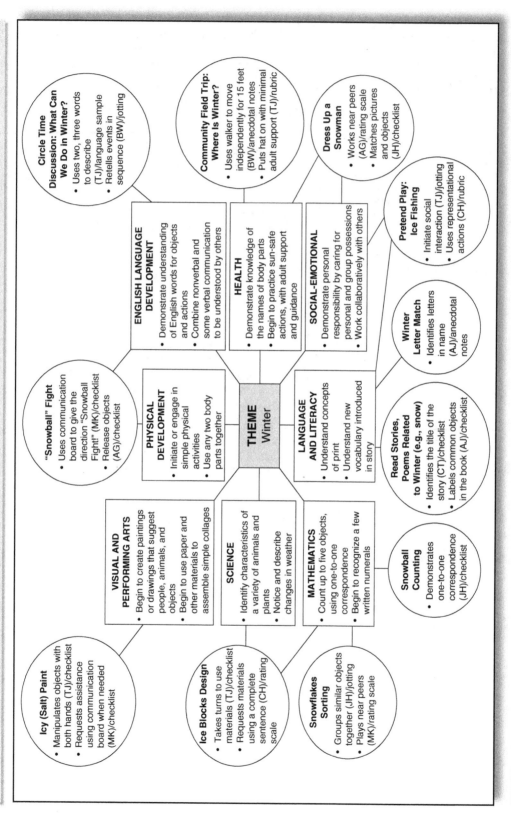

*Source:* Adapted from Grisham-Brown, J., Hemmeter, M. L., & Pretti-Frontezak, K. (2005). *Blended practices for teaching young children in inclusive settings.* Baltimore, MD: Brookes.

## ACTIVITY-BASED INTERVENTION (ABI): EMBEDDING SCHEDULE FOR MULTIPLE CHILDREN

**Focus:** Group  **Setting:** Classroom  **Children's names:** Quan Travers, James Wayne, Alice Vince

**Team members:** Parents: Dawn Travers, Branden Wayne, Kelly Vince  ECSE teacher: Jennifer  Speech-language pathologist: Fran

**Dates schedule will be used:** March 2018

**Daily Classroom Activities and Opportunities to Practice**

| Children and Target Skills | Arrival | Free Play | Circle Time | Center Activity | Snack | Playground |
|---|---|---|---|---|---|---|
| **Child's name: Quan** <br> **1. Follow routine directions** | As Quan arrives, prompt him to put away his backpack. | | | Encourage Quan to put away toys when Center time is over. | Remind Quan to bring the plate and utensils to the sink when he finishes eating. | |
| **2. Request using his communication board** | | Ask Quan to choose an activity he wants to play. | Prompt Quan to request a song. | Give Quan a few pieces of puzzles or blocks, and encourage him to request more. | Offer small amount of food, and prompt him to request more. | When Quan plays on the swing, stop it periodically so he can request more. |
| **3. Demonstrates understanding of one-to-one correspondence** | | | Ask Quan to distribute musical instruments to his friends. | | Have Quan help set the table for the class (e.g., put the mats on the table, and put one cup, one plate, and one utensil on the mat). | |

*(Continued)*

295

(Continued)

| Children and Target Skills | Arrival | Free Play | Circle Time | Center Activity | Snack | Playground |
|---|---|---|---|---|---|---|
| **Child's name: James**<br><br>**1. Sort like objects** | | Ask James to put all of the similar toys (e.g., cars, blocks) together during clean up. | | | After snack, ask James to help clean up (e.g., put all the plates in one bin, cups in another bin). | |
| **2. Say or sign 10 different objects or event labels (e.g., ball, water, apple)** | Ask James what he had for breakfast at home. | Encourage James to label common objects in a book. | | Ask James what he is playing. Encourage him to label the toys. | Provide James two choices of snack items (e.g., pretzels or crackers). | Ask James what he wants to play (e.g., slide, swing, sand). |
| **3. Manipulate objects with two hands** | Encourage James to unzip his coat by himself. | | | Encourage James to play with blocks, puzzles, and other manipulatives. | Provide food that requires spoon use. | |
| **Child's name: Alice**<br><br>**1. Initiate social interaction** | Prompt Alice to greet peers when she arrives. | | | Encourage Alice to greet her friends as she enters a center. | | Encourage Alice to select a peer to play with. |
| **2. Make choices** | | Ask Alice to choose an activity she wants to play given two choices. | Ask Alice to choose a song she wants to sing given two choices. | Give Alice a choice of two favorite centers. | Give Alice a choice of two foods. | Have a peer give Alice a choice of two toys. |

*Source:* Adapted from Johnson, J. J., Rahn, N. L., & Bricker, D. (2015). *An activity-based approach to intervention* (4th ed.). Baltimore, MD: Brookes.

## EXAMPLES OF APPLICATIONS OF UDL IN ECI

| Applications of Universal Design Principles to Class Meetings | |
| --- | --- |
| **Physical Environment** | **Teaching Environment** |
| • Expand the group meeting area so that all children can be present and focus their attention on the activities.<br><br>• Provide varied seating options so each child may lie on the floor, sit on a mat or chair, or use specialized seating.<br><br>• Use other materials of different sizes, textures, and shapes to help each child actively manipulate the objects for learning. | • Vary your expectations for participation and performance. If children are listening to a story and are asked to recall events, some may attend to and repeat back key words; others may recall the names of characters by pointing to pictures or using signs and gestures; and even others may predict what will happen next using complete sentences in English.<br><br>• Present content in multiple formats, including verbal, print, video, or concrete objects, repeating key words and phrases in children's home language and using simple sentences with gestures.<br><br>• Use physical cues to focus children's attention, such as pointing to the picture in the book, giving verbal prompts to help children begin a response, offering language models for children to imitate, and encouraging children to keep thinking and trying. |
| **Health and<br>Safety Practices** | **Individual Assessment<br>and Program Evaluation** |
| • Provide clear, wide paths throughout the classroom so each child may safely and easily reach the meeting area.<br><br>• Ensure safe floor covering for safe passage for any child, including for example a child who is in a hurry, has visual impairments, or uses a wheeled stander.<br><br>• Consider each child's energy level and health conditions in planning activities. | • Request information or action in various ways including complex questions, simple phrases, and emphasis and repetition of key words or phrases.<br><br>• Identify the multiple ways children can show what they learn during activities. For example, the child who waits for another child to respond to a teacher's request, to handle a show-and-tell object being passed around, or to choose the song demonstrates turn taking. Some children, as in the example above, may respond to the request using complete and accurate sentences spoken in English, while others may need to point, sign, or use words in their home language. Others may point to the object or event in the book in response to simple questions. |

*(Continued)*

(Continued)

| Social-Emotional Environment | Family Involvement Practices |
|---|---|
| • Invite and encourage all children to join in, using multiple means of communication (e.g., speaking English and/or children's home language, signing, displaying symbols).<br>• Give simple directions using multiple means (e.g., verbally, signed, in print, modeled) so each child may see, hear, and understand any rules and expectations.<br>• Use books, songs, and communication that involve and represent all children, regardless of cultural predominance or linguistic and skill levels. | • Share information with families through a newsletter written at an appropriate level. Have key phrases translated into families' home languages, and include photographs of children engaged in an activity.<br>• Provide multiple opportunities for families to be involved. Bilingual parents might be willing to translate the information for monolingual families. Families could support their child's involvement by asking specific questions about the activity and/or the book read to the group. |

# REFERENCES

Appelman, M., Vail, C. O., & Lieberman-Betz, R. G. (2014). The effects of constant time delay and instructive feedback on acquisition of English and Spanish sight words. *Journal of Early Intervention, 36*, 131–148.

Bricker, D. (Series Ed.). (2002). *Assessment, evaluation, and programming system for infants and children* (2nd ed.). Baltimore, MD: Paul H. Brookes.

Bronfenbrenner, U. (1979). Contexts of child rearing: Problems and prospects. *American Psychologist, 34*, 844–850.

The Center on the Social and Emotional Foundations for Early Learning. (n.d.). *Resources: PreSchool training modules*. Retrieved from http://csefel. vanderbilt.edu/resources/training_preschool.html

Conn-Powers, M., Cross, A. F., Traub, E. K., & Hutter-Pishgahi, L. (2006). *The universal design of early education: Moving forward for all children*. Beyond Young Children. Retrieved from http://journal.naeyc.org/btj/200609/ConnPowersBTJ.pdf

Division for Early Childhood. (2014). *DEC recommended practices in early intervention/early childhood special education 2014*. Retrieved from http://www.dec-sped.org/recommendedpractices

Division for Early Childhood, & National Association for the Education for Young Children. (2009). *Early childhood inclusion: A joint position statement of the Division for Early Childhood (DEC) and the National Association for the Education of Young Children (NAEYC)*. Chapel Hill, NC: Author.

Dunst, C. J., Trivette, C. M., & Hamby, D. W. (2007). Meta-analysis of family-centered helpgiving practices research. *Mental Retardation and Developmental Disabilities Research Reviews, 13*, 370–378.

Fox, L., Dunlap, G., Hemmeter, M. L., Joseph, G. E., & Strain, P. S. (2003). The teaching pyramid: A model for supporting social competence and preventing challenging behavior in young children. *Young Children, 58*, 48–52.

Fox, L., Hemmeter, M. L., Snyder, P., Binder, D. P., & Clarke, S. (2011). Coaching early childhood special educators to implement a comprehensive model for promoting young children's social competence. *Topics in Early Childhood Special Education, 31*, 178–192.

Grisham-Brown, J., Hemmeter, M. L., & Pretti-Frontczak, K. (2005). *Blended practices for teaching young children in inclusive settings*. Baltimore, MD: Brookes.

Grisham-Brown, J., Pretti-Frontczak, K., Hawkins, S. R., & Winchell, B. N. (2009). Addressing early learning standards for all children within blended preschool classrooms. *Topics in Early Childhood Special Education, 29*, 131–142.

Hartman, A. (1978). Diagrammatic assessment of family relationships. *Social Casework, 59*, 465–476.

Individuals With Disabilities Education Act, 20 U.S.C. § 1400 (2004).

Johnson, J. J., Rahn, N. L., & Bricker, D. (2015). *An activity-based approach to intervention* (4th ed.). Baltimore, MD: Brookes.

McConnell, S. R. (2002). Interventions to facilitate social interaction for young children with autism: Review of available research and recommendations for educational intervention and future research. *Journal of Autism and Developmental Disorders, 32*, 351–372.

McCormick, K. M., Stricklin, S., Nowak, T. M., & Rous, B. (2008). Using eco-mapping to understand family strengths and resources. *Young Exceptional Children, 11*, 17–28.

Odom, S. L., Hanson, M. J., Lieber, J., Marquart, J., Sandall, S., Wolery, R., . . . Chambers, J. (2001). The costs of preschool inclusion. *Topics in Early Childhood Special Education, 21*, 46–55.

Odom, S. L., & Wolery, M. (2003). A unified theory of practice in early intervention/early childhood special education: Evidence-based practices. *The Journal of Special Education, 37*, 164–173.

Odom, S. L., Zercher, C., Li, S., Marquart, J. M., Sandall, S., & Brown, W. H. (2006). Social acceptance and rejection of preschool children with disabilities: A mixed-method analysis. *Journal of Educational Psychology, 98*, 807–823.

Strain, P. S., & Bovey, E. H. (2011). Randomized, controlled trial of the LEAP model of early intervention for young children with autism spectrum disorder. *Early Childhood Special Education, 31*, 133–154.

U.S. Department of Education. (2013). *Annual report to Congress on the implementation of the Individuals With Disabilities Act.* Washington, DC: Author.

U.S. Department of Health and Human Services & U.S. Department of Education. (2015). Policy statement on inclusion of children with disabilities in early childhood programs: September 14, 2015. *Infants and Young Children, 29*, 3–24.

## ADDITIONAL RECOMMENDED READING ON EARLY CHILDHOOD SPECIAL EDUCATION

Copple, C., & Bredekamp, S. (Eds.). (2009). *Developmentally appropriate practice in early childhood programs serving children from birth through age 8* (3rd ed.). Washington, DC: National Association for Education of Young Children.

Grisham-Brown, J., & Pretti-Frontczak, K. (2011). *Assessing young children in inclusive settings.* Baltimore, MD: Paul Brookes.

Noonan, M. J., & McCormick, L. (2014). *Teaching young children with disabilities in natural environments* (2nd ed.). Baltimore, MD: Paul Brookes.

## TOP FIVE WEBSITES TO SUPPORT EARLY CHILDHOOD SPECIAL EDUCATION

➡ http://iris.peabody.vanderbilt.edu

➡ http://csefel.vanderbilt.edu

➡ http://community.fpg.unc.edu

➡ http://ectacenter.org

➡ http://vkc.mc.vanderbilt.edu/ebip

## APPS WE LOVE

- ➡ Choice Works
- ➡ Talk'n Photos
- ➡ My First Voice Lite
- ➡ Social Skill Builder Lite
- ➡ Model Me Going Places 2

# 17

---

# *Focusing on Strengths*

## *Twice-Exceptional Students*

### Claire E. Hughes
*Canterbury Christ Church University, England*

## TWICE-EXCEPTIONAL: GIFTED WITH A DISABILITY

Imagine living in a world where Edison had not invented the light bulb, Einstein had not found the relationship between energy and matter, Harry Potter was played by someone other than Daniel Radcliffe, and where Justin Timberlake hadn't written "Can't Stop the Feeling!" It's a different world, isn't it? Did you know that, while these four people are famous for what they have accomplished, they also had disabilities? If they were in school today, these gifted individuals would likely be receiving special education services: Einstein probably would have been identified with autism spectrum disorder, Edison would have qualified for ADHD, Daniel Radcliffe has dyspraxia (a motor-planning disability), and Justin Timberlake has received services for attention deficit hyperactivity disorder (ADHD). Now, imagine if they received educational services that focused *only* on their disability and did not also highlight and build their areas of talent. Years ago, somewhere, teachers and parents were wringing their hands, saying, "But he won't sit still; he can't write; he won't talk!" There could be an Edison, Timberlake, or Einstein sitting in *your* classroom today, and we would do well to listen to the words that we would have told those long-ago teachers. *Work with the disability, but focus on the ability!*

We need to nurture the abilities of *all* our children, but there are some children whose academic abilities require additional educational interventions to keep learning. While no one can deny that there are children who enter a grade knowing most of the material in a particular content area, who learn faster than most of their peers, and who can come up with unusual, out-of-the-box answers, many people disagree about how to identify these children and what to do to meet their needs. What we *do* know is that if we do nothing, only those from well-off families who can supplement their educational experience will continue to grow. A study by the Jack Kent Cooke Foundation (Plucker, Giancola, Healey, Arndt, & Wang, 2015) found that as children moved through school, children from lower socioeconomic families increasingly fell out of the high-achieving group. By the time they graduated high school, significantly few students from poverty who started out "at promise" ended up in the high performing group—a group overwhelmingly upper middle-class. Students from wealthier backgrounds have families who can supplement what the schools cannot or will not provide. These students attend summer camps, have after school lessons, and are provided with additional enriching experiences. Students from poverty and other at-risk groups often depend exclusively on teachers as their advocates to recognize their abilities and provide opportunities to grow their talent.

You might be wondering why you are reading about gifted education when you picked up this book wanting to learn about students with exceptional needs. Well, guess what? It happens more often than one might think that a child with a disability can also be gifted. In both instances, they would be considered special learners. In fact, estimates indicate that 5% to 10% of children with disabilities are also gifted (Bracamonte, 2010; Hughes, 2011). While the definition of *gifted* changes from state to state, and even from school to school, there will be children who are significantly dif-

**Key Concepts**

Twice-exceptional learners:

- The disability may mask the giftedness
- The giftedness may mask the disability

*Work with the disability, but focus on the ability!*

ferent from their peers who need extra help and extra enrichment to learn and to grow. There will also be children who are wonderfully strong in one area and severely deficient in another. These "mountain peaks and valleys" children are considered twice-exceptional, or 2e. No one argues that children in special education need specialized instruction to learn; gifted children do as well—especially gifted children in poverty. Nowhere is this recognition by teachers and administrators more needed than among children with disabilities, a group that will tend to be overrepresented in poverty (Skiba, Poloni-Staudinger, Simmons, Feggins-Azziz, & Chung, 2005) and underrepresented in their development of talents. When the child has a disability *and* is highly talented, schools, teachers, families, and children themselves are often confused about what to do. It is critically important that teachers, administrators, specialists, and family members become familiar with the characteristics and needs of 2e students so that these unique needs can be more fully met.

## WHAT WE KNOW FROM THE RESEARCH

There are numerous examples of 2e adults throughout history. Walt Disney, Richard Branson of Virgin Airlines, and director/producer Steven Spielberg, to name a few, are individuals who have developed their talents and abilities while overcoming disability obstacles. There is even a recent documentary out about 2e children! Yet, despite the successes of these prominent individuals, programming for 2e children remains very rare.

**Plugged In**

Check out the documentary film about 2e students at www.2emovie.com.

Baum, Owens, and Dixon (2003) described these children as having unusual strengths combined with unusual weaknesses. Recently, the Twice-Exceptional National Community of Practice (Baldwin, Baum, Pereles & Hughes, 2015), a collaboration of individuals representing numerous organizations including the National Association for Gifted Children and the Council for Exceptional Children, released a definition of 2e that states:

> Twice exceptional (2e) individuals evidence exceptional ability and disability, which results in a unique set of circumstances. Their exceptional ability may dominate, hiding their disability; their disability may dominate, hiding their exceptional ability; each may mask the other so that neither is recognized or addressed.

2e students, who may perform below, at or above grade level, require the following:

- Specialized methods of identification that consider the possible interaction of the exceptionalities
- Enriched/advanced educational opportunities that develop the child's interests, gifts and talents while also meeting the child's learning needs
- Simultaneous supports that ensure the child's academic success and social-emotional well-being, such as accommodations, therapeutic interventions, and specialized instruction.

Working successfully with this unique population requires specialized academic training and ongoing professional development. (Hughes, Baldwin, & Pereles, 2015)

As you can see, 2e children are *both* gifted *and* have a disability—and that often creates a child with unusual needs and strengths, often in paradoxical ways. Much as an optical illusion might be seen differently from different vantage points, the 2e child remains uniquely themselves.

*Source:* ©iStockphoto.com/Siphotography

## Paradoxical Characteristics

The characteristics of giftedness and disabilities often exist together and influence each other. They may even appear to be in conflict. Check out the end of this chapter. The table called Paradoxical Strengths and Challenges for 2e Students presents these two opposing perspectives (Montgomery County, 2010; Trail, 2011).

It is important to note that not all 2e children will exhibit these characteristics and that not all characteristics are displayed by every 2e child. Just as all children with disabilities are not the same, and all gifted children are not gifted in the same way, 2e children are truly each unique in their own way.

Identifying 2e children can be rather difficult. There are the students who are identified first as having a disability, those identified first as gifted, and numerous children who are never identified because of the masking effect that each has on the other. The most commonly identified disability areas for 2e children include learning disabilities, ADHD, and autism spectrum disorder (Foley-Nicpon, 2013). Because of the variations in definitions of both disability areas and giftedness found across the country, the most common methods of identification include full-scale psychological assessments and a classroom-based response to intervention (RTI) process. Psychological testing can uncover statistically significant differences in scores, while RTI can uncover how a student performs within a given context, if they are looked at across content areas (McCallum et al., 2013). In both cases, examiners have to be looking for both areas of

**Making Connections**

Check out Chapter 11 on Learning Disabilities and Chapter 13 on Autism Spectrum Disorder.

promise and areas of challenge. Often, schools are overly focused on what a child can't do, and as a result, families are inclined to lose faith in their school's ability to work with their children (Besnoy et al., 2015).

While identification is challenging, providing appropriate programs and instruction can be even more challenging. Best practices state that 2e students require a dual-emphasis approach, one that focuses on strengths and talents while supporting and addressing the disability (Baldwin, Omdal, & Pereles, 2015). While there are lists of strategies that are appropriate for gifted students, and a raft of other strategies appropriate for students with disabilities, the fact that the 2e student requires both types of support at the same time requires an integrated, whole-child approach (Pereles, Omdal, & Baldwin, 2009). Addressing only the area of remediation or only the area of strengths and interests is inadequate. Check out the dos and don'ts offered at the end of this chapter. Consider printing it, laminating it, and taking it to your next staff meeting to share with colleagues (Montgomery County, 2010; Trail, 2011). Have a conversation about what you are doing as educators to support—or perhaps even stifle—children who have both gifts and disabilities.

## STOP FOCUSING ONLY ON THE PROBLEMS

**Teachers:**

- ✗ **STOP thinking that a child with a disability can't be gifted.** They are not mutually exclusive.

- ✗ **STOP thinking that a child who is gifted can't have a disability.** All disability categories, with the exception of intellectual and developmental disability, do not exclude children with high IQ scores or high achievement. Children with high IQs can have a disability—learning, social, language, physical, or emotional. Approximately 10% of the population is considered high ability, and this includes children with disabilities. Since children with disabilities are approximately 10% to 15% of the population, in theory, this would have 1% of all children (10% of 10%) identified as being 2e.

- ✗ **STOP writing goals that only focus on the area of disability.** Goals should reflect all the learning needs of a child, which include any need that requires special education. While gifted education is not mandated, the child can best learn to work with his or her area of disability when it is taught in the context of his or her strength. Goals should be written to allow teachers and the student to use their abilities.

- ✗ **STOP using the area of giftedness as a reward for learning in the area of challenge.** Too often, teachers will say, "You can go do more math problems, read about space, or learn more about WWII when you have finished _____." While *some* use of the preferred behavior

is okay to use as a positive reinforcement, doing this too much
means that you're thinking of
the area of challenge as a motivational issue, not a disability.
Telling a child with ADHD that

**Plugged In**

For a short piece on teaching
reading to 2e students, see
https://youtu.be/Us8-tG6R024.

he can go read about cats once he gets his desk organized is like telling a child who is blind that he can do something once he sees better.

✗ **STOP taking offense when it appears that they are challenging
you.** Typical behavior modification programs often don't work
with 2e children because they don't intellectually understand the
process. Gifted children are highly independent and often want to
understand reasons behind decisions. "Because I told you so" sets
up an unnecessary power struggle when all the child wanted to
understand is the reasoning behind the conclusion. This is not to
say that they won't push your buttons on purpose. They are often
trying to distract the attention away from their area of challenge,
and they can be very good at being very bad.

✗ **STOP drilling! It's killing.** Often, a 2e child will learn backwards;
that is, they learn advanced content before they master easier content. Drill-and-kill does not give them the novelty and complexity
that they crave. Introduce the need for specific memory skills in
unusual ways—give lots of songs, memory tricks, and visual cues.
Try "Most Difficult First" by presenting the most difficult problems
first. If a 2e student can do it at 85% mastery, move on.

Administrators:

✗ **STOP forcing families or children to choose between services
for gifted and services for their area of disability.** A 2e child has
two areas of exceptionality, and they both should be served. If the
school offers a gifted program, the U.S. Department of Education
(2007) has noted that to not allow a student with a disability to
participate in it would be discriminatory.

✗ **STOP requiring *only* an RTI cut score to identify students with
learning disabilities.** Many students who are gifted with learning
disabilities are identified using a discrepancy model, in which the
IQ is significantly higher than the performance area, but the performance area is not significantly lower than the typical student's.
In a Dear Colleague letter, the U.S. Department of Education (2013)
stated explicitly that school districts are not to use predetermined
cut scores to determine a learning disability and that "it would
be inconsistent with the IDEA for a child, regardless of whether
the child is gifted, to be found ineligible for special education and

related services under the SLD category solely because the child scored above a particular cut score established by State policy. . . . and the regulations clearly allow discrepancies in achievement domains, typical of children with SLD who are gifted, to be used to identify children with SLD" (p. 2).

✗ **STOP denying a child admission to an enriched or accelerated program based on scores in other areas.** If the child has a D in reading, he or she should still be able to try for accelerated math. Some 2e children have amazing problem-solving skills; they can be doing algebra before they fully master multiplication. Often, these children have "mountain" scores—very high or very low—in very different content areas. Teach them based on where they are in the content, not based on where the book says they should be, or by where their typically developing peers are.

## DO FOCUS ON THE POSSIBILITIES

Teachers:

✔ **HELP students identify their gifts.** Creating a strengths-based instructional plan should start with the identification of the students' learning strengths and interests. There are several tools available to help with this process:

- **Ask the student.** Interest forms, such as the Scales for Rating the Behavioral Characteristics of Superior Students (Renzulli et al., 2010), ask about areas of learning, creativity, motivation, and leadership as well as information on content areas, the arts, communication, and planning.
- **Ask the parents.** An interest form (Yssel, Adams, Clarke, & Jones, 2014) for parents to fill out requests information about the student's favorite books, after-school activities, and vocabulary, which can be used to help augment the student's areas of strength.
- **See what they've done already.** The Interest-Alyzer Family of Instruments (Renzulli, 1997) is a survey for students that requests information about activities in which the student has already been involved to create opportunities for further investigation or creative productivity.

✔ **DEVELOP the gift/ACCOMMODATE the disability.** Take whatever it is that they're good at (e.g., math, history, train time schedules) and make *that* the center of the lesson. It will help with motivation, and it will allow students to develop whatever it is they excel at and love . . . and it's that thing that they're good at that they're going to do for their adult life. Very few of us made a career out of something because we needed more work in it; we made a career out of something we loved and were strong in. We go into an area because that's our passion. Teachers have the awesome responsibility of helping kids find and develop that passion, even if the child has a disability. Help them learn to work around the disability and develop the ideas and fascination in their area of strength. See the end of the chapter for a graphic on differentiating twice.

✔ **ACTIVATE prior learning, while also activating creativity.** Remind and ask. Remind and ask again—in a different way. Twice-exceptional learners often lose information in their memories, but once that memory is activated, they can work with it in unusual ways. Many students will benefit from this repetition; repetition aids retention. But at the same time, a gifted child craves novelty. Repeat the same information in a different way. It is important that we model how there are many ways to access and use information. Doesn't this sound like multiple means of representation, a key component of Universal Design for Learning (UDL)? See the graphic at the end of the chapter for differentiating twice, using UDL principles.

**Making Connections**

Check out Chapter 4 on Instructional Strategies and Universal Design for Learning.

✔ **ALLOW compensatory strategies and technology.** Provide the calculator. Allow him or her to write it out on the computer. Teach the child to talk out his or her paper. Use an electronic calendar. Teach specific strategies. Do not let the area of disability get in the way of the child expressing his or her ability.

✔ **TEACH ahead and circle back.** If a child appears to be stuck in a content area, teach concepts ahead of the concept the child is struggling with, and then reteach the basic concept when the child sees the need for the application of the concept. Compacting and independent study are strategies to use for 2e children because they allow students to move ahead while still learning and applying essential skills. I once taught a child in fifth grade, who was struggling with multiplication tables, the basic concepts of the quadratic equation. He understood how to do the quadratic equation, and his multiplication significantly improved when he had to use that skill in the more complex material. Similarly, if a child *can* understand more complex material, try teaching that first and circling back to material with which you know he or she is struggling. One teacher taught parts of speech by analyzing Shakespeare's sonnets. It's more important to take subject matter deep and complex than to stop a child from moving ahead until it's perfect.

✔ **TEACH the "why" of remediation.** Teach the history of zero. Teach the history of letters. Teach the complex rules of phonics. Do not just teach phonics, but embed them into a story that makes sense and is interesting. Spelling may be difficult. Show how spelling has changed over the years. So often, 2e children can become masters of their own learning if they understand *why* they are being taught to do these particular skills. Share the purpose and goals of the remediation efforts with the students. They can understand and will become more invested.

✔ **INCLUDE them in the creation of a behavior management plan.** Cognitive behavioral interventions work very well with these children because they process so much cognitively. Ask them what they want to work for. Ask them if they can find another way to do something. Ask them if they see a way around an obstacle. Ask them how you could remind them of consequences. Approach them with love, understanding that a bad attitude often means that they are going through a bad time and that together you can help them figure out what to do. Being 2e often means that they have the impulse control of a child with ADHD and the perfectionism of the gifted child, meaning that they can frequently be even more sensitive to issues and challenges than other children.

**Making Connections**

Check out Chapter 8 on Positive Behavior Supports.

✔ **TEACH them about other 2e people.** Twice-exceptional children experience high levels of stress and anxiety because they know that they *should* be able to do something, or they can conceptualize how to do it. Concurrently though, they also realize they don't have the skills or the organizational abilities to complete the activity, which can lead to bad attitudes and lack of motivation. Showing them that other people—famous people and successful people—experienced this frustration as well can help them believe in their abilities and allow them to work *around* their challenges and not be stopped by their disabilities. Social and emotional support is key to helping 2e children overcome their disability and realize their giftedness.

Administrators:

✔ **ENCOURAGE your staff to look for problems *and* possibilities.** It is important to look for the child who is "at promise" as well as who is at risk.

✔ **ENCOURAGE a positive growth mindset in your staff so that all children are encouraged to grow.** This mindset will ensure that 2e children are not overlooked. If all talents are respected in all your children, those children with unusual talents from unusual groups will not be overlooked.

✔ **ENCOURAGE parents to see their child as complex and capable and talented.** Encourage them to develop their child's ability as best as they can. Help them seek enrichment opportunities. Some external programs may ask only for test scores and will need a letter of recommendation explaining the child's tal-

**Plugged In**

For a description of summer activities and possibilities, check out http://www.nagc.org/sites/default/files/Publication%20PHP/bonuscontent/Exploring%20Summer%20Camp%20Options%20042013.pdf.

ents; offer to write that letter. Send families information about Duke TIP (https://tip.duke.edu) and summer camp options. Teach them to be advocates for their child.

✔ **PROVIDE professional development on inclusive strategies for your teachers, including your gifted education teachers, mentors, and coaches.** Include information on co-teaching in a gifted environment (Hughes & Weichel, 2001)! Provide professional development to your special educators about gifted characteristics because they will often be looked at as the expert on children with special needs.

✔ **PROVIDE acceleration opportunities as well as remediation experiences in your programs.** If the curriculum were to meet the child where they are, both advanced and developmentally, 2e students could be better served. Allow for flexibility in scheduling. Alex may need to go from his AP chemistry class to a co-taught basic English class.

## PARADOXICAL STRENGTHS AND CHALLENGES FOR 2E STUDENTS

| Strengths | Challenges |
|---|---|
| **Cognitive**<br><br>• Verbal skills<br>• Visual spatial skills<br>• Reasoning ability | **Cognitive**<br><br>• Memory<br>• Executive function<br>• Processing speed |
| **Math**<br><br>• Problem solving<br>• Relating math to alternative situations<br>• Logical connections | **Math**<br><br>• Computing<br>• Recalling math facts<br>• Staying organized; staying sequential |
| **Language Arts**<br><br>• Comprehension<br>• Vocabulary<br>• Connecting to background knowledge<br>• Topics and insights<br>• Creativity and elaboration | **Language Arts**<br><br>• Decoding phonics<br>• Fluency<br>• Translating thoughts to paper<br>• Basic skills (e.g., handwriting, conventions) |

## CONTENT-BASED INSTRUCTIONAL DOS AND DON'TS FOR TWICE-EXCEPTIONAL STUDENTS

| DOs | DON'Ts |
|---|---|
| **Cognitive**<br><br>• Use questioning strategies<br>• Teach about Bloom's taxonomy and how to use it<br>• Use think-alouds<br>• Use multiple modalities for instruction<br>• Teach organization skills<br>• Use strategic instruction to help remember steps for skills | **Cognitive**<br><br>• Assume that they understand how to organize their thinking<br>• Assume that because they know a lot, they remember everything<br>• Emphasize the small details<br>• Assume they will be equally strong across all content |
| **Math**<br><br>• Preassess skills and start with the highest set of mastered skills<br>• Teach concepts and application first<br>• Use hands-on programs (e.g., Hands-on Equations)<br>• Use a multi-disciplinary approach to math, integrate with science, ELA, etc. | **Math**<br><br>• Focus on computation<br>• Insist on copying problems from the book<br>• Withhold the use of a calculator<br>• Give numerous problems to solve<br>• Withhold learning complex material until basic skills are memorized |
| **Language Arts**<br><br>• Focus on legibility<br>• Use mechanical pencils and grips<br>• Focus on comprehension<br>• Use high-interest above grade-level materials with support<br>• Encourage creativity and elaboration | **Language Arts**<br><br>• Focus on handwriting<br>• Use round-robin read-alouds<br>• Emphasize phonics exclusively |

## DIFFERENTIATING TWICE

In order to meet the needs of the whole 2e child, it is necessary to *both* mediate the area of difficulty *and* develop the ability. Teachers, parents, and schools must understand the relationship between the various aspects of the child and work to help the child grow and advance, particularly in their area of strength. Just as watch gears work together in seemingly opposing directions to move the mechanism forward, a dual emphasis can help a child move forward in all aspects of their life.

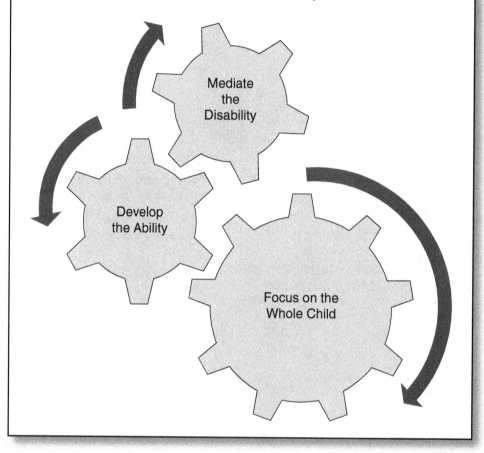

## DIFFERENTIATING TWICE THROUGH UDL PRINCIPLES

### General Input Principles

- Make it visual
- Make it sequential
- Make it interesting

### General Process Principles

- Make it require creativity
- Make it require critical thinking

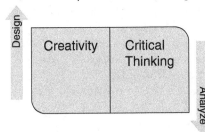

### General Output Principles

| Make it complex | Make it challenging | Make it connected |

One of the challenges of differentiating is that it means so many things to so many people. Gifted education has one view, in which acceleration, novelty, and enrichment are the expectations, and special education has another, in which inputs, processes, and outputs are varied to meet the multiple needs of students. Neither of these contradict each other and can be used together.

This graphic describes how you can differentiate using both sets of principles.

**Input:**
To meet the needs of students with possible language, attention, and skill deficits, the presentation has to rely on visuals and be sequential and task sequenced, while relating to the interests and the strengths of the 2e child.

**Processes:**
While students have to engage with the content, they should be able to use their imagination and their critical-thinking abilities to design and analyze the information, in a top-down and bottom-up approach.

**Output:**
What you ask students to produce has to relate to other topic areas and be challenging for them, but structured in such a way that it is connected to what they know and can do.

**For example:** Teaching place value by researching the history of zero and demonstrating how place value came about in a slide presentation.

*Images source:* clipart.com

## REFERENCES

Baldwin, L., Baum, S., Pereles, D., & Hughes, C. (2015). Twice-exceptional learners: The journey toward a shared vision. *Gifted Child Today, 38*(4), 206–214.

Baldwin, L., Omdal, S. N., & Pereles, D. (2015). Beyond stereotypes: Understanding, recognizing, and working with twice-exceptional learners. *TEACHING Exceptional Children, 47*(4), 216–225.

Baum, S., Owens, S. V., & Dixon, J. (2003). *To be gifted and learning disabled*. Mansfield Center, CT: Creative Learning Press.

Besnoy, K. D., Swoszowski, N. C., Newman, J. L., Floyd, A., Jones, P., & Byrne, C. (2015). The advocacy experiences of parents of elementary age, twice-exceptional children. *Gifted Child Quarterly, 59*(2), 108–124.

Bracamonte, M. (March, 2010). Twice-exceptional students: Who are they and what do they need? *2e: Twice-Exceptional Newsletter*. Retrieved from http://www.2enewsletter.com/article_2e_what_are_they.html

Foley-Nicpon, M. (2013). *Gifted Child Quarterly's* special issue on twice-exceptionality: Progress on the path of empirical understanding. *Gifted Child Quarterly, 57*(4), 207–209.

Hughes, C. E. (2011). Twice-exceptional learners: Twice the strengths, twice the challenges. In J. Escalante (Ed.), *A kaleidoscope of special populations in gifted education: Considerations, connections, and meeting the needs of our most able diverse gifted students* (pp. 153–174). Austin, TX: Prufrock Press.

Hughes, C. E., Baldwin, L., & Pereles, D. (2015, March). *Twice-exceptional students: A collaborative definition, curricular implications, and counseling*. Council for Exceptional Children Annual Conference, San Diego, CA.

Hughes, C. E., & Weichel, W. A. (2001). Collaboration and co-teaching: Lessons learned from special education. *Gifted Child Quarterly, 45*(3), 179–184.

McCallum, R. S., Bell, S. M., Coles, J. T., Miller, K. C., Hopkins, M. B., & Hilton-Prillart, A. (2013). A model for screening twice-exceptional students (gifted with learning disabilities) within a response to intervention paradigm. *Gifted Child Quarterly, 57*(4), 209–223.

Montgomery County, Maryland. (2010). Twice-exceptional students at a glance. Retrieved from http://www.montgomeryschoolsmd.org/uploadedFiles/curriculum/enriched/programs/gtld/2010%20Twice%20Exceptional%20Students-At%20A%20Glance.pdf

Pereles, D. A., Omdal, S. N., & Baldwin, L. (2009). Response to intervention and twice-exceptional learners: A promising fit. *Gifted Child Today, 32*(3), 40–51.

Plucker, J., Giancola, J., Healey, G., Arndt, D., & Wang, C. (2015). *Equal talents: Unequal opportunities*. Washington, DC: Jack Kent Cooke Foundation. Retrieved http://www.excellencegap.org/assets/files/JKCF_ETUO_Report.pdf

Renzulli, J. S. (1997). *Interest-A-Lyzer Family of Instruments: A manual for teachers*. Waco, TX: Prufrock Press.

Renzulli, J. S., Smith, L. H., White, A. J., Callahan, C. M., Hartman, R. K., Westberg, K. L., & Sytsma, R. E. (2010). *Scales for rating the behavioral characteristics of superior students: Technical and administration manual* (3rd ed.). Waco, TX: Prufrock Press.

Skiba, R. J., Poloni-Staudinger, L., Simmons, A. B., Feggins-Azziz, L., & Chung, C. (2005). Unproven links: Can poverty explain ethnic disproportionality in special education? *The Journal of Special Education, 39*(3), 130–144.

Trail, B. (2011). *Twice-exceptional gifted children: Understanding, teaching and counseling gifted students*. Naperville, IL: Source Books.

U.S. Department of Education. (2007). Dear Colleague letter: Access by students with disabilities to accelerated programs. Retrieved from http://www2.ed.gov/about/offices/list/ocr/letters/colleague-20071226.html

U.S. Department of Education. (2013). Dear Colleague letter to Dr. Jim Delisle. Retrieved from https://www2.ed.gov/policy/speced/guid/idea/memosdcltrs/122013delisletwiceexceptional4q2013.pdf

Yssel, N., Adams, C., Clarke, L., & Jones, R. (2014). Applying an RTI model for students with learning disabilities who are gifted. *TEACHING Exceptional Children, 46*(3), 42–52.

# ADDITIONAL RECOMMENDED READING ON TWICE-EXCEPTIONAL LEARNERS

Baum, S. E., & Owen, S. (2004). *To be gifted and learning disabled: Strategies for helping bright students with LD, ADHD and more*. Waco, TX: Prufrock Press.

Colorado Department of Education. (2009). *Twice-exceptional students: Introductory resource book*. Retrieved from https://www.cde.state.co.us/sites/default/files/documents/gt/download/pdf/twiceexceptionalresourcehandbook.pdf

Hughes-Lynch, C. E. (2010). *Children with high-functioning autism: A parent's guide*. Austin, TX: Prufrock Press.

Hughes-Lynch, C. E. (2011). *Teaching children with high-functioning autism*. Austin, TX: Prufrock Press.

National Education Association. (2006). *The twice-exceptional dilemma*. Retrieved from http://www.nea.org/assets/docs/twiceexceptional.pdf

Warshaw, M. (2012). *Tips for parents: Meeting the needs of twice-exceptional children*. Retrieved from http://www.davidsongifted.org/db/Articles_id_10140.aspx

Webb, J. T., Amend, E. R., Webb, N. E., Goerss, J., Beljan, P., & Olenchak, F. R. (2005). *Misdiagnosis and dual diagnosis of gifted children and adults*. Scottsdale, AZ: Great Potential Press.

Whitmore, J. R., & Maker, C. J. (1985). *Intellectual giftedness in disabled persons*. Rockville, MD: Aspen Systems.

# TOP FIVE WEBSITES TO SUPPORT TWICE-EXCEPTIONAL LEARNERS

➡ http://www.hoagiesgifted.org/twice_exceptional.htm

➡ http://www.2enewsletter.com

➡ http://www.wrightslaw.com/info/2e.guidebook.pdf

➡ http://www.nea.org/assets/docs/twiceexceptional.pdf

➡ http://www.uniquelygifted.org

## APPS WE LOVE

➡ Code Academy

➡ Dragon Box

➡ Evernote

➡ Oregon Trail

➡ Presidents v. Aliens

➡ Space Physics

➡ Story Dice

➡ Doors

➡ Wolfram Alpha

# SECTION IV

*What Really Works Beyond the Classroom*

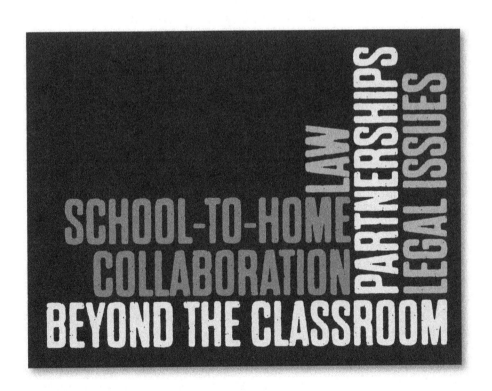

# 18

---

# *It's the Law!*

## *Legal Issues in Special Education*

### Christine A. Hayashi
*California State University, Northridge*

A s a classroom teacher, you want to know what steps to take to get a student assessed for special education services. As a parent, you are upset with your child's placement and want to know how to file for a due process hearing. Or perhaps the new assistant principal will be the immediate supervisor for special education issues and needs to rely on your expertise as a special education teacher. Regardless of your role, the legal issues surrounding individuals with disabilities may impact you. Where do you go to find the necessary responses? How does a school remain in compliance with the numerous and complex special education laws?

The answers to these and many other questions regarding issues concerning students with disabilities can be found in the federal and state statutes, codes of regulation, and case law. Don't worry. This information is increasingly accessible. Teachers and administrators can stay up to date on changes in these laws by subscribing to school law newsletters, attending annual professional development, and/or staying in contact with school district attorneys. While familiarizing oneself with the law may seem daunting, this chapter helps set the stage for understanding the basics and provides some tips for what to do and what not to do. The first step in knowing what really works in special education as pertains to the law is getting to know the law itself!

# THE INDIVIDUALS WITH DISABILITIES EDUCATION IMPROVEMENT ACT

The Individuals with Disabilities Education Improvement Act (IDEIA) of 2004 is the federal statute that provides the rules for special education (IDEA, 2004). The intent of the IDEIA statute (often still known as IDEA, a term we will continue to use throughout this text) is to provide students with disabilities with a free appropriate public education (FAPE), meaning that school districts will provide students with special education and related services at public expense in conformity with the individualized education program (IEP) as required by the IDEA (2004). The IDEA is a huge statute and there are many provisions, but there are several main areas of the law that are especially important for school personnel to understand (Weishaar, Weishaar, & Borsa, 2014). These include:

### Child Find

All children with disabilities residing within each state, regardless of the severity of their disabilities, must be identified, located, and evaluated by the local education agency (LEA) or school district. Additionally, school districts may not turn away a child with a disability or deny the child an appropriate program. Even though you may think that a child's needs are too severe for your school to address, the IEP team must determine how the district will provide services for that child (IDEA, 2004).

### Assessment and Eligibility

Once the children are found, they must be assessed. All assessments must be administered so as not to be racially, culturally, or sexually discriminatory, and they must be provided in a student's native language when possible. The student must be assessed in all areas of suspected disability, no single measure can be used as the sole criterion to determine disability, and tests and assessment materials must be administered by trained and knowledgeable personnel. Eligibility is two pronged: First, the child must have one of the listed disabilities, which include "mental retardation, hearing impairments including deafness, speech or language impairments, visual impairments including blindness, emotional disturbance, orthopedic impairments, autism spectrum disorder, traumatic brain injury, other health impairments, or specific learning disabilities" and, second, the child must *need* special education and related services (IDEA, 2004).

### The Individualized Education Program (IEP)

The IEP Team is a school-based team that includes the parent, general education teacher, special education teacher, representative of the local education agency (LEA) who is qualified to supervise special education, an individual who can interpret the assessment results, the student when appropriate, and other professionals as necessary. Once a child has been assessed and the IEP team has made a determination that a child is eligible for special services, the team must develop an IEP for that student (IDEA, 2004). The IEP is "essentially a blue print of special education services needed by the student" (Weishaar et al., 2014, p. 56). It includes present levels of performance, measurable goals, specialized instruction and related services, and the "extent, if any, to which the child will not participate with nondisabled children in the general education classroom" (La Morte, 2012, p. 263). This leads us to the concept of least restrictive environment.

### Least Restrictive Environment (LRE)

This means that, "to the maximum extent appropriate," (IDEA, 2004) children with disabilities must be educated with children who do not have disabilities. Students will only be removed from the general education environment if the nature and severity of their disability is such that they cannot progress satisfactorily even with supplementary services (IDEA, 2004). Meeting the needs of students with disabilities in the general education classroom is also sometimes referred to as *inclusion*. The IEP team determines the appropriate LRE for each student. Based on the principles of LRE, however, any amount of time that a student is not in the general education setting must be justified. The goal is to educate children with their nondisabled peers as much as possible.

### Due Process Hearings

Parents have the right to file for a due process hearing with the state when they believe the district is not providing a free appropriate public education to their child, and/or if they disagree with the LEA or district's identification, evaluation, or placement of their child. School districts are required to provide parents with a written copy of the procedural safeguards that protect parents' rights regarding special education programs and the provision of a FAPE (IDEA, 2004).

### Parent Participation

Parents, guardians, and care givers must be notified of and given the chance to participate in meetings regarding their child, be given the opportunity to be a part of the decision-making surrounding any changes in their child's placement or services, and generally be included as a partner in their child's education (IDEA, 2004). Research is clear that students succeed when there is home-school collaboration (Murawski, Carter, Sileo, & Prater, 2012), so this isn't just the law—it is what really works!

**Making Connections**

Check out Chapter 19 on School-to-Home Collaboration.

### High Academic Achievement Standards

Educational systems serving students with disabilities must "maintain high academic achievement standards and clear performance goals for children with disabilities, consistent with the standards and expectations for all students in the educational system, and provide for appropriate and effective strategies and methods to ensure that all children with disabilities are expected to achieve" (IDEA, 2004). It is not acceptable to have low or no expectations of progress for students with disabilities. This seems like it should be a given, doesn't it? And yet the legislature felt compelled to add this provision to the statute when it was revised in 2004 because we just weren't seeing those high expectations nationally.

## IDEA: DISCIPLINE ISSUES

Once you have figured out all the above, do you know what to do when your school's dean of discipline asks if she can suspend a student who has an IEP? Have you ever felt frustrated when one child gets a different consequence for the same infraction as a nondisabled peer? Are there separate disciplinary rules for students with disabilities? Let's examine these issues.

Under the IDEA, students with disabilities can be suspended for up to 10 cumulative school days in one year, for similar reasons applied to general education students. The difference is that school officials must begin to provide special education services to the student with a disability, in an interim alternative setting for any additional days of removal beyond 10 days. The school must also conduct a functional behavior assessment (FBA) and create a behavioral intervention plan (BIP) as part of the student's IEP (IDEA, 2004). Unfortunately, this may result in a school either suspending a

**Making Connections**

Check out Chapter 8 on Positive Behavior Supports and Chapter 12 on Emotional and Behavioral Disorders.

student with disabilities for fewer days than the infraction deserves or to simply stop suspending a student once the 10 days have been reached.

If a student with a disability violates school rules that may result in an expulsion, the school must first determine whether the act was a *manifestation* of the student's disability. If the conduct was caused by or had a direct and substantial relationship to the child's disability, or if the conduct was the direct result of the school's failure to implement the IEP, the behavior is a manifestation of the disability and the student cannot be expelled. While some behaviors may appear to have nothing to do with a child's disability, it can be difficult to determine whether certain inappropriate actions are a direct result of a disability where that disability impacts a student's attention, emotion, behavior, or learning. However, that doesn't mean that the school must allow a student to disregard school regulations! If the student's violation involved weapons, drugs, or infliction of bodily harm, the LEA may remove the student with a disability to an interim alternative setting for up to 45 school days, even if it was a manifestation of his or her disability. Additionally, if a student with a disability violates school rules that are not a manifestation of the disability and that do result in expulsion, special education services must continue during the time of the expulsion (IDEA, 2004).

## SECTION 504 OF THE REHABILITATION ACT

Another federal statute that provides protections to persons with disabilities is Section 504 of the Rehabilitation Act of 1973. What is a Section 504 plan and how is it different from an IEP? Under Section 504, "[n]o otherwise qualified individual with a disability in the United States . . . shall, solely, by reason of his or her disability, be excluded from the participation in, be denied the benefits of, or be subjected to discrimination under any program or activity receiving Federal financial assistance" (Section 504, 1998). Public schools receive federal funding. Does that mean they fall within the definition of this civil rights statute? What kinds of disabilities are covered? Does failing to provide accommodations for a student with a broken leg or a student with occasional asthma constitute discrimination?

Schools need to be able to determine whether the appropriate action is to provide the student with reasonable accommodations under Section 504 or to recommend assessment to determine eligibility for special services under the IDEA. Many LEAs put together collaborative teams, similar to IEP teams, to help make that determination. Under IDEA, a student must have one of the listed disabilities in the statute but under Section 504 of the Rehabilitation Act, a student may have *any* condition that meets the legal definition of disability within the law. Under the Rehabilitation Act, the definition of an individual with a disability is "any person who has a physical or mental impairment which substantially limits one or more of such person's major life activities; has a record of such an impairment; or is regarded as having such an impairment" (Section 504, 1998). Major life activities include "caring for oneself, performing manual tasks, walking, seeing, hearing, speaking, breathing, learning, and working" (Section 504, 1998).

Therefore, let's revisit our student with the broken leg. He is otherwise qualified to be a student in the school, the school receives federal monies, the student has a physical impairment, and walking is one of the major life activities. It looks like the school should provide reasonable accommodations for the student. Perhaps the school could provide the student a longer pass time between classes or someone to carry his books. Is a formal 504 plan required? Maybe. Although a written plan is not always necessary for a school to provide accommodations, it documents the measures the school is taking to avoid disability discrimination and ensures that the parents and school have agreed on an appropriate action that will meet the needs of the child.

**Key Concepts**

To qualify for a 504 Plan, does the student:

- Have a physical or mental impairment that substantially limits major life activities;
- Have a record of such an impairment; or
- Is he or she regarded as having such an impairment?

Let's also consider the student with occasional asthma. The student does not meet the definition of a person with a disability when her asthma is in remission. However, one of the major life activities is listed in the regulations as "breathing," and during the times the child is gasping for breath and unable to attend to school work or activities, that child would be covered under the statute (Section 504, 1998). So what should the school do? Special education services are not needed, yet she requires some accommodation. Thus, an appropriate Section 504 plan might be an option for this student, making sure the child is getting necessary support, such as being excused from physical education activities without penalty during attacks, and also providing documentation that the school district is not discriminating against the student.

As if these laws are not enough to review, in addition to the federal statutes we have covered so far, each state has parallel statutes applying the federal laws to their own state and adding state-specific provisions. That is not all. Read on to see how federal and state statutes are supplemented by federal and state regulations.

## CODE OF FEDERAL REGULATIONS (CFR)

The Code of Federal Regulations (CFR) provides additional information regarding the administration of the IDEA statute, and, as with the statutes, individual states have parallel regulations applying the laws to their own state (CFR, 2007). While the IDEA is a statute that was enacted through the federal legislative branch of government, the CFR is created through the executive or administrative branch of the federal government, through the U.S. Department of Education. Each state also has a Code of Regulations created through the governor's office, often through a State Department of Education that includes a State Board of Education and a Superintendent of Public Instruction (CFR, 2007). These regulations give us more details about how to administer the statutes. An example would be that the Americans with Disabilities Act (ADA, 1990; the federal statute) states that a person with a disability must have an impairment that substantially limits a major life activity (ADA, 1990) and the CFR (the federal regulations) explains further that a major life activity includes walking, breathing, learning, and so on (CFR, 2006).

We have now reviewed a number of statutes and regulations. Are you wondering how important it is to remember all these laws? Very important! Although it would be almost impossible to memorize everything, knowledge of the law can help your district avoid time consuming and expensive due process hearings. What's even more important, however, is that knowing these laws will help you provide a meaningful FAPE to each of your students with special needs.

## KEY RESEARCH AND CURRENT LEGAL TRENDS

The area of special education is very statute driven (as you can see from our review above) and also a highly litigated area in education (Erlichman, Gregory, & St. Florian, 2014; Pazey & Cole, 2012); thus, it would be beyond the scope of this chapter to cover all the due process hearings and pertinent case law. Therefore, we focus on trends and outcomes in recent special education litigation. In a study that reviewed the special education court cases that occurred in 2010, researchers found that special education litigation, an area of high cost to school districts, was generally concentrated in the areas of discipline, including manifestation determination disputes, the evaluation process, and transition services (Katsiyannis, Losinski, & Prince, 2012). Researchers recommend that administrators take steps to implement schoolwide discipline policies that encompass general and special education populations, provide early intervention for at-risk students in general education, and finally, make sure that each student's transition plan is individualized to meet the specific postsecondary needs of each student. So, yes, we need to address early education to postsecondary education and everything in between.

Disciplinary procedures were also identified as an issue of concern in a study that addressed the disproportionate representation of racial and ethnic minority groups in special education disciplinary action (Bird & Bassin, 2015). Overrepresentation of minorities in school discipline practices, such as office referrals, suspensions, and expulsions has been noted in a number of studies and can result in special education students dropping out of school and becoming part of the "school-to-prison pipeline"

(Wald & Losen, 2003, p. 11). Bird and Bassin (2015) advocate alternatives to disciplinary actions and referring special education students to more restrictive environments by first halting zero tolerance practices that result in further disproportionate exclusion of minorities from their education, and second, by providing preventive services that may help reduce the incidences of inappropriate behaviors. These practices include: expanding school mental health approaches by collaborating with outside clinical and community agencies to reach students not receiving adequate services, providing multitiered support systems such as schoolwide positive behavior intervention and support, and encouraging "positive psychology practices for developing protective factors in at-risk students" (Bird & Bassin, 2015, p. 22).

**Making Connections**

Check out Chapter 15 on English Language Learners.

According to Zirkel (2013), in another study of recent litigation, educators need to pay specific attention not only to parent permission for services, but also revocation of services. This means that if a parent requests services after previously revoking them, the district must treat the matter as an initial evaluation. Additionally, in districts using a response to intervention (RTI) approach in the general education classroom, administrators need to make sure to fulfill their obligation under Child Find by "conducting evaluations for children reasonably suspected of being eligible under the IDEIA" (p. 320).

Special education students are often at higher risk of injury when they are engaged in activities in a general education setting (Daggett, 2014). To minimize the risk of injury to special education students, Daggett recommends that schools provide general education staff with training and information about individual students and that schools engage in schoolwide and individual safety planning. In other areas where more training is advised, Nichols and Sheffield (2014) found that administrators need to support special education students through further training of special and general education teachers in the areas of cultural sensitivity and providing more time for building co-teaching relationships (Murawski & Lochner, 2011).

**Making Connections**

Check out Chapter 6 on Culturally Responsive Teaching and Chapter 9 on Co-Teaching.

Regarding Section 504 of the Rehabilitation Act, Madaus and Shaw (2006) found that although Section 504 has been around since 1973, it was ignored for many years, partially because schools were under the impression that compliance with IDEA was sufficient, and partially because Section 504 is not funded. They found that while the statute is widely in use, there are hardly any studies that look at how the law is currently implemented in schools (Madaus & Shaw, 2006). As IDEA has never been fully funded (Parrish, 2006), broader implementation of Section 504 plans may benefit school districts as well as students by being a viable alternative for students who may benefit from reasonable classroom accommodations but who are not in need of the full specialized instruction provided by an IEP (Madaus & Shaw, 2006). This is an evolving area that administrators may want to watch for further development.

## AVOID THESE LEGAL PITFALLS!

✗ **STOP separating students in self-contained classes from activities with the general education population.** Make sure that you create opportunities in your school for all students to participate in schoolwide activities regardless of individual placement in special or general education classrooms. Work to remove exclusive barriers.

✗ **STOP assuming that educators are the experts.** Walking into a meeting as the expert or failing to listen to a family's questions and concerns can prevent family members and parents from being true partners in their child's education. Remember that any change in placement must be determined by the IEP team, which includes the family.

✗ **STOP rushing through IEP meetings and then expecting the parents to understand the IEP process.** Use an agenda for every IEP meeting so that the meeting remains organized and all necessary items are discussed and agreed on. If you are unable to accomplish everything within the allotted time, schedule another meeting. Let parents know that their contributions are important by providing sufficient time to address all their questions and concerns.

✗ **STOP failing to build stronger relationships within the IEP team.** Respect everyone's opinion, and don't bully team members into accepting your point of view. Work together as a team for the success of the student. Never sign or expect another teacher to sign an IEP asserting you attended an IEP team meeting if you did not do so.

✗ **STOP pretending that there is never any need to negotiate with a parent.** Resolve issues at the local level and save the cost of contentious due process hearings. Practice your negotiating and conflict resolution skills. Digging in your heels alienates parents, stops the dialogue, and a due process hearing becomes inevitable.

✗ **STOP allowing students to stay too long in RTI and student study team (SST) processes in the general education classroom.** Many teachers complain that these teams have begun to serve as a holding place for struggling students. We need to be sure the teams have concrete time lines for working with teachers and students. The concept of Child Find requires school districts to assess those students suspected of having disabilities that require special services. In addition, districts *must* respond when a parent or teacher requests an assessment and eligibility determination.

✗ **STOP placing students in a general education classroom without appropriate accommodations to ensure satisfactory progress.** In the past, many special education students were kept unnecessarily segregated in self-contained classes. Now, however, the fear is that districts may not provide adequate support for students with disabilities placed in the general education classroom. Increasingly, as more students with disabilities are taught in the general education classroom, IEP teams need to be prepared to determine the supports required to help a student be successful in that placement— academically, behaviorally, and socially.

✗ **STOP automatically offering a Section 504 plan when a student is not eligible for special education and related services.** A Section 504 plan should not be a consolation prize for the student who has been assessed and found not to be eligible for special education services. A Section 504 plan provides a student with a disability the appropriate accommodations to make that child's education commensurate with that of children who do not have disabilities. If a child does not have a disability, a Section 504 plan is not appropriate. Remember, the Section 504 plan is a legal document and is overseen by the Office of Civil Rights; it should not be provided lightly.

✗ **STOP perpetuating the myth that students with disabilities can do whatever they want and they cannot be disciplined.** Know what constitutes a change in placement for students with IEPs and what actions trigger the need for a special IEP meeting to determine if students' behaviors were a manifestation of their disability. Do not ever punish a child for having a disability, but do provide consequences for those students whose disability has no nexus to the behavior. One concrete step to take to help parents and teachers understand this issue is to meet with them as soon as a student is struggling behaviorally and present this information.

✗ **STOP having family members act as interpreters at IEP meetings.** While it can be difficult to find qualified interpreters, it is unfair and inappropriate to expect family members or the student to translate for meetings. Conversations can include complex concepts and language that the family may not understand and may not be able to interpret correctly. Budget accordingly for professional interpreters.

## SIGN ON TO THESE STRATEGIES FOR SUCCESS

✔ **COMMUNICATE clearly and listen carefully.** Keep lines of communication open between parents, teachers, and administrators. Hone your communication skills—listen carefully, listen respectfully, rephrase for clarity, and work with an interpreter when appropriate. Be there fully when a parent or colleague is relating a concern. Let parents and other educators know that you are truly listening and that the IEP process is in place to support the success of the child with a disability.

✔ **SHOW family members they are an equal member of the team.** Let them know in advance of any meeting that they will be invited to share information on their child. Provide them with guiding questions. Give them paper and pen at the meeting so they are able to take notes. Create name tags with each individual's role and name. Have water and snacks available, if possible, to make everyone feel comfortable. Show respect for the opinions and expertise of the family members through your actions.

✔ **FOLLOW an agenda at IEP meetings.** Having an agenda, such as the example at the end of this chapter, can make parents and other guests feel more comfortable and keep everyone on task. Be sure to include the names and positions of everyone expected to attend, and make sure there is a place noted on the agenda for parents to speak. Stick to your agenda, honor time limits, and be prepared to continue the meeting on another day should you be unable to finish your agenda. Before the parents leave, make sure you've addressed all their questions and concerns. Know and adhere to all parts of the IDEA during the IEP process and implementation.

✔ **BUILD trust and team relationships.** It is important to understand the role and frame of reference of each person at a meeting. Show respect and listen when others talk. Especially in an initial hearing, be sure to take the time to make the family members comfortable. A hasty meeting can end up in a lengthy hearing.

✔ **ENSURE that the appropriate team members are present at important meetings.** The IDEA statute requires a general education teacher to be part of the IEP team. However, just asking any general education teacher to show up at the IEP meeting is not appropriate. Be sure that the invited general education teacher is someone who knows the student, is aware of the student's struggles and successes, and preferably has that student in class. The general education teacher should always know why he or she has been invited to the meeting and what materials to bring for meaningful collaboration.

✔ **PRACTICE good negotiation and conflict resolution skills.** Use your listening and communication skills to negotiate with the other party. Be reasonable. Even if you are legally within your rights to deny a request, sometimes providing a service that is within the means of the district and will not harm the student can bring successful resolution to a situation. Try to come to an agreement before bringing in the advocates and attorneys. The longer the negotiations, mediation, and due process hearing, the more money gets paid to lawyers and the longer the student waits to receive a free and appropriate public education.

✔ **HAVE methods in place to "find" all children with disabilities within the service area of your school, including children in private schools.** To find students in public schools, use pre-referral methods such as SST or RTI. To find students in private schools, provide local private school representatives with district protocol for assessing students with suspected disabilities. The public school district where the private school is located has the duty to assess the student, even if the student lives in another school district area.

✔ **BE PREPARED for discipline issues.** Know that students with disabilities must have a manifestation determination meeting prior to any suspension or expulsion. Consider creating a laminated card, such as the one at the end of this chapter, for team members that gives a short explanation of the legal guidelines for discipline issues and the manifestation determination process. Also, have information prepared regarding creation of a Behavior Intervention Plan (BIP) for students so that the IEP team can discuss ways to support positive student behavior and avoid future discipline issues.

✔ **UNDERSTAND the differences between a Section 504 Plan and an IEP.** The Rehabilitation Act is a civil rights statute that ensures that institutions that get federal dollars do not discriminate against people with disabilities. IDEA provides special services for a small eligible group of students with certain specified disabilities through the IEP process. Have a 504 coordinator identified at your school who can oversee the 504 process and keep data on students who have 504 plans.

✔ **CREATE a "cheat sheet" of special education statutes and regulations.** Keep the sheet updated and available for all administrators, teachers, and team members. Having a quick reference will save time and help you stay in compliance with the law.

✔ **STAY abreast of changes in the law.** The IDEA has not been reauthorized since 2004, but although the statute itself has not changed, there have been many due process hearings and court cases that provide new insight into what constitutes FAPE. The Americans with Disabilities Act Amendments Act (ADAAA) was enacted in 2008 and expanded the definition of disability under the ADA and Section 504 to include new major life activities (e.g., functions of the immune system, digestive, bowel, bladder, and respiratory systems) and impairment that is episodic or in remission (e.g., peanut allergies, asthma). Go to legal workshops, subscribe to school law newsletters, talk to your general counsel in the district, and stay informed. Not a lot of time? There are plenty of short webinars that you can watch while relaxing at home. Legal issues may not be your current area of expertise, but it is important to stay updated to best support your students. Save your school funds for student programs and education, not for lawsuits!

**Plugged In**

Keep abreast of legal changes by joining professional organizations that work with special education.

- www.cec.sped.org
- www.nichcy.org

## THE INCLUSIVE ADMINISTRATOR:
## 10 TIPS FOR SUCCESS

1. Create an inclusive atmosphere on your campus.

2. Keep lines of communication open between parents, teachers, and administration.

3. Follow an agenda at IEP meetings.

4. Build trust and team relationships.

5. Practice negotiation and conflict resolution skills.

6. Have methods in place to "find" all children with disabilities within the service area of your school, including children in private schools.

7. Understand that Least Restrictive Environment is determined by the IEP team.

8. Know the sections of the IDEA that relate to discipline to ensure that students continue to receive a FAPE.

9. Train faculty to understand the differences between a Section 504 Plan and an IEP.

10. Know where to find resources.

## SAMPLE INDIVIDUAL EDUCATIONAL PROGRAM (IEP) MEETING AGENDA

Introduce team members and guests:

Name: _____ Role: _____
Name: _____ Role: _____
Name: _____ Role: _____
Name: _____ Role: _____
Name: _____ Role: _____
Name: _____ Role: _____
Name: _____ Role: _____

Purpose of the IEP meeting and meeting guidelines

Procedural Safeguards: Provide parent with a copy of parents' rights at least once per year.

Share present levels of performance:

    a. Strengths

    b. Areas of concern

    c. Assessment data, testing results, progress reports

    d. Parent input and concerns

    e. Student needs

Determine Eligibility (initial meeting) or Review Eligibility (triennial meeting)

Update Behavior Support Plan (if applicable)

Develop specific measurable annual goals

Determine services to be provided and placement

    a. Services: Time, frequency, and accommodations

        i. Extended School Year (ESY) (if applicable)

        ii. Transportation (if applicable)

        iii. Assistive technology (if applicable)

    b. Placement and least restrictive environment

Update Transition Plan (age 16 years or older)

Next steps; meeting minutes

Signatures

Closing: Thank you for attending!

## DISCIPLINE FOR STUDENTS WITH DISABILITIES TENT

**Directions:** Laminate and fold in the center to create a quick reference "tent."

### Discipline for Students With Disabilities

If a student with a disability violates school rules that may result in expulsion or long-term (more than 10 days) suspension, the school must hold a manifestation determination meeting. The team must determine:

○ Was the conduct caused by or have a direct and substantial relationship to the child's disability? OR

○ Was the conduct the direct result of the school's failure to implement the IEP?

If either of the responses to the above questions is YES, then the conduct is a manifestation of the student's disability and the school cannot apply the same discipline used with students who are not disabled. Instead:

○ Conduct a behavior assessment to determine the circumstances surrounding the inappropriate action, AND

○ Create a behavior intervention plan to assist the student in more appropriate behaviors. If the student already has a behavior intervention plan, it should be reviewed and modified, if appropriate.

If the response to either of the questions above is NO, then the school can provide the same disciplinary procedures applied to students without disabilities, BUT the school must continue to provide a free appropriate public education (FAPE) in an interim alternative setting to allow the student to continue to make progress in the IEP goals.

· · · · · · · · · · · · · · · · · · · · · · · · · · · · fold · · · · · · · · · · · · · · · · · · · · · · · · · · · ·

### Discipline for Students With Disabilities
### For Violations Involving Weapons, Drugs, or Infliction of
### Serious Bodily Injury

- If the student's violation involved weapons, drugs, or infliction of serious bodily injury, the school may
  ○ remove the student with a disability to an interim alternative setting,
  ○ for up to 45 school days,
  ○ even if the conduct was a manifestation of the student's disability.

### Important!!

- If a student with a disability violates school rules that are not a manifestation of the disability and that do result in expulsion, **special education services must continue** during the time of the expulsion.

## REFERENCES

Americans with Disabilities Act of 1990. 42 U.S.C. §126 *et seq.* (2008).

Bird, J. M., & Bassin, S. (2015). Examining disproportionate representation in special education, disciplinary practices, and the school-to-prison pipeline. *Communique: National Association School Psychologists, 43*(5), 1–24.

Code of Federal Regulations, 29 C.F.R. §1630 *et seq.* (2007).

Code of Federal Regulations, 34 C.F.R. §300 *et seq.* (2006).

Daggett, L. M. (2014). Reasonable supervision of special students: The impact of disability on school liability for student injury. *Journal of Law and Education, 43*(3), 303–366.

Erlichman, R., Gregory, M., & St. Florian, A. (2014). The settlement conference as a dispute resolution option in special education. *Ohio State Journal on Dispute Resolution, 29*(3), 407–459.

Individuals with Disabilities Education Improvement Act of 2004 [IDEA]. 20 U.S.C. §1400 *et seq.* (2004).

Katsiyannis, A., Losinski, M., & Prince, A. M. T. (2012). Litigation and student with disabilities: A persistent concern. *NASSP Bulletin, 96*(1), 23–43.

La Morte, M. W. (2012). *School law: Cases and concepts.* Upper Saddle River, NJ: Pearson Education.

Madaus, J. W., & Shaw, S. F. (2006). School implementation of Section 504 in one school. *Physical Disabilities: Education and Related Services, 24*(2), 47–58.

Murawski, W. W., Carter, N. J., Sileo, N. M., & Prater, M. A. (2012). Communicating and collaborating with families. In N. M. Sileo & M. A. Prater (Eds.), *Working with families of children with special needs: Family and professional partnerships and roles* (pp. 59–90). Upper Saddle River, NJ: Pearson.

Murawski, W. W., & Lochner, W. W. (2011). Observing co-teaching: What to ask for, look for, and listen for. *Intervention in School and Clinic, 46*(3), 174–183.

Nichols, S. C., & Sheffield, A. D. (2014). Is there an elephant in the room? Considerations that administrators tend to forget when facilitating inclusive practices among general and special education teachers. *National Forum of Applied Educational Research Journal, 27*(1 & 2), 31–44.

Parrish, T. (2006, March). *National and state overview of special education funding.* Presented at Kansas Association of Special Education Administrators, Lawrence, KS.

Pazey, B. L., & Cole, H. A. (2012). The role of special education training in the development of socially just leaders: Building an equity consciousness in educational leadership programs. *Education Administration Quarterly, 49*(2), 243–271.

Rehabilitation Act of 1973, Section 504, 29 U.S.C. §794 (1998).

Wald, J., & Losen, D. J. (2003). Defining and redirecting a school-to-prison pipeline. *New Directions for Youth Development, 99*, 9–15.

Weishaar, M. K., Weishaar, P. M., & Borsa, J. C. (2014). *Inclusive educational administration* (3rd ed.). Long Grove, IL: Waveland Press.

Zirkel, P. A. (2013). Recent legal developments of interest to special educators. *Intervention in School and Clinic, 48*(5), 319–322.

## ADDITIONAL RECOMMENDED READING

Community Alliance for Special Education (CASE) & Disability Rights California (DRC). (2011). *Special education rights and responsibilities*. San Francisco, CA: Author.

McLaughlin, M. J., & Nolet, V. (2004). *What every principal needs to know about special education*. Thousand Oaks, CA: Corwin.

Osborne, A. G., Jr., & Russo, C. J. (2006). *Special education and the law: A guide for practitioners* (2nd ed.). Thousand Oaks, CA: Corwin.

Thomas, S. B., Cambron-McCabe, N. H., & McCarthy, M. M. (2009). *Public school law: Teachers' and students' rights*. Boston, MA: Pearson Education.

Yell, M. L., Conroy, T., Katsiyannis, A., & Conroy, T. (2013). Individualized education programs and special education programming for students with disabilities in urban schools. *Fordham Urban Law Journal, 41*, 669–714.

## HELPFUL WEBSITES AND PROFESSIONAL ORGANIZATIONS

- The American Bar Association: www.americanbar.org
- The Council for Exceptional Children: www.cec.sped.org
- National Dissemination Center for Children with Disabilities: www.nichcy.org
- United States Department of Education: www.ed.gov
- Wrightslaw Special Education Law & Advocacy: www.wrightslaw.com

## APPS (AND BLOGS) WE LOVE

- Ask a Lawyer: Legal Help
- BernieSez
- A2zeducationaladvocates.blogspot.com
- www.wrightslaw.com/blog/home
- http://specialeducationlawblog.blogspot.com
- http://specialedlaw.blogs.com

# 19

# The Importance of Partnerships

*School-to-Home Collaboration*

Bethany M. McConnell
*University of Pittsburgh at Johnstown*

Wendy W. Murawski
*California State University, Northridge*

## NAVIGATING SCHOOL-TO-HOME CONNECTIONS

Teachers want families to oversee homework, support learning, and emphasize the importance of a good education. Families want teachers to teach academics, as well as manage behavior, keep them informed of what is happening in school, and find ways to make connections with their children so they are able to learn even the most challenging of content. These all seem doable, right? Not so fast. It turns out that school-to-home collaboration and communication are way more complex than it may seem.

What are the issues that impact communication between home and school? Naturally, they are varied. Major issues include different family dynamics and makeup, cultural differences, lack of adequate professional development for teachers, and the expected role of parent as shared educator. Let's take a stab at each of these as they relate to typical home-school collaboration. Then we'll address the added issues that arise when working with special learners!

Family households look very different than they did 30 years ago. Between 1970 and 2012, the share of households that were married couples with children under 18, shifted from 40% to 20%. There are now more blended families, grandparents, same-sex couples, and single parents raising children (Vespa, Lewis, & Kreider, 2013). Educators cannot presume that children are coming from a two-parent household. As families change and evolve, so too must our ability to accept differences. This means that teachers need to be thoughtful of information sent home that might imply a two-parent household or the presence of a father and mother.

Consider the other assumptions we also make when working with families. Not only might we assume that children live with their parents, but we may also make assumptions about how our students' families will communicate with us. Different cultures value education differently, emphasize collaboration differently, and communicate with those in positions of authority differently (Abadeh, 2014). For example, Asian American and Middle Eastern American families often look at educators as authority figures and are less likely to question or engage in coequal problem solving than other ethnicities (Khateeb, Hadidi, & Khatib, 2014; Song & Murawski, 2005). Understanding potential cultural differences can help teachers work proactively to improve the effectiveness of their communication with culturally and linguistically diverse family members. Learning more about each individual student's family and background will help us become more effective in individualizing and differentiating our instruction, while also serving to provide more information for working collaboratively with the student's family.

Teachers need strategies to develop effective practices to work with families. As educators, we need to (a) listen to the family's story, (b) avoid assumptions based on stereotypes, and (c) disconnect our personal family experiences from the family experiences of our students. Families' stories help connect teachers to the very real situations that parents face and help

>  **Key Concepts**
>
> Want to connect with families?
>
> - Find out their story.
> - Avoid assumptions.
> - Disconnect your own personal experiences from those of your students.

develop sensitivity to students with diverse backgrounds (Lightfoot, 2003). This can be intimidating for secondary educators who work with 150 students each day, but research is clear that connecting with students on a personal level is one of the most powerful actions a teacher can take in helping a student be successful in school (Hoover-Dempsey et al., 2005).

How do you find out more about a student's "story?" It's simple—just ask! There are a variety of ways to ask questions, based on time, comfort level with technology, and cultural norms, for you as the teacher and your family groups. You can glean information through surveys, questionnaires, "parking lot" boards posted around the room, student assignments, lunch meetings, small group discussion groups on related topics, and even home visits (for those of you able to do those). Listen, read, and observe actively and without bias. Avoid making assumptions, filling in the gaps with your own personal experiences, or jumping to conclusions. People are unique; find out what makes your students who they are. This will lead to being able to better communicate with the individuals who share a home with them.

Just as family dynamics and cultural differences have changed over the years, so too has the way in which we prepare educators for the classroom. Though connections with families remain a staple of teacher education in theory, many preservice and in-service teachers lack professional development in how to effectively work with families (U.S. Department of Education, 2014). In an era when teachers are told to focus on Common Core Standards and a rigorous curriculum, it can be difficult to emphasize anything other than content knowledge. However, research is clear that making a connection with students and capitalizing on their backgrounds makes a significant difference in their success (Abadeh, 2014). This is especially true when it comes to culturally and linguistically diverse students. Whitbread, Bruder, Fleming, and Park (2007) emphasize that teachers should approach their relationship with parents as a learning experience— a learning experience that never ends.

**Making Connections**

Check out Chapter 6 on Culturally Responsive Teaching.

The final major hurdle we are addressing in this chapter is the notion of parent as shared educator. How many times have you given homework, only to be frustrated when a student doesn't do it? How many times do you think to yourself, "Why didn't Evan's mom make him do it?" or "Why didn't Sparrow's uncle sit down and explain this to her so I don't have to? I have 26 other students to teach today!"? We pay lip service to the fact that family members are experts on the student and that we are experts on the curriculum, but we still also expect that learning is continued at home on a regular basis. Parents are expected to be the *first teachers* of their children. When children come to preschool or kindergarten, we judge what they bring to the classroom. Did they have a literature-rich environment that led to an understanding of letters, words, and reading? Were students taught how to pay attention, listen to the authority figure, sit quietly, and follow directions? Simply speaking, some were not. Those skills become even more complex as the student gets older. Now we want parents to support their children in reading, writing, math, and other content areas, not to mention organizing their binders, studying for tests, and completing work online. Educators must consider that not all families are comfortable or prepared to teach academic skills in the home. They may need resources and supports to provide appropriate instruction at home (Doyle & Zhang, 2011). We're not suggesting that you need to teach adult skills classes at night or send calculators home to all your families! We are, however, suggesting that you consider what you *can* do to help them; we provide concrete ideas for this throughout this chapter.

## HOME-SCHOOL COLLABORATION WITH EXCEPTIONAL LEARNERS

Okay, so we know that it is important for teachers and administrators to collaborate and communicate with families. We know that students have better outcomes when families are engaged participants and decision makers in their children's education (Edwards & Da Fonte, 2012). So far, so good. Now, however, let's add in the notion of our special learners (e.g., English language learners [ELLs], gifted, disability). We've already mentioned the importance of understanding our culturally and linguistically diverse population. Working to support our gifted learners, especially those who also have a disability and are considered twice-exceptional, can be remarkably challenging. Students who are ELLs and have a disability and students who are twice-exceptional

**Making Connections**

Check out Chapter 6 on Culturally Responsive Teaching, Chapter 15 on English Language Learners, and Chapter 17 on Twice-Exceptional Learners.

share the fact that, since they qualify for special education services, they will have an individualized education program (IEP), just like other students with disabilities. Under the Individuals with Disabilities Education Improvement Act (2004), teachers are required to incorporate parent involvement and provide regular updates home on the child's IEP goal progress. Yet, despite this federal mandate, many teachers and administrators still report feeling unprepared to build these relationships (U.S. Department of Education, 2014). So let's address that right here!

We want you to have concrete strategies for building relationships with parents, for going beyond simply sending home grades or having the short perfunctory meeting. Let's start with having you use a McGill Action Plan (MAP; Vandercook, York, & Forest, 1989). We've included a form at the end of this chapter. A MAP is one way for teachers to learn more about a student and his or her family's history by finding out the visions they have for the future. It is quick and easy and can be used at any grade level. You may need to find a colleague to help you translate it into different languages, but you can also read it aloud into a Voice Memo on your phone and then text or e-mail it to parents. You can put it in an e-mail or website like Google Docs to get electronic responses. You can add pictures and provide sample responses to support family members who do not read or don't read well. You can make phone calls and do the MAP orally with those parents who prefer not to write or who tend not to return written work. Worried that this might take too much time? Remember, you don't need to do a MAP interview with all your students, just those students with exceptionalities you are trying to learn more about in order to better meet their unique needs.

Let's say you now have this basic information. You'll want to continue to build this relationship so the family members recognize that you truly want open communication that is two-way. One way to do this is through ongoing communication of a student's progress. Many students with special needs struggle academically; their families are used to only knowing how they are doing when they see the failing grades on the report card. You can change that culture! Consider sending home regular e-mail updates on upcoming assignments, positive behavior changes, and strategies for test-taking. These e-mails don't have to be too lengthy or time-consuming, but they will make a very large and positive impact on your families! Technology can be a useful tool for communicating with families. Please note that as students progress through each grade, there is a marked decrease in communication (McConnell, 2014). Given that, secondary educators more than ever need to make strategic attempts to reach out and find ways to support families in the home. Technology just might be your answer to communication and sanity!

### Plugged In

Want great apps and online resources that help you communicate regularly with families? Try:

- Remind
- Class Messenger
- SchoolSync
- Powerschool

You're feeling good about your efforts to communicate. You've reached out frequently. You've made positive calls home. You've asked for parent feedback and input . . . but you're just not getting it. So much for the two-way street! What's happening here?

There are a few reasons parents might not be communicating. It could be that they have no time, maybe they've had a negative experience in the past (Amatea, Cholewa, & Mixon, 2012), or perhaps their culture considers the teacher the authority figure so they see no need to communicate in response. However, there can also be a hierarchical struggle between school and home (deFur, 2012). If families believe the teacher controls all interactions, they may feel as though their opinions are not important and thus see no reason to share them. Conversely, what if we are clear that we are looking to the family to be the expert on their child? This can also add to difficulties in collaboration (McConnell, Goran, & Bateman, 2015). While we are reaching out and being open to parental feedback, they may still be learning about their own child's disability or may feel ill-prepared to give strategies on how to address the educational needs of their child. Again, this all boils down to the importance of clear communication. Work on letting parents know that they are equal participants in the decision-making process, but that you are there to support them in any way necessary.

One of the ways you can know what parents may need is to recognize their comfort level with various types of parent involvement. Epstein (2001) presented a framework of six types of parent involvement to help teachers and administrators think about the range of two-way communication that occurs between school and home. We've provided the list of those types, as well as examples to go with each one, at the end of this chapter.

Communication and collaboration between educators and family members of any school-age child can be fraught with difficulty; the addition of a disability simply adds more elements to that mix. However, since we know that home-school collaboration can make a substantial and positive difference for children (Hoover-Dempsey et al., 2005), it is definitely worth it. Take note of these critical and practical dos and don'ts and see how you can improve your own communication with the family members of your students.

## THINGS WE DO THAT HINDER COLLABORATION

**Teachers, STOP doing this:**

✗ **STOP calling to give parents only bad reports.** If your main point of contact is always to discuss negative behavior, you've lost them. Though parents need to know what is happening in your classroom, don't you think they are tired of only hearing when their child has done something wrong? If a student with an emotional/behavioral disability or attention deficit hyperactivity disorder (ADHD) is acting out, we shouldn't be surprised and call the parent to complain. It is our educational and professional responsibility to consider the function of the behavior and try various replacement behaviors. Clearly if we have called home 10 times and the student is still acting out, then the phone call home must not be working (Curwin, Mendler, & Mendler, 2008).

✗ **STOP assuming that parents don't care.** Just because a parent does not make it to parent-teacher night or make sure that homework is completed, does not mean that the parent does not care about his or her child's education. When the family does not meet your communication expectations, check your attitude. Instead of assuming you know why, try to find out what is going on.

✘ **STOP complaining to other professionals about what a student is doing or what the family is not doing.** You wouldn't want them to talk negatively about you with their friends, would you? Instead, turn it around and ask those colleagues for strategies to try. Use the teacher lounge as a place to get ideas rather than a place to vent.

✘ **STOP the "Yakety-yak."** Teachers are comfortable leading and talking; it is what we do. However, we need to rein in our talking, and instead actively listen to parents. See the end of this chapter to learn the "LAFF, don't CRY" strategy for active listening (McNaughton & Vostal, 2010).

✘ **STOP coming to IEP meetings as the professional authority figure.** Be human; be approachable. These meetings can be very intimidating to families. Some families have only ever had negative experiences at IEP meetings. Reach out and introduce yourself immediately. Smile warmly. Speak without using jargon and focus on as many positives about the child as you can. Seek out the parent's feedback and take notes on what *they* say.

## Administrators, STOP doing this:

✘ **STOP highlighting diversity through monthly celebrations.** Individuals often report that they feel uncomfortable by the spotlight they are given for a 30-day time slot. It makes students feel even more isolated and different than their same aged peers, because their culture is not embedded like everyone else's. Find other, more meaningful ways to support diversity and various cultures. Also, consider celebrating diversity beyond racial diversity. What about a day to recognize the work of single parents or one for those who work in law enforcement? You might have a place in your classroom where students can give suggestions for "Who should we honor today?"

✘ **STOP implementing one-hit wonder family workshops.** When learning new skills, families need ongoing support, feedback, and examples. Create a committee that can organize meaningful and engaging activities for families. Attend these events to provide support. Be certain that there is always at least one representative there who understands the philosophy of inclusive practices and will be responsible for bringing up the needs of exceptional learners.

✘ **STOP relying on traditional Parent Teacher Associations (PTA) as your only form of parent connection.** Expand parent outreach beyond the small group of active parents who design school-to-home outreach. Find ways to connect with families to enable them to share their perspectives and get involved in different ways. Use the Epstein types of parental involvement to recognize that there is value in more than just school meeting participation.

✗ **STOP allowing teachers to blame parents for difficult situations.** Encourage your teachers to meet families where they are emotionally, scholastically, culturally, and linguistically. Think about how difficult it is to teach a child with a disability—now imagine raising that child! Have empathy yet?

**Making Connections**

Check out Chapter 13 on Autism Spectrum Disorder.

# ENJOYING THE JOURNEY OF COLLABORATION

**Teachers, DO this:**

✔ **REACH OUT to make positive phone calls.** Focus on your students who have been rumored to "challenge the rules" and catch them being good, so you can start the year off with an encouraging story to share with the family. Recognize that parents who have a child with difficult behaviors regularly receive phone calls about the child's behavior and about what the child is doing wrong. By calling these parents with positive stories in the first week of school, you start to build an alliance with these families.

✔ **REACH OUT to the family.** See what you can do to support them in meeting your expectations for collaboration and contact. If a parent does not come to meet you at Back to School Night, find another way to reach out or communicate. See if they prefer to text, talk on the phone, Skype, WeChat, Viber, FaceTime, or send written materials back and forth. If they prefer written notes, find out if they can access them in English. Find out what times of the day and week are best for communication. Keep a log for yourself with all this information on each family.

✔ **PROVIDE ways for families to share their feedback about you.** When you give out report cards to students, provide an opportunity for you to be evaluated as well. Be sure to only ask questions that you are prepared to receive answers to. Use the Teacher Report Card at the end of this chapter as a guide for questions that can help you reflect on your teaching based on family feedback. When working with children with disabilities, add in questions related to how you are differentiating, addressing IEP goals, or managing caseloads. Be aware—it can be scary to get a report card back on yourself!

✔ **HELP parents communicate with their children.** Consider putting out a weekly blog or newsletter. Have prompting questions sent to families via these tools or through group text, on the class webpage, or in a weekly note home. Provide questions that can help parents generate conversations. Family members can also learn more about what is happening in your classroom through these questions. Make sure there are a variety of questions, including some about content they learned and some about their social interactions during the day. Many students with learning disabilities have family members who struggle with the same needs, so having prompting questions might help those who lack strong communication skills. Using basic vocabulary will make the questions more accessible. Having them available auditorally and in different languages will also help if you are able.

✔ **EMPOWER caregivers at IEP meetings.** Prior to the meeting, call the home and let them know the purpose of the IEP meeting, even if the student has been receiving special education services for years. See what questions they have and let them know what to expect. Send home a short list of questions that they can be prepared to respond to at the IEP meeting. These can be questions about their child's sleep, homework and eating habits, their facility and access to technology, their social skills and friendships, their use of time at home, interests and hobbies, and anything else that might help educators work with the student. When the caregiver arrives at the meeting, provide that individual with paper and pen so they are not the only one without paper in front of them. Offer refreshments when possible; even a bottle of water can be comforting. Encourage parents to stop the meeting if jargon is used or they do not understand something. Let them know that if the meeting isn't concluded in the time allotted, you will simply reschedule for an additional time. Above all, talk *to* them, not *at* them. Respect them, and you will in turn receive the same respect.

✔ **FIND ways for families to support the school each month.** Be sure to include a variety of options: those that cost money and those that do not. For example, you might generate a list of needed school supplies for the classroom (e.g., tissues, recycled boxes for projects). You might request a guest reader or volunteer for specific activities. You may also identify tasks that support the school but can be done at home in parents' free time (e.g., cutting/pasting in preparation for a class activity). Many families of special learners are so busy with therapies, doctors' visits, and tutoring that they have little time for volunteering. Provide them with opportunities that work for them and will result in their feeling more connected to the school—and allow their child to see them participating as well!

✔ **MAKE IT EASY for families to visit your classroom.** Visiting your school may require getting clearances; this is free in many states, but it may involve paperwork. Help families by providing a "how to" link to show them how to submit for required clearances. Be aware that some family members may not be able to complete the paperwork (due to language, health, or immigration status) so do not judge those who do not participate. Instead, find ways to bring the school to them (e.g., virtual tours, field trips, online meetings)!

✔ **ASK families questions about homework completion.** Students with disabilities often struggle with homework! Find out what is going on at home. Is it taking too long for the student to complete? How much time is that? Is it difficult to get the child to understand the concepts? Remember, homework is meant to be a review of previously learned material (Archer & Hughes, 2011). Therefore, differentiate homework assignments to match students' ability levels, just like you differentiate instruction in the classroom.

**Making Connections**

Check out Chapter 5 on Using Technology and Assistive Technology.

✔ **ASK QUESTIONS and be an active listener.** Ask sincere questions to learn about the family member's thoughts, feelings, and wants, encourage elaboration, and gather more facts and details. Be prepared to listen and learn more before trying to immediately solve the problem. Sometimes people just need to be listened to and heard. Try very hard to avoid being in a rush to resolution; families deserve your time.

## Administrators, DO THIS:

✔ **PROVIDE a snapshot of your curriculum and any new program initiatives in your building.** Help parents answer these questions in laymen's terms: "What is my child expected to learn this year? What resources can you provide me with to support learning in the home? What will happen if my child is having a hard time following school rules?" Help families of students with exceptionalities know the types of accommodations their child might receive with the curriculum, if determined necessary.

✔ **BE PRESENT and exhibit full participation in IEP meetings.** By being present, you are able to support both the parents and your IEP team at this time.

**Making Connections**

Check out Chapter 18 on Legal Issues.

Understanding your role in this process and the need for your active involvement can reduce the likelihood of legal action.

✔ **GET BACKGROUND information when faced with difficult situations.** Before making assumptions or digging in your heels, try to gather information from parents, educators, and other stakeholders. By learning more from all sides, you can support the IEP team and hear the needs of the family to help facilitate the first steps toward a solution.

✔ **EVALUATE your school's level of parent involvement with Epstein's Six Types of Family Involvement.** Are you meeting the interests of all families in your classroom? Are there some activities that will unintentionally leave some families out? Use the chart at the end of this chapter to label the types of involvement you already have in your school. Compare the types of involvement that you already have, and generate new events that will welcome all families, including those with special needs and those from different cultures. Survey family and student interests so that you can incorporate their needs, strengths, and experiences. Elicit feedback from a variety of stakeholders in the community as well.

✔ **IMPLEMENT new traditions in your school that embrace and highlight diversity within your school.** Be sure to include family members to create these celebrations. These examples should be embedded throughout the school year. Have guest speakers and family members of students with special needs, or even those who have disabilities themselves, come and speak. Artwork, books, videos, and music should be incorporated into the curriculum that were created by individuals with exceptionalities. Also, always double-check: Does this activity embrace all learners, and is it accessible to all abilities?

✔ **HAVE CONFIDENCE in your teachers.** Families of individuals with disabilities have historically had to advocate for their children's rights; don't be surprised when they may approach the educational system defensively or even threaten legal action. Though it is your job to mediate difficult situations, please direct family members to contact the teacher first. When you try to fix problems before the teacher has a chance to work with the family, you are sending a message that your teacher cannot handle the problem. Instead, honor the family's concerns and let them know you take those concerns seriously, but let them know that you want to be sure to include the teacher so real change can occur. Then follow up with the teacher to see if he or she needs additional support.

## A MCGILL ACTION PLAN (MAP)

| | |
|---|---|
| **MAP Interview for:** _____ (name of student) | |
| Person interviewed: _____ (name and relation of family member) | |

| | |
|---|---|
| What is the student's history? | |

| | |
|---|---|
| Who *is* the student? | What are the student's strengths, gifts, and abilities? |
| What would the student's ideal day at school look like? | |

| | |
|---|---|
| What is your dream for the student? | What is your nightmare regarding the student? |
| | What are the student's needs? |

| |
|---|
| What must be done to address those needs? |

*Source:* Adapted from Vandercook, T., York, J., & Forest, M. (1989). McGill Action Planning System (MAPS). *Journal of the Association for Persons with Severe Handicaps,* 23(2), 119–133.

## EPSTEIN'S FRAMEWORK OF SIX TYPES OF INVOLVEMENT

| Six Different Types of Involvement Families May Be Interested in | Example of How a School Might Address and Support This Type of Involvement | What Does This Look Like at Your School? |
|---|---|---|
| **Parenting:** Help all families establish home environments to support children as students | Develop family support programs to assist families with health, nutrition, and other services; consider specific needs of children with disabilities | |
| **Communicating:** Design effective forms of school-to-home and home-to-school communications about school programs and children's progress | Develop a regular schedule of useful notices, memos, phone calls, newsletters, and other communications; consider that not all parents read or speak English | |
| **Volunteering:** Recruit and organize parent help and support | Create a family room or center for volunteer work, meetings, and resources for families; have materials in different languages | |
| **Learning at home:** Provide information and ideas to families about how to help students at home with homework and other curriculum-related activities, decisions, and planning | Provide information for families on skills required for students in all subjects at each grade; have a list of possible adaptations for individuals who are special learners | |
| **Decision making:** Include parents in school decisions, developing parent leaders and representatives | Implement active PTA/PTO or other parent organizations, advisory councils, or committees for parent leadership and participation; ensure that diverse families are not left out and that meetings are accessible to all | |
| **Collaborating with the community:** Identify and integrate resources and services from the community to strengthen school programs, family practices, and student learning and development | Share information on community activities that link to learning skills and talents, including summer programs for students with and without special needs | |

*Source:* Adapted from Epstein, J. L. (2001). *School, family, and community partnerships: Preparing educators and improving schools.* Boulder, CO: Westview Press.

## LAFF, DON'T CRY

| A Teacher Employs LAFF During a Conference With a Parent | |
|---|---|
| Listen, empathize, and communicate respect | Parent: *My son, Ethan, is having trouble in his math class. He's gotten a D or an F on the last three quizzes.* Teacher: *That must be frustrating. I appreciate you coming in to talk with me.* Parent: *He really struggles with his homework each night.* Teacher: *May I take notes so I can be sure to remember all your concerns?* Parent: *Sure, that's fine.* |
| Ask questions | Teacher: *What does Ethan say?* Parent: *Ethan says he can't keep up with the teacher in class, so he doesn't understand what he is supposed to do without help.* Teacher: *Let's talk more about the homework; what do you see when Ethan is working at home?* Parent: *He gets some of his homework done in resource room, but by the time he gets home he's confused again. He works through the example problems, but he can't figure out where he's making his mistakes.* |
| Focus on the issues | Teacher: *I want to make sure I have got all this, so I'd like to check my notes with you. You are saying that he has struggled on the last three tests; he can do his homework at school when he has help, but he really struggles at home. Have I got it? Is there anything you would like to add?* Parent: *Yes. Our nights are getting pretty frustrating. We try to help him, but that's not working very well.* |
| Find a first step | Teacher: *As a first step, I'd like to meet with his math teacher. I want to find out what he is seeing. I will call you by Friday, and we will make a plan for next steps.* Parent: *Thanks for listening. I wasn't sure quite what to do, but I'm glad I came in.* |

| A Teacher Demonstrates CRY Behaviors During a Conference With a Parent | |
|---|---|
| Criticize people who aren't present | Parent: *My son, Ethan, is having trouble in his math class. He's gotten a D or an F on the last three quizzes.* Teacher: *Ethan has Mr. McDonald, a first-year teacher. He may not be familiar with Ethan's accommodations, and he's known to be pretty rigid.* |
| React hastily and promise something you can't deliver | Parent: *Ethan had a first-year teacher last year also! Why should he have to suffer because there is so much turnover?* Teacher: *That's really frustrating. You know, there are other algebra sections, other teachers. Maybe I can switch Ethan to a more experienced teacher.* |

| A Teacher Demonstrates CRY Behaviors During a Conference With a Parent | |
|---|---|
| Yakety-yak-yak | Parent: *What is going to happen about the low quiz grades he's already gotten? Why should Ethan get bad grades because things are so disorganized?* Teacher: *I understand how important grades can be. My daughter is applying to colleges and she is under so much pressure.* Parent: *But what are you going to do for Ethan? Perhaps I should talk to the principal about our problem.* |

*Source:* Adapted from McNaughton, D. B., & Vostal, B. R. (2010). Using active listening to improve collaboration with parents. *Intervention in School and Clinic, 45*(4), 251–256.

## TEACHER REPORT CARD

| **Please let me know how I am doing . . .** |
|---|
| What is going well this school year? |
| What is something that I could do to improve on to better help your child? |
| How long does it take for your child to complete homework at night? Does this seem like a reasonable amount to you or your child? |
| What else can you tell me about your child or your family that will make me a better teacher for your child this year? |
| What grade would you give me, and please explain why: (A = Outstanding; B = Above average; C = Average; D = Below Average; F = Failing) |

# REFERENCES

Abadeh, H. (2014). Home-school communications: Multicultural parents of children with disabilities. *International Journal About Parents in Education, 8*(1), 1–10.

Amatea, E. S., Cholewa, B., & Mixon, K. A. (2012). Influencing preservice teachers' attitudes about working with low-income and/or ethnic minority families. *Urban Education, 47*(4), 801–834.

Archer, A. L., & Hughes, C. A. (2011). *Explicit instruction: Effective and efficient teaching.* New York, NY: Guilford Press.

Curwin, R. L., Mendler, A. N., & Mendler, B. D. (2008). *Discipline with dignity: New challenges, new solutions* (3rd ed.). Alexandria, VA: Association for Supervision and Curriculum Development.

deFur, S. (2012). Parents as collaborators: Building partnerships with school- and community-based providers. *TEACHING Exceptional Children, 44*(3), 58–67.

Doyle, A., & Zhang, J. (2011). Participation structure impacts on parent engagement in family literacy programs. *Journal of Early Childhood Education, 39*(3), 223–233.

Edwards, C. C., & Da Fonte, A. (2012). The 5-point plan: Fostering successful partnerships with families of students with disabilities. *TEACHING Exceptional Children, 44*(3), 6.

Epstein, J. L. (2001). *School, family, and community partnerships: Preparing educators and improving schools.* Boulder, CO: Westview Press.

Hoover-Dempsey, K. V., Walker, J. M., Sandler, H. M., Whetsel, D., Green, C. L., Wilkins, A. S., & Closson, K. (2005). Why do parents become involved? Research findings and implications. *Elementary School Journal, 106*(2), 105–130.

Individuals with Disabilities Education Improvement Act of 2004, 20 U.S.C. § 1400 *et seq* (2004).

Khateeb, J. M. Al, Hadidi, M. S. Al, & Khatib, A. J. Al (2014). Addressing the unique needs of Arab American children with disabilities. *Journal of Child and Family Studies, 24*(8), 2432–2440.

Lightfoot, S. L. (2003). *The essential conversation: What parents and teachers can learn from each other.* New York, NY: Ballantine Books.

McConnell, B. M. (2014). Increasing parent-teacher communication to improve school attendance for a student with a learning disability: A case study. *Betwixt and Between: Education for Young Adolescents, 1*(2), 30–41.

McConnell, B. M., Goran, L., & Bateman, D. F. (2015, November). *Sharing stories: How interviewing families of students with disabilities impacts dispositions of teacher candidates.* 38th Annual Conference of the Teacher Education Division, Tempe, AZ.

McNaughton, D. B., & Vostal, B. R. (2010). Using active listening to improve collaboration with parents. *Intervention in School and Clinic, 45*(4), 251–256.

Song, J., & Murawski, W. W. (2005). Korean-American parents' perspectives on teacher-parent collaboration. *Journal of International Special Needs Education, 8*, 32–38.

U.S. Department of Education. (2014). The dual capacity framework for building family-school partnerships. Retrieved from http://www.ed.gov/family-and-community-engagement

Vandercook, T., York, J., & Forest, M. (1989). McGill Action Planning System (MAPS). *Journal of the Association for Persons with Severe Handicaps*, 23(2), 119–133.

Vespa, J., Lewis, J. M., & Kreider, R. M. (2013). *America's families and living arrangements: 2012*. Retrieved from http://www.census.gov/library/publications/2013/demo/p20-570.html

Whitbread, K. M., Bruder, M. B., Fleming, G., & Park, H. J. (2007). Collaboration in special education: Parent-professional training. *TEACHING Exceptional Children*, 39(4), 6.

## ADDITIONAL RECOMMENDED READING

Auerbach, S. (2015). Fantastic family collaboration: What really works with family collaboration in the elementary classroom. In W. W. Murawski & K. L. Scott (Eds.), *What really works in elementary education* (pp. 319–333). Thousand Oaks, CA: Corwin.

Edwards, P. A. (2009). *Tapping the potential of parents*. New York, NY: Scholastic.

Murawski, W. W., Carter, N. J., Sileo, N. M., & Prater, M. A. (2012). Communicating and collaborating with families. In N. M. Sileo & M. A. Prater (Eds.), *Working with families of children with special needs: Family and professional partnerships and roles* (pp. 59–90). Boston, MA: Pearson.

Prater, M. A., & Sileo, N. M. (2015). Fantastic family collaboration: What really works in family collaboration in the secondary classroom. In W. W. Murawski & K. L. Scott (Eds.), *What really works in secondary education* (pp. 322–334). Thousand Oaks, CA: Corwin.

Turnbull, A. A., Turnbull, H. R., Erwin, E. J., Soodak, L. C., & Shogren, K. A. (2015). *Families, professionals, and exceptionality: Positive outcomes through partnerships and trust*. Boston, MA: Pearson.

## TOP FIVE WEBSITES TO SUPPORT SCHOOL-TO-HOME COLLABORATION

➡ www.cec.sped.org

➡ www.pacer.org

➡ http://www.ncld.org

➡ www.ed.gov/parents/needs/speced/iepguide/index.html

➡ http://www.parentsasteachers.org

## APPS WE LOVE

➡ Bloomz

➡ Remind

➡ Appletree

➡ MyKiddo

➡ Eckovation

# *Index*

AAC (alternative and augmentative communication) devices, 83, 90 (figure), 254–255

Abadeh, H., 339, 340

Abedi, J., 264

ABI (activity-based intervention), 295–296 (figure)

Access, 283

Accommodations, 61, 63 (box), 329
  apps for, 78 (box)
  for assessments, 62–63
  defined, 62
  embedding into instruction, 63–64
  evidence-based practices for, 64–65
  and explicit instruction, 65
  in mathematics, 12–13
  and peer tutoring, 65
  for students with LD, 203 (figure)
  things to avoid, 67–68
  things to do, 68–70

Achievement standards, 323

Active listening, 344, 347, 351 (figure)

Activity-based intervention (ABI), 295–296 (figure)

ACT limit setting model, 213

Adams, C., 308

Adams Becker, S., 81

Adaptations, 61, 63 (box)
  defined, 62
  examples of, 71 (figure)
  in IEPs, 63–64
  things to avoid, 67–68
  things to do, 68–70

Adger, C. T., 105

Administrators
  and accommodations, 68
  attitudes toward technology, 81

and brain-based learning/memory, 125–126, 127–128

and co-planning time, 155

and co-teaching, 160–161, 163, 288–289

and EBD, 212

and ECI, 288–289, 291

and ELLs, 269–270, 273

and home-school collaboration, 344–345, 347–348

and inclusion, 333 (box)

and legal issues, 333 (box)

and PBS, 138, 141–142

and progress monitoring, 173

and students with ASD, 233, 237

and students with EBD, 216

and students with LD, 193–194, 197–198

and students with moderate-to-severe disabilities, 251, 255

and technology, 87, 89

and 2e learners, 307–308, 310–311

and writing, 48, 51

Affective networks, 67

Alberto, P. A., 29, 217 (figure)

Alexander, P., 45

Alexandrin, J. R., 171

Alley, G. R., 45

Allik, H., 230

Allington, R. L., 26

Alshreed, F. M., 210

Alternative and augmentative communication (AAC) devices, 83, 90 (figure), 254–255

Amanti, C., 101

Amatea, E. S., 342

American Federation of Teachers, 24

American Psychiatric Association, 227
Americans with Disabilities Act Amendments Act (ADAAA), 332
Angell, M. E., 83
Anxiety reduction, 235, 240 (figure)
Apichatabutra, C., 26, 45
Appelman, M., 285
Appleton, J., 7
Appleton, R., 7
Applied behavior analysis (ABA), 254
Apps
    AAC devices, 83
    for accommodations, 78 (box)
    for brain-based learning, 132 (box)
    for brain training, 93 (figure)
    for collecting data, 151 (box)
    for co-teaching/collaboration, 168 (box)
    for culturally responsive teaching, 116 (box)
    for data collection, 144 (figure)
    general, 97 (box)
    for home-school collaboration, 355 (box)
    for learning, 92 (figure)
    for legal issues, 337 (box)
    for literacy, 92 (figure)
    for math, 22 (box), 91 (figure)
    for organization, 93 (figure)
    for PBS, 151 (box)
    for presentations, 93 (figure)
    for progress monitoring, 175–176, 185 (box)
    for reading, 41 (box)
    for strategies, 78 (box)
    for supporting ECSE, 301 (box)
    for supporting students with ASD, 243 (box)
    for supporting students with EBD, 224 (box)
    for supporting students with LD, 206 (box)
    for supporting students with moderate-to-severe disabilities, 261 (box)
    for time management, 93 (figure)
    for 2e learners, 318 (box)
    for working with ELLs, 281 (box)
    for writing, 55 (figure), 59 (box), 91 (figure)
Archer, A., 9, 26, 30, 65, 73, 347
Ardoin, S. P., 170
Arndt, D., 303
Artiles, A. J., 103, 265
ASD (autism spectrum disorder). *See* Autism spectrum disorder
Asher-Schapiro, A., 82
Assessment
    co-assessing, 157–159
    in co-taught classes, 160–161
    and differentiation, 158
    of ELLs, 269–270
    formative assessments, 158, 170, 171–172, 177 (figure)
    and IDEA, 321
    of learning disabilities, 264–266
    in mathematics, 15, 17 (box)
    and planning, 174–175
    response to intervention, 51, 305, 307, 327, 328
    summative assessments, 171, 173
    tiered, 74–75 (figure)
    of 2e learners, 305–306, 307–308
    using data to alter instructional delivery, 175
    of young children, 289
    *See also* progress monitoring
Assessment, Evaluation, and Programming System (AEPS), 289
Assessment accommodations, 62–63
Assignments, differentiating, 69, 272
Assistive technology (AT), 81 (box), 82, 83
Auditory processing, 190–191, 196–197
Autism spectrum disorder (ASD), 225–243
    anxiety reduction, 240 (figure)
    apps for supporting students with, 243 (box)
    attachments, 230
    attentional issues, 230
    causation, 227–228
    diagnosing, 226, 228, 238 (figure)
    and environment, 226
    evaluating ideal interventions for, 239 (figure)

and intellectual ability, 230
and interacting with police, 237
labeling, 226–227
and medical issues, 230
and movement, 236
prevalence of, 227
and repetitive behaviors, 229–230
resources for, 247
SCARED (Safe, Calm, Affirmation,
    Routine, Empathy, Develop
    Strategies), 233, 239 (figure)
and social communication issues,
    228–229, 230–231
stimming, 229, 235
symptoms, 228–230
things to avoid, 231–233
things to do, 233–237
and transitions, 229
websites for, 136–137, 231 (box),
    243 (box)
Avramidis, E., 155

Bailey, R. L., 83
Baker, S., 26, 45, 49
Baldwin, L., 304, 305, 306
Baranek, G. T., 229
Baron-Cohen, S., 228
Bashinski, S., 61
Bassin, S., 326, 327
Bateman, D. F., 342
Baum, S., 304
Bauwens, J., 156, 164
Beck, M. M., 10
Beebe-Frankenberger, M., 218 (figure)
Behavior
    and academic interventions, 211
    ACT limit setting model, 213
    applied behavior analysis, 254
    and ASD, 236
    classroom practices, 210–211
    and CRT, 112
    and data, 137, 138 (box), 140,
        144 (figure), 151 (box)
    EBPs for, 202 (figure)
    and families, 141
    functions of, 148 (figure), 209,
        209 (box), 213–214, 236

and learning, 123
modeling, 139, 216
monitoring progress toward
    goals, 175
nonresponders, 149 (figure)
Positive Behavioral Interventions and
    Supports (PBIS) World, 14
and punishment, 138
replacement behaviors, 136,
    138, 254
and restraint, 233
SCARED (Safe, Calm, Affirmation,
    Routine, Empathy, Develop
    Strategies), 233, 239 (figure)
strategies for addressing difficult
    behavior, 148 (figure)
and students with ASD, 230, 233,
    239 (figure)
and suspensions, 212
things to avoid, 211–212
things to do, 233–237
and 2e learners, 307, 310
universal preventative
    strategies, 214
See also behavior intervention plans;
    check-in/check-out programs;
    discipline; emotional and
    behavioral disorders; functional
    behavioral assessments; Positive
    Behavioral Interventions and
    Supports
Behavior, repetitive, 229–230
Behavior intervention plans (BIPs),
    134, 136, 137, 138–139, 142,
    143 (figure), 209, 323
    and families, 141
    and IEP, 209
    resources for developing,
        218 (figure)
    websites for, 135 (box)
Behavior management system, 105
Belfiore, P. J., 210
Belgard, T. G., 228
Bells, 125
Bernhardt, P., 154
Berninger, V. W., 45
Besnoy, K. D., 306

Bevans, K. B., 209
Binder, D. P., 286
BIP (behavior intervention plans).
    See Behavior intervention plans
Bird, J. M., 326, 327
Black, P., 172
Blair, C., 122
Blakely, R. D., 238
Blanks, B., 171
Blogs, for legal issues, 337 (box)
Blood, E., 214, 219 (figure)
Blumberg, S., 230
Boardman, A., 27
Bolt, S., 170
Boon, R. T., 191
Borsa, J. C., 321
Bos, C. A., 219 (figure)
Boulware-Gooden, R., 191
Bovaird, J., 61
Bovey, E. H., 283
Bowman-Kruhm, M., 154
Bowman-Perrott, L., 212
Bracamonte, M., 303
Bradshaw, C., 134, 209
Brain-based learning, 117–132
    apps for, 132 (box)
    guidelines for developing
        strategies, 129 (figure)
    things to avoid, 123–126
    things to do, 126–128
    websites for, 132 (box)
Brain training, apps for, 93 (figure)
Brann, A., 81
Bricker, D., 284, 289, 293, 296
Brigham, F. J., 135, 209, 218 (figure)
Brinkmann, J., 154
Bronfenbrenner, U., 290
Browder, D. M., 248
Brown, C., 226
Brown, M., 226
Brownell, M. T., 247
Bruder, M. B., 340
Bruhn, A., 218 (figure)
Bryant, B. R., 189
Bryant, D. P., 189
Bryson, T. P., 119
Bulgren, J. A., 190

Bullying, 232–233
Burdette, J., 124
Burke, M. D., 191
Bursuck, W. D., 32, 62, 64

Calculators, 11, 12
Calkins, L. M., 43
Cameron, D. L., 267, 272
Cardenas-Hagan, E., 277 (figure)
Carnine, D. W., 26
Carreker, S., 191
Carter, N. J., 323
Cascio, C. J., 229
CASE (Council for Administrators of
    Special Education), 291
Cassidy, J., 24
CEC (Council for Exceptional
    Children), 291
Center on the Social and Emotional
    Foundations for Early
    Learning, 290
Chamot, A. U., 268
Chard, D., 7, 26, 45
Chau, T., 83
Check-in/check-out (CICO)
    programs, 135, 139–140, 141, 142,
    146–147 (figure)
Chen, J. A., 228
Cheung, A. C., 81
Child Find, 327, 329
Chinn, P. C., 103
Choices
    in problem solving, 15
    and technology, 86
    in writing, 50
Cholewa, B., 342
Chow, K., 83
Christensen, C. M., 80
Chromebooks, 82–83
Chung, C., 304
Chunking, 69, 271
CICO (check-in/check-out)
    programs. See Check-in/check-out
    programs
Ciullo, S., 191
Clarke, L., 308
Clarke, S., 286

Classroom, inclusive
  number of special learners in, 160
  *See also* inclusion
Co-assessing, 157–159
Code of Federal Regulations (CFR),
  325–326
Cognitive instruction, for students
  with LD, 191–192
Cognitive load, 45
Cognitive strategy instruction, 9–10,
  14–15
Co-instructing, 156–157
Cole, H. A., 326
Coleman, M., 219 (figure)
Collaboration, 152, 159, 161, 198
  apps for, 168 (box)
  vs. co-teaching, 153
  and co-teaching, 154
  and EBD, 212
  and supporting students with
    LD, 193
  technology for, 94 (figure)
  websites for, 168 (box)
  *See also* co-teaching
Collaboration, home-school. *See*
  Home-school collaboration
Collaborative Teaching Improvement
  Model of Excellence (CTIME),
  163, 198
Collier, S., 263, 267
Color-coding, 69
Colvin, G., 232
Commercials, 119–120, 127
Common, E. A., 219 (figure)
Common Core State Standards
  (CCSS), 23
  mathematics, 8
  writing, 43, 46, 47
Common Core State Standards
  Initiative (CCSSI), 7
Communication
  PROSE checklist, 253, 259 (figure)
  technology for, 94–95 (figure),
    342, 345
  *See also* families; home-school
    collaboration; parents
Comprehension, in reading, 24
Compton, D. L., 29

Concrete-representational-abstract
  (CRA), 8–9, 10, 12
Conderman, G., 154, 156, 157,
  158, 171
Connor, C. M., 29
Conn-Powers, M., 284, 298
Consistency, 127
  and behavior, 141–142
Cook, B. G., 65, 189, 248, 256 (figure),
  257 (figure), 267, 272
Cook, L., 154
Co-planning, 155–156, 161, 174
  table tent, 164 (figure)
Coronado, J. M., 158
Co-teaching, 152–168, 172, 198
  approaches to, 156, 162, 164 (figure)
  apps for, 168 (box)
  and assessment, 157–159, 160–161
  benefits of, 155
  co-assessing, 157–159
  co-instructing, 156–157
  vs. collaboration, 153
  and collaboration, 154
  Collaborative Teaching
    Improvement Model of
    Excellence (CTIME), 163, 198
  co-planning, 155–156, 161,
    164 (figure), 174, 255
  core competencies, 161, 165 (figure)
  Co-Teaching 2.0, 154–155
  Co-Teaching Lesson Planner,
    158–159
  and data, 157
  and ECI, 288–289
  parity in, 156, 162
  in reading, 26
  required components of, 153,
    155–161
  things to avoid, 159–161
  things to do, 161–164
  websites for, 160, 161 (box),
    168 (box), 195 (box)
Co-Teaching 2.0, 154–155
Co-Teaching Lesson Planner, 158–159
Council for Administrators of Special
  Education (CASE), 291
Council for Exceptional Children
  (CEC), 283, 291

Courtade, G. R., 248, 256 (figure), 257 (figure)
CRA (concrete-representational-abstract), 8–9, 10, 12
Cramer, S., 159
Creativity, technology for, 94 (figure)
Critical thinking, technology for, 95 (figure)
Crnobori, M., 218 (figure)
Cross, A. F., 284, 298
CRT (culturally responsive teaching). *See* Culturally responsive teaching
CTIME (Collaborative Teaching Improvement Model of Excellence), 163, 198
Culturally responsive teaching (CRT), 100–116
    apps for, 116 (box)
    defined, 101
    vs. differentiation, 101
    and ELLs, 267
    experts on, 102–105
    learning about students, 110, 111–112, 113–114 (figure)
    and motivation, 104
    and prior knowledge, 106–107
    purposeful teaching, 104–105
    and racial justice, 103
    things to avoid, 106–109
    things to do, 109–112
    websites for, 116 (box)
    and whole child, 106, 107
Culture
    and celebrating diversity, 344
    defined, 102
    and home-school collaboration, 339
    influence on learning, 102
    and prior knowledge, 106–107
Cummins, J., 267, 269
Curriculum, pacing, 125
Curriculum augmentation, 61, 62–63
Curriculum-based measurement (CBM), 170, 171, 172, 173
Curwin, R. L., 343
Cyber Listening Lab, 272

Da Fonte, A., 341
Daggett, L. M., 327

Damer, M., 32
Danielson, L. C., 247
Data
    and behavior, 137, 138 (box), 140, 144 (figure)
    and co-teaching, 157
    and decision-making, 215, 252
    importance of, 212
    lesson plan template, 181 (figure)
    portable collection methods, 175
    using to alter instructional delivery, 175
    *See also* progress monitoring
Davies, R., 80
Dean, M., 128
Deatline-Buchman, A., 10
DEC (Division for Early Childhood), 283, 291
Decoding, 25–26, 29 (box)
Deficit based thinking, 107, 111, 268
DeFur, S., 197, 342
De la Paz, S., 50
DeNisco, A., 265
Deno, S. L., 171
Department of Education, U.S., 265, 283, 307, 340, 341
Department of Health and Human Services, U.S., 283
Desai, T., 83
Deshler, D. D., 45, 190
*Diagnostic and Statistical Manual (DSM-V)*, 227, 245
Dictation tools, 51
Dieker, L., 68, 155, 157, 158, 160, 162, 163
Dietz, S., 7, 9, 192
Differentiation
    and assessment, 158
    of assignments, 69, 272
    vs. culturally responsive teaching (CRT), 101
    and 2e learners, 309, 314–315 (figure)
Digital devices, 81. *See also* technology
Digital divide, 80
Dingfelder, S., 10
DiPipi, C. M., 10
Discipline, 323–324, 326–327, 329, 331, 335 (figure). *See also* behavior

Disproportionality, 103, 265.
    *See also* overrepresentation
DISSECT Strategy, 32, 37 (figure)
Diversity, 344, 348
Division for Early Childhood (DEC),
    283, 291
Dixon, J., 304
Doabler, C., 26, 45
Dollar store finds, 258 (figure)
Domnwachukwu, C. S., 103
Donehower, C., 83
Dopamine, 126
Downing, J. E., 245
Doyle, A., 341
Drasgow, E., 170, 172
Drill-and-kill, 307. *See also* worksheets
Duke TIP, 311
Dunlap, G., 286, 292
Dunst, C. J., 286

Early childhood inclusion (ECI),
    282–301
    access in, 283
    activity-based intervention in,
        295–296 (figure)
    embedded intervention in, 285,
        294–296 (figure)
    naturalistic instructional strategies
        in, 293 (figure)
    participation in, 283–284
    PBS in, 286
    promotion of social-emotional
        competence in, 285–286, 290,
        292 (figure)
    supports in, 284
    teaching pyramid in, 292 (figure)
    things to avoid, 287–289
    things to do, 289–291
    UDL in, 284, 297–298 (figure)
    *See also* early childhood special
        education
Early childhood special education
    (ECSE), 284–285
    apps for, 301 (box)
    websites for, 300 (box)
    *See also* early childhood inclusion
EBD (emotional and behavioral
    disorders). *See* Emotional and
    behavioral disorders

ECI (early childhood inclusion).
    *See* Early childhood inclusion
Ecological systems theory, 290
Eco-mapping, 290
ECSE (early childhood special
    education). *See* Early childhood
    special education
Edgar, B., 118
Edgemon, E. A., 62
Educational technology (ET), 81 (box)
Edwards, C. C., 341
Elementary and Secondary Education
    Act (ESEA), 189
ELLs (English Language Learners).
    *See* English Language Learners
Embedded intervention, 285,
    294–296 (figure)
Embodied cognition, 126
Embury, D. C., 156
Emotional and behavioral disorders
    (EBD), 207–224
    and academic interventions,
        211, 219 (figure)
    apps for supporting students with,
        224 (box)
    interventions, 208–211
    opportunities to respond tracking
        form, 221 (figure)
    and peers, 211
    recommended reading,
        217–219 (figure)
    things to avoid, 211–212
    things to do, 213–216
    use of term, 208
    websites for supporting students
        with, 216 (box), 224 (box)
Emotional regulation, and memory, 121
Enders, C., 7, 192
Engagement
    goals underlying, 84–85
    and mathematics, 15
    and technology, 80, 84–85
English Language Learners (ELLs),
    263–281
    approaches to working with, 263
    apps for working with, 281 (box)
    assessment of, 269–270
    learning difficulty vs. language
        barrier, 264–266

overrepresentation of in special
        needs education, 265
    prevalence of, 263
    and reading, 32
    referring for assessment, 266
    strategies for working with,
        274–276 (figure)
    teaching, 266–268
    things to avoid, 268–270
    things to do, 270–274
    twice-exceptional, 270
    websites for supporting,
        277–278 (figure), 280 (box)
Environment, and ASD, 226
Epstein, J. L., 343, 350
Equal, vs. fair, 196
Erlichman, R., 326
Ertmer, P. A., 80–81
Estrada, V., 81
Etscheidt, S. K., 170
Every Student Succeeds Act (ESSA),
        23, 247
Evidence-based practices (EBP)
    for accommodations, 64–65
    for reading, 31
    and students with LD, 189–190,
        194–195, 202 (figure)
    and students with moderate-to-
        severe disabilities, 247–248,
        256–257 (figure)
Expectations, 28–29, 104–105, 107, 112,
        211, 267, 272
Explicit instruction
    and accommodations, 65
    elements of, 73 (figure)
    in reading, 30
Eye contact, 232

Facilitated support, 162–163
Fair, vs. equal, 196
Fairbanks, S., 134
Falk, K. B., 219 (figure)
Families
    and ASD, 234
    blaming, 345
    classroom visits by, 347
    communication with, 102–105,
        259 (figure), 342–343, 345
    and CRT, 106, 107, 109, 110, 111–112

    and ECI, 289–290, 291
    and eco-mapping, 290
    and ECSE, 286
    and ELLs, 270
    feedback from, 345, 352 (figure)
    and IDEA, 322–323, 341, 345
    opportunities to support school, 346
    and PBS, 141, 142
    relationships with, 328, 330
    and students with EBD, 216,
        216 (box)
    and students with moderate-to-
        severe disabilities, 250, 253
    support for, 344
    teachers' expectations of, 340–341
    and 2e learners, 311
    types of involvement by, 348,
        350 (figure)
    See also home-school collaboration;
        parents
Family structures, 339
FAPE (free appropriate public
        education), 321, 322, 326,
        332, 333 (figure)
Farkis, M. A., 210
Farley, C. A., 65, 189
FBAs (functional behavioral
        assessments). See Functional
        behavioral assessments
Feedback, from families, 345,
        352 (figure)
Feedback, from peers, 105
Feedback, in mathematics, 16–17
Feggins-Azziz, L., 304
Fein, D., 226
Fernandez, N., 265
Fernandez-Lopez, A., 83
Ferriter, B., 85
Fine motor skills, and mathematics, 7
Fleming, G., 340
Focus, websites for, 127 (box)
Focus drills, 127, 128, 132 (box)
Foegen, A., 171
Foley-Nicpon, M., 305
Ford, M. P., 157
Fore, C., 191
Forest, M., 341, 349
*Formative Assessment Made Easy*
        (Cornelius), 174

Fortner, S., 75
Foundational learning, 124
Fox, L., 286, 292
Freeman, A., 81
Friedlander, B., 46
Friend, M., 62, 64, 154, 156
Friendship skills, 290
Frustration, 108
Fulk, B. J. M., 193
Functional behavioral assessments
    (FBAs), 134, 135–136, 137, 138–139,
    143 (figure), 209, 254, 323
  and ASD, 233
  and data, 140
  and families, 141
  resources for developing, 217 (figure)
  websites for, 135 (box)
Funding
  for reading materials, 33
  for technology, 88, 88 (box), 89

Galvan, M. E., 158
Garcia, M. S., 128
García-Orza, J., 127
Gargiulo. R. M., 208
Garrett, S. D., 24
Gay, G., 101, 102, 104
Geary, D. C., 7
Gersten, R., 7, 49
Geschwind, D. H., 228
Giancola, J., 303
Gibbs, J., 7
Gifted learners, 265, 303, 341.
    *See also* twice-exceptional learners
Ginsberg, M. B., 104
Gischlar, K. L., 170
Gleason, M. M., 26
Goldin-Meadow, S., 126
Gonzalez, N., 101
Google Earth, 16
Goran, L., 342
Gordon, D., 85
*Go Talk Now*, 83
Graber, A., 81
Graduated instructional sequence, 8–9,
    10, 12
Graham, S., 43, 44, 45, 46, 52
Grammar, 48
Graphic organizers
  for math, 19 (figure)

for students with LD, 191
  for writing, 47, 49, 53 (figure)
Graves, D., 43
Gray, T., 81
Gregory, M., 326
Griffin, C. C., 10
Grisham-Brown, J., 285, 294
Grouping, 105, 157, 158
Grudges, 108
Guardians. *See* Families; Parents
Guardino, D., 134
Guides, visual, 13. *See also* graphic
    organizers
Gurganus, S. P., 8
Gutman, D., 119

Hadidi, M. S. Al, 339
Haenlein, M., 81
Hagan-Burke, S., 68
Hall, J. A., 210
Halverson, R., 81
Hamby, D. W., 286
Hansen, S. N., 227
Harris, K. R., 43, 44, 45, 46, 52
Harris, T. L., 27
Harry, B., 103, 265
Hartman, A., 290
Hawken, L. S., 135
Hawkins, S. R., 285
Healey, G., 303
Hedin, L. R., 154, 156, 157, 158, 171
Hemmeter, M. L., 285, 286, 292, 294
Henderson, L. M., 230, 234
Henderson, N., 114
Henry, H. R., 210
Hermann, D. J., 119
Hermeling, A., 82
Hicks, A., 81
Highlighting, 69
Hinkley, S., 190
Hippocampus, 118, 119, 120, 124,
    125, 128
Hodges, D., 124
Hodges, R. E., 27
Hoff, K., 10
Hojnoski, R. L., 170
Holmes, D. L., 128
Homeostasis, 126, 127
Home-school collaboration, 323,
    338–355

apps for, 355 (box)
challenges to, 338–341
communication with families,
    342–343
and culture, 339
home visits, 289, 291
LAFF, don't CRY, 344, 351 (figure)
McGill Action Plan, 341–342,
    349 (figure)
and parents' comfort level, 343
strategies for, 339–340
Teacher Report Card, 345,
    352 (figure)
things to avoid, 343–345
things to do, 345–348
types of family involvement, 348,
    350 (figure)
websites for, 354 (box)
Home visits, 289, 291
Homework, 347
    differentiating, 69
    for math, 11
Hoover-Dempsey, K. V., 339, 343
Hoppes, M. K., 191
Horn, M. B., 80
Horner, R. H., 134, 135
Hosp, J. L., 103, 170
Hott, B. L., 135, 143, 209, 210, 211
Hourcade, J., 156, 164
Howard, E., 105
Howard, L., 155
Hua, Y., 209
Hudson, M. E., 248
Hudson, P. J., 7, 9
Hughes, C., 9, 30, 32, 37, 65, 73, 158,
    230, 234, 303, 304, 305, 311, 347
Hurley-Chamberlain, D., 154
Hutter-Pishgahi, L., 284, 298

Ialongo, N., 209
IDEA (Individuals with Disabilities
    Education Act). See Individuals
    with Disabilities Education Act
Identification, of special learners,
    264–266, 321, 327, 329. See also
    assessment
Identity, 234
IEP (individualized education
    program). See Individualized
    education program

Iland, E., 237
Inclusion
    culture of, 198
    meaning of, 251
Inclusion, of special learners in general
    classroom, 101–102, 152–153,
    251, 322
    and accommodations, 329
    and administrators, 333 (box)
    ELLs, 266
    improving, 195
    and severity of disability, 246–247
    and students with moderate-to-
        severe disabilities, 248–249
    See also co-teaching; early childhood
        inclusion
Independence, teaching strategies for, 70
Individualized education program
    (IEP), 61, 322, 328, 330, 341
    adaptations in, 63–64
    and BIP, 209
    and determining which strategies to
        use, 63
    least restrictive environment in, 246,
        282, 283, 291, 322
    lesson plan template, 181 (figure)
    meeting agenda, 334 (figure)
    meetings, 346
    and planning process, 172, 174
    and progress monitoring, 170,
        178 (figure)
    vs. Section 504 plan, 331
    things to avoid, 67–68
    things to do, 68–70
Individuals with Disabilities Education
    Act (IDEA), 61, 189, 246, 251, 282,
    291, 307, 321–324, 330
    achievement standards, 323
    and assessment, 321
    Child Find, 321, 327, 329
    and definition of emotional
        disturbance, 208
    and discipline issues, 323–324
    due process hearings, 322
    lack of funding for, 327–328
    and LRE, 246, 282, 283, 291, 322
    and parent involvement, 322–323,
        341, 346
    See also individualized education
        program

Innovation, disruptive, 80
Inserra, A., 265
Instruction
    high-quality, 76 (figure)
    tiered, 74–75 (figure)
Intellectual disability (ID), 248
Interests, of students, 113 (figure), 120
International Society for Technology in
    Education (ISTE), 85, 88
Internet. *See* Apps; Technology;
    Websites
Interpreters, 270, 329–330
Interruptions, 125
Intervention, embedded, 285,
    294–296 (figure)
Interventions, academic, 211
Interventions, behavioral, 219 (figure).
    *See also* behavior intervention
    plans; check-in/check-out
    programs; functional behavioral
    assessments; Positive Behavioral
    Interventions and Supports
IPads, 82, 83
Isbell, L., 143

Jablonski, B. R., 62
Jalongo, M. R., 191
Jitendra, A. K., 10, 191
Johanson, D. C., 118
Johns, B. H., 62
Johnson, C. W., 80
Johnson, J. J., 284, 285, 293, 296
Johnson, L., 81, 82
Jones, R., 308
Joseph, G. E., 286, 292
Joshi, R. M., 191

Kame'enui, E. J., 26
Kamei-Hannan, C., 28, 35
Kanner, L., 227
Kaplan, A. M., 81
Karpinska, K., 126
Katsiyannis, A., 326
Kauffman, J. M., 218 (figure)
Kellogg, R. T., 45
Kena, G., 101, 103
Kennedy, M., 8
Ketterlin-Geller, L., 26, 45
Keyword strategies, 190, 195

Khateeb, J. M. Al, 339
Khatib, A. J. Al, 339
Kiely, M. T., 247
King-Sears, M. E., 154
Kiuhara, S., 45
Kleinheksel, K. A., 190
Klingner, J. K., 27, 102, 103, 265
Knowledge, prior, 28, 106–107, 272
Knowles, M., 219 (figure)
Korinek, L., 197
Koth, C. W., 209
Kozleski, E. B., 265
Krawec, J., 7, 192
Kreider, R. M., 339
Kroeger, S. D., 156
Kurth, J. A., 249

Ladson-Billings, G., 102, 104
LAFF, don't CRY, 344, 351 (figure)
La Morte, M. W., 322
Landreth, G. L., 213
Lane, K. L., 209, 218 (figure),
    219 (figure)
Language arts, for 2e learners,
    313 (figure)
Larrson, J.-O., 230
Lathrop, M., 134
Laurienti, P., 124
LD (learning disabilities). *See* Learning
    disabilities
Leaf, P. J., 134, 209
Learning, apps for, 92 (figure)
Learning disabilities, students with,
    188–206
    apps for supporting, 206 (box)
    and cognitive instruction, 191–192
    and evidence-based practices,
        189–190, 194–195, 202 (figure)
    and graphic organizers, 191
    strategies for, 195 (box), 195–197
    strategies for developing auditory
        processing, 190–191
    strategies for developing memory,
        189–190
    strategies for developing
        metacognition/
        self-regulation, 191
    strategies for developing visual
        processing, 190

things to avoid, 193–194
things to do, 194–198
websites for supporting, 195 (box),
    205 (box)
Learning styles, 11, 118
Least restrictive environment (LRE),
    246, 282, 283, 291, 322
Lee, D. L., 209
Legal issues, 320–337
    and administrators, 333 (box)
    apps for, 337 (box)
    blogs for, 337 (box)
    Code of Federal Regulations,
        325–326
    current trends, 326–328
    and discipline, 326–327
    professional organizations for,
        337 (box)
    Section 504, 324–325, 327–328, 329,
        331, 332
    things to avoid, 328–330
    things to do, 330–332
    and 2e learners, 307
    websites for, 331 (box), 337 (box)
    *See also* individualized education
        program; Individuals with
        Disabilities Education Act
Lembke, E. S., 171
Lenz, B. K., 32, 37, 190
Leon-Carrion, J., 127
Lerner, J., 10
Lesson plan template, 181 (figure)
Letter strategies, 189–190, 195
Levy, S., 219 (figure)
Lewis, J. M., 339
Lewis, M. B., 83
Lieberman-Betz, R. G., 285
Lietsala, K., 82
Lightfoot, S. L., 339
Lignugaris/Kraft, B., 65
Linan-Thompson, S., 170, 172
Lipsky, J., 233, 239
Listening, active, 344, 347,
    351 (figure)
Listening comprehension, websites
    for, 272
Literacy
    apps for, 92 (figure)
    changes in, 46

EBPs for, 202 (figure)
Little, T. D., 62
Lleras, A., 125
Lloyd, J. W., 62
Location, and memory, 124–125
Lochner, W. W., 163, 165, 198, 327
Losen, D. J., 103, 327
Losinski, M., 326
LRE (least restrictive environment),
    246, 282, 283, 291, 322
Lumsden, J., 126
Lylo, B., 209
Lyon, K. J., 249

Macaro, E., 45
Maccini, P., 9
MacFarland, S., 245
MacLeod, K. S., 135
Macrae, C. N., 126
MacSwan, J., 264
Madaus, J. W., 327, 328
Mancl, D. B., 8, 9
Marketing, 120
Martinez-Segura, M. J., 83
Mason, B. A., 214
Mason, L. H., 43, 46
Mastropieri, M., 46, 65, 69, 155, 189,
    190, 192, 193, 199, 201
Mathematics, 6–22, 214
    accommodations in, 12–13
    apps for, 22 (box), 91 (figure)
    assessment in, 15, 17 (box)
    calculation devices, 18 (figure)
    cognitive strategy instruction, 9–10,
        14–15
    EBPs for, 202 (figure)
    and engagement, 15
    failure rates, 7
    and fine motor skills, 7
    graduated instructional sequence,
        8–9, 10, 12
    graphic organizers for, 19 (figure)
    metacognitive strategies instruction,
        10, 14
    monitoring comprehension, 17
    number sense, 7, 11
    pegwords, 190, 196
    Planning Pyramids, 12
    practice in, 14, 16–17

problem-based, 6
problem solving, persistence in, 13
problem-solving skills, 15, 192
questions, 15
real-world problems, 16
schema-based instruction, 10, 13–14,
　　19 (figure)
*Solve It!* 10, 14, 192
standards, 7, 8
things to avoid, 11–12
things to do, 12–17
for 2e learners, 313 (figure)
understanding, 13
vocabulary for, 14, 15
websites for, 21 (box)
Whole Brain Math, 17
word problems, 9–10, 13–14
Mathematics keyword
　　strategies, 190
Matias, C., 103, 104
Matthias, L., 75
McCallum, R. S., 305
McClelland, M. M., 128
McConnell, B. M., 342
McConnell, S. R., 283
McCormick, K. M., 290
McDuffie, K. A., 155
McGill Action Plan (MAP), 341–342,
　　349 (figure)
McKeown, D., 45
McLeskey, J., 64, 76, 189, 251
McNaughton, D. B., 344, 351
Medical issues, of students
　　with ASD, 230
Memory, 117–132
　and commercials, 119–120
　and emotional regulation, 121
　and life success, 122
　and location, 124–125
　long-term memory, 45, 120
　mnemonics, 192–193
　and position, 124–125
　short-term memory, 45, 118–120, 125
　strategies for, 121, 129 (figure),
　　189–190
　things to avoid, 123–126
　things to do, 126–128
　and writing, 44–45

Mendler, A. N., 343
Mendler, B. D., 343
Mensebach, C., 121
Menzies, H. M., 209, 218 (figure)
Metacognition, strategies for
　　developing, 191
Metacognitive strategies instruction,
　　10, 14
Meyer, A., 85
Miles, L. K., 126
Miller, E. K., 126
Miller, S. P., 7, 8, 9
Miller, T. D., 128
Milstein, M., 114
Minorities, overrepresentation of in
　　special needs education, 103
Missall, K. N., 170
Mitchell, M. M., 134
Mixon, K. A., 342
Mnemonics, 69–70, 192–193
Moderate-to-severe disabilities,
　　244–261
　apps for supporting students with,
　　261 (box)
　and evidence-based practices,
　　247–248, 256–257 (figure)
　lack of clear definition of, 246
　things to avoid, 249–251
　things to do, 251–255
　websites for supporting students
　　with, 261 (box)
Modifications, 61, 63 (box)
　defined, 62
　for students with LD, 203 (figure)
Moll, L. C., 101
Montague, M., 7, 9, 10, 192
Morgan, T. H., 10
Morrison, F. J., 128
Moseley, A., 230
Motivation
　and CRT, 104
　for reading, 33
　and success on early tests, 126–127
Motze, F., 83
Movement, 124–125
　and ASD, 236
　and problem solving, 125
Mulcahy, C. A., 9

Mumford, L., 83
Munakata, Y., 122
Murawski, W. W., 26, 54, 68, 113,
    143, 153, 154, 155, 156, 157, 158,
    160, 161, 162, 163, 164, 165, 183,
    198, 231, 263, 272, 323, 327,
    334 (figure), 335 (figure), 339, 352
Myelination, 126

Nagro, S. N., 251, 259 (figure)
Nass, C. I., 127
National Assessment of Educational
    Progress, 24
National Association for the Education
    of Young Children, 283
National Autism Center (NAC), 247
National Center for Education
    Statistics, 103, 152, 263
National Education Association
    (NEA), 33
National Education Technology Plan
    (NTEP), 82
National Professional Development
    Center on ASD (NPDC on
    ASD), 247
National Reading Panel, 24, 25, 27
National Secondary Transition
    Technical Assistance Center
    (NSTTAC), 248
Nation's Report Card, 7
Neel, R. S., 219 (figure)
Neff, D., 101
Nelson, J. R., 27
Nichols, S. C., 327
No Child Left Behind (NCLB), 6, 23, 247
Nowak, T. M., 290
Number sense, 7, 11
Nusbaum, H. C., 126

Oakes, W. P., 209
O'Connor, C. M., 25
O'Connor, R. E., 29
Odom, S. L., 286, 289, 290
O'Malley, P., 83
Omdal, S. N., 306
Ophir, E., 127
Opportunities to respond (OTR),
    210, 214

tracking form, 221 (figure)
Orfield, G., 103
Organization, apps for, 93 (figure)
Ortiz, A., 265, 266
Osher, D., 265
Overrepresentation, in special needs
    education, 103
    and discipline issues, 326–327
    of ELLs, 265
    and poverty, 304
Overton, C., 81
Owens, S. V., 304
Owiny, R., 75

Pace, of curriculum, 125
Pak, M., 27
Palmer, S. B., 62
Papert, S., 80
Paraprofessionals, 29
Parents
    blaming, 345
    communication with child, 345–346
    in IEP meetings, 346
    as shared educators, 340–341
    See also families
Parent Teacher Associations
    (PTA), 344
Parity, in co-teaching, 156, 162
Park, H. J., 340
Parner, E. T., 227
Parrish, T., 328
Participation, in ECI, 283–284
Partnerships. See Families; Home-
    school collaboration; Parents
Pazey, B. L., 326
PBIS (Positive Behavioral Interventions
    and Supports). See Positive
    Behavioral Interventions and
    Supports
PBS (Positive Behavioral Interventions
    and Supports). See Positive
    Behavioral Interventions and
    Supports
PDQ model of anxiety reduction, 235,
    240 (figure)
Pea, R., 128
Peer coaching, 105
Peer feedback, 17, 105

Peer relationships, and early childhood education, 285–286, 288, 290, 292 (figure)

Peers, on inclusion of students with moderate-to-severe disabilities, 248–249

Peer tutoring, 17 (box)
 and accommodations, 65
 and EBD, 210, 215
 planning form, 222 (figure)

Pegwords, 190, 196

Peltz, A., 230

Peñagarikano, O., 228

Perdomo, M., 105

Pereles, D., 304, 305, 306

Pérez-Santamaría, F. J., 127

Perin, D., 43, 45

Perron-Jones, N., 10

Persistence, in problem solving, 10, 13

Phonemic awareness, 24, 25

Phonics, 24, 25–26

Planning
 and assessment, 174–175
 lesson plan template, 181 (figure)
 Planning Pyramids, 12
 *See also* accommodations;
  individualized education
  program; Universal Design for
  Learning

Planning Pyramids, 12

Plucker, J., 303

Police, interacting with, 237

Poloni-Staudinger, L., 304

Popham, W. J., 158

Position, and memory, 124–125

Positive Behavioral Interventions and Supports (PBIS/PBS), 133–151, 208–211
 apps for, 151 (box)
 described, 133–134
 in ECI, 286
 nonresponders, 149 (figure)
 overarching model for, 135–136
 *Positive Behavioral Interventions and Supports (PBIS) World*, 14
 practical issues, 135–136
 research on, 134–135
 settingwide support examples, 145 (figure)
 strategies for addressing difficult behavior, 148 (figure)
 things to avoid, 136–139
 things to do, 139–142
 Tier 1, 134
 Tier 2, 134, 141
 Tier 3, 134, 142, 143 (figure)
 websites for, 141 (box), 151 (box)
 *See also* behavior intervention plans;
  check-in/check-out programs;
  functional behavioral
  assessments

*Positive Behavioral Interventions and Supports (PBIS) World*, 14

Potts, E. A., 155

Power struggles, 214, 307

Practice
 in mathematics, 14, 16–17
 and memory strategies, 121
 for reading, 32–33
 for writing, 48–49

Praise, and EBD, 210–211, 214

Prater, M. A., 323

Preschool. *See* Early childhood inclusion

Presentations
 apps for, 93 (figure)
 technology for, 95 (figure)

Pretti-Frontczak, K., 285, 294

Prince, A. M. T., 326

Prior knowledge, 28, 106–107, 272

Problem solving
 and movement, 125
 technology for, 95 (figure)

Problem-solving skills, 9–10, 13, 14–15, 192

Professional organizations, for legal issues, 337 (box)

Progress monitoring, 170–185
 apps for, 175–176, 185 (box)
 collection sheets, 179–180 (figure)
 and curriculum-based measurement, 171, 172
 daily tracking sheet, 182–183 (figure)
 and data, 174, 289
 described, 170–172
 formative assessments, 171–172, 177 (figure)
 and individualized education program, 178 (figure)

summative assessments, 171, 173
things to avoid, 172–173
things to do, 174–176
websites for, 185 (box)
Project Tomorrow, 81
PROSE checklist, 259 (figure)
Prosody, 26
Public Law (PL) 94–142, 282
Public Law (PL) 99–457, 282
Puig, M. V., 126
Pullman, M. Y., 122
Pull-outs
in ECSE, 288
and ELLs, 269
Punctuation, 48
Punishment, 138. *See also* behavior;
discipline
Pyramid Model for Promoting Social-
Emotional Competence in Young
Children, 285–286

Question-Answer Relationships
(QAR), 32

*Race to Nowhere* (film), 12
Racial justice, 103
Rahn, N. L., 284, 293, 296
Randall's Cyber Listening Lab, 272
Raphael, T. E., 32
Rawlings, L., 135
Raybeck, D., 119
Readability formulas, 31, 31 (box)
Reading, 23–41, 31 (box), 34–35 (figure)
apps for, 41 (box)
connecting to other subjects, 28
decoding in, 25–26
DISSECT Strategy, 32, 37 (figure)
and English Language Learners, 32
evaluating needs, 34 (figure)
evidence-based practices, 31
and expectations, 28–29
explicit instruction in, 30
goal of, 31
guided oral reading, 26
individualizing instruction, 28, 30
model of service delivery, 28
and motivation, 33
and older students, 29
phonemic awareness, 25

phonics, 25–26
practice time, 32–33
promoting independence, 32
Question-Answer Relationships
(QAR), 32
reading aloud, 31–32
reading comprehension, 27, 32
reading fluency, 24, 26, 38 (figure)
selecting texts, 31
skills for, 24–28
and support, 33
things to avoid, 28–30
things to do, 30–33
vocabulary, 26–27, 29, 36 (figure),
37 (figure)
websites for, 40 (box)
Reading comprehension, 27, 32
*Reading Connections* (Kamei-Hannan
and Ricci), 28
Reading fluency, 24, 26, 38 (figure)
Recognition networks, 66
Reeves, J. R., 267
Regrouping, 105, 157, 158
Reinforcement, in PBS, 140
Reis, S. M., 158
Renzulli, J. S., 158, 308
Repetition, 123
and short-term memory, 119
Reschly, D. J., 103, 245
Resiliency chart, 114 (figure)
Resource binders, for math, 13
Resources. *See* Apps; Graphic
organizers; Websites
Response to intervention (RTI), 51, 305,
307, 327, 328
Reutebuch, C., 191
Reynolds, R., 81
Ricci, L. A., 28, 35
Richards, W., 233, 239
Robertson, K., 278
Robinson, A., 85
Rodriguez-Almendros, M. L., 83
Rodriguez-Fortiz, M. J., 83
Rolstad, K., 264
Rose, D., 85
Rosenberg, M. S., 251
Rous, B., 290
Rule of 9, 14
Rules, 105

SAFER (Successful, Anxiety-Free, Engaged Reading), 31–32
Sahni, J., 135
Salvia, J., 170
Scaffolding, 123
SCARED (Safe, Calm, Affirmation, Routine, Empathy, Develop Strategies), 233, 239 (figure)
Schaffhauser, D., 82
Schedules, and ASD, 236
Schema-based instruction, 10, 13–14, 19 (figure)
Schendel, D. E., 227
Scheuermann, B. K., 210
Scholte, R. H. J., 233
School climate, 126
School-to-home collaboration. *See* Families; Home-school collaboration; Parents
Schumaker, J. B., 45, 190
Schwarz, N., 128
Scott, K. L., 54, 113, 143, 183, 231, 334 (figure), 335 (figure), 352
Scott, T. M., 209
Scripting, 234–235
Scruggs, T., 46, 65, 69, 155, 189, 190, 192, 193, 199, 201
Sczesniak, E., 10
Section 504, 324–325, 327–328, 329, 331, 332
Self-control, 122
Self-efficacy, 111
Self-monitoring, 14, 191
  and EBD, 210, 215
  for students with LD, 196
  for writing, 49
Self-regulation, 122, 122 (box), 124, 126, 191
Self-worth, 105
Shaffer, L., 154
Shamberger, C., 154
Shaw, S. F., 327, 328
Sheffield, A. D., 327
Sheltered instruction, 263
Shogren, K. A., 249
Shora, N., 211
Siegel, D. J., 119

Silbert, J., 26
Sileo, N. M., 323
Silver, H., 85
Silver-Pacuilla, H., 81
Simmons, A. B., 304
Sinclair, J., 234
Sindelar, P. T., 247
Sirkkunen, E., 82
Skiba, R. J., 304
Skills, technology, 85–86
Skinner, C. H., 210
Skipper, J. I., 126
Slavin, R. E., 81
Small, S. L., 126
Smedge, H., 230
Smith, A., 81
Smith, P., 190
Snyder, P., 286
Social bookmarking, 86, 86 (box)
Social communication, in students with ASD, 228–229, 230–231
Social justice, 103
Social reinforcement, 228
Social skills instruction, 128, 253, 285–286, 290, 292 (figure)
Social Story, 234–235
Socioeconomic status, and gifted children, 303
*Solve It!* 10, 14, 192
Song, J., 339
Soraya, L., 235
Soukup, J., 61, 62
Speak Up, 81
Speech-to-text tools, 57 (figure)
Spelling, 47, 50, 50 (box)
Spencer, S., 45, 49, 52, 53, 57, 162
Spencer, V. G., 191
Sreckovic, M. A., 219 (figure)
SRS resources, 214 (box)
Stakeholders, 108
Standards
  effects on students with disabilities, 8
  mathematics, 7, 8
  for technology, 88, 89
Stecker, P. M., 171, 172
Steele, C., 105
Steele, M. M., 190

Steen, M., 124
Stenhoff, D. M., 65
Stereotypes, 110–111
St. Florian, A., 326
Stimming, 229, 235
Stivers, J., 159
Stone, D., 83
Stoner, J. B., 83
Strain, P. S., 283, 286, 292
Strategic networks, 66
Strategies
    apps for, 78 (box)
    choosing, 287
    and curriculum augmentation, 62–63
    for ELLs, 267–268, 271,
        274–276 (figure)
    for home-school collaboration,
        339–340
    for supporting students with LD,
        189–193, 195 (box), 195–197
    transferability of, 197
    websites for, 78 (box)
Strategy instruction, 69–70
    in writing, 45–46, 47, 49, 52 (figure)
Strengths-based approach, 111
    and twice-exceptional learners,
        302–318
Stricklin, S., 290
Strogilos, V., 155
Strong, R., 85
Student-centered teaching, 13
Student response systems (SRS), 214
Successful, Anxiety-Free, Engaged
    Reading (SAFER), 31–32
Sugai, G., 105, 134, 232
Sugarman, J., 105
Suk-Hyang, L., 62
Sullivan, A. L., 264
Summy, S. E., 190
Supports, in ECI, 284
Surveys, 112
    for identifying 2e learners, 308
    to learn about students,
        113–114 (figure)
    websites for, 110 (box)
Suspensions, 138, 212
Swanson, H. L., 45

Swarup, V., 228
Syllables, 26, 36 (figure)
System of least prompts, 285

Tarver, S., 26
Teacher preparation, 340
Teacher Report Card, 345, 352 (figure)
Teaching, purposeful, 104–105
Teaching pyramid, 292 (figure)
Technology, 79–97
    accessibility, 84
    alternative and augmentative
        communication devices, 83,
        90 (figure), 254–255
    assistive technology, 81 (box), 82, 83
    barriers to integrating, 80–81
    bring your own device (BYOD), 81
    and choices, 86
    for collaboration, 94 (figure)
    and communicating with families,
        342, 345
    for communication, 94–95 (figure)
    for creativity, 94 (figure)
    for critical thinking, 95 (figure)
    digital divide, 80
    educational technology, 81 (box)
    and engagement, 80, 84–85
    and focus, 128
    funding for, 88, 88 (box), 89
    needed skills, 85–86
    for problem solving, 95 (figure)
    standards for, 85–86, 86 (box), 88, 89
    teachers' attitudes toward, 81
    things to avoid, 86–87
    things to do, 87–89
    and 2e learners, 309
    and Universal Design for
        Learning, 69
    user-created content, 81–82
    websites for keeping up with,
        97 (box)
    and writing, 46, 47, 49, 49 (box),
        50 (box), 54 (figure),
        55–56 (figure), 57 (figure)
    See also apps; websites
Temple-Harvey, K. K., 214
Templeton, T. N., 219 (figure)

Test, D. W., 248, 256 (figure),
    257 (figure)
Testing accommodations, 62–63
Theory of mind, 228
Thomas, L. E., 125
Thomas-Brown, K., 154
Thornhill, A., 191
Thousand, J., 153, 160
Time delay, 285
Time management, apps for, 93 (figure)
Tomlinson, C. A., 156
Torres, C., 65, 189
Townsend, B. L., 102
Trail, B., 305, 306
Transferability, 197
*Transforming American Education*
    (NTEP), 82
Transitions
    practicing, 128
    and self-regulation, 124
    signaling, 125
    and students with ASD, 229
Traub, E. K., 284, 298
Trent, S. C., 265
Trivette, C. M., 286
Troia, G. A., 44
Troutman, A. C., 217 (figure)
Twice-exceptional learners (2e), 265,
    302–318, 341
    apps for, 318 (box)
    content-based instruction for,
        313 (figure)
    definition of, 304–305
    and differentiating twice,
        314–315 (figure)
    ELLs, 270
    in gifted programs, 307
    identifying, 305–306, 307–308
    lack of programs for, 306
    paradoxical strengths and challenges
        of, 312 (figure)
    participation in gifted programs
        by, 308
    things to avoid, 306–308
    things to do, 308–311
    websites for, 307 (box), 317 (box)
Twice-Exceptional National
    Community of Practice, 304
Twiford, T., 154

2e learners. *See* Twice-exceptional
    learners

Uberti, H. Z., 189, 193, 199, 201
Ullman, M. T., 122
Universal Design for Learning (UDL),
    11, 65–67, 85, 197, 198
    apps for, 78 (box)
    in ECI, 284, 291, 297–298 (figure)
    and ELLs, 271
    examples of, 72 (figure)
    and technology, 69
    things to avoid, 67–68
    things to do, 68–70
    and 2e learners, 309, 315 (figure)
    websites for, 78 (box)
Universal preventative
    strategies, 214

Vachon, V. L., 26
Vadasy, P. F., 27
Vail, C. O., 285
Valadez, C. M., 24
Vandercook, T., 341, 349
Vannest, K. J., 68, 214
Van Roekel, E., 233
Vaughn, S., 27, 170, 172, 219 (figure)
Veenstra-VanderWeele, J., 238
Vespa, J., 339
Villa, R., 153, 160
Visual processing, 190, 196–197
Vocabulary
    DISSECT Strategy, 37 (figure)
    keyword strategies, 195
    for math, 14, 15
    and reading, 24, 26–27, 29,
        36 (figure), 37 (figure)
    strategies for developing,
        199–201 (figure)
Voice, varying tone of, 124
Vostal, B., 209, 344, 351

Wagner, A. D., 127
Wald, J., 327
Waldron, N. L., 64, 76, 189
Walker, J., 135, 143, 209, 210
Wallace, M. T., 229
Wang, C., 303
Warger, C., 10

Weaver, K., 128
Websites
    for assessment in math, 17 (box)
    for autism spectrum disorder,
        136–137, 231 (box), 243 (box)
    for brain-based learning, 132 (box)
    for choice making, 15 (box)
    for co-teaching/collaboration, 160,
        161 (box), 168 (box), 195 (box)
    Council for Exceptional Children,
        291 (box)
    for culturally responsive teaching,
        116 (box)
    for data-based decisions, 252 (box)
    for EBD, 216 (box), 224 (box)
    for ECSE, 300 (box)
    for ELLs, 277–278 (figure),
        280 (box)
    for FBAs/BIPs, 135 (box)
    for focus, 127 (box)
    for home-school collaboration,
        354 (box)
    for keeping up with technology,
        97 (box)
    for LD, 205 (box)
    for legal issues, 331 (box), 337 (box)
    for listening comprehension, 272
    for math, 12 (box), 13, 16 (box),
        17 (box), 21 (box)
    for PBS, 141 (box), 151 (box)
    for peer tutoring, 17 (box)
    for Planning Pyramids, 12 (box)
    for progress monitoring, 185 (box)
    for reading, 29 (box), 40 (box)
    reputable, 287 (box)
    for social skills instruction,
        253 (box)
    SRS resources, 214 (box)
    for strategies, 78 (box)
    for student-centered teaching,
        13 (box)
    for summer activities, 311
    for supporting students with
        moderate-to-severe disabilities,
        261 (box)
    for surveys, 110 (box)
    for 2e learners, 307 (box), 317 (box)
    for UDL, 78 (box)
    for vocabulary, 27 (box)
    for working with special learners,
        273 (box)
    for writing, 49 (box), 55–56 (figure),
        59 (box)
Wehby, J. H., 219 (figure)
Wehmeyer, M. L., 61, 62
Weichel, W. A., 311
Weishaar, M. K., 321, 322
Weishaar, P. M., 321
West, R., 80
Westling, D. L., 251
What Really Works in Elementary
    Education (Murawski and
    Scott), 231
What Really Works in Secondary
    Education (Collier), 267
Whitbread, K. M., 340
Wilkins, R., 124
William, D., 172
Wilson, M. G., 9
Winchell, B. N., 285
Wlodkowski, R. J., 104
Wolery, M., 286
Wong, C., 229, 230, 231, 247,
    256 (figure), 257 (figure)
Wood, L. A., 248
Word problems, 9–10, 13–14
Worksheets, 11, 29, 269
Woynaroski, T., 229
Wright, P. D., 61
Wright, P. W. D., 61
Writing, 42–59
    apps for, 55 (figure), 59 (box),
        91 (figure)
    changes in, 46
    choices in, 50
    cognitive processes of, 44–45
    and dictation tools, 51
    explicit instruction in, 45–47
    genres in, 47, 50
    graphic organizers for, 53 (figure)
    and memory, 44–45
    modeling, 50–51
    need for foundation in, 44
    practice in, 48–49
    priorities in, 47–48
    research on, 43–46
    strategy instruction in, 45–46, 47, 49,
        52 (figure)

and technology, 46, 47, 49, 49 (box),
54 (figure), 55–56 (figure),
57 (figure)
things to avoid, 46–48
things to do, 48–51
websites for, 49 (box), 55–56 (figure),
59 (box)

Xin, Y. P., 191

Yell, M. L., 170, 172
York, J., 341, 349
Yssel, N., 308
Ysseldyke, J., 170

Zhang, J., 341
Zirkel, P. A., 327
Zurcher, A., 236

A SAGE Publishing Company

Helping educators make the greatest impact

**CORWIN HAS ONE MISSION:** to enhance education through intentional professional learning.

We build long-term relationships with our authors, educators, clients, and associations who partner with us to develop and continuously improve the best evidence-based practices that establish and support lifelong learning.

Council for Exceptional Children

The Council for Exceptional Children is a professional association of educators dedicated to advancing the success of children with exceptionalities. We accomplish our mission through advocacy, standards, and professional development.